BLOOD, BULLETS AND BODIES
SEXUAL POLITICS BELOW JAMAICA'S POVERTY LINE

Imani M. Tafari-Ama

Cover Art: Elgo

Fifth Edition

Fifth Edition

First published 2006

This edition published by Beaten Track Publishing

CATALOGING IN PUBLICATION DATA

Tafari-Ama, Imani M.

Blood, Bullets & Bodies ~ Sexual Politics Below Jamaica's Poverty Line

By Imani M. Tafari-Ama

Includes introduction, footnotes, index, bibliography, photographs, poems and original artwork.

1, Sexual Politics. 2, Bodies. 3, Poverty. 4, Jamaica. I Title
5, Political Economy. 6, Gender Embodiment. 7, Power.
8, Crime. 9, Violence. 10, Inner-City. 11, Language.
12, Parenting. 13, Rastafari. 14, Reggae/Dancehall.

Print ISBN: 978 1 78645 136 1
eBook ISBN: 978 1 78645 137 8

Beaten Track Publishing, Burscough, Lancashire.
www.beatentrackpublishing.com

~LIVICATION~

To the Subjects and Agents in Southside

and

in other Inner Cities

And to the

Activists

who still

struggle

for social change

FOREWORD

Two decades ago, I embarked on the research journey to produce the data for my doctoral thesis, which resulted in the first edition of *Blood, Bullets and Bodies: Sexual Politics Below Jamaica's Poverty Line*. The production of this book invoked my multiple identities of academic, womanist action researcher, multimedia journalist, poet and author in a critical deconstruction of the contradictory discourses of power, which characterise Jamaica's political economy. The panoramic perspective that I applied in tackling this problematic entailed delving into the colonial history in order to demonstrate the direct connection between past and present damage to the capacity of the African majority population to enjoy development, as demonstrated by endemic violence. A decade after that initial step, I published the second edition of *Blood, Bullets and Bodies* in 2006, at a time when the escalation of the masculinist discourse of violence was widely acknowledged as the principal obstacle to Jamaica's sustainable development. Another decade on, this fifth edition is being released as the northern Caribbean island has descended further into the abyss of underdevelopment denoted by the colossal failure of successive political and social leaders to staunch the flood of *Blood, Bullets and Bodies*, which is literally draining the lifeblood from our desirable future.

While producing this edition of the book, I am also international fellow and curator of an exhibition entitled '**Rum, Sweat and Tears: Danish Colonialism and Legacy in Flensburg, Ghana and the Virgin Islands of the United States**' – a critical reflection on the political economy of the centennial of Denmark's sale of the land and the people of the so-called 'territory' to the United States of America for $25 million in gold of questionable origin – over $509 million in today's money – 69 years after the African majority had won their emancipation from 250 years of the racist terror entailed in *the Maafa* – the Holocaust of African dehumanisation and enslavement. I am also Fulbright Scholar in Residence in the anthropology department at Bridgewater State University in Rhode Island, tasked to teach four courses to facilitate students critically reflecting on issues of identity politics directly related to the intersectionalities among colonialism, the world economy and attendant contradictory race, class and gender relations, undergirded by discourses of power expressed as violence.

In the course of myriad mulltidisclipinary experiences, I have come to the conclusion that there are indisputable linkages to be drawn among the violence that African people experienced in the Maafa and the violence and underdevelopment entrenched in contemporary expressions of endemic violence in communities predominantly populated by the progeny of the people who suffered this principal crime against humanity. The psychosocial damage is so great that the majority of African people currently define themselves by racialised standards of spirituality, self-representation, social relations and aspirations. It is also no coincidence that the same nations that constituted the colonising protagonists now enjoy the dubious distinction of development while those who bore the brunt of this brutality are designated disadvantaged and underserved.

Describing this construction of oppositional dichotomies of world power as an intentionally designed and racist political economy, the Rt. Hon. Marcus Mosiah Garvey, Pan-Africanist, observed that,

> The attitude of the white race is to subjugate, to exploit, and if necessary exterminate the weaker peoples with whom they come in contact. They subjugate first, if the weaker peoples will stand for it; then exploit, and if they will not stand for subjugation nor exploitation, the other recourse is extermination.[1]

Unfortunately, successive African leaders, on the Continent and in the Diaspora, have failed to adopt a politics of *social transformation*, which would rid us of the shackles of mental slavery, the precursor for tackling the endemic internalisation of the violence entailed in the colonial experience and its unmitigated reproduction as a frightening feature of the postcolonial era. **Blood, Bullets and Bodies** draws these connections, based on evidence-based research in Southside, and from where I now deploy my multidisciplinary skills as a curator, I can testify that the need for crafting a *transatlantic trialogue*, which deconstructs the colonial amnesia attending Euro-American development and protracted African alienation from transitional justice, is even more urgent than it was at the time of Garvey's enunciation at the turn of the twentieth century.

We now live in an era when the masks of Western civilisation have been cast aside to reveal the long-lurking spectre of racist terror, which characterised the dehumanisation drama entailed in the Maafa. It does not take rocket science to recognise that this ongoing threat galvanised the United Nations' Declaration of an International Decade for People of African Descent (2015-24) on the three-pronged platform of Justice, Recognition and Development. Former United Nations' Secretary General, Ban-Ki Moon declared in this context that 'we must remember that people of African descent are among those most affected by racism... [and] denial of basic rights such as access to quality health services and education'. The General Objectives of this Decade are stated as:

> To promote respect, protection and fulfilment of all human rights and fundamental freedoms by people of African descent, as recognized in the Universal Declaration of Human Rights. This main objective can be achieved through the full and effective implementation of the Durban Declaration and Programme of Action, the outcome document of the Durban Review Conference 6 and the political declaration commemorating the tenth anniversary of the adoption of the Durban Declaration and Programme of Action, and through the universal accession to or ratification of and full implementation of the obligations arising under the International Convention on the Elimination of All Forms of Racial Discrimination and other relevant international and regional human rights instruments.[2]

---

1 Garvey, M. *The Philopophy and Opinions of Marcus Garvey*, p. 11, http://www.black-matters.com/books/Marcus-Garvey-Phil-and-Opinions.pdf, retrieved May 29, 2017.

2 http://www.un.org/en/events/africandescentdecade/pdf/A.RES.69.16_IDPAD.pdf, retrieved September 15, 2015.

Despite these lofty ideals, the International Decade for People of African Descent is an eventuality about which many people are seemingly unaware. Yet this Declaration is also a desperate search for mechanisms to reinstate lost African humanity, routed by racist European nation states and compounded in this particular case study, by the comprador relationship that has existed in countries like Jamaica between *de facto* leaders and their *de jure* external interests, exacerbated by denial of Black (i.e. African) power, despite paper-thin emancipation.

In the search for solutions to the twin problems of poverty and violence, again, irrevocably established by several well-meaning research projects in which I have also been multiply involved, we deny the efficacy of the wisdom bestowed on us by sages like Marcus Garvey. I concur with his conclusion that 'we... realize that if (with our knowledge and experience of western civilization) we allow the world to adjust itself politically without taking thought for ourselves, we would be lost to the world in another few decades.'[3]

By re-publishing this edition of ***Blood, Bullets and Bodies: Sexual Politics Below Jamaica's Poverty Line*** at this juncture, I express my unwavering commitment to contributing to the discourses of dissent against all forms of domination and, especially, those stymying sustainable Pan-African development.

Imani M. Tafari-Ama, Ph.D.
Flensburg, 2017

---

3 Ibid. p. 24, http://www.black-matters.com/books/Marcus-Garvey-Phil-and-Opinions.pdf, retrieved May 29, 2017.

ACKNOWLEDGEMENTS

Give thanks to residents in Southside who embraced me with enormous grace and warmth when I conducted research in 1997–99. It is surreal that many of the people you will see photographed in this book do not even look like their pictured image anymore! Children have grown up and become parents; some with straightened hair now wear locks – youthful-looking ones and ones who have undoubtedly aged, while some have transitioned to the land of the ancestors. I also have moved on from being the researcher to metaphorical Sankofa, and I cannot help noticing that the more things have changed, the more they remain the same.

Ethically speaking, data gathering should not only extract and expose subaltern stories through a medium like this book but return this intelligence to its authors to further the initiative of empowerment, already encouraged through a process of critical reflection. Though more needs to be done towards facilitating social transformation in this and other communities, I hope this publication will also be used as a tool by policy-makers, educators, activists and individuals to chart pathways of development, even in incremental steps. I am also heartened that the friendships forged during my journey through the nooks and crannies of Southside so many years ago have stood the test of time, exemplified by the fact that when the second edition of the book was being launched at the Institute of Jamaica's auditorium in 2006, Donovan Rowe, Mauricia 'Molly' Malcolm and Tamara 'Birdie' Richards, were among the principal speakers testifying about their involvement in the production of this manuscript. I was also moved when I introduced the book to some youth who grew up in Southside and had migrated many years ago and saw their emotional response to the photographs of loved ones and read their contributions to the complex discourse analysis of the **Blood, Bullets and Bodies** drama, intertwined with the enactments of Sexual Politics Below Jamaica's Poverty Line, as expressed in this case study.

I have tried to identify the residents of the Southside community with whom I came in touch as widely as possible in the study in fulfilment of the status conferral function of the media and as a contribution to countervailing the social stigma associated with Jamaica's inner cities. However, where such recognition has not been possible for security reasons, rest assured that much respect is still due to you.

Heartfelt gratitude to successive editorial teams who have ensured that this edition has improved from its original thesis incarnation; with each version, the text has visibly improved, even as Southside – prototype for other inner-city communities – remains stagnant, loudly echoing Jamaica's rapidly downward-spiralling citizen security climate. The extraordinary behind-the-scenes labours of love ensured safe delivery of each new birthing.

BLOOD, BULLETS AND BODIES

SEXUAL POLITICS BELOW JAMAICA'S POVERTY LINE

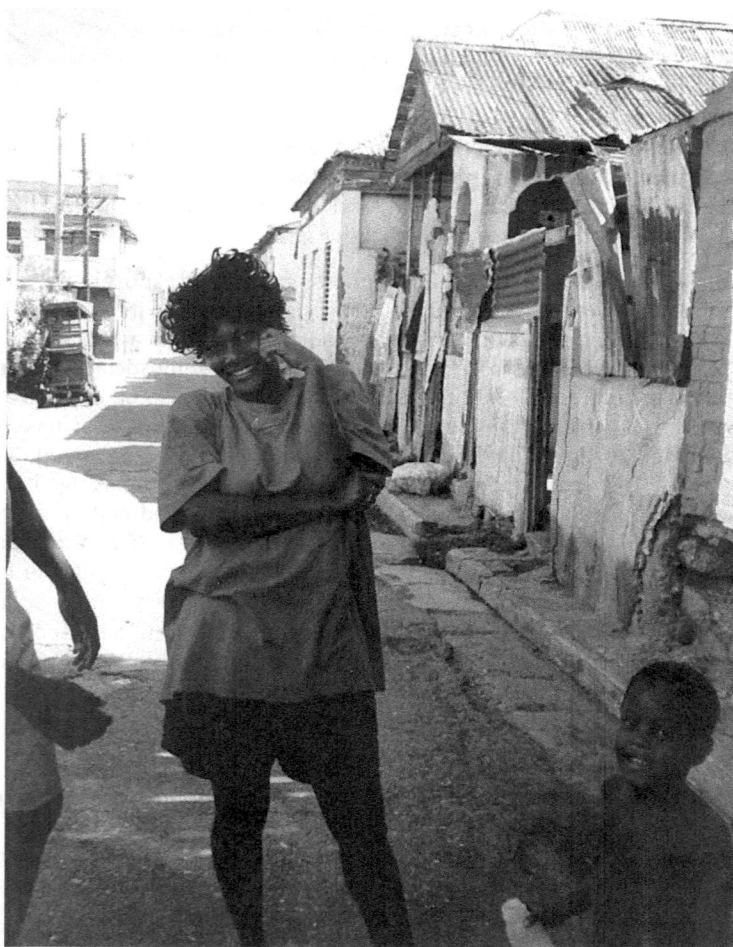

In the environment of poverty and violence,
subordinated subjects subvert structures of power by
exercising agency through embodied actions such as parenting

Imani M. Tafari-Ama

TABLE OF CONTENTS

CHAPTER 7

HEGEMONIC MASCULINITIES, SUBORDINATE FEMININITIES

CHAPTER 8

THE SOCIALLY INSCRIBED BODY

CHAPTER 9

THE BODY AS A RESOURCE FOR EXERCISING AGENCY

PROLOGUE

From the 1970s until now, a lot has been written about mainstreaming gender analysis and having a race and class perspective for a 'holistic' approach, about the need for participatory research in which the researcher learns from the researched and vice versa. This is, however, the first time that I have seen all these aspects combined is such a symbiotic way. What is most important for me is that this research experience has taken place in an inner-city community in Jamaica, where many Jamaicans would never set foot out of fear, thinking that only gunmen and criminals live in these communities. Many uptown people just wish they would all kill each other and disappear. Such are the schisms of Jamaican society.

But that is not all that is remarkable about this book. Sister Imani has decided to include every major aspect of inner-city and national life – culture, economics, politics, sociology her-story and history, socialisation and childcare and parenting, and – believe it or not – SEX! – that terrible word which brings down the condemnation of most church leaders, men and women – if they talk about it at all. Denial of sexual reality, and attempts to confine the conversation to 'acceptable' forms of sexual relationship, with the corollary of condemnation of all that does not 'fit', define the national discourse at the highest levels.

The picture painted by Sister Imani is not pretty – but what is different about this book is that Sister Imani does not engage as if she is talking to some strange species. She engages as a human being talking to other human beings with their own experiences and emotions, showing how the way they see things and act are a consequence of their experiences and the situations in which they exist, and pointing to what has to change for things to be different.

She shows that the inner-city divisiveness and the arming of the gunmen were started by politicians. Now the politicians are afraid, because it has got out of their hands. They are supporting, or being silent about, police brutality, which is the main method being used to try to stamp out the violence and crime. She shows the big-stick attitude by the police, their brutalisation and extra-judicial assassination, their killing of innocent people, for which no policeman has yet gone to jail. She shows the silence of the people in the communities, generated by fear of both the criminals and the police. She shows how the gunmen control the community and decide what people can and cannot do, how the people in the community are prisoners of the 'law' of the gunmen, and that most of the people have no option, since the gunmen are the only ones who bring resources into the community.

She talks about the drugs, and how Jamaica is just part of a large international operation. She defends ganja use for personal purposes, and raises questions about

1

the fact that the same countries which are imposing ganja eradication on Jamaica are changing their laws about ganja and producing it increasingly, yet Jamaica is hesitant to follow suit because the powers-that-be fear the American big stick.

She attacks those uptown people who condemn the way inner-city people live, assuming options that inner-city people do not in fact have. She shows how prostitution operates between uptown and the tourist industry and the inner city, and how the Jamaican elite have no problem when tourists go near naked, but call it nastiness when inner-city women do the same.

She shows the calamity of the macho-man mentality and the male control of everything down to the way people have sex. She shows that lesbianism and homosexuality exist in the inner-city community, that it is condemned in general, but that male homosexuals are fighting back – by having their own gangs of gunmen too! Male socialisation to violence as method therefore crosses the sexual orientation lines. She shows that some of the male homosexuality has a prostitution side, based on uptown demand – but that uptown demand is not the only explanation.

She shows how the women survive by using sex, and how it operates as a kind of slavery, because the men set the limits, and if the women break them, violence is the male response. It is a bit like the slave who eats out of the master's pot but does not have the option to do any other work: her life is totally controlled by the master. Sister Imani shows how competition for the favour of men makes women fight each other, imitating the brutality of the men using ice picks, acid, and so on, which only reinforces the system established by the men. She shows how some women use sex as an empowering factor to show independence, and how that nonetheless reinforces the idea that sex is women's only possible source of power.

But one of the most important things is how Sister Imani shows that the whole situation in the inner-city community goes back to the way men think about themselves and their penises. Domination is the aim, and the gun and the penis that is used to mirror it are twin tools for the purpose. Violence against women and against the community in general, is the outcome. If one gang has a war with another, rape of the other side's women is a form of revenge. As the gunmen are the only ones bringing resources into the area, women have to figure out how to survive in that situation, so they do what they have to do. **So to change the situation, the main challenge is to change the way the men think about themselves and their penises.** In fact, this is not true of the gunmen only. If the politicians did not have the same ideas, they could never agree with what the police are doing in inner-city communities. From the top to the bottom, violence is the main male response to problem-solving. You only have to read the paper to see that men in high places murder their wives or beat them up. This has to change.

As Sister Imani says – and she is brave to say it, because the politicians will not say it because they want votes, so they swallow their consciences and common sense – inner-city people have to take some of the responsibility to change the way they think and act. No matter what else changes, if they do not change that, their situation will not change.

But the politicians also have to ask pardon for their wrongs and change their ways. The police have to begin to have respect for human rights – the people in the inner city are people too, and should not be treated like animals – and it should be recognised that not all inner-city people are criminals. The police have to educate themselves about the situation, and find other ways to deal with the crime. The politicians have to stop encouraging the police to do wrong. The corrupt policemen have to be cleaned out: many are part of the drug trade, and it is rumoured that some politicians are too. We have to get a new kind of policeman trained in human rights as well as in fighting crime. Sister Imani recommends a Peace and Reconciliation Commission like in South Africa, to deal with all the crime, whether from gunmen, police or politicians, because some of the things that have been done to the people in inner-city communities by the police and politicians are criminal too.

Sister Imani says that inner-city development has to be a serious thing. It has to have a budget and money: because we live under capitalism, and those who do not have capital will have to have work, or the guns will continue to rule. The people in the inner city have to sit and analyse the situation, and organise themselves to get out of the rut. They have to be part of the planning, and they have to work together to make the plans work. The plans have to be budgeted as a matter of priority, because this is not something that concerns only the inner cities: it concerns the whole of Jamaica, the way we live, our reputation abroad, how we are going to make money in this world, and how we are gong to make sure that everyone gets a fair chance in this Land We Love.

Those who are already trying to change the situation must continue, and not be discouraged. Whether it is Parents of Inner City Kids or the women's groups like Sistren and AWOJA and Media Watch, and the Association of Female Artists who are trying to change the way men think about women and how women think about themselves, or Sister Punky with the people on S-Corner – they need to keep on keeping on. Anyone who can help them reach more people should do so. Those in the media should stop promoting songs that glorify gunmen and violence. They should promote songs that show the situation as it is and point the way to solutions. They should promote 'Love and Unity' instead of 'War and Crime'. And we should stop imitating what we see in the American films we get here, which are filled with violence and destruction and sex as a weapon; film, song, theatre – all should be used to build consciousness all over the country so we can strengthen our working together for change. The struggle has to get BIGGER, because this concerns Jamaica's future, who we are, and how we are going to live with one another.

Not everyone in the inner-city community of Southside lives off gunmen. Some people work outside. However, the gunmen determine when they can walk and how they must live when they are inside. Some people do not like it, especially the older people – and the Rastafarians do not defend that way of living at all. That is why Sister Imani says that Rastafari must start to play a bigger role, like they did in 1978 when they helped to arrange the Peace Treaty. It's true that politicians broke it up afterwards, but people are wiser now. Rastafari must use their Peace and Love power again, to help to stop the war and to get people to think differently. Rasta women must come forward and defend their rights and those of women in general – and make their voices heard and work to make the children have a better life in their youth, and a better future.

But listen to this! Sister Imani says **we must listen to the children** – let them express themselves. They have things to say about how all this affects them, and how they want to live. They are our future. We must listen. Sister Imani lets them speak in her book.

One of the best parts of the book is where Sister Imani quotes from the *Convention on the Rights of the Child*. You should read that too! How are we going to make sure that the children can enjoy their rights?

Sister Imani is going to do a video version of her book, so look out for that too. The Sister is powerful! Electric-light power, not gun power! Get some of the light!

Joan French
Gender & Development Expert
and former United Nations Representative
[including in Burkino Faso]

INTRODUCTION

No matter how long a log stays in the water, it doesn't become a crocodile
Bambara Proverb ~Mali

Power, Gender and The Body

Sitting on a sidewalk in Southside with young girls all with chemically straightened hair
Talking about boys and periods of bloody encounters
Of sex of pregnancy of just feeling bodies changing and wondering
How to manage these transitions
I too talked of my encounters with the pleasure pain and perplexity
and of the confidence that
I being a woman assert and the
art of loving it
I will return I said and maybe even live here for a while and share some more as you grow
through your changes
No Miss! You can't live here!
The panic and distress in the response from the girl was unmistakable
Others nodded in unison
You can't live here! She said again Every day gun shot fire down here and every day
some body dead down here miss! We used to it
but you not used to it You can't live here miss!
Silenced, I thought,
These girls take the deadly violence stalking their community as the norm
Their identities are bound up with the acrid texture of its death knell
A young man once told me that because he knows that there is a bullet out there with his
name on it
He would prefer to do it without a condom and die from AIDS
Because he was sure
he would enjoy the sex more!
What comment on cause and effect of violence and poverty could offer comfort in the
face of such raw cynicism?
For one wrong word said you soon could be dead
on this power-filled street
where the gold-teeth don-gorgons meet
Though social lack is a challenge to hope
The socially inscribed body provides options to cope
Then there is the tourism sector

The biggest moneymaker
Far removed from the
Madness and mayhem
But the value of the body
Is the power behind the dollar
Almighty money overrides
The stakes of morality
The youth have seen and they have heard and have learnt to say not a word
They know that Jamaican society
Gives social whiteness top priority
While the African majority
Live with chronic scarcity
Life in a Jamaican inner city
is not pretty
It's a story of the cheapness of life
Yet the rich passion of beauty
Amidst cycles of strife
A power game of who next
Will bite the dust
If poverty is a crime
Then violence is a must

© **imani tafari-ama**

Blood For Blood, Fire For Fire

The underbelly of Jamaica's cosmopolitan façade is not as alluring as its public relations agents desire and make it out to be. This has sorely affected the island's political health and public image. In recent years, the international media have emphasised that this spectacular tourist destination is somewhat less than pristine because of the extreme violence stalking some of the inner-city streets of Kingston. And, because the fickle tourism industry is currently the number one foreign exchange earner, the local authorities have deliberately and continuously tried to sanitise the bloody urban streets of its capital city, in an effort to convince visitors that this amazingly beautiful Caribbean island is a safe destination. They succeed, to whatever extent they do, only because the exclusive 'all-inclusive' tourism activities take place on the showpiece north coast, well away from the flying bullets and the mayhem in the inner-city enclaves of Kingston.

In contrast, this public relations gambit has enjoyed variable success, if any, with most of the local population. Jamaica is, admittedly, a very class-stratified society so it is quite possible for the elite – just like the tourist – to avoid all contact with the danger areas, from the safe distance between the real world and the television screens in their securely gated properties – or guard-patrolled neighbourhoods. However, people living in inner-city communities cannot avoid the harsh reality of their streets. Jamaica, generally, is like a volatile powder keg waiting to explode and for those living below the poverty line the danger is not merely televised, it is live and direct. The law of the urban landscape is 'blood for blood' and 'fire for fire'. Hence, for poor city residents, violence is embedded in their past, pervades their present, and threatens to overrun their future.

Blood, Bullets and Bodies is about the political economy of this endemic violence and the corresponding sexual politics in Southside, an inner-city community in Jamaica's capital, Kingston. This book is also about the gender-power dimensions involved in this violence and their implications for definitions and performances of femininity and masculinity, both in the inner-city environment and in the wider society. This study illustrates how, and why, in the context of dire disadvantage, human bodies, particularly female bodies, have become an indispensable resource for strategic survival and self-realisation. On the one hand, women, themselves, use their bodies to acquire income, influence, protection and prestige. And, on the other hand, women's bodies are seized by men as a prize of conquest in the ongoing turf wars and political confrontations. It is a tragic irony that may be more extreme and explicit below the Jamaican poverty line, but is not necessarily limited to the inner city or to just a Jamaican context.

Some Things about Southside

Percival 'Ites Man' Cordwell (now deceased), recalled that Southside got its name in the early 1970s when some footballers decided that they would call themselves 'Southern Ethiopia' to counteract the designation of the Dunkirk area as 'Biafra', reflecting the conditions of poverty that were akin to the notorious Nigerian situation. Over time, this was shortened to 'South' and when the press caught on to the name, they added the 'side', hence 'Southside'. The Kingston Harbour, one of the largest natural harbours in the world, forms the boundary on the south. The 6,000 residents of the community are, characteristically, poor people of predominantly African descent who are, for the most part, unemployed. Some are self-employed while the minority is wage earning. These residents live in poor housing and socioeconomic conditions and exist under the constant threat of violence, due to the activities of the gangs, security forces and itinerant criminals.

Fishing has long been one of the main economic activities for men in the area. For me, observing the old men making the fishing nets in the New Road Park, next to the South Camp Road border, was an odyssey of grassroots art and popular theatre. News and anecdotes flew freely, between the skilful weaving of knots, recalling that in the past, women bought and sold the fish once the men brought it ashore. In recent times, more and more women have become involved in various other aspects of the fishing industry. They now own boats and go out to sea. Both the men and women involved in this industry complained, however, that they were hampered in the maintenance of their trade by a lack of resources.

On the whole, people in Southside suffer from chronic neglect of the community by the state authorities, whose failure to provide the necessary infrastructural support to the inner-city areas, is reflected in the gruesome tale told in the pictorial story below.

Figure In.1: Fishing boat parked on Fleet Street.

South is like the end of the earth.
When it rains and the garbage is
washed down the gutters
and you have to jump over it
it is so nasty.
The gully is overfull with all kinds of things
from dead dog to baby pampers to all kinds of things.
Sometimes we even think that
people might drown in it because
the gully water high, high.
People put out their garbage but
sometimes for months you see no sign of the garbage truck.
The garbage collection people once brought in
one of the large garbage units
and placed it on the street not far from our house
Because they never used to come and collect the garbage regularly
we had to rebel for them to move it because when that was full
nobody could stay around South
because that would be too stink

Maxine, 35, Higholborn Street

Figure In.2: In spite of the garbage receptacle, garbage spills over into the streets.

This destitution stands in sharp contrast to what Ras Carlie remembers as a community that was once home to a middle-class population. The dramatic decline coincided with the departure of the formerly well-to-do residents from the area.

> It was mostly Jews, Syrians and Chinese running business. It was as if this community was the economic base for Kingston. From the early sixties and by 1970, most of them were gone. When they constructed Newport East, and Newport West, then most of the industries left the area and went into that area. When the powerful people moved out, people mostly from the rural areas moved in.[4] I was about twelve, thirteen at the time. People were always moving, because you had development taking place in other areas, better housing and so on. When those people moved out, people did not restructure the houses or refurbish them. They just stayed and people came and lived in them.[5]

(Ras Carlie, Laws Street)

When the Brown people moved out of Southside, they went to the uptown areas of St. Andrew, the suburban area surrounding Kingston. Only magnates like the Matalons (and GraceKennedy Limited.) retained their property and presence in the area. The Mechala Group of Companies – including the Multicare Foundation,[6] owned by the Matalon family – has its head offices on the Harbour Street section of the Southside community.

The corporation has contributed to the development of Southside, in recognition of the adverse impact that the debilitating social profile of the inner city has had on the political economy of downtown Kingston as a whole.

Dr. the Hon. Aaron Matalon, former head of Mechala, gave the Twelfth Annual Bustamante Lecture on February 26, 1998, at the Jamaica Conference Centre. He recounted some of his experiences of growing up and managing a commercial concern in the downtown Kingston area that now includes Southside, and lamented the drastic changes that have taken place due to the escalation of political and gang-related violence.

> There is the perception that crime and violence in the inner cities make downtown Kingston a fearful place in which to do business. We cannot deny that the level of violence in our inner cities is intolerably high. The older political tribalism and the new 'donmanship' that exists have made any action at the community level very difficult. Drug use and abuse are on the increase...

---

4 Cohen documents that the unemployment rate in the rural areas at this time exceeded that in the urban area, which was increasing. Rural-urban migration was the order of the sixties even as emigration accounted for the numbers who were uprooted due to political and economic necessity. He points out that '[t]he most visible consequences of changes in rural life were evident in Kingston, where those pushed from the land set up their shacks and swelled the ranks of the urban poor...' (1977, 25).

5 From other oral accounts, many people came from rural as well as other urban areas.

6 Mechala sponsored the initial video documentary which I did on the Southside community, and during my PhD research period, the company contributed J$50,000 towards the production of the one-month series of children's workshops as an indication of their commitment to the development of the community. I am grateful to Ms. Janet Carvalho, Mr. Liebert Grant and Dr. Neville Ying for their support.

So what happened to the Kingston that I knew? To answer this question would require a socioeconomic and political analysis, which is not within the ambit of this talk. What I will assert as strongly as I can is that we should not; we must not let our city die. There is too much of our history, of our very beings wrapped up in this city of ours...I believe that, despite everything, Kingston does have a future – but it will require the will and commitment of the widest possible cross-section of Kingstonian...

Many commercial businesses survive unmolested in inner-city areas today because of the protection money which they pay to 'area dons' to guarantee the security of their premises. Of course, this is not to suggest that the Matalons pay protection money, but it is worth mentioning because protectionism is, in fact, a big money transaction, particularly for businesses located in close proximity to certain inner-city communities.

When I went to Southside for the first time in the fall of 1995, the bright mid-morning sun which bounced off the zinc fences was as dazzling on the eyes as were the welcoming smiles reflecting the hospitable warmth of the people I met. I was working with a team of researchers whose objective was to find out whether there is a direct correlation between poverty and violence in inner-city Jamaica. This project was sponsored by the World Bank and the University of the West Indies, Mona, and was the precursor to the establishment of the Jamaica Social Investment Fund from that 'debt forgiveness' pot of World Bank/International Monetary Fund (IMF) money. We worked in a total of nine urban grassroots communities located in the Kingston metropolitan area, Spanish Town – the original capital – and Montego Bay – the second city. We used Participatory Rapid Appraisal (PRA) methods to find out what people saw as problems and solutions to their cultural development.

Figure In.3: The Breezy Castle Sports Complex on Harbour Street was a gift from the Mechala Group of Companies, the headquarters of which is located on the opposite side of the street.

We did not need binoculars to see the connections between poverty and violence. The research findings revealed that 'respect' is what people crave most (Levy, 1996). They felt that it was the institutionalised *dissing* by the System that caused the approximately half a million inner-city residents to be living in the jaws of poverty. The residents perceive this as being directly related to the violence snaking its way throughout their lives. People said that if the youth were not chronically unemployed, they would not feel impelled to get involved in illegal activities in order to get some form of gain – whether psychosocial or material. Others noted that because reprisal 'blood for blood' killings are the order of the day and conflict resolution capacities were at an all-time low, the syndrome of violence could never cease. Still others said that gang warfare over turf, guns and drugs fuelled the internecine conflicts. Many concluded that these combined factors, actually prevent them from fulfilling their needs and wants.

After that inaugural PRA project, I returned to Southside in 1996 to use drama and audiovisual documentation to work with children on issues of identity and social relations, teaching them in the process how to use the camera and facilitating their play-making capabilities. This culminated in the production of a video documentary called *Living, Loving and Losing in Southside*, which was screened on local cable channels. The children participated in a workshop at the then Consortium Graduate School of the Social Sciences, where they shared their perspectives on their lives with professors from the school.

When I came back to Southside in 1998, it was to spend a year and a half doing an intensive, and extensive, intergenerational study of violence and sexual politics. I completed a thesis on the subject and achieved the PhD objective from this work, but, for me, the experience went beyond being just another academic exercise. My PhD research benefited from my involvement in a Participatory Rapid Appraisal project initiated by the Jamaica Social Investment Fund (JSIF) and to which I referred earlier.

My involvement in the JSIF project culminated in the formation of a local group, the *Grassroots Youth Organisation*, to tackle some of the social problems that they had identified. However, the development of this group has been severely challenged by the need for investment in long-term organisation building, as much as by the violence in the area. For example, a social trip, organised to engender community goodwill, had to be cancelled on Boxing Day 1999 because the brother of a member of the group was murdered. And, despite the determined attempts to pursue the painstaking process of community development, the efforts of the group are challenged by everyday insecurity issues.

It is impossible to have engaged as intimately as I did with quite a number of people in the community and not been profoundly impacted by the experience. As the photograph (Fig. In.4) shows, it is not even desirable to be aloof in a situation where the quality of the data generated is greatly enhanced by virtue of the closeness of the relationships which I formed.

I conducted several in-depth interviews with Mauricia Malcolm, popularly known as Molly Marshall, whose voice became a recurring point of reference in my thesis and a device that I used to create linkages between the issues that I explored. I also became involved in consciousness-raising efforts as part of my commitment to producing research that leaves the cultural environment positively affected by its encounter with academia. Molly and others were candid about the fact that while they might not have received direct threats, people in communities like Southside generally live on the edge of danger, twenty-four seven. They also bear the scars of the stigma assigned to people subsisting in the inner-city space and the exclusions that go along with residing in that social space. Chronic lack of trust and the absence of empowering social relations in the community, as well as the poor physical infrastructure, all serve to erode psychosocial well-being. The obvious question is whether the political will even exists to tackle the taproot causes of the poverty and the rising incidence of violence, which is now endemic to the inner-city areas.

While working on the research, I lived with the Shepherd family at 51 Higholborn Street, although I also had an uptown home base in Jacks Hill. Becoming part of this tremendous extended family has been one of the most enriching experiences of my life. We still relate to each other as family in that special way that does not confine the notion of family to blood. Blood becomes a metaphor for love, support and friendship, and an indicator of an institutional support system that is responsible for the retention of social sanity in spite of the prevailing blood-for-blood nightmare. The closeness of my relationship with my family, which has meandered into the present, also demonstrates the benefits of adopting a participatory approach to conducting research.

Figure In.4: Here, members of the project team, comprised of consultants, institutional representatives from the Social Development Commission (a JSIF partner) and community trainees, are involved in a community mapping exercise in the HEART Trust's building at the corner of Maiden Lane and Barry Street.

The Shepherd family also explodes stereotypes about the dysfunctionality of those living in the ghetto. I cannot claim to have gone native in the true sense of the term, but I can certainly testify that the rich depths of the human condition that we were able to explore, threw up tremendous gems of beauty, passion, self-confidence, brilliance[7] and all the other desirable attributes for citizens living in an underdeveloped society. The collective creative genius of each and every one – my mother,[8] siblings, nieces, nephews – is also a statement of strategic parenting mixed with talent that produces the will to survive creatively despite the dehumanising living conditions of the social environment.[9]

Figure In.5: Here I share one of many memorable moments with Molly (left) and a friend (right) in her 'South Pole' bar on Tower Street.

Moving between my two living spaces was symbolic of the binary opposition embedded in the coexistence of the two vastly different ways of life between 'uptown' and 'downtown' Kingston. Another paradox was that as an outsider, I was able to cross boundaries that some residents saw as forbidden, due to deadly demarcations of turf. Significantly, several persons said that my Rastafari self-identification was the main reason that they were confident to be open with me about their 'inside' experiences and feelings. Additionally, as a woman, albeit a Rasta woman, I was also able to probe into intimate personal details that no man could have.

This almost automatic conferral of status is directly linked to the leadership and peacemaking roles played by people in the community who live a *Rastafari Livity or Way of Life*. I have, therefore, paid very close attention to ethical standards of representation in this recounting, bigging up the status of people by naming them, where it is safe to do so, and avoiding such naming where the security of the speaker would be compromised. The diverse multimedia and culturally informed research

---

7 For example, Faye's son Bruce, a chartered accountant at PriceWaterhouseCoopers, has the distinction of holding the record of the youngest person to have qualified as a chartered accountant in the Caribbean. And he was born and raised in Southside.

8 Her spirit lives through memories, constant recollections and performances of various skills related to the tailoring skills she taught.

9 One of the greatest things to happen to me was being in traffic the other day and seeing my nephew Chunny walking down the road in his Kingston College uniform. I was so pleased to see this handsome boy, who had grown from the bright five-year-old baby he was in 1999 to genius material in 2005 that I held up the line for a few minutes to chat with him and send a message home. was the main reason that they were confident to be open with me about their 'inside' experiences and feelings. Additionally, as a woman, albeit a Rasta woman, I was also able to probe into intimate personal details that no man could have.

methods used were contoured to raise the consciousness and self-esteem of the participants, while enabling me to gain access to a wealth of data, which I returned to the said participants in various forms of *cultural communications*. Defined by Paulo Freire as cultural action achieved through praxis, this approach is designed to contribute to the process of social change (Freire, 1979, 180). Nevertheless, I was able to immerse myself in the experience while still maintaining critical analytical distance. Even so, I also acknowledge that this form of knowledge (re)production is liable to reinforce power differences between the (activist) researcher and the subjects with whom she engages. Be that as it may, in the final analysis, I trust that people in Southside will agree that I represented them well.

Imani Tafari-Ama
August 2008

CHAPTER 1

CAUGHT IN A TRAP

*Jankro say im nyam ded meat fe pain a toomuck,
but dawg nyam i fe craben.*

*John Crow says he eats dead meat
because of pain in the stomach,
but Dog eats dead meat because he is gluttonous.*

*Some people do unpleasant things out of sheer
necessity, while others will do the same things
without good reason.*[10]

Fact or Fiction

It is said that 'fact is stranger than fiction' and this is certainly true for the story we are about to tell. It is a disturbingly ironic story about how blood, bullets and bodies below the poverty line in a tourist paradise have turned a vacation heaven into a living hell. It is a compelling story about how inner-city Black bodies, especially Black female bodies, have become prized possessions and highly valuable commodities, to be bargained with as a means of survival (sex for sale), or to be seized by force as a sign of conquest (sex on demand). It is a thought-provoking story about the integrated set of sociopolitical and socioeconomic historical circumstances that has made crime and violence – bullets, blood and dead bodies – the number one problem in late twentieth- and early twenty-first-century Jamaica. It is a story that needs to be told. It is a riveting story of sex, violence, political intrigue, mass mental (psychosocial) manipulation and generations of survival, by any means necessary. It sounds like a blockbuster movie, and one day it will be, but the worst thing about this strange story is, it is all true. It is indeed fact, not fiction. And, at the time of writing, it is all still taking place at an escalating pace on the streets of Kingston.

The high propensity for violent, ballistic behaviour by young Jamaican members of the so-called '*Jamaican Posse*' and '*Yardie*' criminal gangs is now well known in places like the United States, Canada and England. However, the real reasons and root causes for the violent actions of such Jamaican gangsters living overseas are not as well known in those countries. Back in the Caribbean homeland of the '*Yardies*', the problem of extreme violence is now so endemic to the society that modern Jamaica has experienced and accepted a normalisation of pathological behaviour by its younger inner-city residents as an unavoidable occurrence. Thus, blood, bullets and bodies

---

10   See Morris Brown (1993: 90).

have become a fact of life. The abnormal pathology behind the widespread violence can be heard in the language of the streets, as might be expected, but, surprisingly, a pathological psychology can also be detected in the language used by, supposedly, civil society, if one listens with informed ears. That same violent pathology can also be seen in the *body language* of Black ghetto residents as much as in the body language of even 'Brown' suburban residents. All this is enacted against the backdrop of a corresponding unspoken (and literally 'foreign') body language, which is enunciated silently by skimpily clad, visiting, White tourists lazily sunning themselves on picture-perfect, north-coast beaches, not that many miles away.

Just as it is true that fact is, indeed, stranger than fiction, it is also true that perspective is everything and that socialisation and choices define our identities – who we say we are – and influence how we construct meaning. As we will soon see, perspective and socialisation shape the choices we make and how each and every one of us acts in a social setting. Such perspectives, socialisation and definitions of choice are highly influenced and shaped by the everyday (body) language and words we use, whether spoken or unspoken. Unfortunately, words don't always mean what we want them to mean, or what we think they mean. Or, conversely, words can mean exactly what we want them to mean (beyond mere semantics) at any particular time.

This, then, is the dilemma we face: separating fact from fiction and finding real and enduring meaning, as we narrate this strange story and try to dissect and analyse the prevailing sociopolitical psychology and *body language* of the violent pathology exhibited on the inner-city streets of Kingston. This is the dilemma we face: separating fact from fiction in order to find real and enduring solutions that will reduce the distressing flood of blood, bullets and bodies. We hope that by highlighting some of the facts and exposing much of the fiction, this book will be a catalyst in motivating the *political will* necessary to find and implement such enduring real-time solutions.

Selling Sex

Sex sells. Everyone knows that. People – men and women – think about sex repeatedly and regularly many times a day. That is why sexual innuendos and sexualised body images are used to sell everything: movies, cars, sneakers, cigarettes, boats, records, sports, cosmetics, beer, clothes and even vacations in the Caribbean. Sex is used, universally, by the advertising media to shape and influence the fashion, appetite, lifestyle and minds of millions. Obviously, then, sex and the gendered bodies that are inscribed with sexual identities, and which perform programmed sexual roles, are all central elements in the lives of everybody, everywhere, every day – no matter the race, nationality or religion.

Sex and the human body form a nerve tonic that interconnects with all other facets of human life in many ways. Therefore, sex, what is said about sex, and the embodied meanings ascribed to sexualised words are appropriate tools with which to analyse societal problems in Jamaica, precisely because sex and embodied sexualised issues interconnect with so many other areas of human life. Hence, given that this book's subtitle is *Sexual Politics Below Jamaica's Poverty Line*, we will be discussing sex and the body, sex and politics, sex and violence, sex and economics, sex and race, sex and history, sex and tourism, sex and words, sex and literature, sex and Jamaica etc., during the course of the upcoming chapters.

Please rest assured that I am not trying to be salacious; nor am I providing mere literary titillation with all this talk of sex, sex, sex. Rather, an intimate and detailed examination of this multifaceted and intriguing subject is necessary for an accurate theoretical deconstruction of the many, nuanced, binary oppositions that work in tandem and against each other in the lives of most ordinary Jamaicans who live in inner-city communities. Sometimes the language used in coming chapters will be as raw as the bloody, bullet-riddled bodies and as profane as the X-rated female bodies that are also under discussion; all that goes with the territory and with this strange story.

Thus, to recap, sex sells, and in Jamaica sex sells very well. Unabashed sexual expression is the near norm on Jamaica's north coast, which is considered to be a tourist haven from lush Port Antonio in the east, through the cruise ship port of Ocho Rios and tourist capital, Montego Bay, all the way to Negril's world-famous beach resorts in the west. By and large, the Jamaican government and local churches turn a blind eye toward the hedonistic lewdness of White visitors and ignore the wet and wild, naked exhibitionism that abounds and is encouraged within the confines of the north-coast resorts. Only when outrageous pictures appear in the newspapers do we hear cries of condemnation. Otherwise, it is business as usual, and one of the most lucrative businesses in the north-coast tourist circuit is selling and buying sex: selling the charms of Black bodies to White buyers for their sexual satisfaction.

In this contrived scenario, the identity markers of race, gender, complexion, age and nationality all matter and all mean something tangible to both the buyers and sellers of sex. But, it is very important to remember that sex and sexuality for and with White tourists vacationing in north-coast hotels is a world apart from sex and sexuality for and with Black people residing in the inner-city areas of Kingston. The body language and social meanings of the interactions are basically all the same in both worlds, but the rules and results are very different. Sex in the tourist world involves escapism of one form or another for everyone. But, in a perverse inversion, sex in the inner-city world only ensures temporary survival in the vicious ghetto trap from which few of the buyers or sellers escape. The politics and economics of sex and violence in this inner-city ghetto environment, far removed from the tourist resorts, is where the primary focus of this book lies.

The Ghetto Trap

The community called Southside is a typical example of the politicised inner-city or *garrison community* phenomenon in Jamaica. **Blood Bullets and Bodies** focuses on the his-/her-story of the lives of the subjects of Southside, their inner-city streets and their ongoing efforts to improve their desperate situation against the background of the contradictory political economy of embodiment. In a very real sense, the disadvantaged residents of inner-city enclaves of Kingston are caught in an economic/ social trap, not of their own making. This ghetto trap of poverty, violence and crime is every bit as vicious a cycle of disenfranchisement and immobility as a bear trap, and is as inescapable for most of those born into these dire social conditions. To get to the root of precisely how this ghetto trap evolved over the past few decades, we first have to talk to the old-timers in the community, like Ras Carlie.

> *The real changes came in the late sixties; after those business people started moving out, the politics set in. This displaced a large number of people*

because of the fear of political violence that escalated by 1967 when one man was shot and killed inside a dancehall called Goldfinger Lawn at 34 Fleet Street. A Chinese family that owned that property used to live in that area until they moved out. As far as I know, it started there. That was the first time that I can recall seeing gun violence in politics. It lulled for a time and then it started again in 1972. In 1969 when Macka, a member of the Maxi Gang lost his life, it caused a split between youths in the area. Politicians came in and labelled one set as Spanglers and one set as Skull. As far as I could understand it, it was people who lived beyond Gold Street at that time, going west, who were the Spanglers while the people on the eastern side of Gold Street were the Skull. From that time until this time, the battle has not ended.

In my view, most of the youths that were involved in the conflicts at that time had nothing to do with politics. It would have faded out if politics had allowed it to and made the youths solve their problems. The youths were youths that grew together. The press presented Spanglers as PNP and Skull as Labourite but as I said before, most youths were not dealing with anything political. It was a press hype to print things and say they were so when they weren't so. In a way, the election in '76 was not as hostile as in the earlier seventies. This was because of the state of emergency and things like that. I can only recall two detainees from here; the two are deceased now. You had Foreign Pants and Rock-I who was more recently killed. People did not fear them because, normally, what they did was not something that involved all of the people, just a number of youths who had conflicts among themselves.

You had the Peace Truce in 1978 and that continued through the rest of the seventies until 1980. Then in 1980, during a political campaign by one of the parties, it started again. You had some shooting and some people got injured. That died down, then you had the Gold Street massacre.

Things got out of hand from there on then. From such time to this time, things have not changed. Or, I should say, it has changed from better to worse because everything from sixties, seventies and even the early part of the eighties was better than now. The nineties are way out of control; you have a divided community right now. One time you could go to any corner, any hours. You could go anywhere freely without fear. Now it is divided up into different gangs who are fighting themselves for reasons unknown. It is only the Almighty that can settle this. I think this is beyond man's control because of how people are thinking now. Most of the youths nowadays, it's like they have been turned into killers. It is hardly likely that they can be reformed. It seems as if better days might come but I know that better ones have passed. The kind of joy and happiness that used to exist in the community no longer exists. Before, it was a twenty-four seven community. Now, I think that we have been reduced to six hours; everyone is living in fear[11] because no one is sure of what is going to happen next. Who might be the next victim.

~Ras Carlie, Laws Street

---

11 Fear is a recurring motif and a concept that I will explain methodologically as directly related to the pervasive violence, which describes the helplessness that many people express.

If we look at Jamaica's evolution as a nation, we will see that the formation of the political parties and their style of personality-driven leadership mimicked the power games of the colonial experience. Since Jamaica attained its political independence in 1962, those who control the state machinery have used force as an organising principle – a tactic fundamental to the British *modus operandi* of divide and rule. The two main parties in Jamaica today, the People's National Party (PNP) and the Jamaica Labour Party (JLP) have been the main contenders for the 60 parliamentary seats, leaving political novices, not versed in the art of partisan politics, to struggle to make back their deposits.

The watershed event that signalled the use of violence in politics came in 1966 when Tivoli Gardens was constructed by the JLP on the ruins of the bulldozed and burnt-out homes of the previous residents of the infamous Kingston ghetto known as 'Back-o-Wall' or 'Dungle'. This bulldozing operation was organised by then Minister of Housing, Edward Seaga, currently the retired Leader of the Opposition JLP. Tivoli Gardens, with its trademark high-rise buildings, was the very first, and still is the best run, and most successful example of a *garrison community*. In the three decades that followed the Foreshore razing, Jamaican politicians from both sides of the divide constructed many other *garrisons*. Residents are allowed to live unmolested in these politicised areas based on party affiliation while, in a clientilist exchange, party loyalists are rewarded with scarce benefits like housing, labour contracts and phallic prizes of deadly gun weaponry, the modern archetype of masculinity.

In this context and environment, Kingston, and hence Southside, is all too often the scene of violent deaths. Anthony Woodburn notes that this trend has been growing from the sixties and has now reached crisis proportions:

> The two-year period 2000–2001 shows an uncanny appetite for murders totalling 2,026, exceeding the total murders for the period 1960-1974, a total of 1,767 murders. The total murders and shootings reported between 1960 and 2001 are 18,058 and 36,430 respectively.

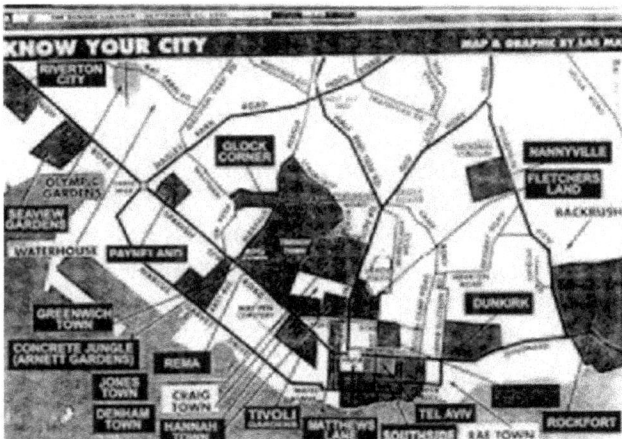

Figure 1.1: Map of some of the inner-city communities of Kingston & St. Andrew.

Enlightened sociologists now accept that to a large extent, poverty and crime go hand in hand. Thus, the song by the group Still Cool, 'To Be Poor Is A Crime' (re-sung by Freddie McGregor), is an important truism. The map in Figure 1.1 shows the inner-city communities of Kingston and St. Andrew that are adversely affected by the triple scourges of poverty, crime and violence. Southside is located between Rae Town and Matthews Lane in the south-eastern (bottom-right) section.

By instigating the partisan violence, politicians, in effect, primed the ghetto trap and provoked a vicious cycle of reprisals, the original cause of which many in today's Southside cannot even remember. Gang feuds have been reinforced by feelings of 'blood for blood' revenge arising out of the human losses that families have suffered during the years of conflict. The syndrome of 'fire for fire' revenge is also fraught with gender power dynamics, since those who perceive that they have been injured, in turn, lash out on those whom they recognise to be weaker, due to lack of symbolically phallic gun weaponry and the authority this emblem connotes. In addition, the legal system is so corrupt that many injured parties do not see it as a viable avenue through which to achieve justice, and as a popular international slogan points out: 'No justice – no peace!' Thus, gunfire, gushing blood and bullet-riddled bodies abound.

Ballistic Affair

Throw whey yuh gun
Throw whey yuh knife
Let us all unite
Everyone is living in fear
Just through this ballistic affair

~Leroy Smart ('Ballistic Affair')

The need for revenge was thought to be diminishing as more and more people migrated from the inner-city areas to North America in search of a better way of life. Of course, some local gangsters established business connections with their overseas counterparts called *Posses* in the USA (Gunst, 1995: 140) and *Yardies* in England and Canada. Many of these international business affiliations mushroomed on the ashes of partisan Jamaican politics. Some of the political activists/gunmen fled Jamaica to escape the long reach of the law, repatriating material support, including high-powered guns, which are easily obtainable in the USA. These ballistic weapons found their way into the eager hands of men in inner-city communities like Southside, stoking the fires of already red-hot cycles of violence and revenge. Thus, the 'blood for blood' and 'fire for fire' mentality has now become a socially entrenched pattern of behaviour.

Nowadays, the recurring and spiralling violence has surged beyond the boundaries of politics. Clive, a community activist, poetically agonised over the deteriorating conditions in his area, characterised by the proliferation of the gangs and crews that control corners in his community.

The Other Side of the Coin

The other side of the coin is when
People flipped it up and forgot
that the smooth side was all about
Love and unity
People then started to live on the edge
and that was all about drugs, dons,
Guns, fast living, and corners
McWhinney Street and Stephen Lane
Raiders, Charlotte Street
to Tower Street South Camp Road and Gully Massive
Old Man Corner, Fleet Street or Renkers
Tiger Fort, Buck Town, Site, First Street, which takes in
Love in the House, Stallag 17, Super Dollar and Super Stud
Coolers, Okro Slime, Pow and Young Pow
Max and Breadfruit Tree
That's it till you reach to Tel Aviv and Spoilers
That's how the power struggle comes about
About who to run where and what
Who has the most guns who is the baddest ma
Any one man can control anywhere in this community
because the man who owns his own gun
is not about to take any talk from another man
about what he should or should not do
because he becomes his own don
and that leads to death and destruction
yet all this derives from politicians
and the distribution of guns
till the so called dons got the opportunity
of leaving and of sending
guns with the aim of arming the corners
the whole government is at a loss
as to how to solve what they call
the problems of the ghetto
where you find man and man
living on the edge
at four and five
not knowing the language to strive
to resolve the conflicts
at two and three
how can it be
that we cannot remember
how to create unity in the community

~Clive, 33, Higholborn Street

Figure 1.2: Spray-painted slogan of the Jamaica Labour Party, JLP.

When the political battle lines were drawn, Southside was on the side of the JLP,[12] an identity which was established when party opponents were forcibly removed or 'roped out' of this community in the run-up to the 1980 general election. This pattern of disembowelling communities in the name of partisan pursuits has resulted in the separation of family members and the splintering of community relations, which are the main causes of the present syndrome of citizen insecurity. The graffiti that is splattered across the walls of the community proclaim this partisan allegiance in symbolically enlightening statements.

Although the JLP has been the more influential party in Southside, they 'never really did anything much for the people of Southside', as then Leader of the Opposition Edward Seaga confessed to me in a telephone interview. The photograph in Figure 1.3 depicts Southside's cultural heroes. At left is the local government councillor at the time of my research, Taffawa Nesbeth, who was subsequently defeated. He was the first independent candidate to get the unanimous support of the traditionally JLP community. His father, Rock-I, and two brothers were murdered early in 1999, sparking a series of reprisal killings. Taffawa was himself imprisoned in the aftermath of these incidents, on suspicion of being implicated in an incident of revenge killings on a proverbially Bloody Sunday when the murderers used his car in the drive-by shooting of youths playing football in the streets.

Next to Nesbeth is a drawing of Edward Seaga, superimposed on the Jamaican flag. A former Prime Minister, Minister of Finance and Leader of the Opposition, Seaga was leader of the Jamaica Labour Party for just over two decades and is widely regarded as a formidable political leader. Despite the support that many hard-core JLP activists in Southside give to the JLP, the low level of the party's actual involvement in their particular community belies this confidence.

---

12 Some sections of the community are affiliated to the PNP, however; e.g. 'The Site', the four-storey walk-up constructed by the PNP in the 1970s.

Figure 1.3: Cultural icons in Southside. L-R: Former Local Councillor, Taffawa Nesbeth; Leader of the Opposition, Edward Seaga; Drop-Pan gambling score; JLP Caretaker, Olivia 'Babsy' Grange; Hon. Robert 'Bob' Marley; and Reggae star Shabba Ranks.

To the right of Seaga's picture, at the corner of the wall, are the scores for 'drop pan', a Chinese gambling practice, which has been absorbed into poor urban communities by Africans. Knowledge of the practice, which is managed by local 'bankers', has been passed down over the years to those who are interested in reading *rakes* or the signs incorporated into everyday living, as ways of making their fortune (see Chevannes, 1989).

Next in the frame is Olivia 'Babsy' Grange,[13] who was the local JLP caretaker for many years. Grange is also outstanding as one of the longest-running women in politics and has been a successful producer of Reggae music; Shabba Ranks and Carlene Davis were some of her artistes. Bob Marley, whose songs speak to the joys and despair of the subordinated majority class, is beside Shabba Ranks, the popular Dancehall DJ.

Despite the dominance of JLP loyalties in Southside, some support for the PNP persists, resulting in the evolution of partisan allegiances that cut across family and geographical lines. Therefore, the bizarre reality is that clashes have occurred on contiguous corners between party supporters, with members of the same family falling on opposite sides of the battle lines.

Nevertheless, family also provides a cultural buffer in the midst of all the instability created by the partisan tactics of divide and rule. Ironically, however, family loyalties are often the root cause of the cycle of revenge killings. The pain suffered by relatives who lose loved ones to gun violence fuels the reprisals, invariably enacted by male family members. In addition, a man who perceives that he or a member of his inner circle has been dissed in any way often feels obliged to retaliate with violence in order to save the perceived family honour. This revenge motive feeds the cycle of ballistic warfare.

---

13 Within the JLP administration formed when the party came to power in September 2007, Ms. Grange was Minister of Information, Culture, Youth and Sports. At the time of publication, she is the Minister of Sports, Culture, Entertainment and Gender Affairs.

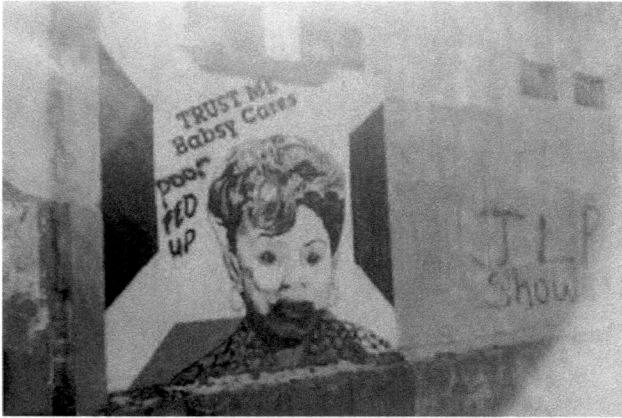

Figure 1.4: 'Poor Fed Up': Disgust with the political machinery and particularly the JLP representation is evident in this statement superimposed on the image of then JLP representative for the area, Babsy Grange.

Despite the doom-and-gloom currency in the speech of many residents, there have been instances when representatives of the power structures have attempted to implement social welfare programmes. In the 1970s, when then Prime Minister Michael Manley was the Member of Parliament for the Central Kingston area, Southside was used as a test case for the PNP's attempt to improve the lives of women and children by providing support for households as a whole. Alicia Taylor, who played a vital part in that experiment, recalled that this project was fraught with political contradictions from start to finish.

> We were looking at the child and the care of children. So we trained women who were working in the impact programme to be child minders. I worked on the issue of basic school education and I worked with the Bernard van Leer Foundation, headquartered in Holland, which provided the funds for the upgrading of women who worked as teachers and auxiliaries in basic schools. We assisted in the primary schools whenever we could and for the secondary schools, we had an after-school programme to prepare them for final high school exams. That was the forerunner to the current YESS[14] programme run by KRC.[15]

> We worked with the churches, particularly seeking assistance to care for the elderly who are the people who were left behind in the great migrations that took place in the '50s. The elderly men, in particular, had not become attached to any of their families so they were there, in need of care in their old age so we wanted the church in particular to work with us in this aspect of the programme.

---

14 Youth Empowerment

15 Kingston Restoration Company, an organisation which has done much to facilitate capacity building and infrastructural development in Kingston's inner-city communities. However, some argue that these efforts could be strengthened by the integration of the political will to address the fundamental causes of the problems that provide the raison d'être for their philanthropy.

Unfortunately, this project was hijacked when the government changed hands in 1980. This hiatus in political development and direction (and even reversal in some cases), compounded the stagnation in the national economy. The subsequent two decades are distinctive for the steady decline in standards of living for people of all classes, but particularly for inner-city residents like those in Southside.

Figure 1.5: Map locating Jamaica in the northern Caribbean, close to
Central America and juxtaposed between the continents of North and South America.

Meanwhile, those few men behind the cold barrels of the state-of-the-art guns highlight the fact that citizen security is one of the most pressing development problems in these enclaves, in particular, and in the country as a whole.

The ballistic weapons of the political dons and the *rude boys* (i.e. gangsters not necessarily affiliated to the parties) proclaim the downside of Jamaica's strategic location in the middle of the Caribbean Basin in the proverbial backyard of North America. South Florida's proximity to Jamaica makes metro-Miami the foremost 'American gateway to the Caribbean' for illegal arms shipments. The island's proximity to South America allows the Colombian dons not only to transship contraband and weapons through Jamaica but to, increasingly, control the retail drug trade on the streets of Jamaica. Besides guns and ammunition coming in from both North and South America, ballistic weapons and paraphernalia are now also coming from – of all places – Haiti, which was flooded with guns as a precursor to the US-coordinated ousting of democratically elected, former Haitian President Jean-Bertrand Aristide in February 2004.

In more ways than one, then, the discourse of violence in inner-city *garrison communities*, like Southside, is now out of the control of the local security forces, which are themselves also regarded as a clear and present danger because of their internationally recognised and chastised penchant for illegal 'law enforcement', corruption and outright criminality.

Adding salt to these wounds, American cable channels are now available to the most deprived households and, as a result, inner-city residents have received deep doses of cultural penetration by foreign values and lifestyles. Pre-programmed values are reinforced through representation – for example, of violent men as heroes.[16] Ironically, the phallic threads that run through people's lived experiences and which are institutionalised in the fabric of society, serve to portray ballistically violent manhood as sexy. This contradiction is graphically depicted in the following mural (Figure 1.6), which adorns a wall on Fleet Street in the Southside community.

The *Renkers Crew*, is the name of a ruthless gang that extended its influence to the infamous *yardie* posses in the USA. This celebration of 'real manhood' as violent is shown by the alignment of thug identity with the street, sweet-boy expression, 'gal dem man'. Translated from Jamaican Patwah into English, this means 'the girls' man'. The relevant syllogism is that a real man performs violence, women want real men, and therefore women want men who perform violence. On the right of the picture, the influence of North American culture is unmistakable in the 'name-brand' sportswear and the National Basketball Association (NBA) artefacts.

Figure 1.6: Violent, hegemonic masculinity and sexuality.

Rude Boys

Out of this murderous milieu emerged Jamaica's now infamous rude boys who, like sheep to the slaughter, would become grist for the murder mill and bait for the ghetto trap. As a cultural icon, the *hot-stepping rude boy* was constructed in the *popular culture discourses* of the late 1960s. Back in the day, this identity idiom was transmitted via the music and translated into a designation of a real man as a bad man, who was as fearless as he was feared. Ska, an up-tempo beat that had predominated in the early 1960s, was replaced in the summer of 1966 by the slower and more sensuous sounds of rocksteady. The lyrics accompanying the slinky rocksteady rhythms were symbolic

---

16   Increasingly, violent policemen are also the avant-garde heroes, again suggesting a definition of masculinity that correlates desirability with violence.

of the popularity of the rude boy, whose inclination to violence using imported German ratchet knives as an idiom of real manhood, was the harbinger of the political intonations that were to be added to this musical innovation.

> [I]n 1966, two new words entered the vocabulary of Jamaican pop music to go with the new rhythm. The words were 'rude boy' and they referred to youths who hung out on the slum street corners. They were mostly unemployed and had taken to carrying German ratchet knives and hand guns. They could be anything from 14 to 25 years old and came from all over West Kingston. And above all, the rude boys were angry. Conditions in West Kingston had hardly improved with the passing years. Rather than buckle to a life spent doing menial work or no work at all, the rude boys took to the streets and to crime.
>
> (Hebidge, 1987: 72, emphasis in original)

The rude boys were also fastidious in their dressing and their general entertainment habits. In fact, as Hebidge notes, the rude boy phenomenon can be traced back to as early as 1962, when 'Roland Alphonso released an early Ska record...which dealt with the *Rude Boys*. However, it wasn't until 1966, when the Wailers produced the track 'Rude Boy' for Clement Dodd, that the cult [sic] really took off inside Jamaican pop music' (Hebidge, 1987: 73). Other releases from an outstanding array of artistes, who exemplified the notoriety of the rude boy phenomenon, included The Wailers' 'Rule Them Rudie' [and 'Steppin' Razor'], Derrick Morgan's 'Tougher Than Tough' and Prince Buster's 'Too Bad'. The latter song boasted, 'Rude Boys never give up their guns, no one can tell them what to do' (Hebidge, 1987: 73), an assertion that foretold the defiant fearlessness of the present-day version of the rude boy personae, the *shotters*, who have come to dominate the posse and *yardie* gangs of today.

The popularity of the rude boys extended to the Reggae era, which started in 1968. The paraphernalia of the idiom – the dark (Mafia) glasses, the *bopping walk*, the dapper dress styles and the characteristically *phallic* symbols of ratchet knife, motorbike and guns, have also persisted as part of the identity gears of the rude boys – or raggamuffins as they were known in the 1980s. Nowadays, the more affluent posse-affiliated rude boys sport tinted Toyota 'deportee' or other imported vehicles and the ubiquitous cell phone, are necessary technological tools of their trade. This *phallic* array suggests that meanings of violence and sexuality are intertwined in prevailing notions about how to enact a space-specific definition of real *manhood*.

The politicians, in typical opportunistic mode, courted some of the rude boys to act as their clients in the urban grassroots. But not all of the men who became party thugs were rude boys, and not all rude boys were seduced by the scarce-benefits-and-spoils practices of persuasion. Nevertheless, the insertion of the rude boys[17] into the partisan political project of inner-city turf contestation had pronounced implications for the

---

17 For historical accuracy, I must distinguish between rude boys as a cultural construct for masculinist identity and the men who provided the 'hard core party support' (Stone, 1986: 49). Although some rude boys are party activists, most function independent of direct party affiliation. However, as Stone's analysis shows, backed by the activism of the party thugs, popular support for the political parties 'fluctuates between an estimated bottom line of 90,000 to 110,000 and grows as large as 150,000 to 160,000 when the party's fortunes are on the ascendancy' (Stone, 1986: 49).

social security of the country as a whole. The rise to power at the subaltern level of the politicised rude boys was reflected in the late 1960s in the proliferation of warring gangs. Terry Lacey's summation of the main gangs that operated in the west Kingston area in 1966–7, is still relevant although the sociopolitical order of things has changed dramatically and the number of names has burgeoned way beyond this estimate.

> Trench Town, Denham Town, Back O' Wall, Moonlight City – these names of parts of western Kingston conveyed images of youth gangs, political gangs, Rastafarians, of Prince Henry's gang, the Max gang, the Blue Mafia, the Dunkirk gang, the Phoenix gang, the Vikings, or the Roughest and the Toughest. These gangs symbolised the latent power of the lumpen proletariat. In the period 1966-7 many were armed to provide the 'soldiers' for a battle between the PNP and JLP in Western Kingston. After this short introduction to politics within the system, some of the gangs reverted to ordinary criminal activities, others turned to more revolutionary politics and used their newly-acquired guns to terrorise the rest of society.

> (Lacey, 1977: 32)

The type of consciousness required for the revolution suggested here, is certainly not reflected in the present spraying of blood, bullets and bodies all over the urban landscape. And while a number of killings can be traced back to gang conflicts and politics, there is still an element of itinerant violence connected to the drug trade and dominated by ongoing revenge dynamics that make people throw up their hands and say 'it can't done!' In other words, those trapped below the poverty line often feel there is virtually no escape from the death trap in which they are caught – like flies in a web or fish in a net.

Here, we should be careful not to 'lumpen-proletariatise' the youth, as this would avoid the necessary interrogation of a political system whose experiment is long out of control. Ever since the introduction of the *discourse of violence* into political divide-and-rule practices in the late 1960s, the staging of general elections have been marked by a dramatic escalation of political violence in Jamaica's inner-city communities. Adding gun violence to the political process was like pouring muddy water into the quicksand of the ghetto trap, resulting in an absolute social quagmire. Ever since, guns have done the talking for the violence-prone political partisans of both sides.

The Peace Treaty

The most intensely contested Jamaican elections were held in 1967, 1972, 1976 and 1980. Mirroring the apparent heroics of the movie stars, local gangsters like Claudie Massop (JLP) and Bucky Marshall (PNP), emerged as the stars of the inner-city dramaturgy, which was all the more tragic because this bizarre production of 'real manhood' was no fiction but harsh reality. The blood, bullets and bodies were all real. The various roles that the politicians and security forces have played in this war effort identify them as co-villains, whose autographs have been written in and with the very blood of the pawns in their political power game of bourgeois democracy.

> The level of political violence in the run-up to the 1976 elections got so high that the Prime Minister declared a State of Emergency. A Gun Court was set up in the centre of Kingston and a law was passed whereby anybody found carrying a gun could be immediately arrested and detained for an indefinite period...The situation only began to improve when Claudie Massop and Buckie Marshall, the Rude Boy gunmen for the two political parties in Kingston's slums, signed a truce and decided to work together to improve local conditions...This move was started by the Rastafarians. The shift from violent to peaceful solutions to Jamaica's problems was reflected in the next phase of the island's pop history – Reggae. [18]

(Hebidge, 1987: 74)

During the late 1970s, hard-core political activist Claudie Massop controlled Tivoli Gardens, the JLP-identified area of western Kingston, while the equally tough Bucky Marshall dominated the PNP stronghold of Kingston Pen.

> The battle had been bloody. Bucky's PNP boys had powered in hard and wiped out a lot of Massop's JLP boys, and not just no-hopers, they got a few ranking party members as well – and Massop's boys had come back with a vengeance late in the day and massacred entire households of PNP supporters, until it seemed like there was no stopping the epidemic of political violence and nobody even tried very hard.

(Thomas and Boot, 1982: 85)

However, in the midst of the chaos, the socially stabilising influence of Rastafari by their production of myriad *discourses of cultural resistance* became unmistakable. First and foremost, Rastafari reclaimed race as a site of struggle and resistance and thereby provided a direct foil to those men who chose to express their identities in the idiom of violence. In the face of the vicious tribal warfare all over inner-city areas, the role of the Rastafari has always been to keep the flood of blood down by encouraging rival gangs to make peace instead of taking 'blood for blood' and fighting 'fire with fire'. In the late 1970s, the Rastafari refrain of 'Peace and Love' politics found great resonance with the urban gangsters who, after all, grew up among members of that homegrown, Afrocentric *Livity*.[19] Touched by the very same Black-consciousness energy that flowed through the USA in the 1970s, grassroots man and man[20] realised that Black man killing Black man in Jamaica must stop. Rastafari provided the spiritual *grounding*[21] that is eschewed in the political realm, but which was so crucially needed to put the internecine conflicts on pause.

Thus, in the late 1970s, leading and influential inner-city Rastafarians persuaded the political gunmen from both sides to share ganja 'peace pipes' with each other, and while the marijuana-filled, water-filtered chalices were passed from hand to

---

18 I will deal in more detail with the Rastafari impact on popular culture and the discourse of resistance in upcoming chapters.

19 See Murrell et al ((eds.), 1998) for a comprehensive exposé on Rastafari.

20 Men is used to describe homosexuals in local parlance, hence the plural term 'man and man'.

21 Used here in the metaphoric electrical sense, this word also speaks to the Rastafari expression for reasoning in a group.

hand, the Rasta-led reasoning about the bread-and-butter and life-and-death issues at stake took place. After evaluating the ways in which they had, senselessly, been fighting against each other, the top-ranking, political gunmen decided to call a halt to hostilities in order to stem the flood of blood and cool down the fire in the inner city. Much to the astonishment of the politicians, as well as the conflicted enclaves and the society at large, the warlords decided to heed the Rastafari call to 'cease fire',[22] and came together in a determined effort to end the bloodbath which had been unleashed on the inner-city communities. In the immediate aftermath of the signing of the *Peace Treaty*, the street fighters wanted Bob Marley to headline a special concert to mark the occasion. Marley had himself been shot and injured in a politically motivated 'Ambush in the Night', as he dubbed one of his many hit songs, just prior to the 'Smile Jamaica' concert, which heralded the 1976 general election.

Figure 1.7: Rastafari, gangsters and politicians: then Prime Minister Michael Manley (L) and Opposition Leader Edward Seaga (R) are 'united' in a symbolic gesture mediated by Rastafari Reggae maestro Bob Marley at the historic *Peace Concert*. (courtesy Bob Marley Foundation).

In order to avoid further political entanglement, Marley subsequently left the island and resided in England for a few years. However, this did not deter him from returning to perform at the politically unprecedented *Peace Concert*, when personally invited to do so by Claudie Massop. Officially entitled, 'The One Love Concert', the *Peace Concert* as it was popularly known, was held at the National Stadium, in Kingston. It was no coincidence that the mammoth event was staged on April 21, 1978, the twelfth anniversary, to the day, of Ethiopian Emperor Haile Selassie I's arrival on his 1966 State Visit to Jamaica. The open-air stadium was the site of the civic welcome ceremony put on for the visiting Ethiopian Regent by the government and people in the Jamaican capital. Holding the 1978 show on the anniversary of that significant date and at the same venue was symbolic of the overriding Rastafarian influence on the organising of the *Peace Concert*.

22 Bunny Wailer, who was an original member of the Wailing Wailers, sang a powerful hit in this era called 'Cease Fire', which was didactic of the conflict-ridden tenor of the day.

Appropriately, therefore, the historic *Peace Concert* featured a long who's who list of prominent Reggae/Rasta artists and brought together opposing political leaders Michael Manley and Edward Seaga, as well as the gang leaders themselves, who had agreed to relinquish the warfare. So it was Peter Tosh, the Rasta man, who stopped the music and verbalised the sentiments and the social agenda of the poor in an explicitly candid tirade during his set. And, under a full moon with a natural mystic (Herb) blowing through the air, it was Bob Marley, the Rasta man, who was captured for posterity by all the cameras, holding aloft, above his head, the joined hands of Jamaica's opposing political leaders as a symbol of unity. There could be no doubt, thereafter, but that the Rastafari were Jamaica's homegrown apolitical peacemakers.

The spontaneous peace truce encompassed key rival political communities including Tivoli Gardens, Arnett Gardens (a.k.a. 'Concrete Jungle'), Matthews Lane and Payne Land. However, despite the spiritually loaded shot in the arm of Rastafari philosophy and pragmatic politics, inner-city peace proved easier to broker than to maintain. Those advocating peace were swimming against the tide of blood left behind by those cut down 'for reasons unknown', as a baffled Ras Carlie put it. In the aftermath of the highly successful concert, the leaders of the said peace effort were unceremoniously and brutally eliminated, bringing the notoriety they had enjoyed to an abrupt end...to be continued...only...in the memories of the elders.

Figure 1.8: This mural celebrating the Max Corner is located at the corner of Gold Street and Tower Street. The painting above the caption is a tribute to the survivors of the Green Bay Massacre, which I will address in Chapter 6.

Despite – or maybe because of – the boldness of the gesture of the peace pact brokered by the gangsters themselves, the security forces, many say acting on the direct orders of their political superiors, subsequently eliminated these one-time street leaders. Unfortunately, in their determination to promote peace, that generation of gang leaders also demonstrated their redundancy to the traditional political leadership in the island.

> Claudie and Bucky had big plans. They actually signed a Peace Treaty. Everybody held their breath. It was crazy, but it was symptomatic...And here you had two brassy thugs from the Jungle giving the orders...However, a few weeks later Claudie and Bucky were dead.

> (Thomas and Boot, 1982: 89)

Claudie Massop's ambush and brutal murder sent shock waves over Kingston's inner-city communities for quite a long time. His was only one among a series of legally sanctioned high-profile eliminations, a trend which prompted noted Reggae artiste Peter Tosh to pen the sardonic lyrics, 'all who signed the Peace Treaty now resting in peace in the cemetery'. Indeed, all the leading figures in the Peace Concert, including Tosh and Marley, were eventually killed one way or another. Massop's legacy is still felt in the centralised form of leadership which has been retained in the west Kingston area, which is strikingly different from the amorphous style of turf leadership that characterises other communities like Southside. Naturally, after the elimination of most of the top-ranking rude boy peace advocates in the late 1970s, the gang feuding in the conflicted areas intensified as demonstrated by the subsequent over-proliferation of rival gangs in the 1980s.

Gun Men Gone Wild

The level of blood and violence that has washed over the inner-city areas since 1980 has taken a cruel toll on an entire generation. When the statistics are collated, it is frightening to think of the proportion of men per capita in a little island of two and a half million people who are biting the dust in the tit-for-tat, life-for-a-life, 'blood for blood' and 'fire for fire' ballistic free-for-all.

Figure 1.9: Ironically, the inscription of 'How the South Was Won', the wild west gun-slinging image of the American cowboy hero, provides the foreground inscription against the understated cry for 'Love, Peace and Change'. This contradiction shows that on the one hand, media images reinforce the notion that heroes gain ascendancy through gunplay, imagery which reifies hegemonic masculinity in the idiom of violence. On the other hand, the inscription on the right emphasises that this value system is a minority viewpoint: the majority of the citizens in Southside desperately desire an end to the warring and a change in their social space. When I returned to the community in January 2000, six months after I took this photograph, at the corner of Gold and Barry Streets, the mural had been blotted out. This erasure suggests that efforts are being made to subvert the stereotype of violent masculinity as the dominant code of behaviour for man and man in the community.

[W]e have to recognise the degree to which, in Jamaica, men, especially young men, are killing each other and inflicting violent acts on each other. In 1993, 45 young men aged 13-18, 182 aged 19-25 and 157 aged 26-30 were killed. Although the numbers get lower after this age group, they are not insignificant. In over half of the cases, one man shot another. Figures for 1994 are even more staggering: 197 men between the ages of 19-25 were murdered, and 82 died aged 13-18. Male on male violence for just one month was 579 and of course, this is an under-reported number.

(Hanif, 1995: 4)

Although the current figures and murder totals were not disaggregated at the time of writing, the murder rate for 2004 was a record 1,471. An analysis of crime statistics in *The Gleaner* in August 2004 predicted this kind of gloomy outcome for a year when violence ran at many paces faster than lawmakers and the security forces were able to match.

Major crimes listed by the police as of 2003 are murders, shootings, sexual offences, felonious woundings and robberies. Felonious woundings were not listed among major crimes up to 2002.

Since January, there have been more than 900 murders almost as many as the 975 killed in 2003 alone. At the current rate, the number of murders may well pass the record 1,139 in 2001 if actions are not taken to stem the carnage.

(*Jamaica-Gleaner Online*, August 29, 2004)

Although the community enjoyed a refreshing break in the first two years of the installation of the Central Kingston Task Team – a community development organisation sponsored by the Grace and Staff Community Development Foundation – Southside is back on the murder map. Criminal forces have defied the attempts made by a broad-based community grouping to work across differences to cut the crime rate. Once again, an attempt is being made to reconfigure the images of masculinity in terms of the stereotypes of violence that represent people in the inner city as undifferentiated and violent.

It is an ongoing debate whether the *political will* exists to improve the chances of identity recovery for the subordinated, who have no recourse but to live with poverty and violence. As the following drawing by the Gully Massive crew illustrates (Figure 1.10), youths are sucked into the maelstrom through the systematic social exclusion that leave some with no choice but to react in the codes that they create to deal with this experience of dehumanisation.

A community discussion about this pictorial analysis expanded on the causes of the violent conflicts in Southside. The phrase 'red eye' means that jealousy – in this case over gun ownership – is evident in the current gang feuding. The same meaning is conveyed in the reference 'man a mek dem name' (men are making names for themselves), denoting the ego-defensive motivation of men seeking to realise a sense of gender power through violence. The prevalence of rape emphasises the gendered nature and impact of masculine expressions of power. The sexual violation of women's bodies as part of the war discourse denotes the super-subordination of womanhood in the equations of the inner-city discourse of violence. Poor women are thus disadvantaged by men's performance of hegemonic masculinity on several levels. These women, therefore, experience oppression and exploitation in terms of class, race/colour, gender, sexuality and age.

Gun Shooting
from long time
war a gwaan
man a mek
dem name
Gun
Red Eye

EFFECTS
ROBBING
RAPE
Cant Walk
Cant GET WORK
Cease fire is not peace;
Shot can fire any time a man dead
Gully Massive
Pieces

Figure 1.10: Drawing by mixed-gender group of youths on Gully Massive corner, at the intersection of South Camp Road and Tower Street.

Although high unemployment was also linked to criminal activities in the group discussion, it was still evident that men opt for violent alternatives to survive to an extent that women do not. Some men perceive 'menial' work to be unbecoming for a *man*, whereas being the predominant heads of households circumscribes the options from which women are able to choose in their strategies to survive. In the discussion, an ironic twist accompanied the explanation offered for peace. The participants in the discussion offered a *double entendre* to the concept. They said that in spite of attempts to defuse the hostilities among the warring factions through numerous peace agreements, the frequency with which the peace is broken leaves only pieces of human lives shattered by the use of the 'phallic piece', or gun.

Attempting to gain materially through the patronage only reinforces violent masculinity, which ultimately has devastating effects on the ones who use this means of achieving selfhood. At the same time, this discourse strengthens the more dominant and deadly violence of the privileged class, represented by the state and its machinery. The subtext of this discussion, therefore, is that the subordinated inner-city residents fit into the agenda of the hegemonic order, while internalising the notion of acting in their own interests (Gramsci, 1957; Lukes, 1986).

While those who have died can, in one sense, be conceived as victims, in living memories, some of them are actually deemed to be heroes. They are perceived, symbolically, as giants for their enacted performances of wickedness, or defiance, or fearlessness or other inferences of power – the very same reasons for which they may also be derided, even in death. Contradictorily, these traits are attractive to aspire to because they counteract material lack, which connotes hopelessness. However, while some of the living may be seen as hapless victims, the majority of residents, more accurately, embody survivor status.

The monster of violence is not peculiar to the poor, but is the flip side of the extraordinary privileges that the well-to-do enjoy.

> [T]his 'gun man' community is not separate from the selfishness, materialism and self-centredness of the privileged…[which] would spend more on a dog than a poor person who works in their garden. The privileged person feels that he has no responsibility for anyone other than himself and barricades his house under the false consciousness that he has done nothing to warrant his victimisation. In truth the "gun man" wants to be the privileged man, and perhaps if he did not have the technology of the gun he would be forced to inculcate discipline and patience.
>
> (Hanif, 1995: 7-8)

Getting out of the bottom of the barrel is easier said than done, as far as the 'gun man' is concerned. Having grown accustomed to surviving by the fear caused by his 'tool', many inner-city men do not know how to be powerful without it. Some women, also, define themselves as powerful by being violent. They fight *matey wars*, usually over the *possession* of a man. So many men have died, are in prison or abroad as a result of the cyclical conflicts, that fewer and fewer are available to women. The rivalry between mateys is also enacted in the Dancehall environment in practices locally called *modelling* or showing off. Modelling entails competitions among women and is expressed in material and symbolic terms.

Again, the insidious influence of the political economy is evident in this symbolic and sometimes physical form of violence. For example, one gains power by being able to outfight one's rival, dress more expensively and dance more creatively, especially in a sexually explicit fashion suggestive of who, through superior sexual expertise, is more capable of capturing the man who might be the object of competition. Ultimately, these competitions reinforce prevailing patriarchal norms, which place men's desires at the centre of not only their own interests but also preoccupy the women who are interested in them.

Rude Girls

I sat on the sidewalk on Foster Lane one day reasoning with a group of women about this phenomenon. These women actually call themselves *rude girls*, an example of women buying into the dominant male discourse of violence and mirroring male interpretations of power in defining themselves. One of the women teased another that her matey[23] *sat on her*[24] when they were fighting. The other woman defended herself by saying,

> Mi bite har pon her breast! She pull my hair and she do nuff things. I defend myself and let her know that I am not fighting over man. She is the one who is fighting over a man because she says that the man want her.

---

23 The other woman having a relationship with the man she is in a conjugal partnership with.

24 In addition to being a literal allusion to a decisive moment in the fight, this is also a symbolic reference to someone who attains dominance over another.

Another woman said that if she had a man, and a woman took him away, she would 'beat her and chop her in her head'. The other two women demurred, saying that they would defend themselves if a woman attacked them, but that they would not take the initiative to fight over a man, because it was a man's prerogative to pursue a woman and not the other way around. This opinion clearly reflected the internalisation of a patriarchal perspective on the production of gender relationships, which also entails prescribed material roles for women and men. This material value system also has direct implications for the enactment of the discourse of violence, because, invariably, the men engaged in this gender performance have a better chance of wooing and winning women.

The rude girls agreed, though, that when women fight over men, it is a weak victory for the winner and mainly serves to boost the ego of the man in question. 'They (the men) love it' was the enthusiastic consensus. A healthy discussion ensued, however, when the suggestion was put forward that although it was public knowledge in the community which men and women are sexual partners, some women persist in the practice of forcing themselves onto men who are otherwise engaged. Ironically, this competition is intensified because the violent conflicts among men make it difficult for women to secure sexual/material partners.

'Mi haffi beat the gal if she is along with my man,' one woman insisted, 'because you know that you can't fight a man.'[25] One woman in the group of five said that she would walk away rather than give the man the satisfaction of seeing her fighting another woman over him. Molly was also succinct in her analysis of the problem:

> It's like this. You know Tom and I see Tom and Jane and all of a sudden, Tom and I are together. You take Tom from Jane and Tom and Jane already have five, six, seven or eight years together or even ten years. And you just come and take Tom and then Tom and Jane could have three or four kids in a union and you just come in and mash up Tom and Jane's union and you probably just have one kid for him. Then, a little after you mash up that life, you and him mash up; then you just go again and interfere with a next person's relationship. I don't give in to that; I feel that you are supposed to look for a person for yourself[26] and not wait till Jane has Tom to take him away, because probably Tom was there all the time.

Many women in the inner-city areas, like Southside, have not evolved sufficiently out of the popular *monogamous mode* to the emotional stage of sufficiently accepting extra-union relationships, to be able to shift their way of having relationships. Although they might tolerate sharing their mate for the sake of maintaining the relationship with the man, many are not happy with this situation. They demonstrate, in no uncertain terms, the extraordinary lengths they will go to in order to *keep a man*. In the matey tradition, the more powerful perceives herself to be *number one*, in vexed if not violent

---

25 This is also a strong statement of strategic deployment of power; the matey wars demonstrate a recognition that it is expedient for women to fight each other because they cannot with any equanimity match the strength and violence which men may be able to muster up.

26 Paradoxically, this proclamation of monogamous precedents for pursuing a conjugal relationship is belied by the paucity of males, whose numbers have been reduced thanks to the normalisation of the bloody reproduction of bodies (corpses), the converse of creativity, in the inner-city environment.

competition with her mate or matey, whose shortcomings are gauged based on various criteria.

The cultural acceptance of *monogamy for the woman but not for the man*, is a schizophrenic value system that allows men to have multiple partners and promotes a political economy of contested relations between women who do not subscribe to this practice. Women who have multiple relationships with men are stigmatised as *sketels*, which is not a good thing.

Subordinated Women

One could say the violence that women display towards each other in contestations over men reflects a choice, but it also indicates the extent to which women's identities are a function of the dominant discourse of power. Located at the fulcrum of this power paradox, poor and disadvantaged Black women attempt to resolve the conflicts that seep through the cracks of their larger problems by the use of a range of weapons – acid, machetes, ice picks, their bodies, words – in an odyssey of *modelling* against their adversaries. These power dramas erupt into fights with such monotonous regularity that people who witness these performances – especially children – cynically treat them as everyday street entertainment. They choose sides to see who will win, cheering on the opponents as they would boxers in a ring.

It is interesting too, that the women do not usually tackle their male partners on the issue of their infidelity. A subliminal imperative of this patriarchal discourse impels some women to attack other women who seize the prize of 'their man'. This other woman, mind you, is as disadvantaged as the attacker in the larger power matrix and is therefore more vulnerable than the 'strong man' in the triangle, who wrote the script and directed the production. In power games, the strong invariably seek ways to disadvantage those weakest in options and choices.[27]

An inner-city woman may also choose to be in a relationship with a man who is violent because he can provide her with social security – money that he might procure from criminal activities – and with the social value of being protected because she is associated with a man who is feared and respected in the community. Thus, the issues surrounding the beneficiaries of the violence are as complex as those who suffer it. Such strategic transactions that valorise violence have resulted in the routinisation of criminality as an expression of power to such an extent that many people have become increasingly desensitised to the danger posed by this enigma which is so deeply embedded in everyday values and attitudes. Popular beliefs and norms hold that men prove themselves as men when they kill, whereas women are socially stereotyped by their reproductive capabilities.

The subordination of women is an inevitable outcome of a system of male domination based on violence. While not homogeneous, women are particularly disadvantaged in the inner-city scenario where their bodies are literal battlefields in the reproduction of structural, discursive and gendered power dynamics. Women are often raped

---

27   See Post (1996) for an elaboration of these concepts.

as a statement of conquest over some men by other men. Considering that it was only as recently as October 2001 that the War Crimes Tribunal in The Hague finally acknowledged rape as a war crime and as a crime against humanity, it is no wonder that, for the women in Southside who have experienced such violations, the benefits of this new legislation seem as remote as the European city of its genesis.

Gun Talk

Everything you draw you 'lass
Everything you run for your gun
Everything you fling rockstone
Hear this
Throw down your arms and come
Drop them!

~Burning Spear ('Throw Down Your Arms')

Finally, a brief word about some of the lethal firearms that are intrinsic to this strange but true story of blood, bullets and bodies. Virtually every make of gun manufactured in the world has somehow found its way into Jamaica. If we were just talking about handguns like the GLOCK, that would be bad enough; even more damaging is the glut of high-calibre machine pistols and military-style assault rifles that have shattered the arteries carrying Jamaica's social and economic life-blood.

GLOCK, the Austrian defence contractor that originated the pistol of the same name, claims sales of over 2.5 million handguns in over 100 countries. The M-16, the primary general issue infantry rifle of the United States military, is one of the primary banes of Jamaica. Manufactured by Colt and Fabrique Nationale (FN Herstal) among others, there are an estimated 8 million-plus M-16 assault rifles in existence. Too many of them are now in Jamaica.

The world's most famous assault rifle, the Russian built Kalashnikov AK-47, is also very popular and very much present in Kingston's inner cities. Produced by Russian manufacturer Izhmash, and used in many Eastern bloc nations during the Cold War, the AK-47, along with its numerous variants, was produced in greater numbers than any other assault rifle in the twentieth century. It is estimated that over 100 million units were produced, making it the most prolific small arm of the second half of the twentieth century. Since its introduction in 1947, the AK-47 has been manufactured in modified forms in dozens of countries, and has been used in hundreds of conflicts and countries, including Jamaica. During most of the Cold War, the Soviet Union and China supplied their arms and technical knowledge to numerous countries under a military assistance program. In addition, another policy saw the supply of arms, free of charge, to pro-communist fighters such as the Sandinistas in Nicaragua and the Viet-Cong in North Vietnam. This policy was mirrored by the West, with the United States providing arms to such groups as the anti-communist Afghan Mujahideen (now known as the Taliban).

Another very popular weapon in Jamaica is the Bushmaster. Bushmaster Firearms Inc. is the manufacturer and distributor of a semi-automatic pistol and rifle variants that use the AR-15 design. As of 2003, Bushmaster was, reportedly, the best selling brand for AR type firearms in the United States. The company participated in a $2.5-million settlement for survivors and families of victims of the 2002 Beltway sniper attacks around Washington DC, allegedly carried out by 'two Jamaicans'. (Only one, Lee Boyd Malvo, was actually a Jamaican). Also much in demand in Jamaica is the Uzi machine pistol, manufactured by Israel Military Industries (IMI), Fabrique Nationale and others. The Uzi was used until recently by the Israeli special forces. Total sales of the pistol, up to the end of 2001, netted IMI over US$2 billion, with over 90 countries using the weapons either for their soldiers or in law enforcement. In Jamaica, however, the Uzi, along with a wide range of other guns, is also used by law breakers.

Figure 1.11: Some of the illegal, but popular, assault rifles in Jamaica are
(L-R) the American M-16, the Israeli Uzi and the Soviet AK-47.

Clearly, Jamaica has a deep and ingrained gun culture. Thus, many young Jamaicans are infatuated with guns. They know the brand names, know how they look, know how they sound, know how to break them down and clean them, and they know how to load and shoot them too. Accordingly, gun-talk is popular on inner-city streets, and young Dancehall entertainers regularly sing and DJ about ballistic weapons when they are live at stage shows and dances and also on their studio recordings. Having grown up watching cowboys shooting Indians and cops shooting robbers on TV and at the movies, the inner-city gunmen want to shoot someone or something themselves. Thus, their daily gun-talk is symptomatic of and synonymous with the prevailing non-verbal *discourse of violence*, which is taken for granted in everyday life in the ghetto.

In the meantime, there are no accurate or official figures for the number of illegal automatic and semi-automatic assault rifles and high-calibre handguns on the streets of Kingston. Nevertheless, it is still very obvious that there are indeed far too many of these portable killing machines in the hands of both the political and criminal gunmen. The indiscriminate, illegal importation of such weapons of war has resulted in unbridled bloodletting and has led Jamaica to the brink of social disintegration. No wonder, then, that guns were described as a 'wicked invention' by Reggae vocalist Edi Fitzroy in his hit song, 'The Gun'.

CHAPTER 2

SEXUAL POLITRICKS IN SOUTHSIDE

It revolves and causes a chain reaction: *people start to get confused, people become violent against each other, not because they want to be violent but because they want things and they can't get them.* Then some guy comes along and says to you "those guys over there are fighters and you might want to get rid of them." So he issues some guns. In the meantime, someone else arms Tom and Harry over there. So now, they have two sets of man from both sides, properly armed. Then the politicians just stepped out of the middle of it, leaving us to fight it out, and they are out of the country. Out of the country versus inner city.

(Clive, Higholborn Street)

Introduction To Hybrid Analysis

In this chapter, I am going to begin by introducing the theoretical tools of analysis that we will be using to deconstruct the problem under consideration – crime and violence. Then I will move on to take our first detailed look at other important and relevant topics such as gendered discourses of violence, dominant masculinities and subordinated femininities, the subtle and sometimes not so subtle nuances of body language, and, of course, creative sexual survival strategies. A working comprehension of these and other concepts utilised in this story is vital for a proper appreciation of the role '*sexual politricks*' plays in the daily lives of inner-city residents living below the poverty line.

The scenario sketched in the previous chapter put the violent power dramas played out in Southside within the broader theoretical context of the political economy. At the same time, the human body and its inherent sexuality is clearly up front and centre in the power struggles enacted at every level of this all too real-life drama. In this chapter, and at this point, we need to take a more analytical look at the various ways in which politics and its attendant ills have served to trick people at the grassroots level into believing that they are actually better off when they align themselves to one or the other of Jamaica's two main political parties.

Even more crucial, is an examination of how politicians from both sides have duped people below the poverty line into believing that their party affiliation should be sufficient cause for them to go to war with other equally disadvantaged people. This kind of partisan political con game and political usury is what is known in Jamaica as 'politricks'. Accordingly, the objective and subjective conditions that prompt people to use their body as a sexual commodity and survival tool, in this deeply divided and partisan political environment below the poverty line, is what we are referring to as 'sexual politricks'.

Our analysis will examine (i) the gendered discourse of violence, which haunts the inner-city space; (ii) the dichotomy of *dominant masculinities* and *subordinate femininities*; and (iii) *body language* and the underlying racism, sexism and classism inherent to Jamaican society as a whole, and which are also expressed in Southside. Finally, we come to the grim realisation that despite their disadvantaged social position, women, men, adolescents and children in Southside have perfected survival strategies related to their use of sexual advantage for material gain. Please note that we will also detail several alternative ways of expressing identity that defy what is dictated by cultural norms. The stark fact is, given the limited options that are available to them, Southside residents often choose to use these sexual survival strategies with 'mucho gusto' and no apology.

If we truly want to remove the obstacles inhibiting the cultural development of the majority class, we have to make a concerted effort to unravel the conceptual knots that inhibit analytical clarity. In view of the fact that these bonds of domination have been woven securely over centuries of systematic subjugation, we need to loosen the outer threads of the social status quo in order to get at the main strands of the power structures. Class, political economy, gender, patriarchy, the body and agency are the elements that the weavers of the politricks-of-the-day, have threaded into the complex tapestry of poverty and violence in inner-city areas like Southside.

A counter-weaving process is required to reveal the patterns of resistance, which emerge with monotonous regularity, on the other side of the tapestry. Just like rats caught in a trap, we have to weave our way through the mazes of the power and mind games that are stock in trade in the politrickal arena in which inner-city residents find themselves. And, given that the sum of an entity is greater than its constituent parts, my hybrid of analytical approaches to the problem permits the 'diversity of inquiry' (Hall, 1999: 177) recommended for a fuller understanding of the complex problem we are contemplating. Conceptual hybridity is particularly useful because 'specialisation leaves gaps between subfields…whereas a synthesis brings a humanisticunity, a new interpretation, a personal or stylistic achievement' (Dogan and Pahre, 1990: 63-64).

In addition, I utilise a Black *feminist/womanist* standpoint in my research because coming to the table of analysis with a particular perspective is an important part of the process of unravelling the power mechanisms that are entrenched in all social relationships. When one develops the kind of engagement politics specific to this viewpoint, it is easier to override the power plays that govern differences in the production of knowledge. Some Black feminists even call themselves '*womanists*', in order to distinguish themselves from White feminists who would like to claim the domain of Women's Liberation from all forms of oppression as their inalienable territory. *Womanists* are of the view that 'the subjects of historical knowledge have the most legitimate right to carry out research and to write about themselves' (Nkululeko in Qunta (ed.), 1987: 89). So, although I am in fact an outsider to the inner-city experience, I also gained firsthand, inside knowledge while conducting this enquiry. In addition, I am as committed to the struggle to transform this scenario as most native insiders (Collins, 1990).

Womanist standpoint politics also challenges the ways in which the human body has been used to institutionalise systems of oppression and exploitation. As a counter-discourse, *womanists* promote the use of *strategic essentialism*, which means that they reclaim the female body as a resource for expressing power. The centrality of the physical body to all of these opposing discourses, opens up a Pandora's Box of sex, sexuality and gender, all of which have to say their piece in the groundings.[28]

The Gendered Discourse of Violence

Discourse consists of a set of meanings that are conveyed and reproduced through various media of cultural, political and social communication. According to Foucault (1980) and Weedon (1999), it is the means by which power is made intelligible in the thought processes, language systems, institutional referents and the behaviour patterns that channel the meanings of such authority apparatuses in a given social context. A *discourse* incorporates the meanings of power in both structural and resistance applications.

Discourse is also directly related to the use of violence to establish structural and embodied authority. Thus, Post (1996: 271) contends 'discourse, as a medium through which the agents of power make ideology effective, has to be seen in company with violence and coercion'. However, while systems of domination grant privileges to some social actors while objectifying others, those who are subordinated in this relationship, inevitably, also tend to produce *discourses of resistance* through various processes of struggle (Post, 1996: 278). *Discourses of resistance*, which are mediated through embodiment, demonstrate that power does circulate throughout the body politic in the myriad ways by which social agents of *discourse* negotiate to give meaning to their everyday lives.

> Discourses define what it means to be a woman or man and the available range of gender-appropriate and transgressive behaviour. We learn who we are and how we think and behave through discursive practices.
>
> Moreover, subjectivity is embodied, and discursive practices shape our bodies, as well as our minds and emotions, in socially gendered ways.
>
> (Weedon, 1999: 104)

In the Jamaican inner-city context, a *discourse of violence* denotes prevailing power relations, which demonstrate that Jamaica's politicians have propagated a system of bourgeois democracy, saturated with copious amounts of patriarchy, in order to manipulate notions of masculinity to make inner-city men carry out acts of violence. The deployment of this *discourse* by the politicians is a part of their hegemonic strategy of dividing and ruling the electorate. As enacted in Southside, a *discourse of violence* conveys the message that a 'real' man will engage in acts of interpersonal violence. It is structured around such acts, as well as being expressed verbally in terms that have immediate meaning for the men who both receive and transmit the message. Because of its content and the consequent action, the message is also conveyed to women and affects their lives and perceptions. Some women have internalised and reproduced their own versions of violence as illustrated in their competitive encounters to secure

---

28 Rastafari word for reasoning.

the scarce 'commodity' of a 'man'. This shows the extent to which men have become resources to be acquired to reinforce womanpower, which, in a vicious cycle, dovetails into the *discourse of violence* that denotes a particular brand of masculinity. Sex is therefore conflated with violence in the identity drama played out on the torrid streets of the inner city.

Genetically speaking, sex refers to the biological features that distinguish male from female. Sexuality, on the other hand, encompasses the additional social and political meanings that are constructed around sex and sexual differences in order to establish power hierarchies between men and women and among social groups. Patriarchy is an integral part of such power set-ups, because, as we now know it, sexuality is a 'social construct of male power, defined by men, forced on women, and constitutive of the meaning of gender' (MacKinnon, in Nicholson, (ed.), 1997: 159).

Sex has traditionally been defined as a binary opposition between female and male. However, the present possibilities for transcending one's given biology through gender reassignment, or for superseding the heterosexual dyad by choosing to define oneself as lesbian, queer, gay, bisexual or transsexual/transgender, all demonstrate the extent to which a 'given' sex has become a cultural construction. In this sense, it is more appropriate to recognise that

> [s]ex and sexuality are social phenomena shaped in a particular history. But also called into question is any idea of a unitary 'society' which can construct 'sexuality'...There are sexualities, not a single sexuality.

> (Weeks, 1985: 178-179)

When we look at the interwoven strands of racism, sexism and classism around the body, then we see that what is called 'sexuality' is the outcome of this nexus. The political meanings of identity that are incorporated in discourses about the body are in fact the plural sexualities of which Weeks spoke above. Fortunately, or unfortunately, identity is susceptible to the norms and prohibitions related to sexual preferences and performances.

Essentialists argue that the biological differences between men and women, which constitute the sex of the physical body, are positive attributes endowed by nature. They suggest that *natural* functions of the body, like reproduction, are fundamental to the social roles that women and men should perform as gendered beings. They also suggest this reductionist approach as the method that women from various social categories can strategically use to transform embodied oppression into embodied resistance. This tactical negotiation with biological determinism encourages women like those in Southside who experience oppression, to take economic and social advantage of their bodily assets as a way of overcoming their experiences of disadvantage.

Criticisms of such essentialist views come from social constructionists who contend that gender-specific cultural discourses about the body engender oppressive and exploitative relations between men and women. In their view, 'the factors shaping sexualities and identities are appropriated and created differently by females and males *because of the way sexed bodies are culturally interpreted and defined*' (Blackwood and Wieringa, in Blackwood and Wieringa (eds.), 1999: 48, emphasis added). Sexuality and politics, therefore, interact to produce a cross-current of contradictions in the power relations tide against which inner-city residents have to struggle on an everyday basis in order to survive.

> To suggest that the sexual might be continuous with something other than sex itself – something like politics – is seldom done…even by feminists. It is as if sexuality comes from the stork…To explain gender inequality in terms of 'sexual politics' is to advance not only a political theory of the sexual that defines gender but also a sexual theory of the political to which gender is fundamental.

> (MacKinnon, in Nicholson (ed.), 1997: 160-161)

In terms of sex and sexuality then, gender refers to the roles that females and males 'should' perform in 'public' and 'private' domains. Such prescriptions make differences between women and men fundamental to the organisation of the political economy. In this matrix, women's capacity to bear children is used as just cause to assume that a woman's place should be in the ('private') home. On the other hand, men are deemed guardians of the public sphere. These indicators of gender identities shape how norms, boundaries and transgressions are defined in embodied performances. Gender, embodiment and identity, therefore, combine to form a nexus that is fundamental to the deployment of power in all social relationships (Foucault, 1980). Conceptions of gender are institutionally guarded and reproduced by the ideological apparatuses of hegemony that reinforce structures of power (Gramsci, 1957). In the final analysis, therefore, gender is central to the maintenance of all power regimes and is a crucial element of *sexual politricks* below the poverty line in inner-city Jamaica.

In the tense inner-city scenario, transgressions of gender norms are severely punished. The most emotionally charged issue I encountered was the heterosexist cultural prohibition against *bowing*, a term that includes a wide range of *deviant* embodied practices. This only adds fire to the already raging fury of the *real man* as *bad man* syndrome. Heterosexuality is definitely the cultural norm in Jamaica, while homosexuals (called 'battymen' or 'chi chi men') are violently outlawed. Clamorous anti-battyman sentiments are expressed in diverse forms and stinging content in the society in general. These messages are amplified in the inner city.

It is important for power brokers to enforce strict codes about sexual 'transgressions' in order to preserve the prevailing gender and political orders. Such prohibitions make a charade of everyday gender 'performances'.

> [T]hat culture so readily punishes or marginalises those who fail to perform the illusion of gender essentialism should be sign enough that on some level there is social knowledge that the truth or falsity of gender is only socially compelled and in no sense ontologically necessitated.

> (Butler, in MacKinnon (ed.), 1997: 412)

Gender is thus seen to be an embodied space where norms of identity, which relate to sexual preference, notions about morality and issues of subjectivity and representation are inscribed. In other words, gender is a metaphor for the multi-layered deployment of power in society.

[G]gender permeates the meanings women [men, girls and boys] make of experience and the possibilities for…generating the meanings and the possibilities for action…To recognise a connection between experience and meaning…is to call attention to the ongoing construction of reality and the placing of oneself within it, that takes place in everyday life.

(Gregg, in Fisher and Davis (eds.), 1993) 195)

The foregoing theory leads us to one obvious conclusion: that gender is a very important concept for explaining the *discourse of bloody violence* that pervades the inner-city communities of Jamaica. Although inner-city residents are subordinated as a class, patriarchy enables even men in the lowest social categorisation to occupy a position of power in relation to women. And although men, *per se*, are not the cause of the problem, it is an unlikely coincidence that men are at the peak of social power systems in general, and also at the peak of power below the poverty line in the inner-city context in particular.

We, also, cannot ignore the intersection of race with class and gender in this discussion that is really focusing on identity politics. Critical *womanists* claim the space of difference in order to draw a definitional distinction between themselves and mainstream White feminists. In so doing, they have defined their own political and cultural distinctiveness in the process of creating meaning. Yet even among Black women there are many sites of diversity. These differences determine the combination of perspectives from which women experience systems of power, which affect their capacity to exercise agency. Embodied identities are, thus, sites of political and subjective contradictions, and as such, reflect the fact that '[t]he body is central to the discourses of superiority/ inferiority on which sexism and racism are based' (Allen, in Barrow (ed.), 1998: 276).

Divide & Rule

The *Lynch doctrine* which perfected the 'divide and rule' strategy is a prime example of the manipulation of differences as a mechanism of power and control. Willie Lynch, said to be an infamous plantation owner from the British West Indies, explained his invidious methods to a slave-owner meeting on the banks of the James River in Virginia in 1712, thus:

I have a foolproof method for controlling your Black slaves. I guarantee every one of you that if installed correctly, it will control the slaves for at least 300 years…I have outlined a number of differences among the slaves, and I take these differences and make them bigger. I use fear, distrust and envy for control purposes…On top of my list is "AGE" but it is there only because it starts with an "A"; the second is "Colour" or Shade, there is INTELLIGENCE, SIZE, SEX…now you have a list of differences, I shall give you an outline of action – but before that *I shall assure you that DISTRUST is stronger than TRUST and ENVY is stronger THAN ADULATION, RESPECT OR ADMIRATION*.

(Lushena Books, 1999: 8, emphases in original)

Beyond the mundane implications of this speech, it is important to recognise that Lynch is also the metaphoric explanation of the all-too-real methods of subjugation that have historically characterised relations between the Whites and various races of coloured peoples. Of course, power is not a discretely dichotomised black-and-white issue, as evidenced by inter- and intra-rivalries across the race spectrum. Suffice it to say that those responsible for establishing hierarchal systems of social difference should be held accountable and made to compensate the disadvantaged for their cumulative losses. This debate therefore places the issue of 'accountability...[in the context of] larger structures of domination (sexism, racism and class elitism) and [indicts] the individuals – often [socially] white, usually male, but not always – who are hierarchically placed to maintain and perpetuate values that uphold these exploitative and oppressive systems' (hooks, 1994: 117).

Physical differences are fundamental to the maintenance of antagonistic power relations in Jamaica between the state/elite classes (perceived as the political and socioeconomic centre of society) and the mass of the population (seen as peripheral). Thus, discourses of difference sustain ideological hegemonies of dominant over subordinate classes. In neo-colonial spaces like Jamaica, such antagonistic social relations have distinct race/colour, class and gender implications.

> In...societies where whiteness is hegemonic, skin colour and phenotype are inescapable markers of difference. However much an individual might want to escape racial categorisation and be seen merely as an individual, s/he finds her/himself confined by white societies' implicit and explicit definitions of whiteness and racial otherness. These definitions are not merely the property of prejudiced individuals, they are structural, inhering in the discourses and institutional practices of the societies concerned.
>
> (Weedon, 1999: 152)

Furthermore, the minefield of identity politics in Jamaica is so saturated with racist, classist, sexist and ageist discourses of power that poor Black women and girls end up as the most disadvantaged constituents. This canker of inequality, which is relentlessly eating away the flesh and shedding the very lifeblood of the society, is the outcome of corrupt historical and political practices. This syndrome of social decay is expressed through discourses that create the ideal conditions for the reproduction of culture. In everyday life, discourses (including conversations and the words used in those conversations) operate as sites of power relations and are thus intrinsic to identity politics. Identities are constituted in discourse and discourse is also a mechanism that is employed, or deployed, in the re-constitution of displaced identities.

> We learn who we are and how we think and behave through discursive practices. Moreover, subjectivity is embodied, and discursive practices shape our bodies, as well as our minds and emotions, in socially gendered ways...The individual is the site for competing and often contradictory modes of subjectivity, which together constitute a particular person.
>
> (Weedon, 1999: 104)

Coming straight out of Willie Lynch's little white Pandora's Box of politricks, the meanings of colour is one of the most divisive elements of identity politics in Jamaica today. For example, '*Brown*' denotes a state of mind that has very real meaning for those who both benefit from and are disadvantaged by having or lacking this *marker of embodiment*. The Chinese, Lebanese and Jewish migrants who came to the island toward the end of the nineteenth century were crucial to the development of the Brown class in modern-day Jamaica. Since those first-generation, local Brown people initially went into the professions,[29] their descendants have come to dominate the merchant class, consolidating the economic distance between themselves and the majority Black class.

Generally speaking, therefore, people of African descent have been socioeconomically disadvantaged.

> The small and medium scale business sector is made up of a minority of middle income persons with brown or light skin racial type, and a substantial majority of persons of Black complexion as well as a minority of Asian and Chinese. The big business sector consists of owners drawn from the privileged racial minorities of Jews, Syrians, Lebanese and Whites, and a small minority of brown complexion. The foreign-owned enterprises of this big business sector are managed increasingly by a multiracial mixture of Whites, Blacks, Asian Indians, Chinese, and persons of brown complexion.

> (Stone, 1986: 37)

The key point to note here is that the main racial contradiction in Jamaica has been between Africans, who comprise just over 75 percent of the population, and Browns, who account for roughly 20 percent, as Carl Stone emphasises.

> The larger size of the Jamaican society and its more historically pronounced pattern of sharp divisions, distinctions and separation between status groups and its older and more entrenched rural and urban middle class make its social and political life quite different from that of most of the eastern Caribbean islands Similarly, the metropolitan area of Kingston and St. Andrew is populated by approximately half a million people in a crowded urban setting characterised by systems of wealth and poverty in contrast to most of the small and relatively homogeneously poor rural communities in many of the rural parishes.

> (Stone, 1973: 1)

Many perceive the upper-class Blacks and Browns as 'socially White' (Beckford and Witter, 1980: 68) or representing the privileged sector. In reality, Jamaica's private sector is run, to this day, by an infamous 'twenty-one family' syndicate that still practices intergenerational inter-marrying, thereby solidifying business-class *alliances*. C.Y. Thomas clarifies just how this family syndicate's *comprador* relations with external interests served to further consolidate their privilege as the elite class of Jamaica.

---

29   The Browns were teachers initially; later their status improved as doctors, lawyers, bankers and, eventually, government officials. Africans have also moved through the ranks to enter the professions, but there is still a social notion of difference to their status vis-à-vis the Brown elites.

> [T]here was evidence of continued consolidation of the society's traditional hegemonic groups, with 21 families accounting for 125 of the 219 directorships in corporations registered in Jamaica. These same families also supplied approximately 70 per cent of the chairpersons of the various corporate boards. Not one of these firms was in Black hands, although Blacks made up 80 per cent of the population. Of the 219 directorships only six were held by Black people and, of these, two were government appointments in joint-venture arrangements. There was also extensive foreign ownership in the major sectors of the economy, with 100 per cent in mining, 75 per cent of manufacturing, 66 per cent of transport, over 50 per cent of communications, storage and tourism and 40 per cent of sugar in foreign hands. The Jamaican bourgeoisie was thus economically subordinate to North American and British capital.
>
> (Thomas, 1988: 212)

Despite the acuteness of Thomas' analysis, his allusion to Blacks should more correctly be interpreted here as *Brown*, with the particular meanings of social status that this connotes in the Jamaican context. Carl Stone's research coincides with Thomas' argument, emphasising how these families have strengthened their position as the managers of the Jamaican political economy.

> In the transition from a plantation-dominated economy in which there was an ascendant White rural planter class to a more diversified urban-centred economy there has emerged a powerful grouping of urban-based wealthy families mainly of Jewish and Arab ethnic origin...They have penetrated and dominated many areas of the Jamaican economy...Included among these are the following 15 families who are perhaps the most powerful, active, and influential families in the economic and political power domains of the country and they represent an important segment of the effective class leadership among the rich capitalists in Jamaica:
>
> Powerful business families
> Matalon, Ashenheim, Hendrickson, Facey, Mahfood, Issa, Hart, Henriques, Desnoes, Geddes, DeLisser, Clarke, Rousseau, Stewart, Kennedy.
>
> (Stone, 1986, 38-39)

These families started out as 'importers and commission agents of foreign companies' (Stone, 1986: 38). And, although the bulk of their fortunes have been produced on local industrial and commercial soil, their primary business loyalties extend beyond Jamaica's shores. There is, therefore, a *client* or *comprador* socioeconomic relationship between local capitalists and their external controlling interests, particularly those located in North America (Beckford and Witter, 1980: 67). Thus, beyond the machinations of the political parties, we need to trace the roots of this socioeconomic canker in order to understand how the tree comes to be bearing the fruits of 'Clientilism gone mad!', to paraphrase calypsonian, The Mighty Sparrow.

This undoubted power mechanism is what discourse analysts say we have to analytically deconstruct in order to reveal how structures of power are configured and how they can be dismantled. This de-/re-construction is no easy task, as is clear from the diverse *domination discourses* at large in Jamaica today. This is not to suggest that Black people are hapless victims. However, calling the majority class the greatest survivors runs into the danger of glorifying oppression. But it remains true that, 'every heart knows its own sorrow'. Black self-assertion challenges cultural values that privilege people of lighter complexion over those of a darker hue. Still, over the past 30 years or so, there has been an increasing trend of Black people gaining upward social mobility through education, business and technical skills. In addition,

> [l]arge scale migration of lighter skinned ethnic minorities from Jamaica in the 1970s opened up wider opportunities for Black middle class Jamaicans to be recruited into the ranks of the professional managers. This trend has diluted the earlier pattern in which the educated Black middle class was located entirely in public sector jobs while the management of the private sector was monopolised by the ethnic minorities.

(Stone, 1986: 40)

Despite this modern trend, internalised racism is really the centrepiece of the identity crisis currently being expressed outwardly in the vicious forms of violence in various inner-city communities. Violence to the self is the order of the day as disadvantaged people try to reconfigure themselves into the 'Brown' ideal – literally and figuratively. Practices such as skin bleaching and hair straightening are commonplace. Some people describe bleaching as a 'style' which is adopted to achieve a sexually and socially desirable body. This practice takes on macabre implications when parodied as the route to self-validation. For the desperate unconscious, gaining Brownness, even in caricature mode, is worth the effort because, in their view, they acquire some measure of improved status.

Thus, my use of the term 'African' to describe the subjects of this study is more reflective of my own point of entry into the discussion on identity politics, rather than material reality. Using African to refer to the majority class may be an analytical fiction on my part, because except for a minority, Black people who live in Southside would never call themselves 'African'. African descendants in this urban space have inherited the dubious legacy of being inserted into the Jamaican society's vicious maelstrom of race, class and gender-specific identity configurations, which have, themselves, become a much taken-for-granted social fact. It is little wonder then, that some people express their traumatised psychosocial status through violence. These subjects are caught up in a web whose strands are intricately woven into Jamaica's bloody history.

We need to remember in this context, that downtown Kingston was the location of an auction block on which Africans captured on the mother continent were bought and sold from the fifteenth to nineteenth centuries. At the time, this northern Caribbean island was under the control of British planters who had won it from the Spanish in 1655. The latter had held Jamaica for 263 years and executed extreme terrorism against the indigenous Tainos (more popularly referred to as Arawaks). The Spanish quickly decimated the Tainos and were forced (or rather, chose) to import Africans in their stead.

The Africans who had miraculously survived the horrors of the Middle Passage holocaust were culturally stymied when they realised that White people owned the land on which they were made to work under the most dehumanising conditions. The notion of land ownership was anathema to these enslaved Africans because they came from cultures that accepted that the land belongs to the Ancestors. Back in Africa, various communities knew the meaning of sustainability because the fundamental principle of the collective was to care for the land in the present on behalf of the Ancestors, and to hold it in trust for future generations.

Debilitating culture shock set in when the enslaved realised that apart from their slave-labour relationship to the land, their only other access to this sacred benefit of Nature was via their paltry provision grounds. Conditions improved only marginally in the post-emancipation period, and this created hunger and anger in the rural peasantry and the urban poor, which eventually erupted in the 1938 labour rebellions.

Dominant Masculinities & Subordinated Femininities

The poverty and violence in urban grassroots Jamaica today is characteristic of inner-city communities the world over. These areas are usually underdeveloped and violent because there are high political stakes in the construction of marginality (Castells, 1983). As a motif of both old- and new-world globalisation, the so-called ghetto is typically confined to the most deprived sector of the urban landscape. World powers that (legally) manufacture weapons for individual and mass destruction promote the notion of masculinity being akin to violence, in order to sell their penile products of war for huge profits. Nationhood is predicated on the *phallic* objects of bombs and bullets – the bigger, the better – or worse as the case may be.

The arms industry is one of the few major growth industries in the world today. Their market objectives push them to contrive and artificially sustain a need for violence. This industry rationalises turning men into killing machines as part-and-parcel of their power drama. The fight against an *enemy* is contrived to justify the crime as being a heroic gesture of nation and self-building. Similarly, inner-city 'soldiers' have become casualties of this industry of death production – without even the 'benefit' of a cause to soften the mortal blows for the families. Possession of the *ballistic phallus* and its fatalistic power, galvanises the men hell-bent on this death production pursuit into vicious actions against fellow citizens and the society at large. Jamaican politicians are known to have been instigators of the inner-city violence although as 'politricksters', they take no responsibility for either this method of manipulating the electorate, nor for the out-of-control monster of gang warfare that this practice has spawned.

Under certain circumstances, particular notions of masculinity come to dominate as *hegemonic masculinities*. Thus, a range of masculinities have to be considered in order to explain how dominant gender power comes to be constructed in masculinist and/ or violent terms.

> This did not eliminate other masculinities. What it did was marginalise them: and this created conditions for new versions of masculinity that rested on impulses or practices excluded from the increasingly rationalised and integrated world of business and bureaucracy.

> (Connell, 1987: 131)

Those who control the state have a vested interest in promoting particular 'social relations of gender' (Connell, 1987: 126) and have encouraged the construction of masculinist ideology and practices in the violent idiom as the dominant gender order. This has resulted in the problematic definition of inner-city men's masculinities in violent terms; thus, a *real man* has to be a *Bad Man*.

> The state both institutionalises hegemonic masculinity and expends great energy in controlling it. The objects of repression, e.g. 'criminals', are generally younger men themselves involved in the practice of violence, with a social profile quite like that of the immediate agents of repression, the police or the soldiers. However, the state is not all of a piece. The military and coercive apparatus has to be understood in terms of relationships between masculinities: the physical aggression of front-line troops or police, the authoritative masculinity of commanders, the calculative rationality of technicians, planners and scientists.
>
> (Connell, 1987: 128-129)

The correlation between violence and 'real manhood' is expressed, for example, in the valorisation of the gun as the modern weapon of warfare. By extension, the *phallus* symbolises nationhood and in all its violent glory, the trailblazer on the road to sovereignty.

> It is not the possession of a penis which provides the basis for male dominance over women. Rather it is systems of patriarchy, which enable the penis to be represented or understood in ways that express domination…[I]t is clear that the dominations that are being discussed do not simply refer to domination of men over women. We are also dealing with dominations of men over other men, and the possible and complex links between these and other patterns of domination.
>
> (Connell: 1987: 75)

Structural power is translated at the ground level into patriarchal authority, which privileges the sexuality of men over that of women, while stereotyping women as objects of men's sexual desire. Just like cultural robots, women and men are programmed to perform their identities/gender roles within this patriarchal idiom (Butler, in Nicholson (ed.), 1997). Femininity is therefore oftentimes defined in male terms, even when it is conjugated as an expression of agency by and on behalf of women.

Body Language

As Kingston's industrial development peaked in the 1960s–70s, the waterfront community of Southside was exposed to another wave of body trading. Many ships docked to do business, and while deals were struck in the fledgling private sector, the sailors' entry into Southside also heralded a syndrome of sex work, transactions which left behind a legacy of *Browning offspring*. These colour-coded children had huge implications for how values of beauty and sexual desirability are configured and perpetuated in this urban grassroots space. During that time, prostitutes called 'sports' used their highly prized bodies to gain material advantage – a strategy of survival and agency expression contoured by their material and psychosocial needs and wants.

Contemporary embodied practices of survival below the poverty line reflect this 'sporting' tradition that has been dubbed the oldest profession in the world. There is a cultural understanding in the inner-city environment that women will have sex with men in exchange for the receipt of material goods. This acts as a survival strategy and an identity reclamation symbol, and illustrates that those who are subordinated will also inevitably produce *discourses of resistance* through various processes of struggle (Post, 1996: 278). And, because the human body is the physical interface between *discourses of domination* and *discourses of resistance*, body language – in a specific definition of the term – constitutes a colossal example of how meanings are conveyed in *unspoken discourse*.

In classical communication contexts, *body language* refers to the non-verbal meanings that can be inferred through the medium, movements and profile of the body. This entails an elaborate array of transactions that can be read from gestures, eye movements, posturing and many combinations of signals from different limbs. Recall that language is one of the primary elements of *discourse* and that *body language* actually transcends conscious and sub- or unconscious language.

Here, however, I am actually more concerned with what is said about the body, than what is said by it. For example, when those who control the power structures manipulate what is said about the body, they deliberately create registers of social differentiation, which are then used as the basis of social inclusion or exclusion. What people say in everyday interactions reflect the positive meanings that are applied to bodies – e.g. 'Brown and pretty', or the so-called negative meanings like 'Black and ugly'. In Jamaica, just as in the USA, attitudes to race have, in fact, regressed considerably since the sixties and seventies, when slogans like 'Black is Beautiful' re-marked the Black body as a space for resistance. But history will remember that some Blacks/ Africans never succumbed to the culturally fatal seductiveness of disempowering discourses.

The construction of concepts of masculinity and femininity is directly related to structures and *discourses of power*, and incorporates identities of class, race/ colour, sexuality, gender, patriarchy, age and social geography. Therefore, '[w]e are increasingly aware that...what we call "sexual" is as much a product of language and culture as of nature. But we earnestly strive to fix it, stabilise it, say who we are by telling of our sex...' (Weeks, 1985: 186).

Of course, the definition that I have presented here is not the sum total of meanings of *body language*. As Weeks also notes, embodied identities are, at best, fragmentary and unstable (ibid.). However, citing the links between politics, identity and sexuality is crucial for clarifying the connection that I am drawing between discourse and power, since beyond language, discourse should be regarded in relation to power and identity politics; it is embodied and shaped by structures and institutions of power (Foucault, 1980).

Further, unpacking the power motifs that recur through *body language* reveals the insidious thread of patriarchy, which is entrenched in cultural norms and taboos that prevent women from exercising full agency. Patriarchy can be defined as the articulation of structural and discursive systems of power, which necessarily entails the domination of females by males (Post, 1996; Bulbeck, 1988; Coward, 1983). This is one of the most prevalent examples of the construction and application of a binary opposition as a mechanism of domination. Patriarchy serves elite-class interests and cuts across social categories, even while facilitating class alliances between privileged women and men against their lower class counterparts. However, in cases like Southside, patriarchy also allows for alliances between upper-class (politician) men and lower-class (gun) men in enacting the violence drama.

Therefore, while derogatory *discourses* about the body marginalise African people as a class, across classes, men are still able to oppress and exploit women on the basis of their gender identities. This challenges some of the assumptions that the experiences of slavery – or contemporary material insolvency, for that matter – have served to undermine the capacity of Black men to exercise power. The fact that Black men, women and children experience the vagaries of structural and discursive power as a class, does 'not change the reality that men in patriarchal society automatically have higher status than women – [and] they are not obliged to earn that status' (hooks, 1981: 88).

Yet, as mentioned earlier, disadvantaged women who have little or no other choice resort to trading sex as a survival strategy. They also deliberately have children in order to fulfil the normative matriculation requirements for cultural stability. The fulfilment of such actions by objects of domination gives *meaning* to their lives and, in the process, allows them to rescue a sense of selfhood and gain material advantage. Although these actions might not be regarded as particularly compelling in development terms since they do not sufficiently disrupt the entrenched power structures, they nevertheless qualify as discursive power.

> [T]he messy reality of multiple identities will continue to be the experience out of which social relations are conducted. Neither peasants nor proletarians deduce their identities directly or solely from the mode of production, and the sooner we attend to the concrete experience of class as it is lived, the sooner we will appreciate both the obstacles to, and the possibilities for, class formation.

> (Scott, 1985: 43)

Here, Scott contextualises patterns of embodied resistance in the everyday experiences of objects of domination (i.e. the residents) living in Southside. However, there is an inherent problem in rationalising all forms of resistance expressed in this cultural context, as being viable ways of exercising agency. In other words, because some actions of resistance are actually outcomes of internalised oppression, they might not only serve to reinforce the very power structures that make recourse to such choices necessary in the first place, but may also preclude the possibility for social transformation to achieve social justice. The people of Southside are caught in another trap. Thus, despite the fact that in the urban grassroots, a number of subordinated subjects have often achieved the status of agents, theirs can be viewed as an existence of multiple contradictions because their '...counter-interpretation of experience, counter-use of symbols, counter-constitution of knowledge...identity etc., [are] but reinterpretations... In that sense, in such a process of resistance through double inversion a sort of refraction takes place, since one image does not lead back directly to the other, but at an angle, like a stick seen through water' (Post, 1996: 286).

This limitation is a crucial consideration when trying to understand why, despite the undoubted strategies that show that the citizens are not all victims of domination, there is still such a strong syndrome of sociopolitical paralysis or apathy in enclaves like Southside. And yet the positive outcome of the limited agency exercised by subjects at the ground level, is the reconfiguration of their personal self-definitions in idioms of their own construction. Most significantly, their physical body provides a ready resource for replacing depreciating definitions of identity and power with self-assertive symbols, some of which, paradoxically, sometimes bear the hallmark of internalised oppression.

> Subjectivity is [therefore] embodied, and discursive practices shape our bodies, as well as our minds and emotions, in socially gendered ways... The individual is the site for competing and often contradictory modes of subjectivity, which together constitute a particular person. Modes of subjectivity are constituted within discursive practices and lived by the individual as if he or she were a fully coherent subject...[I]t is only by assuming forms of subjectivity, which include the dimension of agency, that we can think, communicate and act in the world.
>
> (Weedon, 1999: 104)

Anthony Giddens' (1999) insightful interpretation of the make-up of society as being a series of negotiations between structure and agency is useful for explaining the structural and discursive elements of power that I am exploring. He suggests that tensions accrue in the process of self-production, which account for the wider social systems and relationships that, eventually, impact on the individual or group. This tension generates complex responses, which, in turn, define the social actor as possessing the potential for expressions of agency or active resistance, notwithstanding the overall mitigating social circumstances.

Giddens also suggests that the language in popular use is crucial for the construction of discourses of resistance. He notes that everyday practices from which ontological meanings may be inferred, are most significant if they can be defined as having intended and/or unintended consequences. This distinction accounts for the difference between action that reinforces existing power structures and action that clearly reflects the exercise of independent consciousness by the subject/object of domination.

Still, resistance to *discourses of domination* is not always a public display; therefore, a paradigm shift from such limiting definitions certainly creates more conceptual space to explain power relations in terms of people's lived and embodied experiences. The embodiment theme used here is of course, my own emphasis; Giddens fails dismally to put a gender to his social actors, so they might be mythical, angelic beings with no sexual apparatus for all we know. Yet other theorists, like Lois McNay, underscore the importance of embodiment to expressions of agency, which should be seen as an intricate tapestry.

> [T]here is a shift, therefore, from understanding the sex-gender system as an a-temporal structure towards an alternative concept of a series of interconnected regimes whose relations are historically variable and dynamic. This idea of gender as a historical matrix, rather than a static structure, is regarded as offering a more substantive account of agency.
>
> (McNay, 2000: 13)

McNay efficiently analyses agency in relation to the dynamics of gender and power. She presents a balanced view of the symbolic meanings of subjectivities that are constituted within specific historical, political and economic conjunctures, and about the effects of normative discourses on the construction of strategies for self-realisation. As she emphasises,

> [t]he relationship between symbolic and material practices can begin to be understood more adequately with the shift from a determinist to a generative account of subjectification and agency. When the formation of subjectivity is understood not in one-sided terms as an exogenously imposed effect but as the result of a lived relation between embodied potentiality and material relations then an active concept of agency emerges.
>
> (McNay, 2000: 16)

Agency has to be seen as a dynamic concept, especially in view of the changes that are constantly taking place in the states of power under question.

> It is crucial to conceptualise these creative or productive aspects immanent to agency in order to explain how, when faced with complexity and difference, individuals may respond in unanticipated and innovative ways which may hinder, reinforce or catalyse social change.
>
> (McNay, 2000: 5)

This emphasis on consequence is a dramatic departure from the more static formulation offered by Giddens, which suggests that any action – with intended or unintended consequences – could be considered agency. Instead, as McNay emphasises, one has to uncover the meanings underlying the intentions that motivate actors, as well as the consequences of those actions, particularly when considering power relations between gendered subjects.

> With regard to issues of gender, a more rounded conception of agency is crucial to explaining both how women have acted autonomously in the past despite constricting social sanctions and also how they may act now in the context of processes of gender restructuring...[A]ttendant on the conceptualisation of a creative dimension of agency are renewed understandings of ideas of autonomy and reflexivity, understood as the critical awareness that arises from a self-conscious relation with the other.
>
> (McNay, 2000: 5)

McNay proposes that post-structuralist feminists have also imposed dualistic notions of agency onto the subject, and as a consequence, they have produced deterministic formulations of agency, which are limited to the discursive realm. Although theorists in the Habermasian mode have taken a more grounded approach to the discussion, 'the concept of agency that emerges is limited because its understanding of inter-subjective relations is underpinned by an implicitly domesticated concept of difference' (2000:12). In other words, a comprehensive analysis of agency has to incorporate explicit political concerns, as well as nuanced interpretations of what constitutes the subject and how the subject experiences and reconstitutes self through active engagement with and production of cultural discourses.

Sanctioning the Chi Chi Men

In Chapter 8, we detail how the human body symbolises a bridge or physical interface between the culture of the surrounding macro-world and the internal micro-world inside the body/head of each individual. As the metaphoric bridge between the wider culture and the individual, the *body* is therefore a site of the inscription of social values and their institutionalised causes and effects. In short, the body is the major site of the binary oppositions which serve to prescribe, circumscribe, proscribe and sanction engendered values, identity definitions and embodied practices. What is said about the body becomes culturally normalised and institutionalised and becomes the yardstick by which transgressors are demonised and endangered. Unpacking the norms and taboos in the culture reveals the political stakes that are vested in the maintenance of a patriarchal gender order and specific embodied practices, which in the case of Southside, are all defined and confined by violence.

Case in point is the strong stream of homophobia currently running through the vista of violence in which inner-city values and attitudes are rooted. This trend can have catastrophic consequences for ordinary folk who fail to fall into the line of the prevailing yardstick. Of course, the batty man/chi chi man (homosexual male) is by definition, taken to be geometrically opposed to Jamaica's rigidly enforced patriarchal gender order.

As we point out in Chapter 5, anti-chi chi man (i.e. anti-homosexual) sentiments are most vocally represented in the Dancehall space where the body is reconstructed in line with popular notions of permissible and taboo sexualised performances. 'More Fire' is the chant of the day as turbaned artistes pound lyrics of damnation, taboos, boundaries and sanctions on the sensibilities of all and sundry who come in earshot of their vinyl and CD volumes.

The judgemental pronouncements speak directly to the sanctions (potentially) imposed against taboo practices, and are enunciated with deadly emphasis and pinpoint precision in the lyrics of many artistes. One of the most popular Reggae songs in Jamaica for 2001, entitled 'Chi Chi Man', is a composition which is virulently homophobic.

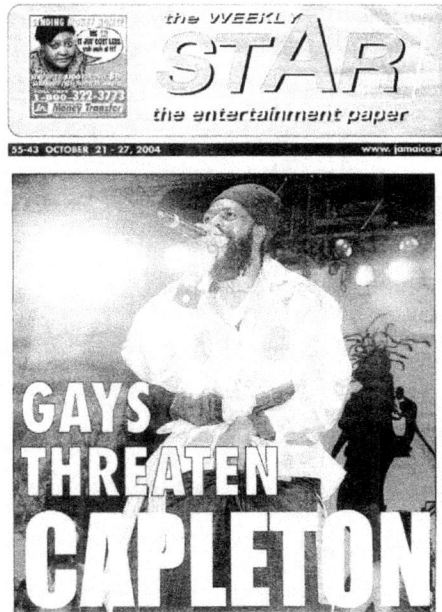

Figure 2.1: The Star newspaper reported that gays in Europe and the USA were threatening to prevent popular DJ Capleton from performing at venues in their cities because of his alleged homophobic lyrics.

Chi-Chi Man

O.K. niggers, Yow, Yow, Yow
My crew, my dogs
Set rules, set laws,
We represent for the lords of yards
A gal alone a feel up mi balls
(Only a girl can fondle my balls)
Chorus:
From dem a par inna chi-chi man car
(Since they are driving in a homosexual's car)
Give me fire make we bun them
(Give me some fire to enable us to burn them)
From dem a drink inna chi-chi man bar
(If they are drinking in a bar owned by a homosexual)
Give me fire mek we done dem
(Give me fire and we will kill them)
So mi go so: do you see what I see
Niggers why you doing that
nuff a dem inna crew
(A lot of them are together in a group)
dem a carry all dem dirty egg

(They are carrying their dirty eggs, suggesting pollution)
nuff a dem a lick di pipe
(A lot of them are licking the pipe – suggesting fellatio)
if dem bring it to we
full them up a copper shot
rise up every collie come we rata tat tat
(Let us rata tat tat i.e. shoot them up)
every chi-chi man haffi get flat
(Every homosexual has to die)
me and me niggers a go make a pact
(My friends and I are going to make a pact)
chi-chi man fi dead and it's a fact
(Homosexuals have to die and that's a fact)
Chorus
So mi go na na na na na na na na na
Nah go mek no chi-chi man walk right ya so
(We are not going to permit homosexuals to walk here)
From a boy a do that
(If a boy i.e. not a man is doing that)
We a go done him right now
(We are going to kill him right now)
Lef him whole family inna sorrow
(Leave his entire family in sorrow)
See him from far, me and him naw go par
(I can recognise him from afar and know we cannot be friends)
A nuff a dem boy deh a smoke man cigar
(Many of those men are sucking other men's penises)
Me and him coulda never inna rum bar
(He and I could never socialise in a rum bar)
Dem boy deh flex too bizarre
(Those boys' behaviour is too bizarre)

From this song, it is apparent that in the inner-city context, there is a direct correlation between the *discourse of violence* and the interpretation of normative practices of manhood in the vocally virulent heterosexual idiom. The artistes threaten, with impunity, to murder transgressors of this well-established gender-identity-embodiment cultural contract. The message of this song recalls the example that I used to open this discussion: that the use of this theme by politicians to appeal to the homophobic interest in the popular culture shows the pervasiveness of the patriarchal dividend in the popular culture.

This verbal assault is commonplace in Jamaica, although at the international level the adoption of this stance poses a tremendous financial risk for errant artistes,[30] ever

---

30 Prominent Reggae artiste Shabba Ranks felt the harsher effects of this backlash when his musical career was abruptly aborted by the lobbying campaign of the homosexual community in the United States. Ranks had made statements in support of Buju Banton to the effect that homosexual practices are wrong

since Buju Banton achieved notoriety with his 'Boom Bye Bye' (in a Batty Boy head). The 'chi chi man' antagonism is a current cultural sentiment of violent homophobia which is sanctioned by the presiding Judaeo-Christian Ethic. This sentiment is openly and articulately expressed by the objecting artistes, and is reinforced by legislation that still outlaws homosexual practices.

The increase in such severe pronunciations against homosexuality from popular Reggae Dancehall artistes is resoundingly echoed at the ground level. The rapid thrusts against sexual deviants parallels the ever-increasing number of violent crimes in the society. In a vicious cycle, a crisis in masculinity is expressed as a patriarchal dividend (Connell, 1987; 1995) invested in this double whammy, which feeds upon and into the homophobic hysteria. Men, who may feel the need to quiet their own anxieties about what defines them as *real men*, often project their insecurities onto others. By exerting authority over what is said about the (male) body, they define cultural peculiarities in the domain of sexuality and by extension, of politics, over moral codes and behaviours.

Sexual Survival Strategies

Applying all this theory to Southside, we see that some women have used status-seeking practices, like hair straightening and skin bleaching (see Chapter 8), to refract the racist, classist and sexist discourses that have been projected onto their psychically fractured African bodies. Through these efforts to achieve the symbolic goal of *social whiteness* (Beckford and Witter, 1980: 67), the disadvantaged subjects hope to achieve a sense of improved social status and sexual desirability. Such expressions of internalised racism tell us how deep-seated the problem of underdevelopment is in inner-city communities, and highlights the necessity of venturing into the difficult dimension of the human (un)consciousness, if we are to achieve the vaunted ideal of social change. The effects of internalised oppression are probably a more challenging problem to solve than those of the entrenched structures of power we have already examined.

Sexual Politrickery

Remember that piece of poetry
From Reggae maestro Bob Marley
Emancipate yourselves
from mental slavery
none but ourselves can free our mind
he sang this to me
because he could clearly see
when the powers-that-be
would rather we be blind
to the conspiracy

– as sanctioned by the Bible. Shabba, whose image is etched in many of the murals adorning the walls of Southside, suffered this ignominy because he had inadvertently inserted himself into a political equation that was beyond his capacity to solve.

underlying poverty
violent masculinity
and subordinate femininity
the entrapped condition
of the African majority
is all about how the money
stops short of the inner-city
partisan manipulation
and politricks of sexuality
now the human tragedy
is that to survive
yeah just to stay a-live
some women have no choice
but to sell their body.

© **imani tafari-ama**

Since they live in such a volatile political situation with social chips so firmly stacked against them, many disadvantaged women resort to selling their sex as a survival strategy. Poor women often have no recourse but to bargain with their bodies to gain materiality and social advantage. The extraordinary pragmatism that is entailed in this contradictory social fact was, for me, one of the most definitive indicators of how resistance discourses are shaped by and contoured to specific social circumstances. It also shows how the strands of gender, identity and embodiment are interwoven into language, practices and institutions – the discourses of everyday life (Foucault, 1980).

Parenting is an intimate bedfellow of the survival strategy of selling sex for materiality. Some women use their role as mothers to counteract the psychosocial pains of subordination, as well as to establish fertility as an indicator of their sexual viability. Conversely, those who do not conform to this essentialist notion of their 'natural' role of reproducing the species, are perceived as socially deficient and are subject to ridicule. Women who do not conform to the heterosexual norm and bear children are viewed as abnormal and called mules. The biblical injunction to 'be fruitful and multiply' is used by religious institutions to reinforce this gendered popular belief. Thus, the choice to be a parent is intricately bound up with normative stereotypes of masculinity and femininity, which confer social legitimacy on the biologically reproductive on the one hand and stigmatise barrenness and homosexuality on the other.

By and large, then, women in Southside gain some psychosocial advantage by appropriating their roles as re/producers as a way of offsetting material lack. Parenting has been used as an important practice of identity recovery. Such embodied practices are opportunities to gain visibility, which, in turn, enables women to proceed beyond the boundaries that are intrinsic to their gendered location *below the poverty line*. However, norms governing parenting practices are supersaturated with specific 'power' assumptions about womanhood.

Thus, despite all the joys people experience as parents, this practice of identity reclamation also has the potential to reinforce the subordination of women. While youthful parenthood might satisfy compelling cultural norms of self-realisation, the financial responsibility entailed oftentimes militates against the social advancement of the mothers. In some cases, the psychosocial satisfaction of motherhood (and fatherhood) is counter-foiled by chronic social lack. As several women told me, early childbearing and consequent parenting tasks have prevented them from making advances in their own lives.

For girl children, who are socialised in inner-city communities like Southside, identities of femininity converge around fertility as proof of womanhood. The general emphasis on selfhood reclamation through reproductive sexuality is thus a *gendered discourse*. Paradoxically, parenting also enables victims of social exclusion to defy disadvantage because of the new way they see themselves. Parenting also gives new meaning to their lives.

The act of parenting is, therefore, loaded with contradictions. Material lack and social powerlessness mitigate the effectiveness of this act of empowerment and building of self-esteem. Seductive norms that prescribe fertility and fecundity as necessary features of womanhood, actually give more power to patriarchy. Yet, a child of resistance is constantly being conceived within the womb of the parenting ideal. The local proverb 'Children are poor people's riches' is thematic of one of the prevailing strategies of self-realisation and survival. Seen in this light, children are the social capital in the self-realisation repertoires of their parents.

On the other hand, several parents defined their poverty in terms of their own hunger and inability to provide food for their children on a day-to-day basis. The fact that many parents residing in inner-city communities like Southside remain materially beneath the poverty line indicates that their achievement of discursive power needs to be balanced by changes to the structures of power that predetermine their destitute material circumstances. Normative *cultural discourses* need to change too, as the values and attitudes that surround parenting are directly connected to other institutionalised forms of power.

Youthful parenthood might satisfy prevailing norms of self-realisation, but where did those norms come from? Who gains from women's parenting practices? Fatherhood cannot happen without motherhood, so there is a great deal of meaning to be inferred from the phrase 'having a baby for a *man*'. In actuality, the phrase tells of the patriarchal investments in women's bodies. Parenting also validates poor men's existence. But does parenting hamper the social advancement of the mother who many times assumes sole responsibility for the child?

Children Learn What They Live

So far, my exploration of gender power has addressed the contradictory relations that obtain between men and women and how structural factors of domination exacerbate the disadvantages that citizens at the subaltern level of the Jamaican society experience in their everyday lives. However, it would be remiss of me not to consider how children live through these power relations. Childhood is also a hotbed of social, political, gender and embodied contestations, which are not easily resolved

(Bradley, 1996). This dilemma persists because of the stakes that power holders have in maintaining this social category – childhood – as another realm of subordination. Children and youth represent a particularly impressionable and also creative stage of identity formation. As such, the institutions that reinforce ideological hegemonies invest tremendous material and human resources to ensure that the status quo is maintained via the values and attitudes that are employed as major instruments in the socialisation of children.

However, by no stretch of the imagination can young people in the inner city be seen as mere hapless victims, notwithstanding the grinding poverty and severe social degradation that they experience. But, because of the multiple levels of disadvantage that are inherent to the inner-city environment, children's rights to self and social determination, which are guaranteed by the *United Nations' Convention on the Rights of the Child*, are often overlooked. As stated in the introduction of this Charter,

> [c]hildren have the right to be provided with certain things and services, ranging from a name and nationality to health care and education. They have a right to be protected from certain acts such as torture, exploitation, arbitrary detention and unwarranted removal from parental care. And children have the right to participate in decisions affecting their lives as well as the community as a whole.

> (UNICEF, 1990: 2, emphasis in original)

Although this charter requires its signatories to develop the legal framework which will promote and protect the inalienable human rights of girls and boys, there is notable gender blindness in many of the articles. This is reflected in the failure of many policy-makers to develop gender-specific programmes for children's development. This caveat needs special attention, particularly in the inner-city context where identity politics and material circumstances are such conflicted and gendered terrains. And, despite these UN requirements, it is also clear that class differences militate against some children's capacity to access these internationally sanctioned mechanisms of support.

Despite the fact that children in general and disadvantaged children in this case study in particular, display a capacity to exercise agency, it is rare for their knowledge bases to be validated in academic or even development projects. I have, therefore, included children's voices in this analysis in recognition of the extent to which age acts as an obstacle to self-realisation for young people. This all-inclusive approach is important because ageism means using differences in chronological years as a power control mechanism. It is also crucial to recognise, as Bradley observes, how gender differences among children constitute yet another mechanism for exercising power.

> [C]hildhood and adolescence are crucial periods for gender relations, as times when young women and men have to make many choices which are vital to their later lives. Yet these are made in the context of differentiated gender expectations and of discourses of masculinity and femininity which promote male dominance.

> (Bradley, 1996: 110-111)

The age concept, therefore, enriches my aforementioned theoretical hybrid and allows me to analyse the matrices of domination in Jamaica from the most inclusive perspective possible. Children and adolescents are, intrinsically, culture bearers or recipients of identities and value systems, a truism which speaks to the matrices of power into which and by which children are socialised. They define their identities within discursive constructions of femininity and masculinity, which reify specific power prescriptions. Add on all the social challenges that their adult counterparts have to contend with, and we see that children and adolescents who emerge from inner-city communities perform their programmed and rehearsed gender roles within a power play of innumerable contradictions.

Critiquing 'A Culture of Poverty'

Oscar Lewis' work, which is the closest relative to my own research in the literature, is based on his research on poverty and violence in the slums of Puerto Rico, the Caribbean state annexed by the USA. His detailed representations of inner-city life in that Caribbean country was designed to avoid a stereotyping of the residents who have no recourse but to live under such challenging socioeconomic conditions, as either virtuous or dysfunctional (1967: xxxix). As Lewis explains,

> the culture of poverty can come into being in a variety of historical contexts… The culture of poverty is both an adaptation and a reaction of the poor to their marginal position in a class-stratified, highly individuated, capitalistic society. It represents an effort to cope with feelings of hopelessness and despair which develop from the realisation of the improbability of achieving success in terms of the values and goals of the larger society.

(ibid.: xl-xli)

While focusing on the negative aspects of the culture, Lewis also validates the many positive features that are characteristic of the nation's attempts to pursue a pathway of development. I find this emphasis relevant because I am also highlighting some of the most forbidding aspects of Jamaican culture. However, this concentration on the most problematic aspects of the culture is designed to identify the taproot of the problems and suggest solutions. As Orlando Patterson wrote in analysing the events of July 3–7, 2001, when there was a flare-up of violence between gangsters in Tivoli Gardens, western Kingston and the security forces,

> [t]he bad news is that Jamaica's attempts at economic development have largely failed. Here, as in Puerto Rico and most other Caribbean islands, post-independence attempts at industrialisation have fallen apart. Jamaica now has vast shantytowns; unemployment at depression levels; and high rates of economic inequality, crime and drug abuse.

(*The New York Times*, July 23, 2001)

Like Lewis, my interest in the issues of social disintegration is intended to stimulate improvement of the conditions analysed, rather than to exploit and sensationalise the subjects of the study. Furthermore, this analysis is as comprehensive as it is because I want to demonstrate that the portrayals of masculinity and femininity related to violence and embodied practices of survival are not isolated instances of social dysfunction. On the contrary, the critical assessments have to be understood in the context of prevailing political, economic and social conditions that have, as Lewis describes, constituted dominated subjects and consequently determine the course of their lives. I also share Lewis' view that protracted social exclusion has a deleterious effect on those who experience such marginalisation. However, I disagree with his conclusion that those who experience the *culture of poverty* are somehow also responsible for the cycle of deprivation in which they are embedded. He argues for example, that

> once it [the culture of poverty] comes into existence it tends to perpetuate itself from generation to generation because of its effect on the children. By the time slum children are age six or seven they have usually absorbed the basic values and attitudes of their subculture and are not psychologically geared to take full advantage of changing conditions or increased opportunities which may occur on their lifetime.

(Lewis, 1967: xli)

By presenting this reductionist outlook, Lewis fails to tackle the structural and discursive power relations that are intrinsic to the situation that he so comprehensively researches. These class, gender and age-specific relations of power prevent most of the children born and raised in Kingston's inner-city communities from being able to escape the vicious cycle of disadvantage in which they are trapped. In addition, Lewis' argument does not take full cognisance of the many children from the *'ghetto'* who succeed in overcoming the limitations imposed by the circumstances of their birth. Further, Lewis posits that this 'culture' is a by-product of evolutionary changes in society, rather than situating the phenomena of poverty and violence within the context of the prevailing political economy of the polity that he studies. He suggests that

> [m]ost frequently, the culture of poverty develops when a stratified social and economic system is breaking down or is being replaced by another, as in the case of the transition from feudalism to capitalism or during periods of rapid technological change. Often it results from imperial conquest in which the native social and economic structure is smashed and the natives are maintained in a servile colonial status, sometimes for many generations.

(Lewis, 1967: xli)

The violence is half a century old but, of course, rooted in the colonial past. The fact that there is intentional and involuntary colonial amnesia compounds our incapacity to solve this entrenched crisis of social dysfunction. That is a terribly long transitional period, if we buy into his evolutionary argument (which I do not). I consider that approach to be an over-generalisation of the problems of poverty and violence. Puerto Rico's development experiences are historically similar to Jamaica's even if different in contemporary details. They, therefore, have to be referenced against the specific modes of production experienced, as well as against the development models with which state powers have experimented in specific periods. In addition, Lewis studied the problems of poverty and violence within the family environment as a means of extrapolating about what obtains in the wider society. He came to the conclusion that

> [t]he women…show more aggressiveness and a greater violence of language and behaviour than the men…Indeed, a great deal of the aggressiveness of the women is directed against men. The women continually deprecate them and characterise them as inconsiderate, irresponsible, untrustworthy and exploitative. The women teach children to depend upon the mother and to distrust men.

> (1967: xxv)

My own research results suggest the opposite perspective. While, as I discuss, women engage in violence in the household as well as in wider social relationships, the violent behaviour exhibited by men is more pervasive and intimidating. As I have argued, this violence is an intrinsic part of the patriarchal discourse that is characteristic of hierarchical class relations, which undergird power relations in the wider society. Lewis also fails to problematise the embodiment of his research subjects, but takes for granted their gender identities as well as the roles into which women and men have been normatively constituted.

Because of their social demography, urban 'marginalised' subjects are generally perceived as a security threat, or, as (erroneously) implied by Lewis' model of the *culture of poverty*, to be inherently dysfunctional due to their own intergenerational social practices. This impression of the dangerous influence of the ghetto on the rest of the society is, also, often associated with the gun violence practised by some men – usually the minority – who reside in these communities. Furthermore, the high statistics of teenage pregnancy among ghetto residents is also seen as an immoral influence that contributes to the underdevelopment of the areas (Wacquant, in Calhoun (ed.), 1993). Where I find congruence with Lewis' model and my critique of the structures of power is in his suggestion that the 'culture of poverty' is perpetuated because of the systematic social exclusion that the poor experience. In this regard, he argues that,

> [t]he lack of effective participation and integration of the poor in the major institutions of the larger society is one of the crucial characteristics of the culture of poverty. This is a complex matter and results from a variety of factors which may include lack of economic resources, segregation and discrimination, fear, suspicion or apathy, and the development of local solutions for [macro] problems.

> (1967: xlii)

Ultimately, however, Lewis' model reflects a tendency to ascribe blame for the persistence of poverty and violence to the slum dwellers. It thereby avoids a confrontation of the hegemonic *construction* of the cycles of disadvantage that permeate inner-city communities, which derive from the structures of power that dominate the wider society. Nevertheless, the actions of the residents, which do reflect complicity with the hegemonic project, also have to be unpacked in the analysis of how various power mechanisms come into being and are maintained. Therefore, the poor should be seen as participants in a power game in which the circumstances of their history, geography, political sociology and embodiment have allocated them to the losing roles of pawns. Thus, the call for accountability from the subalterns who perpetuate this political dramaturgy is at once passionate and frustrated, because of the mitigating circumstances of its enactment.

Finally, I use the specific term *discourse* instead of 'culture' (as in '*discourse of violence*' rather than 'culture of violence') in order to emphasise the contrived and permeable nature of the circumstances that I am addressing. The broader definition of discourse (as I have already defined it), enables me to traverse a wider range of analytical possibilities than is suggested by the specific term culture.

CHAPTER 3

EMBODIED DISCOURSES OF RESISTANCE

Now that we have established the theoretical framework of this strange yet true story in Chapter 2, it is time to outline some of the socio-historical factors that gave rise to Kingston's inner-city communities, and we will do that in Chapters 3 and 4. However, we cannot discuss sexual practices in inner-city Kingston without also considering Jamaica's place in the international sex trade.

Sexually Inscribed Tourism

Jamaica is historically celebrated as a sexual paradise and has long held the dubious distinction of being a party island where the rum flows as fast and freely as the abundance of fine female flesh.

The historical high point (or low point, depending on where you're coming from) occurred during the colonial era when the British buccaneers/pirates made their headquarters in what would become known as Kingston Harbour, whence they could conveniently hoist the 'Jolly Roger'/Skull and Crossbones and attack the bullion-laden Spanish galleons sailing out of nearby Cuba – all for queen and country. Back in those days, before there was a city called Kingston, 'party central' in Jamaica was located at the infamous Port Royal, the seaport located at the tip of the sand-spit Palisadoes peninsula where the pirates and privateers spent much of their stolen loot. Port Royal became known, at the time, as the 'wickedest city on earth' because of the violence, drunkenness and prostitution that occurred there. The earthquake of 1692 in which (a tsunami) the Caribbean Sea swallowed up and destroyed about a third of the now infamous Jamaican 'sin city' was, even then, widely seen as divine judgement on an outrageously wicked place.

Nevertheless, that concept of a Caribbean island paradise where White men could indulge themselves freely in copious amounts of wine and women has endured, right up to the present, and is the hidden and unstated secret attraction of Jamaica. Now, White people in general, that is both men and women, seeking rum and fun in the sun, see Jamaica as a premiere tourist destination to fulfil their dreams of a fantasy vacation, which not only involves drinking themselves into oblivion, but also tasting the 'forbidden' but oh-so-exotic delights of the 'primitive', 'semi-savage' Black natives of the island. In this way, White tourists have inscribed their own contrived reality onto the Black bodies of their hosts, who are expected to meekly act out their assigned embodied roles in the all-inclusive vacation package.

Accordingly, spring break in Negril for US college students is all the rage, while the *Jerry Springer Show* has repeatedly brought its trash-TV antics to north-coast venues like the world-famous Hedonism II, where White guests can strip naked and cavort like children to the amusement of the natives. Naturally, many of the male tourists are trying to sample as many local Black women as they can land, while the female tourists are laying themselves nude on the beach as human bait to be sampled by as many of the local Black men as they can entice. Most importantly, the economic power of the foreign dollar/pound/euro or whatever, usually keeps the power equation balanced in favour of the visitors.

Europe is, of course, still a major source of visitors to Jamaica, and the Jamaica Tourist Board has run television advertisements in key markets like England, Germany and Italy for years. As a result, European visitors to Jamaica increased by an estimated 22 percent in 2003. Male European sex tourists have been travelling to 'Third World' countries for many years, and in this context there is certainly nothing new about the sexual exploitation of local women. Indeed, there is a long history of sexual exploitation of Black/coloured women under colonial rule and White men have long projected their racist sex fantasies onto the once enslaved 'primitive'/natural other.

At the same time, White women have long lusted for and have frequently given themselves up bodily to the charms of their fancied big, Black, hard-bodied, 'Mandingo' buck. These days, especially with the advent of the internet, the major tourist industry players have turned this kind of postcolonial fantasy into an item of mass consumption. Everything from go-go girls and female strippers, to well-endowed and muscular young men, to sex resorts where anything goes, are all being advertised at online Jamaican websites for the benefit of both male and female sex tourists. Jamaica has even become a popular location to shoot homemade X-rated videos and photo sessions of tourist-like holiday 'sexcapades'.

Jamaica, just as other economically underdeveloped regional holiday destinations like Brazil, the Dominican Republic and Cuba, is marketed as a culturally 'different' place, and all European tourists are encouraged to view this 'difference' as a part of what they have a right to consume on their holiday. The construction of this theoretical difference takes place around ideas such as 'natural' vs. 'civilised', leisure vs. work, exotic vs. mundane, rich vs. poor, sexual vs. repressive, and powerful vs. powerless. Sex guides written by White men, such as *Travel and the Single Male* by Bruce Cassier, tap into the idea of embodied 'difference' to justify the sexual exploitation of Black women in these countries. A key component of sex tourism is the objectification of a sexualised, racialised 'other', therefore the racist stereotype of the exotic and erotic Black woman, is the main subliminal image that is used to sell sex tourism to Europeans.

By all accounts, sex tourists are not a homogeneous group: they may be men or, increasingly, women; White, Asian or even Black; heterosexual or, increasingly, homosexual; and they are not all rich these days, as more and more middle-class or working-class people are buying into the dream-vacation idea. Numerically, the main group of sex tourists are still Western, White, heterosexual men, who like travelling to poor countries because it reinforces the illusion of a restoration of the proper order of life between the genders and between the races. Beautiful chocolate- or coffee-coloured women and girls are at their sexual beck and call, while Blacks or Hispanics and Asians are serving them, shining their shoes, cleaning their rooms etc. As far as White men are concerned, that is exactly what life should be like, in paradise.

Back wherever they come from, a combination of Black political activism and feminist politics have both challenged and undermined the previously unquestioned power which gave most White men their gender and racialised identity: i.e., their sense of self. In this context, male sex tourists find that their masculinity and racialised power is affirmed in places like Jamaica, in ways that it is not 'back home'. Ironically, while in their own countries, sex tourists may often feel unable to approach Black men and women, but when they travel overseas they 'get close' to 'Others' and really manage to bridge differences. And, it is not only anxieties about racialised power that are calmed, but also anxieties about gender. Male sex tourists are very resentful of the perceived power of the White western woman and fear her ability to reject their sexual advances and are alarmed by her demands for female equality.

This is the conclusion of two sociologists from Leicester University in England, Jacqueline Sanchez Taylor and Julia O'Connell, who interviewed over 250 sex tourists in eight different countries as part of research project for the End Child Prostitution and Trafficking campaign and the Economic and Social Research Council. Many of their interviews were recorded and were eventually made into a radio programme for BBC Radio 5 Live.

In an excerpt from 'Sex Tourism in the Caribbean', found on The New West Indian Website,[31] Sanchez-Taylor notes that in 1997, she conducted preliminary research on female sex tourism in Negril, Jamaica. She conducted semi-structured interviews with 45 individuals involved in the informal sex industry and with female sex tourists. She also gathered data from a questionnaire administered to a sample of 86 tourists and disclosed that the survey found that almost half of the single female tourists had entered into one or more sexual relationships with Jamaican men while on holiday. Her, admittedly, non-scientific conclusion was that some women travel for sex in much the same way that some men do. Continuing, Sanchez Taylor writes

...it seems that female sex tourists are very similar to male sex tourists in terms of their attitudes and motivations and the narratives they use to justify their behaviour. Just as male sex tourism can be understood as an attempt to affirm a given racialised and gendered identity, so female sex tourism appears to reflect a concern to reverse and restore a particular order and to ensure their own position and power within that order. Women have traditionally used travelling as a way of masculinising their identities rather than as a way of affirming their femininity. Today, some female sex tourists are travelling in order to penetrate traditional male domains, claiming traditional male powers to reaffirm their femininity.

31 http://www.awigp.com/default.asp?numcat=sextour

The article goes on to note that

> [i]t is important for many female sex tourists to affirm their sense of 'womanliness' by being sexually desired by men. Women who feel rejected by men in the West for being 'sort of fatter and older, you know, 35, but their faces, they look 40', find that in Jamaica all this is reversed. Here they are chased and 'romanced', sweet-talked and 'loved' by men and once again find that they exist as sexual objects. Sex tourism allows some Western women to sexualise their bodies in ways that would be difficult to achieve back home and to be desired by highly desirable men...

The objectification of the bodies of people of colour in the context of tourism is exemplified by the fact that

> Black bodies become commodities which allow affluent Western women (both Black and white women) to experience an alternative form of embodied power. In this case they are allowed to be in control of masculinities which are 'Black', 'hypersexual' and 'dangerous'. This type of female sex tourist does not want to establish a loving relationship with a Jamaican man and take him back to meet her parents nor does she challenge racism back home. Rather such women accept the notion of a racial hierarchy and welcome their position in it. Tourist destinations become a safe environment within which female sex tourists can enact control over a masculinity which is imagined stereotypically as aggressive and violent.

> ...Such control means these women can limit the risk of being rejected or humiliated...They can also transgress sexual, gendered, racialised and age boundaries. Where at home they would be stigmatised for having legitimate or casual relations with Black men, younger men, 'womanisers' or for having many sexual partners, in holiday resorts such as Negril they are permitted to 'consume' the Black male, the younger boy, the playboy or as many men as they desire while maintaining their honour and reputation back home. Their sense of racialised superiority in Caribbean countries, together with their economic power also puts them on a level with white men and for once they can experience feeling more powerful than a man.

As the Leicester University sociologist added, the most interesting feature of sex tourism at the theoretical level, is how involvement by locals rests on their using their 'Blackness' as part of the commodity that they are selling. For, along with the actual services, whether it is acting as a guide, fruit seller, artist, procurer of drugs, or gigolo/prostitute, they are also selling a part of their personal selves. Thus, so long as it remains acceptable to market these multiple embodied 'differences' as the Caribbean's unique selling point, the international tourist industry will continue to provide a framework which permits and even encourages sex tourism. Contradictorily, though, this tourist/native sexual interaction serves to entrench not only the inequalities between the West and developing countries, but also the very forms of racism and sexism which structured the existing patterns of exclusion and exploitation in the first place.

As indicated in the opening chapter, the rules and results of the 'pleasure business' are much different for tourists than they are for inner-city residents. Many developing countries are just realising the sociological price their countries are paying for their investment in tourism is far too high. For instance, despite the bare-breasted and hip-thrusting beauties that characterise Carnival and attract thousands of tourists to Brazil annually, authorities in Rio de Janeiro have attempted to tone down Rio's image as a major sex tourism destination. They also tried to minimise the crime that surrounds prostitution, so city prosecutors launched a campaign against sexual exploitation and the use of minors in the sex trade. The drive involved a police crackdown on pimps and brothels as well as a public awareness campaign, and one of its focal points was definitely tourism. The start of this campaign coincided with the beginning of Rio's world-famous Carnival jamboree on February 20, 2004. Press reports in November 2003 quoted a special UN envoy as saying that the problem of child prostitution and sexual exploitation in Brazil was worse than in most other countries because of the combined key elements of poverty, crime and tourism. Non-governmental groups estimate the number of child prostitutes in Brazil at between 100,000 and 500,000, out of a total population of 175 million.

The problem of child prostitution in Jamaica has not yet reached Brazil's alarming level, but with the runaway level of crime and poverty ravaging the island, it is not too early to begin addressing the many potential spin-off problems that can be caused by ongoing sexual tourism. Although the idea of Jamaica being a chaste Christian island is an obvious myth, an influx of openly homosexual and bisexual tourists will no doubt speed up the unprecedented and, largely unwanted, changes in what is publicly accepted as sexually permissible in Jamaica. This is going to happen sooner rather than later. After years of holding out, even Butch Stewart's Sandals Resorts has finally given in to enormous financial pressure exerted by the British gay lobby in particular for the hotel chain to begin catering to gay cruises and gay visitors at all of their facilities in Jamaica and throughout the Caribbean.

In the meantime, we can clearly see the overwhelming importance of the human body and its sexuality. What is said about the (Black and White) body and what is represented by such (male and female) bodies, is one of the main driving forces behind the promotion of one of Jamaica's most critical lifelines – the fickle tourist industry. Like it or not, sexuality is inscribed all over Jamaica's tourism product. But, despite the sexual allure of Black bodies to White tourists, Jamaica's seasonal tourist industry is still liable to be crippled in an instant, if reports of too much shooting and killing in Kingston make the world news headlines. News of an eruption of blood, bullets and bodies anywhere in Jamaica is always anathema to the Jamaica Tourist Board, which is usually trying to convince visitors that the island is indeed just one big safe beach serviced by docile natives.

Embodied Expressions of Identity

Ongoing social and economic inscription by White 'tourism' has thus formed the background against which the embodied identity expressions of Jamaicans have developed. Although many Blacks have acquiesced and succumbed to catering to the sexual whims and fancies of their vacationing White overlords, many others have resisted this temptation. And not even three centuries of systematic oppression and exploitation in Jamaica have been able to quell the highly developed *spirit of resistance* in the island's majority race/class in Jamaica, a spirit which was born of a very strong embodied sense of self. Logically, the Black majority's strong sense of self goes hand in hand with an equally clear perception and acceptance of their own unique identity as Africans, because, as Bob Marley aptly sang, 'We are what we are, and that's the way it's gonna be'. Obika Gray succinctly describes this embodied identity configuration when he observes that,

> the Jamaican poor possess a social power of their own, and that one of the main circuits for the exercise of this power is the ability to define their personae, to protect it against attack and humiliation, and to defend it against the extractive claims of the state and allied groups in civil society... [A] large volume of the social power of the poor can be found not so much in formal organisations, leaders, and political resources, but in "powers of the body" and its associated dramaturgy.

> (Gray, in Social and Economic Studies, 1994:187)

Contributing to a long-established continuum of opposition (Campbell, 1985; Tafari-Ama, 1990), Rastafari have reclaimed race as a discourse of resistance in an attempt to erase the scars of slavery and to impose a level of dignity on a contemporary life dogged by systematic marginalisation. Rastafarian Reggae musician Peter Tosh, for instance, reinforced this embodied Black identity when he sang, 'No matter where you come from, as long as you're a Black man, you're an African...Nuh mind your nationality, you've got the identity of an African...' Thus, by his very persona and dress, and by the way he walks, talks and thinks, the Rasta Man has lived and expressed an embodied identity as an African/Ethiopian. So too has the Rasta Woman. Their whole lifestyle is an *embodied discourse* of identity reclamation and resistance to external (European) domination.

Just like their male counterparts, grassroots women in Jamaica have made tremendous contributions to the island's cultural development. Their contributions have been embodied, expressed and transmitted through their parenting practices in particular, and in general through the use of their physical bodies as buffers between overt domination and their personal expressions of agency. Nevertheless, grassroots women are caught in a web of identity differences and attendant power regimes through which they have to constantly negotiate, as they define who they are and their place in a very confusing, multi-layered world. Many varying strands of binary oppositions are present in these women's lives and are expressed as 'multiple fluid structures of domination which intersect to locate women differently at particular conjunctures...In other words, systems of racial, class and gender domination do not have *identical* effects on women in Third World contexts' (Mohanty, in Mohanty et al (eds.), 1991: 13, emphasis in original).

It is obvious, therefore, that embodied male *discourses of resistance* are expressed and regarded very differently from embodied female discourses of resistance. Upcoming discussions will focus on how these parenting and other embodied expressions feature in the resistance repertoires of women in Southside, so it is useful, here, to start a review of historical resistance from this perspective, in order to take a gendered review of male and female expressions of defiance to dominant systems of power.

Double Jeopardy

Under slavery, women of African descent in Jamaica had to negotiate male domination in all walks of life. In addition to outright and overt forms of resistance, they also developed subversive and covert systems that effectively undermined male authority. Likewise, their male counterparts had to be skilful to deal with the double jeopardy of losing control not only over themselves as free agents, but also over their women who held equal status as slaves.

> [E]very slave was a slave regardless of sex...The ownership of their bodies and labour, and the power of the slave masters to dispose of them and their children at will, gave rise to this equity in relation to land. This was despite occupational inequalities on the estates, where women dominated field work and men the skilled occupations.

> (French, in Wieringa (ed.), 1995:123)

Hilary Beckles is of the opinion that a crisis in masculinity[32] occurred because 'enslaved African men, the social majority, were pressed into labouring activities gendered as "woman's work"' (Beckles, in Barrow (ed.), 1998: 99). This dissonance would have made male slaves partial to the patriarchal norms promoted by the English colonialists and would have spurred them to retrieve some modicum of power by projecting a Creole combination of African and European patriarchal expressions onto their female counterparts. Therefore, the position of women was particularly precarious because they bore the double burden of production and reproduction, while also having to contend with the sexism practised by both the White male masters and their own African men. This type of extreme double jeopardy was faced exclusively by Black/African women.

Thus, 'with women working as hard as men, in the same jobs and generally as competently, gender was an important basis of social hierarchy' (Morrissey, 1989: 16). The multiple roles that grassroots women have always performed in negotiating racism, classism and sexism, can therefore be interpreted as the fundamental artery of their life-streams of resistance.

> In fact, '[t]here is virtually no task in Caribbean commodity production not at some time carried out by female slaves...[and] in the declining years of sugar production women generally outnumbered men and sometimes, with older slaves and children, achieved at least as high levels of per capita labour productivity as earlier generations of young, robust males'.

> (Morrissey, 1989: 33)

Corroborating this evidence, Joan French notes that in Jamaica at the end of slavery, there were more female field slaves than male (French, in Wieringa (ed.), 1995: 123).

Paradoxically, the double roles that women performed in both the so-called private and public domains of household and capital-driven work, resulted in their ability to manoeuvre to some measure of advantage despite the harsh conditions they had to endure. This predominance of women in the slave labour force and in the cultural

---

32 See *Men and Masculinities* (Connell, 1995) for an elaboration of this concept.

construction of the family ensured that patriarchy did not have a chance to take root at the ground level, thereby endorsing the independence of women, especially in relation to their access to land.[33] In addition to negotiating the strictures of patriarchy, applied at the structural authority and interpersonal levels, women, just like men, were also preoccupied with doing what they could to overthrow and/or undermine the White-dominated system of oppression and exploitation.

> As they became established in monotonous work roles on the plantation, women slaves did not succumb to apathy and resignation…They proved difficult and awkward to manage…Other women refused to carry out their set tasks…[W]omen slaves were frequently accused of insolence, shamming sickness, excessive laziness, disorderly conduct, disobedience and quarrelling.
>
> (Bush, 1990: 56, 58)

These acts of passive resistance incensed the slave masters, who had a vested interest in portraying Africans as less than human at worst and at best, as the most derogatory form of humanity. To justify this myth, women were subjected to whippings, chained isolation and more brutal forms of labour, whenever they were perceived to have contravened the boundaries of subservience. However, enslaved African women remained defiant and rebellious. Historical records show that women were prominent protagonists in the drama of poisoning their masters, feigning and deliberately inducing illness, committing suicide, stealing, deliberately destroying equipment, working less hard than expected, and thereby sabotaging the success of the slave economy. Black women were notorious for the whiplash-like tongues that they used to defy domination and to mobilise others to do the same (Morrissey, 1989: 60-61).

Sometimes the so-called 'house slaves' who were located in the 'great house' had divided loyalties and faced their own peculiar brand of double jeopardy. They tended to identify with and become sympathetic to the Whites although their proximity to the slave masters placed them in more jeopardy and made them fearful of challenging their masters' authority. Theirs was perhaps the most paradoxical of roles in the social relations of slave society (Bush, 1990: 60-61), because although some betrayed the proactive resistance plans of the field slaves, not all collaborated with the planter class. On the contrary, '[t]hey, too, refused to acquiesce gracefully to White authority… Female domestic servants were a constant source of irritation, particularly to White women, whose job it was to supervise them' (Bush, 1990: 61).

It is clear, therefore, that the colourful history of public leadership by women in Jamaica and indeed in all of the New World, began way back in the days of slavery, and many individual spokeswomen were often backed by organised groups of women. This is where the phrase, 'petticoat rebellion', used by Jamaican slave owner Matthew G. Lewis, comes from. Lewis wrote in 1816 that on his plantation 'the women, one and

---

33 As French also observes, women's close relationship with the land derived from the roles they performed as primary producers in Africa. However, although they enjoyed the same access to land as men during slavery, this gain was eroded in the post-1838 period when gender norms became more segregated to reflect the expedient capitalist emphasis on the ideal of the male breadwinner, which rationalised paying low or no wages to women. The imposition of this ideology was dependent on separating the roles performed by the sexes in private and public domains (French in Wieringa (ed.), 1995: 123).

all, refused to carry away the [cane] trash…[and] in consequence, the mill was obliged to be stopped; and when the driver on that station insisted on their doing their duty, a little fierce young devil of a Miss Whaunica flew at his throat, and endeavoured to strangle him'. Naturally, resistance like this was full of risks, as there was neither safety in numbers nor in gender solidarity for the enslaved African women, who were as likely to have their challenges to authority met with as severe violence as were Black men.

Embodied African Spirituality – Nanny

These subversive performances by the slaves were augmented by African practices of spirituality such as obeah which 'was worked by individual[s]…who dealt in magic, poisons, herbs and folk medicine' and 'Myalism [which] was concerned more with group worship [and] was used as an antidote against the harmful aspects of obeah' (Bush, 1990: 73). Because of their ignorance of African religions, spiritual practices like obeah invoked tremendous fear in the slave owners, with just cause. Obeah practitioners not only had the power to inflict embodied physical harm, but also provided the organising impetus[34] to galvanise the slaves to commit acts of outright rebellion (Bush, 1990: 74). This explains why Boukman, a Maroon (Myal) priest who escaped from Jamaica, is said to have provided the spiritual impetus that ignited the historic rebellion among Africans enslaved in neighbouring Haiti in the early 1790s. Obeah practices have persisted to the present day in Jamaica, alongside more formal church affiliations, and, as I observed during my research, the practice is resorted to for a wide variety of reasons.[35]

The formal churches have tended to ghettoise and disapprove of obeah, this, supposedly, maverick expression of spirituality, due to the over-emphasis on 'harming others' (Post, 1978: 141). Meanwhile, obeah remains closely linked with Myal, an association that grew out of strategic necessity during slavery. Post goes on to note that 'Myalism was, in fact, the practice of traditional Akan religion, its priests opposed to Obeah but forced to work secretly because under slavery all African religious practices were forbidden' (Post, 1978: 141).

The slave owners' hysterical response of forbidding Africans to give expression to their spiritual beliefs and practices, was rooted in the planters' realisation that spiritual forms of expression provided a *lingua franca* that enabled people of different language groups[36] on the plantations to communicate with each other. This spirituality was expressed in the heartbeat rhythms of the drum's secret messages, replicated in dance, storytelling, jokes, proverbs, laughter, wailing, crying and playing (See Ford-Smith, in Wieringa (ed.), 1995: 147-151). These vibrations were also captured at weddings, feasts, funerals and in institutions such as the wake, which is a gendered space of ritualising resistance. The relentless weaving of such strong threads of spirituality, have held the fabric of grassroots survival intact.

---

34   Acts of dissidence were planned at gatherings for an obeah or Myal ceremony (Bush, 1990: 74).

35   This practice is prevalent as a component of discourses of resistance in the inner city.

36   Africans of similar language groups were deliberately separated in order to create a Tower of Babel (confusion) on the plantation and thereby undermine the chances for the enslaved to plan insurrections. This divide-and-rule tactic is a theme of binary opposition, which characterises the entire slavery experience.

This African spirituality is inspired by a world view that sees time and space as multilateral experiences rather than linear events. In the African mind, therefore, the past, present and future are indivisible. This outlook enabled enslaved Africans to value death as a reconnection with their dearly departed Ancestors, whose spirits always protect the living. This insightful capacity to think outside of the box, helped to absorb the extraordinary shocks of their vicious exploitation and material disadvantage, and, somehow, these embodied objects of domination transcended their destitution.

Jamaica's first and only female national hero to date, the Maroon Queen called Nanny and/or Ni, was reputed to possess strong spiritual powers, which were attributed to her performances as 'an obeah woman' (Bush, 1990: 69). In fact, Queen Nanny was actually a Myal High Priestess, not an obeah woman, and was already recognised as royalty in Africa even before she came to Jamaica. On the one hand, her spiritual powers were said to have enabled her to bounce bullets from British guns off her buttocks. But we should not so mythicise her that we gloss over her many other outstanding attributes. These include her intellectual, managerial, political, medicinal and embodied military stratagems, which all speak to confrontation with, struggle against, and victory over oppressive forces. This is especially significant when we consider the constraints under which this Black Maroon Queen repeatedly and proverbially checked the White colonial king, neutralised his White bishops and knights, and broke the ranks of their conscripted and confused White pawns.

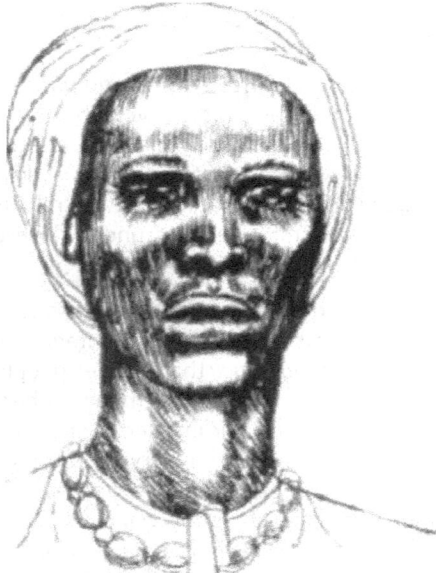

Figure 3.1: Maroon Queen Mother Nanny.

The role she played was crucial to the success of the Maroons during the 1720s and 1730s. Not only was she a tactician and political adviser, but as a spiritual leader she assured communal loyalty and upheld the morale of the Maroons (Bush, 1990: 70).

Queen Ni's embodiment of the 'strong, Black woman' concept, is also a double-edged sociological sword. The perception that African women are capable of enduring extreme forms of hardship while still being able to produce, reproduce and be creative enough to take the harsh edges off multiple registers of oppression, contradictorily rationalises the enforcing of the very same kind of labour relations and *discourses of embodiment* which re-inscribe such norms. Yet survival necessities have made the stereotype an unfortunate truism. Wholehearted embracing of spirituality has been fundamental to the survival and the resistance strategies of grassroots subjects in general and of women in particular.

African women were subjected to such severe experiences of sexual exploitation under slavery that they became acutely aware that the principles of Christian spirituality that emphasised chastity for women, juxtaposed with their perennial experiences of sexual violation, made strange bedfellows. Nevertheless, some African women were still able to turn around what was certainly a masculinist purview, transforming it into a transaction from which they could also reap some measure of benefit.

Dehumanising the Female Body

In Jamaica's historical evolution, the plantation was a space where African bodies, in general, and the bodies of women in particular, were routinely ravished in various ways. African women experienced embodied oppression and dehumanisation, particularly because the racist power relationships that prevailed on the plantations did not allow them to avoid this rampant form of sexual objectification and exploitation. This situation was taken for granted because 'most White and free coloured males owned female slaves. And slaveholders freely engaged in sexual relations with their slaves, as did their staffs, retainers, and guests' (Morrissey, 1989: 69).

Part of the ingrained, racial schizophrenia that has haunted White males for centuries, stems from their public disdain and depreciation of African/Black women, which existed simultaneously with their secret private lust and desire for the same taboo Black flesh. The Caucasian men had heard of the legendary Black Queen of Sheba and many of them, especially the Roman Catholics, had prayed to the 'Black Madonna' at various European shrines. In a contradictory and hypocritical psychological state, White Christian colonists in the Caribbean still harboured erotic desires for the perfect Black woman, who appeared to them in their fanciful secular dreams as the 'Sable Venus'.

The slave-era *sexual politics* of these contradictory desires were immortalised for posterity in the infamous painting by Thomas Stothard, 'The Voyage of the Sable Venus from Angola to the West Indies', which is still considered by many to be one of the most outrageous works 'inspired' by the Atlantic slave trade. It is reproduced in the second volume of Bryan Edwards' 1793 book, *History of the British Colonies in the West Indies* and appeared beside a salacious poem by an unnamed Jamaican author. The poem's coarse message was that African slaves are preferable to English girls at night, because they are accessible, willing and passionate/uninhibited. This is the reason that White male plantation owners would wait expectantly by the dock of the bay for days, literally licking their lips in anticipation of the arrival of their very own *Black goddess* with whom they could have their carnal way and do as they pleased. The 'Sable Venus' propaganda picture seems designed to portray the nautical Atlantic crossing as a benign method of procuring beautiful Black women for the enjoyment of deserving White men.

The painting is filled with telling symbolism and depicts an African woman or 'Creole Hottentot', in a pose similar to that of the famous 'Medici Venus'. The 'Sable Venus' is of course naked, except for a narrow cloth around her hips, and stands on a half-shell lined with an expensive fabric. Her ocean-going seashell is being pulled, gently, with chains of gold across the Atlantic by sea creatures, while chubby pink cherubs fly around in attendance, shielding her from the sun. It is the ultimate pictorial dehumanisation and merchandising of the Black female body. The sea king, Neptune, appears at the left side of the picture, apparently pointing the way to the Caribbean. Nude except for his crown, Neptune projects a strange combination of eroticism and empire as his robust physique serves to heighten the sensuality of the work, His desires for the 'Sable Venus' are signalled by the arrow Cupid (top left) aims at him. The painting is a really obscene and chauvinistic glossing over of the actual horrors endured by African women making the treacherous *Middle Passage* journey aboard the slave ships.

Figure 3.2 The infamous 'Voyage of the Sable Venus' is a painting by Thomas Stothard, and is considered to be one of the most outrageous works 'inspired' by the Atlantic slave trade.

It should never be forgotten that after being captured, rape became a feature in the lives of defenceless, enslaved African women. They were routinely and repeatedly used and abused – beginning in the African slave castles before they set sail; during the two to three months of maritime mayhem on their way to the West, and especially after they were auctioned off to the highest bidder (from amongst the vying White males) and taken to their final destination – the slave plantation. This was the beginning of the White/ European 'Pleasure Business'.

The slave industry was a morally bankrupt enterprise, but the heinous treatment of enslaved Africans, especially women like the 'Sable Venus', was just seen as business as usual. Like the sugar, cotton and tobacco industries and other unsavoury businesses, the slave trade and plantation slavery were highly profitable enterprises for the CEOs of insurance companies, banking establishments, manufacturers and European shipbuilders, as well as for the overall colonial economies of the Caribbean and North America.

Africans provided the necessary slave labour and were the hot commodity of this New World entrepreneurship. Their Black blood, sweat and tears greased the wheels of the Industrial Revolution and the world economy, while their forced free labour changed the way in which European nations did business.

The systematic dehumanisation of Africans, through the physical exploitation of their bodies for capital and pleasure, was saturated with racism and sexism. Even White women, who benefitted from the racist aspects of the slave system, had to comply with the prevailing patriarchal precedents inherent to this rigorous organisation of social stratification.

Despite the obvious disadvantages bred by this power arrangement, some African/Creole[37] women gained advantage because of their sexual relationships with the White 'masters'. Sometimes these liaisons developed into long-term concubinage; through these relationships, enslaved women gained social and material advantage for themselves and their progeny.[38] Children fathered by White men gained their freedom much more readily than children who were born to African parents (Bush, 1990: 117). And, although this kind of collaboration solidified the subordination of women by men, it was simply a case of making the best out of a bad situation. The African women who formed intimate alliances with White men were also likely to be considered for early manumission because of their *Brown* children's status, as well as their own association with the White slave holders.

This embodied sexual transaction set the historical foundations for today's current economic practices of trading sex for material/social advantage. Displaced and dispossessed African women living in deprived inner-city communities in Jamaica are constrained in their survival choices because of the raw deal they have received at the

---

37 Although in my view, Africans intergenerationally remain Africans in the same way that a 'leopard does not change its spots', the use of the term Creole here distinguishes Africans who were born on the African continent and those who were born in the Caribbean.

38 I have to emphasise here that this notion of appropriation of the dominant discourse is deeply contradictory because it suggests a degree of choice, which was not characteristic of the race and gender power relations that obtained in plantation society. In other words, although a few women were able to exercise this degree of agency, we have to bear in mind the oppressive conditions under which slaves lived, which made their sexual exploitation the proverbial last straw in the multiple forms of domination and exploitation to which they were exposed.

hand of history. Brownness – as in the colour of their embodiment – has also evolved as a positive attribute of sexuality and social status, which some of the subordinated, especially women, have long used as a resource for social advancement (Bush, 1990: 117).

Under slavery, women were obliged to have children in order to reproduce the labour force. Some resisted this authority system by refusing to bear or bring up children through practices of pregnancy prevention, abortion and infanticide.[39]

> Some scholars have argued that contraceptive and abortive practices were directly involved in maintaining Jamaica's consistently marginal rate of natural increase, which in turn created a trade policy that preferred African males to females. Others have argued that the birth rate was much higher than figures suggest, and that infants often died soon after birth. This phenomenon would have the same effect in keeping the population increase marginal.
>
> (Elgersman, 1999: 120)

Many women also resisted domination by refusing to subscribe to the short suckling period recommended by the authorities. This colonial recommendation was designed to increase the birth rate, as the release of the hormone prolactin during breastfeeding inhibited conception. However, maintaining the African tradition of extended suckling was also a device for reducing the risk of infection to the child, as well as a mechanism for maintaining strong kinship and affective ties with their progeny (Morrissey, 1989: 130-131, Bush, 1990: 110).

The female strategy of entering into concubinage with slave masters was, therefore, an option of resistance that was explored under extremely trying circumstances. While not formalised as marriage due to the prevailing race and class cleavages, which dehumanised Africans, this arrangement was fairly commonplace.

Prostitution was also institutionalised, 'Jamaican cities were said...to be full of prostitutes...with domestics in taverns and inns serving as prostitutes, the hiring out of individual prostitutes by masters and independent prostitution by slave women themselves' (Morrissey, 1989: 69).

The sexuality of women thus served as both a means and an end. A means for the subordinate (women) to exercise agency, and an end in itself, in so far as exploiting the pleasurable prize of a woman's sexuality brings instant gratification while reinforcing the structural power of the dominant (men). As a consequence of this practice, grassroots women in Jamaica have been kept busy designing devices for dealing with the disadvantages that they have long experienced in the productive sector, simultaneously trying to cope with their sexual exploitation while still negotiating for some advantage.

For their part, the powers-that-be had decidedly sexual and political designs of their own on the reproductive identities of the subordinated women. Those in power promoted the so-called 'nuclear' form of family structure as a means of increasing the

---

39 Morrissey suggests that poor health could also have been a factor (1989: 119)

labour force by natural reproduction during slavery, and as a form of social control in the post-Emancipation period. However, the African population proved to be as intractable as they had ever been.

> Resistance to these and other forms of injustices inherent in this model of male-female relations was evident in the low rate of marriages despite the best efforts of the missionaries and some of the planters.

> (French, in Wieringa, 1995: 125)

Contrary to racist myths about the inferiority of Africans and their proclivity for promiscuity or social dysfunctionality (Elgersman, 1999: 104), many enslaved Africans resisted these stereotyping discourses and developed reinforcing relationships and positive self-concepts based on African values (Bush, 1990). Although slavery disrupted household arrangements, many Africans were able to maintain stable (nuclear) family life especially on large estates, despite the sexual exploitation that many women suffered at the hands of White planters and both Black and White overseers. Again, we see that parenting and reproduction are important to maintaining cultural resistance among people who have experienced intergenerational forms of domination and embodied dehumanisation.

Embodied Family Dynamics

Most grassroots men have been unable to sustain the Western-defined role of patriarch, i.e. sole breadwinner at the household level. Clearly, this is because of the handicapped terms on which they were inserted into the Jamaican society. But even without a sturdy, financial, material base, some men have still been able to promote a *phallocratic* (Post, 1996) definition of gender power, which also affects how women define and conduct themselves. Although socially marginalised men in Jamaica have experienced class oppression, they still benefit from the convergence of European and African patriarchal values in cultural, ideological and institutional norms that result in disadvantage to women (French, in Wieringa (ed.), 1995: 124).

While the nuclear family structure has persisted as an ideal[40] in grassroots Jamaica, this household arrangement is not necessarily sanctioned by marriage.

Visiting unions are even more common. Extended families, which were a legacy of African social organisation, enabled the alienated slave population to retain a system of social relationships and are a cultural form that has persisted to the present. As Bush recalls, '[t]ypes of families other than matrifocal and nuclear accounted for much smaller numbers of slaves, but extended and polygamous units as well as families of more than two generations were more common among urban rather than rural populations' (Bush, 1990: 118).

Conventional definitions suggest that an extended family is identified by a core nuclear structure. However, the version that evolved in Jamaica emerged as a female-

---

40 As Joan French explains, this phenomenon was due to 'British ideology which…informed State policy and became institutionalised in ways which induced some level of conformity. For example, married slaves were given preference in estate housing in the late slave period' (French, in Wieringa, (ed.), 1995: 125-6).

dominated institution including mothers, fathers, grandmothers, aunts, uncles, sisters, children, distant relations and friends. This network is a bulwark of social reproduction and support, identity re-creation and defence from forces that threaten from within and outside of the community.

In slave society, this female-headed institution was an integral component of the *discourse of resistance* to which women were central. This was a crucial resource to fall back on, considering the slave masters' 'paradoxical...claim to possession of an egalitarian ideology, within which Black women were not recognised as inferior or subordinate to Black men...[but] there was no intention on their part of weakening dominant patriarchal systems to which the Black male also subscribed and [by which they were]...partially empowered and privileged' (Beckles, in Barrow (ed.), 1998: 109).

After Emancipation in 1834, the demands of capitalism meant that many men were forced to leave the household environment to seek wage work, reinforcing the ideology of man as the breadwinner. But the corollary concept of the dependent housewife has never been the norm of gender relations at the Jamaican grassroots (French and Ford-Smith, 1983-85). However, the strategic appropriation by both women and men of this discourse shows the reflexive rationality (Giddens, 1993) which informs their actions. They have been able to convert aspects of a bourgeois model into arrangements that allow them to rescue some form of advantage from the jaws of the racist-sexist-classist monster of power.

Conjugal arrangements resurfaced as a site of political contestation in the labour rebellion of 1938 and the troubled years of its aftermath. This had problematic implications for family relations in general as well as for the position of women in the productive and reproductive domains in particular. In the century between 'official' Emancipation and the watershed event of 1938, grassroots women in Jamaica had to struggle, concurrently, on several fronts to gain materiality and improvement in their social status.

Although women's discontent with their diminished wage/labour power was part and parcel of the 1938 uprising, the outcomes of this decisive groundswell were contradictory as far as their political interests were concerned. The uprising was successful to the extent that it forced significant changes to the prevailing social and political orders. However, despite these advances, women still experienced systemic inequality based on sexuality. Following the uprising, the British government organised a Commission of Enquiry, headed by Lord Moyne, to analyse the causes of the social discontent and to make policy recommendations to improve the situation. Interestingly, the Commission suggested the normalisation of society through, of all things, marriage. This was an attempt to deflect attention away from the demands of the oppressed class for material and social justice.

> The solution to female poverty then, was not to pay women proper wages for the work they did, but to deprive them of what little wages they had by establishing families in which men were seen as the providers, and therefore as having the primary right to a wage.

> (French in Wieringa, (ed.), 1997: 131)

The fact that grassroots women have always worked in the public and private spheres, means that they have entirely different social realities from their more economically privileged female counterparts. Some of the latter had the luxury of staying home and being supported by a male wage earner.[41] In many cases, they had domestic servants to do the work in the household (and they still do, even now). Furthermore, the colonial marriage campaign was also a moralising attempt to establish an institutionalised mechanism of keeping women under control. Marriage and the trappings of bourgeois family norms were thus the means by which the Commission attempted to reinforce patriarchal authority and the hegemonic power relations implicit in this structure.

The ulterior motives underlying this initiative are all too familiar. The majority of grassroots subjects in Jamaica are, after all, the progeny of the Africans who had resisted similar overtures at the end of the slave trade. In the two periods, women and men preferred to construct stable family formations, which placed emphasis on parenting and social responsibility, rather than on the mythical marriage ideal. Visiting unions facilitated conjugal independence, which allowed both men and women to have multiple-partner relationships (French, 1994, Chevannes, 1999).

Both women and men have their own reasons, based on their desire for independence, for not getting married. They didn't mind that in this predominantly Christian society, recorded in the *Guinness World Book of Records* as having the most churches per capita, they were kicking against the prick of ideal moral living. Unfortunately, some men have used the quest for independence as the excuse to be absentee fathers. More serious, though, is the fact that chronic unemployment prevents impoverished men from achieving the status of breadwinner, which undercuts their self-esteem and their image of themselves. They feel unable to face their children's mothers as well as their children when they feel that they are social failures. This is the reality of domestic *sexual politics* in the post-slavery era.

This sinister failure syndrome results in many women remaining single by default. Some would be married if the men were available and supportive, but others choose to remain unmarried as a form of resistance to male control. The women who now live in inner-city areas like Southside have, therefore, inherited a complex and contradictory ideological perspective on household and family arrangements. Mostly unemployed themselves, they have had to negotiate with a number of masculinist discourses in a network of power relations that mitigate their capacity to exercise agency independently.

> In Jamaica...approximately 40% of women are unemployed as against 16% of men. Of employed women, 68% are doing unskilled labour and earning less than J$30 per week. At the same time, one third of the women are de facto heads of households.
>
> (Reddock, in Ellis (ed.), 1986: 29)

The years that have passed since this study was done, have seen a continuation in the trend of worsening conditions for women. The urban poor are disenfranchised as a

---

41 However, with the evolution of the women's movement, a few women in this class have problematised this arrangement as being undergirded by patriarchal and thus oppressive ideological precedents.

class, with women bearing the biggest burdens. However, they have continued to draw on the resources of the strong resistance tradition that they have inherited from their forbears. Women use the embodied cultural, sexual and spiritual resources at their disposal to counteract the power structures and discourses arrayed against them. And although grassroots women's socioeconomic precariousness has been exacerbated by their caring responsibilities for children, the aged and the sick, the extended family has also served as a source of happiness and social support. This institution provides the space where the socially dispossessed are able to codify their lives in meaningful emotional, material and spiritual terms.

Embodied African Liberation – Amy Jacques Garvey

Amy Jacques Garvey is an excellent example of a twentieth-century Caribbean woman with a revolutionary world view. Mrs. Garvey was a pioneer Pan-African emancipator who was born in Kingston, Jamaica on December 31, 1895. Frequently overlooked by journalists and contemporary writers, she was the second wife of Marcus Mosiah Garvey and was the mother of his two sons – Marcus Jr. and Julius. Amy Jacques embodied twentieth-century African Liberation and became the first Queen Mother of the US Universal Negro Improvement Association and African Communities League in August 1920.

Mrs. Garvey was an international organiser and race leader in her own right and her discourse in words and deed were trend setting for politically inclined Black women of her day. In the cause for African emancipation, her message was the same as her husband's: 'The hour of Black resurrection is at hand. Black man, Black woman be up and doing for self… – for you can achieve what you will.' She was genuinely concerned with the plight of her fellow Africans, and for this reason she toiled unceasingly, from youth to old age, to spread the teachings of African solidarity and independence. From 1919, when she became the Secretary-General of the UNIA, until her death, 54 years, her life was intricately bound up with the national liberation struggles of African people. Her activities in Jamaica and the United States from 1919 to the 1940s prefaced the defeat of European fascism and the irreversible disintegration of the colonial system which led to the upsurge and triumphs of the African National Liberation Movements. She aided and contributed financial assistance to the workers' movement in Nigeria and was instrumental in organising the Fifth Pan-African Congress held in 1945. Twenty-five years later, she visited Ghana at the invitation of Kwame Nkrumah. She was also a sponsor of the Sixth Pan-African Congress which was convened in Dar Es Salaam, Tanzania in 1974.

Amy Jacques Garvey was one of the most important Black female journalists and publishers of the entire twentieth century, a fact that is often overlooked by historians. Amy Jacques was the Winnie Mandela of her time and stood by her man, Marcus, throughout his trials, imprisonments and tribulations. Even after Garvey's death, Amy Jacques remained true to the ongoing quest for African liberation, championed by her heroic husband, and wrote countless articles and letters.

She came to New York in 1917 and was involved with publishing *The Negro World* newspaper in Harlem from its inception in August 1918. *The Negro World* was a weekly newspaper with worldwide circulation and was created by Marcus Garvey as the official media tool of his Pan-African organisation. *The Negro World* spread Garvey's philosophy of Black Consciousness, self-help, and economic independence. Most noteworthy is the fact that because of its positive *'Black is Beautiful'* stance, the newspaper refused all advertisements for skin lighteners and hair straighteners, which were (and still are) a mainstay of the advertising pages of most African-American newspapers. During her tenure from 1924 to 1927 as a *Negro World* associate editor, Amy Jacques added a page called 'Our Women and What They Think'.

The Negro World enjoyed a broad and influential distribution, reaching not only the entire United States and the Caribbean, but also Central America, Canada, Europe and Africa. At its peak, the publication had a circulation of 200,000 copies and was the most popular Black newspaper in North America, the Caribbean and in colonial Africa. In order to make *The Negro World* more accessible to its broad readership, the Garveys initiated a Spanish language section in 1923 and a French language section in 1924. In addition to all that, Amy Jacques was primarily responsible for the publication in the 1920s of both volumes of *The Philosophy & Opinions of Marcus Garvey*, which became the Black Nationalist 'Bible' for Pan-Africanists around the world. After her husband's death in 1940, the Pan-African heroine and Queen Mother became a contributing editor to a Black Nationalist journal, *The African*, published in Harlem in the 1940s. Amy Jacques also published her own book, *Garvey and Garveyism* in 1963.

Amy Jacques Garvey was awarded Jamaica's Gold Musgrave Medal for her contributions to the Garvey Movement and to the history of people of African descent. She passed on to the Ancestors on July 25, 1973. Her work and memory serve the noble cause for which she stood. As a Pan-African patriot, a pioneering nationalist, a political scientist, and as an organiser, a journalist, an editor, a publisher, a philosopher, a mother, a wife, she ably embodied the female essence of Pan-African Liberation.

The Sistren Theatre Collective

I have been concentrating on the history of grassroots women's resistance because of its importance to present-day sexual politics and the position of women in Southside. However, it is also important to acknowledge that women from all classes have made their voices heard and their presence felt in the process of cultural development. One of the most outstanding moments in the modern phase of the Jamaican women's movement was the emergence of the Sistren Theatre Collective,[42] a feminist organisation that was formed as a result of the collective organising of grassroots and upper-class women in the 1970s. The aim of this collective was to look at the ways in which they all suffered as women (Sistren and Ford-Smith, 1986) and, more generally, to problematise women's experiences of oppression and exploitation, on the bases of race, class and gender discrimination in the Jamaican society.

---

42 Rastafari word for sister or woman is sistren, a word that also denotes the plural for sisters or women.

Sistren effectively used popular theatre and participatory research to interrogate the widespread inequalities in the society in general, and those that women faced in particular. As Ford-Smith emphasises, the methodology of popular education was effective in locating women's place in the social and political formation of Jamaica.

> In particular, it [Sistren] attempted to continue the tradition, exemplified in the work of early nationalist feminist writers Louise Bennett and Una Marson. Both these women have struggled in their writing to come to terms with their experiences as Black Jamaican women. Both strived to build a dramatic movement which would reflect the voices of the working class. Their work also gave legitimacy to the Jamaican language, thus making it possible for working class Jamaican women to speak out and be heard in their own words.

(Ford-Smith, in Wieringa (ed.), 1995: 149-50)

The cultural media to which Ford-Smith refers here, can be considered to be among the 'hidden transcripts' (Scott, 1990) of women who have been cultural architects and repositories of tactics and strategies for negotiating with domination, and who have, thereby, constructed discourses of resistance. This collective has done much to facilitate the kind of consciousness-raising necessary to promote social transformation. Sistren can, therefore, be credited for having advanced discourses about the womanist practices that occur in everyday life, and by so doing, has demonstrated women's capability and practice of coming to voice (Collins, 1990).

The research on *Women's Work* and *Organisation in Jamaica*, 1900-1944 (French and Ford-Smith, 1985), which was carried out by Sistren Research, the affiliate of the Sistren Theatre Collective, interrogated the myths that have obscured the long-standing tradition of proactive *womanism/feminism* in Jamaica. This work revealed that validating the feminist 'herstory' of women is a difficult process, because 'with rare exceptions, women in Jamaica have scarcely become historical subjects' (French and Ford-Smith, 1985: iv). However, by using oral 'herstories', these activists were able to establish that peasant and working-class women have been key agents in the major efforts to undermine the social injustices faced by the subaltern class/race in general and by women in this sector in particular.

Alongside activists like the Sistren Theatre Collective, ordinary women struggled in the 1970s to cope with crippling challenges like the IMF's[43] Structural Adjustment policies and the uncertain political climate fostered by Michael Manley's Democratic Socialism (Payne, 1997; Stephens and Stephens, 1986), as well as the race/colour and class barriers that continued to pose obstacles to their cultural development. At the same time, women in the organised movement expanded the discursive struggles for women's liberation. The Committee of Women for Progress (CWP), the women's arm of the Communist Workers' Party of Jamaica, along with the women affiliated to the political parties, particularly the PNP, were outstanding in their advocacy and organisation of practical initiatives for advancing the political and social status of women. However, some critics suggest that the political activists did not sufficiently acknowledge the resistance continuum that preceded them, but made it seem as if

---

43 International Monetary Fund.

they were actually starting the movement for the first time (French and Ford-Smith, 1983-85).

Despite this myopia, the contemporary efforts have also made their mark. Since the mid-1980s, the Association of Development Agencies (ADA) and the Women's Studies Group[44] at the University of the West Indies (Mona), have been among the more vocal of the activist and intellectual groups which also made significant contributions to advancing debates, research and action in the interest of women's liberation. In 1987, the Association of Women's Organisations in Jamaica (AWOJA) was formed and, during its life cycle, which lasted just over a decade, served to address a cross-sectional array of women's concerns at the grassroots level. Further, non-governmental organisations incorporated in the Association of Development Agencies, all politicised female experiences of subordination and advanced programmes to challenge established patriarchal norms. And in addition to all that, women in the Reggae music industry were sources of inspiration for women's liberation, although many female singers defer to the male-dominated power structures on which the business sector of the music industry rests.

The Language of Resistance

In the Jamaican context, the *de facto* language and literature of domination is English. In contrast, Jamaican-English, sometimes called broken-English, Creole, or Patois/Patwah, (with a variant dubbed 'Rasta/Dread Talk'), is a '*Language of Resistance*' containing significant Africanisms in terms of both words and speech patterns. The evolving social elements comprising the '*Language of Resistance*' and embodied in both Patwah and 'Rasta Talk', would make an interesting case study for linguistic anthropologists. Linguistics is the scientific and humanistic study of language and its accompanying literature. On the other hand, sociolinguistics involves the study of language and linguistic behaviour as influenced by social and cultural factors. This is where semantics comes in, semantics being the study or science of the variable meanings or interpretations of words, sentences and other language forms like *body language*, signs and symbols.

Africans in Jamaica, especially the Rastafari and other popular cultural artists, have creatively changed the meaning of words and have created new words where necessary, or have used folktales from Africa (i.e. Anancy spider stories) in order to maintain their own historical perspective. Armed with this picturesque, hybrid vocabulary loaded with hidden historical and cultural meanings, they utter their colourful phrases with a unique vocal cadence and rhyme, and with flamboyant complementary bodily gestures that make their communication seem like foreign language to non-Jamaicans, especially in written form.

Women have been at the forefront of this *counter-discourse* in Jamaica. The work done by Louise Bennett between the 1970s and 1980s, which embodies the proverb, 'we little but we *tallawah*' (we are small but strong), created a watershed in the development of Jamaican and West Indian literature as far as popularising grassroots women's

---

44   This group evolved into the Centre for Gender and Development Studies.

resistance and establishing the Jamaican *Patwah* as a viable vehicle of literary expression were concerned. Miss Lou, as Bennett is popularly known, legitimised the language of the poor as a persistent act of resistance. Miss Lou epitomises the subaltern use of language and the knowledge it incorporates, as a gendered site of creating counter-discourses to subjugation (Nettleford, 1978, Cooper, 1993). Her poetic satirising of class divisions and her witty celebration of cultural identity evoked the ire of the upper classes, which were ashamed at her elevation of *Patwah* in the public space of strategic theatrical performances.

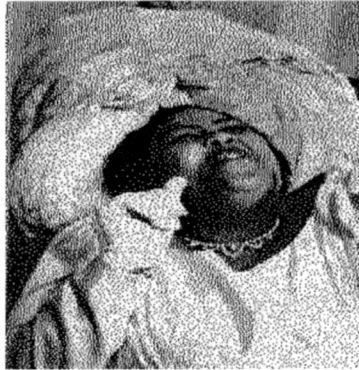

Figure 3.3: The Honourable Louise Bennett-Coverley – 'Miss Lou' – is a poet and actress who was popularly dubbed Jamaica's First Lady of Comedy. This woman celebrated the fact that she took up tremendous space in Jamaican society. She dared to disrupt dominant linguistic discourses in Jamaica from the early 1960s to the early 1980s when she retired from active artistic performances. 'Miss Lou' wrote and performed poetry in Patwah, the language of poor Africans, in celebration of the positive aspects of their culture, while skilfully satirising the structures and practices of social stratification that are typical of the Jamaican society.

Displaced Africans in Jamaica created the indigenous language of Patwah as a *lingua franca* of resistance to colonial domination. However, the colonial period is viewed with shame by both the privileged classes and those of the subordinated category who have internalised *dominant discourses* of self-identification and self-depreciation. This embarrassment hinders the recognition of the local language as a cultural artefact of nationhood. Nevertheless, Miss Lou bravely interrogated the persistence of colonial and racist values inherent in the promotion of English as the standard national language. She simultaneously promoted Patwah, which is the first language of Jamaica's Black majority, despite its previous association with negative self-perceptions and low status.

Bennett used the weapon of language to fire deadly lyrical shots at the prevailing discourses of neo-colonial domination. She triumphed in her appropriation of the language of 'otherisation' as a vehicle for celebrating selfhood. Her 'comic/satirical sketches have presented us with a diversity of social/class values and behaviours that attests to the verisimilitude of Bennett's detailed portraiture. Indirection is the quintessential attribute, and/or dubious distinction of the crafty Jamaican woman, of whom Bennett is, herself, a prime example...' (Cooper, 1993: 47-48).

Bennett paved the artistic way for many other poets and musicians, while giving voice to the poor (and to females) who have been multiply silenced (Hill Collins, 1990). The linguistic divide denotes the prejudices which prevent the national motto of 'Out of Many, One People', from being little more than wishful political jargon. Bennett therefore used language as a metaphor for the African human *being*, in contrast to popular negative representations of self, which make caricatures of Afrocentricity. This creative artist effectively used the power of words and speech to challenge the class prejudice, racism and sexist biases inherent in the colonial interpretation of Patwah as 'lower class language'. Within the ideological and material minefield of Jamaican culture, therefore, inasmuch as language is a principal site of domination, it is also evidently, one of the most significant and symbolic sites of resistance and identity reclamation. This is because we have the power to change the meaning of words and make them mean what we want them to mean, especially when their prior meaning negatively impacted our self-image and cultural identity. And this is how social agents can begin to change the present social matrix, by changing the meanings expressed in our everyday *social discourse*.

Parents of Inner City Kids

The resistance repertoire of grassroots women has stretched across centuries and now encompasses the work of sisters in Southside like Paulette Bennett, not known to be a relative to Miss Lou.[45] At the time I did my research, Paulette was a member of a group called Parents of Inner City Kids (PICK). Parents in Southside, who recognised that the process of parenting was getting more and more problematic with the passage of each generation, got together and formed this group. Over the years, PICK has benefitted from corporate support from the Grace and Staff Community Development Foundation (Jamaica) and the Bernard van Leer Foundation, headquartered in the Netherlands.

Figure 3.4: Headquarters of the Parents of Inner City Kids (PICK), the institution, located at the corner of Tower Street and Maiden Lane, which is mobilising against dysfunctional features of the community through self-empowerment strategies for mothers and children.

---

45 The politics of names and naming is one of the harshest legacies of slavery. All enslaved Africans on each plantation were usually given the last or family name of their respective slave master/owner.

Parents of Inner City Kids (PICK) is an organisation which provides the opportunity for parents of inner city communities to acquire levels of education or communication skills needed to identify and analyse issues which affect their children. PICK have been operating since 1985 with a membership of over 200 parents from inner city communities including Jones Town, Olympic Gardens, Payne Avenue, and August Town. In order to meet our objective, we have been organising a number of parent education programmes through out the year. In keeping with this, this workshop was designed to address the issue of trauma within our children, in light of the fact that community violence is on the increase.

(Miss Carmen Charles, quoted in Sobers, 1997: 3)

Figure 3.5: Paulette Bennett, community activist.

PICK[46] encourages women to recognise the ways in which they have internalised oppression and how such experiences are reproduced in their everyday relations with their own children. The collective defines how women can build effective child-support systems and communicative competence rather than abusive systems of expressing authority.

PICK has thus used the process of parenting to countervail existing notions of how power should be managed in family relations. This strategy has had far-reaching effects on the lives of parents and children alike, and has the potential for altering the oppressive family environments in which youth are usually socialised.

Thus, Paulette Bennett was able to testify that PICK had made a huge difference in her own life.

---

46 This organisation has experienced fluctuations in its membership and activities and continues to be challenged by the obligations of maintaining a consistent focus on community development in the face of overwhelming environmental challenges.

> Through discussions in PICK, I learnt that I was abusing them by saying those things. Sometimes when things got to me, anything I would catch I would use it to hit them. PICK has brought me from that stage. I did not realise that I was passing it on to them until I got into PICK.

Paulette's struggle to deal with the emotional tensions that she experienced as a result of her realisation that her abusive parenting practices have been shaped by her own upbringing, has inspired her choice to change.

> I have gone out and I got knowledge, and I think that it is only fair to pass it on. I am in the same situation and I think that you must try and do your best, but some parents are not seeing the children as the future. They are just seeing themselves as the future and that is where they are going wrong. I don't know when they are going to realise it.

Paulette experienced the liberation that can only be realised through the practice of consistent cultural criticism (hooks, 1990). She concludes on a positive note of personal appreciation for the organisation whose intervention radically interrupted the intergenerational cycle of internalised and external oppression, which has traumatised her and so many others in the community.

> Now I just talk, I do not bother with the hitting. I explain to my children that I have not forgotten the past but because I do not intend to pick it up again, they should just cooperate. I have been to workshops with PICK where I learn that it is frustrating but I just hang on with the coping part.

However, in spite of its tremendous development possibilities, the success of institutions like PICK is mitigated by the prevailing dominance of patriarchal norms, which women internalise and perpetuate through practices of socialising children. It is evident that inasmuch as patriarchal precedents are deeply entrenched in the discourses which chronicle the production of the subject, it will take as much effort to alter the course of these meanings of the self, as it took to develop the taken-for-granted discourse in the first place. In the meantime, the PICK process of intergenerational healing is also contributing to the process of structural change through the acquisition of property. This initiative is designed to facilitate the expansion of the efforts by the organisation to stimulate confidence and social development in the community.

CHAPTER 4

RACE AS A MALE DISCOURSE OF RESISTANCE

The Ultimate Race Man

Jamaican National Hero and Pan-African Philosopher Marcus Garvey was the ultimate and most internationally recognised African-centred '*Race Man*' of the entire twentieth century. The Jamaican native successfully championed the cause of the African race like no one else before or since. He also proved to be the most effective Black leader to politically challenge the worldwide socioeconomic system of racial prejudice, discrimination and exploitation that was collectively promoted by colonising European powers.

By all accounts Garvey was an exceptionally articulate orator, with outstanding motivational powers. He was a printer by trade and a prolific writer and publisher. Thus, because of his copious *discourses of resistance*, Marcus Mosiah Garvey was able to generate remarkable enthusiasm for the cause of African liberation from all forms of oppression.

It is no surprise, therefore, that Marcus Garvey is regarded as the father of the modern *discourse* of racial and cultural resistance in Jamaica, because of his emphasis on the importance of reclaiming African identities as a mechanism of resisting domination. In 1914 he formed the Universal Negro Improvement Association (UNIA) as a means of mobilising the disenfranchised and dispossessed Africans 'at home and abroad', around the issues of repatriation and collective socioeconomic development. He suggested that by returning to Africa, displaced Africans in the Diaspora would reclaim sovereignty over their destinies, and their contact with Africans from the Continent would facilitate an enterprise of universal resistance to neo-colonial domination by Western imperialist powers.

Although a significant number of grassroots people were receptive to this overture, Garvey's message was generally ignored by the still-colonised masses in Jamaica. Nevertheless, Garvey's advocacy for identity reclamation definitely engendered great alarm within Jamaica's elite plantocracy, and its rising mercantile sectors, which regarded him as a serious subversive political threat. Those within the grassroots audience who took Garvey seriously were in two minds about whether to translate his message of racial redemption metaphysically, or to take it to its literal conclusion. On the one hand, the notion of repatriation was interpreted as the basis for reinstating the potency of African identities in the Diaspora, and on the other, as a physical and spiritual return to the land of the ancestors.

He [Garvey] it was who turned the faces of many Jamaicans towards Africa and a generalised Black Nationalism, though he brought to his native island the ambivalence which likewise in the USA had marked the response to his advocacy of a return to the ancestral continent.

(Post, 1978: 161)

Garvey was most discouraged by what he recognised to be internalised racism, which prevented Africans in Jamaica from recognising their own oppression and exploitation. Tony Sewell records that Garvey remarked, 'Men and women as Black as I, and even more so, had believed themselves White under the West Indian[47] order of society' (Sewell, 1990: 28). Rejected by the Brown middle class in Jamaica, because of his attempt to contest elections on the platform of race, Garvey was determined to prove that he could successfully mobilise Africans internationally around the issue of repatriation and redemption. His primary preoccupation was to generate African race pride through the promotion of self-confidence and collective socioeconomic consciousness, with the ultimate vision of repatriation to Africa and the establishment of modern civilisations there, as the mechanism for addressing the perennial problems of displacement and dispossession.

The Race Man stirred up the proverbial hornet's nest because of the vastness of his visualisation of African redemption and the innovativeness of his organisational efforts.[48] The political and legal pressure applied in North America was even more devastating to Garvey's personal reputation and to the success of the movement he spearheaded. The Government of the United States of America put the decisive nail in the coffin of the UNIA's integrity as a resistance and counter-discourse facilitator, when J. Edgar Hoover and the Federal Bureau of Investigation framed Garvey on trumped-up charges of mail fraud, imprisoned him in 1925 and deported him in 1927.

On his return to Jamaica, Garvey continued his political, cultural and publishing activities. He was closely involved in the daily affairs of Kingston and in an editorial in *The New Jamaican* newspaper entitled 'The Life of Gangsters in Jamaica', published on July 16, 1932, Marcus Garvey put the responsibility for causing and solving crime specifically, squarely on the colonial government of the day.

...we are having here gangsters who can well be compared with their brethren in other parts of the world, particularly in Chicago and New York... Crime is generally the result of ignorance or bad conditions; for both, the State is responsible. If the State neglects the education of the people, they generally develop criminal tendencies; if the State refuses to regulate the

---

47 Although many persist in following Christopher Columbus' erroneous naming of the Caribbean as the 'West Indies', I avoid contributing to the perpetuation of this misnomer.

48 As I. Jabulani Tafari elaborates in *A Rastafari View of Marcus Mosiah Garvey*, 'Garvey's resettlement proposal called for the establishment of four modern cities on the continent and Liberia was chosen to become the African headquarters of the UNIA...Behind the scenes however, the British and French governments became alarmed over the implications of Garvey's repatriation movement and in collusion with the multinational Firestone Rubber, led the way in pressuring Liberia to deny access to the UNIA...Before long, the Liberian Government sent a diplomatic note to the US Government announcing that it was "irrevocably opposed both in principle and in fact to the incendiary policies of the UNIA..." The lands promised to Garvey (1 million acres) were instead leased for 99 years to the multinational Firestone Rubber Company of Akron, Ohio.' (Tafari, 1995: 70).

economies of the country and promote a healthy industrial life, then crime naturally will stalk the land...

It is this neglect by the State and the Municipality of Illinois and Chicago that has made Chicago the most criminal city in the world. We want a greater determination on the part of government to educate and influence the adult, and not to allow him to drift from the ordinary elementary school into a career of his own without any direction or good guidance.

When men are left entirely to interpret the ways of life from a primitive beginning then you cannot very well blame them for any harm that they may do to society. These people who are committing crime should be taught by good influence that it does not pay.

Those words are as relevant today, if not more so, in the twenty-first century, as they were when Garvey first wrote them in the 1930s.

In the meantime, present-day Garveyites have sought to secure a posthumous exoneration from the US Government to clear Garvey's name, but thus far, those who control the American state and its apparatuses have refused to officially acknowledge their culpability in tarnishing Garvey's reputation. Presumably, because they had (and continue to have) a vested interest in sabotaging the integrity of this unprecedented attempt by dispossessed Africans to re-generate their psychosocial, political and economic well-being, by securing prime real estate – on the African continent itself.

Figure 4.1: The map of Africa transgresses the boundaries of the socio-geographical space demarcated as the ghetto or the confining island boundaries of Jamaica for that matter. Yearning for the motherland and spiritual communion with the ancestors, is a belief system, which has been important in the survival strategies of displaced Diasporeans domiciled in 'a strange land'.

Nevertheless, Garvey's 'Race First' legacy is a philosophical outlook of self-pride, which has been preserved within many grassroots environments in North America and also throughout the Caribbean. Garvey's two-volume *Philosophy and Opinions* continues to have a profound impact on shaping identity sensibilities in Jamaica, in particular, as illustrated by the preceding and following murals in Southside.

Garvey's philosophy of 'Africa for the Africans, those at home and those abroad', has also been graphically translated onto the Southside mosaic as part of an identity *discourse of resistance*. So although domiciled in the heartland of Jamaican poverty, the possibility still exists for inner-city residents to embrace a larger vision of self, in the Pan-African identity articulated by Garvey.

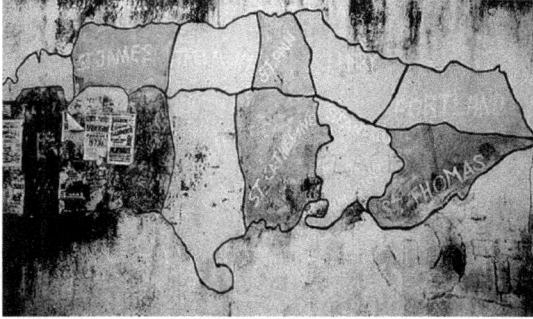

Figure 4.2: Map of Jamaica showing the demarcation into fourteen parishes, painted in the national colours, yellow, green and black. This mural is on a wall on Tower Street.

The UNIA & the Women's Movement

That Garvey succeeded in his confrontation of the race and class injustices facing Africans on the Continent and in the Diaspora, is evident from the subsequent offshoots of his movement, like the Nation of Islam, the Hebrew Israelites and the Rastafari Movement. Yet one of the few limitations to his political campaign was the scant attention that he seemed to pay to power issues related to gender. Having said that, it must be emphasised that Garvey was obviously influenced to some extent by the social climate and prevailing gender discourses of his time.

Nevertheless, because of the *sexual politics* and the women's suffragette movement of his day, he was still far more open to and supportive of female inclusion than were most intellectuals and/or agitators at that time. To his enduring credit, Garvey supported the active participation of women at all levels in the UNIA and surrounded himself with intelligent, self-actualised women who proved ultimately to be as committed to political engagement as he was. However, since gender cannot be discretely separated from race and class in the Jamaican experience or any other for that matter, we have to question the analytical/theoretical myopia concerning female empowerment, which seems to have characterised the UNIA and many of the subsequent African liberation struggles that the Garvey Movement spawned.

This oversight is also unfortunate when one considers that between the late nineteenth and early twentieth centuries, women were as active in the labour force and domestic spheres as they had been during slavery, albeit for low-waged and arduous work. French and Ford-Smith note that

> [i]n 1911 women constituted 37% of the labour force in bananas and in 1921, 42%...In the banana industry, women worked as weeders on the farms, cleared trash and helped to carry the suckers for the men who did the planting.

(1983-85: 44)

In both the USA and Jamaica, two of the territories where Garvey concentrated his activism, Black women were clearly as much in need of the benefits of race and class equality as were men. However, women required even greater liberation because of the gender discrimination that they faced. This situation resulted from the prevailing political and social arrangements governing the society, as well as from the gender myopia of most of the male leaders in the Black liberation movements. The class differences among women in both societies (Jamaican and American) aggravated the disadvantages that Black women experienced. Angela Davis notes in reference to the post-Emancipation division of labour in the United States that,

> [a]s during slavery, Black women who worked in agriculture – as share-croppers, tenant farmers or farm workers – were no less oppressed than the men alongside whom they laboured the day long...In the aftermath of emancipation the masses of Black people – men and women alike – found themselves in an indefinite state of peonage.

(Davis, 1982: 88)

This statement mirrors the data available from Jamaica, In the Jamaican case, women who left the rural areas to work in urban settings gained employment mainly as domestic servants, dockworkers and prostitutes, and endured enormous difficulties as they struggled to make a living. Alluding to the multiple burdens that women had to bear in both wage earning and household work, Post notes that,

> special attention should be drawn to the position of women in the Jamaican working class, not merely in their traditional subjected role in capitalist society as household drudges but also as wage workers. Their important presence in agricultural field labour and on the docks...[makes] it clear that discrimination against them on sexual grounds added a degree of super-exploitation to their position in the casual labour market. It must also be noted that in Jamaica to a large extent domestic service and petty trading were female occupations.

(Post, 1978: 138)

Garvey's perceived avoidance of the gender question is at first baffling, but when one considers that women contributed significantly to the organisation of the UNIA, became loyal rank and file members by the millions and helped in the dissemination of the philosophies of African-centred consciousness, the oversight does seem more apparent than real.

When the record is examined, it is clear that women were an integral part of the Universal Negro Improvement Association from its establishment in 1914. After Marcus Garvey himself, the UNIA's first founding member was a young, 17-year-old woman called Amy Ashwood, who helped to conceptualise the organisation. She spoke in public debates, did social work and became Garvey's first wife. In the organisation's first two years in Kingston, about half of the Association's members were women. The UNIA was also very unusual among organisations of its day, in that it insisted on women taking leadership roles and produced many dynamic women leaders. Accordingly, therefore, when the UNIA headquarters moved to Harlem, New York, women held some of the highest positions in the movement. The UNIA established positions for women as a president and vice-president; the African-American actress, Henrietta Vinton Davis, became an international organiser; and Lillian Galloway was the head of the UNIA's printing press.

After joining her husband in the USA, Amy Ashwood continued to speak in public and became the editor of *The Negro World*. She was an officer of both the Black Star Line and the Negro Factories Corporation and took a bullet meant for Marcus in the failed Harlem assassination attempt of 1918. Even after she and Garvey were divorced, Amy Ashwood continued to be an important and influential member of the Pan-African liberation movement and lived in Ghana in her later years. She is another unsung Jamaican-born heroine who is definitely deserving of a more prominent place in recorded history.

The UNIA formed two paramilitary organisations that functioned like regular armed forces, with members dressing in military uniform and receiving military training. These were the Universal African Legion for men and the Universal African Motor Corps for women, making the UNIA the first organisation in the USA to have had a women's paramilitary group. In the meantime, one of the most powerful and best known of the UNIA's various auxiliary organisations was the *Black Cross Nurses*, which trained women to do social work and taught them healthcare. From a gender perspective, the critique here, of course, is that these roles reinforced women's position as caregivers and nurturers.

Just like Garvey's first wife – Amy Ashwood – his second wife, Amy Jacques, became the editor of *The Negro World*. She, too, was a strong public speaker and was also an important activist and organiser in the UNIA. Amy Jacques was Garvey's secretary in his Harlem heydays, before becoming his wife. She was responsible for the compilation of Marcus Garvey's writings and organised the publishing of his most famous book, entitled *The Philosophy and Opinions of Marcus Garvey.*[49] After Garvey's passing, Amy Jacques Garvey continued to work for the UNIA. She made sure that Garvey's name and his oral and *literary discourse* were not and would never be forgotten.

Despite these facts, it is still my contention that Garvey's political refraction of the prevailing Eurocentric patriarchal culture, in many ways, inadvertently reinforced the patriarchal elements in the very structures of power that he was so passionately committed to contesting. The political implication of this oversight was a dichotomisation of race and gender in the resistance struggle. To some extent, that militates against the effectiveness of Black liberation endeavours in general, and against the emancipation of Black women in particular. Garvey's silence on gender discrimination, can also be seen as the outcome of a choice to treat race as more of a political issue than gender and as a domain for masculinist activism. By default, then, issues of gender subordination were feminised and trivialised.

---

49   For a full treatment on this dimension of the Garvey movement, see Winston James' (1998) *Holding Aloft the Banner of Ethiopia: Caribbean Radicalism in Early Twentieth Century America*, Verso, New York, pp. 147-55.

Figure 4.3 Garvey married two Amys, both of whom worked as his personal assistants. Here he is pictured with Amy Jacques Garvey who compiled the seminal *Philosophy and Opinions of Marcus Garvey.*

In this sense, cultural ideology has been as much responsible for the construction of gender (as a concept and then in the distinctions based on it) as it has for the construction of race and its distinctions. The formulation in which these two hierarchical patterns are enclosed, then, is metaphysical insofar as the hierarchy does not display or logically derive from the ostensible biological properties.

(Lang, in Zack (ed.), 1997: 25, emphasis in original)

From Garvey to Rastafari

Rastafari constitutes a socio-spiritual and political movement that has also emphasised the centrality of race to the *discourse of resistance*. As the self-proclaimed 'true' progenitors of Garvey, Rastafarians have carried the baton of reclaiming the metaphysical, political and embodied dimensions of race, and thereby legitimised the struggle by displaced and dispossessed Africans for social justice in modern Jamaica (and by extension, in the world). Traditionally, the male leadership in Rastafari has also focused on issues of race and class, to the exclusion of gender. Consequently, they succeeded in reinforcing male domination as the norm and thereby portrayed the role of women as supportive and subordinate. However, this contradiction has been challenged, especially in the past couple of decades, by *womanist discourses* circulating in the wider society. Committed but confrontational responses of women in Rastafari, a situation which developed in the 1980s, have also interrogated the sexism inherent to such portrayals of gender power and relations.

The *Livity*, or *Way of Life* of Rastafari, became prominent in Jamaica because the early practitioners (and those who have followed in this tradition) unapologetically declared the Divinity of the Ethiopian Emperor, H.I.M. Haile Selassie I.[50] This recognition coincided with the coronation of Emperor Haile Selassie I and Empress Woizero Menen on November 2, 1930. Haile Selassie was recognised on this occasion as the 225th successor in a line of Judaic Kings in Ethiopia, which stretched back in antiquity to the famed Biblical Kings, Solomon and David. Seventy-two nations (i.e., a representative cross-section of the international community) participated in the unique and elaborate coronation ceremony at which the former Ras turned Negus (King), Tafari Makonnen, was crowned as King of Kings, Lord of Lords, Conquering Lion of the Tribe of Judah, the Elect of God and the Light of this World, among other titles.[51] This event was seen to be the fulfilment of not only Biblical prophecy, but also of a prophecy that Marcus Garvey is alleged to have made a few years earlier, that the dispossessed Africans in the Diaspora should 'look to Africa where a Black King will be crowned', because this event would signal their redemption. Empress Menen was crowned Queen of Queens. (Davis and Simon, 1992: 68).

Figure 4.4: Emperor Haile Selassie I and Empress Menen shared
the coronation ceremonies of November 2, 1930, breaking centuries of tradition.

50   As Horace Campbell remarks disparagingly, it is ironic that Rastafari are defined as 'millenarian' because of this world view while 'those who walked around with pictures of the British King [were deemed] well adjusted' (Campbell, 1990: 69).

51   It was also seen as symbolic that on this occasion King George V of England returned the sceptre that had previously been stolen from Ethiopia by British agents, an action that was interpreted by Rastafari as another fulfilment of prophecy, which signified the Divinity of the King of Kings. This knowledge, which is passed down through oral transmission, alludes to Genesis 49:10 to validate this claim: 'The sceptre shall not depart from Judah, nor a lawgiver from between his feet, until Shiloh come; and unto him shall the gathering of the people...' In other words, Judah will hold the royal sceptre, his descendants will always rule and nations will bring tribute and bow in obedience before HIM.

Interestingly and ironically enough, when Negus Tafari ordered that both he and his Empress-to-be share the coronation ceremony, he broke with centuries-old traditions, and this became the first time in history that a king and queen were crowned at the same time. In this way, the young Emperor set a new precedent for how women were to be regarded, not only in Ethiopia, but throughout the entire African Diaspora. Until very recently, this critical aspect of that historic event has been largely overlooked by most Rastafari brethren.

Generally and apart from exceptional individual cases, Rastas have chosen to avoid alignment to the partisan machinery of political or cultural clientilism that operates in Jamaica. However, the undeniable patriarchal emphases in the ideology and practices of the *Livity* demonstrate that formations like Rastafari, will display 'disciplinary mechanisms which take a material form' in the process of cultural reproduction (Weedon, 1999: 125). Maureen Rowe argues that because the *Livity* has to be seen as a composite of the inherent contradictions within Jamaican society, it was inevitable that within Rastafari the prevailing patriarchal precedents would express themselves as the predominant register of embodied discipline. Yet she correctly suggests further, that the form of patriarchy expressed in Rastafari is actually more African than European, although these two versions of the ideological and material control of men over women are expressed in the wider Jamaican society.

According to Rowe, African patriarchy emphasises the power of men based on their innate masculinity and the support women give to this discourse by, in many cases, expressing their femininity through procreation. On the other hand, she explains, European patriarchal discourse is based more on materiality, with male power being emphasised through the role of the man as 'breadwinner' (Rowe, in Murrell et al (eds.), 1998: 73-74).

The Rastafari construction of family relations and discourses on embodiment, were shaped by and enunciated 'at three points in the evolution of Rastafari: (1) during the widespread acceptance of dreadlocks, (2) at the advent of the Jamaican Rudeboy phenomenon, and (3) with the rise of the women's liberation movement' (ibid.: 75). These conjunctures provide significant liberatory moments for the way in which women were perceived in the Livity.

Rowe designates the 1930–1950 period as 'the formative years'; 1951–1971 as 'the early years'; and 1972 to the present as 'the later years' of the Livity. During the formative years, the Rasta pioneers established a headquarters at Pinnacle in the St. Catherine hills. This community was repeatedly raided by the police starting in June 1941 (Lacey, 1977: 25, Post, 1978: 188–90), and after a number of years of such police attacks, the commune was eventually destroyed. This action reflected the usual anxiety that the colonial state displayed at any sign of grassroots resistance to imperial European domination. Administrative unease also resulted from the fact that ganja (marijuana) production was flourishing (along with a wide variety of other crops) among the African-centred peasants at Pinnacle. These agricultural producers were influenced by the Rastafari proclamation of the Herb as a holy sacrament, as well as by their desperate economic circumstances, which were improved by the sale of ganja on the local and export markets.

This created an anti-government and anti-police environment in remote rural districts, especially since ganja was often grown on government lands by squatters. During the 1960s ganja cultivators grew increasingly bold and might stone or snipe at police raiding parties. Organised crime provided outlets, money and presumably, later in the 1960s, guns.

(Lacey, 1977: 25)

Among Rastafari, the advent of the Dreadlocked Nyahbinghi (Post, 1978: 189) – who would become known colloquially as the *'Blackheart Man'* – also marked the advent of a much more radical sensibility among the youth. This mode of self-presentation provided a decisive symbol of rebellion against colonial Caribbean oppression and exploitation and was even more visually upsetting to the ruling elites than the facial hair which initially had characterised the Rasta man as a *'Beardman'*.

> The Dreadlocks emerged in the course of overturning the authority of the older generation, whom they judged to be too compromising towards the society. They were more separatist, symbolising their ideological stance in their spectacular hair style. To the older generation [of Rastafari] the scissors and razor had been taboo; to the Dreadlocks the scissors, the razor and the comb.

(Chevannes, in Caribbean Quarterly, 1990: 69)

Contrary to Chevannes' dating of the advent of the Dreadlocks to the period of the 'early years', this phenomenon actually started emerging in the early 1940s. Rastafarians stopped cutting and combing their hair and started to grow locks when they claimed a connection with the still mysterious African tradition of Nyahbinghi. The revolutionary roots and consequent discourses of this self-identification is what the colonial authorities found most disturbing, because '[s]ome of them began to call themselves Nya-Binghi (Nyabingi), members of the great conspiracy that was going to destroy the rule of the White man over the Black throughout the world' (Post, 1978: 173). This uncompromising and radical stance was also the taproot of the ambivalence that Marcus Garvey and the more conservative elements in his organisation seemed to have felt towards this new and more hard-core progeny of his movement.

> *[T]hey were growing beards and refusing to cut their hair,* so as to prove that they were Moors and have even gone to the length of changing their Christian names and their surnames, to be known as Mohammed Ali, of Mohammed Bey or some peculiar Moorish or Mohammedan religious mystical name...

(Charles L. James, q. in Post, 1978: 1989, emphasis added)

The turbulent decade of the 1960s was an important turning point in the development of Rastafari and saw the occurrence of a number of watershed events in the growth of the Movement. First, there was the publishing and submission to the government in 1960 of a University of the West Indies Report on Rastafari, prepared by a team of UWI scholars from the Mona campus led by Professor Rex Nettleford. During that same year, the Rasta-inspired Reverend Claudius Henry was implicated in an unsuccessful incident of armed militancy by Black Power advocates. The revolutionaries, including a son of Henry, were eventually slain by the Jamaican security forces.

Next, the Jamaican government sponsored a historic ten-member mission (including Rasta Elder Mortimo Planno) to five African states in 1961. Then, in Easter 1963, the infamous Coral Gardens Massacre took place on the island's north coast, resulting in the killing, beating, maiming and incarceration of a large number of Rastafari brethren. While this roller-coaster ride defined the Movement's evolution during the early 1960s, the flowering Black Power Movement in North America was also contributing significantly to the shaping of the Rastafarians' international political outlook and world view.

However, it was the visit of Emperor Haile Selassie I to Jamaica in April 1966 that proved to be the most significant and culturally enduring event on the Rastafari calendar for that decade. The Emperor's official state visit conferred a new status on the *Livity* that did much to deflect the effects of the syndrome of stigmatisation to which its members had hitherto been subjected. Ironically, the success of the Ethiopian Monarch's visit ran counter to the political objectives of the ruling JLP, which had secretly harboured ulterior motives in endorsing this event.

> In 1966, Haile Selassie was invited to make a state visit to Jamaica by Michael Manley...Although Manley's party was not then in power in Jamaica, the ruling party, the Jamaica Labourites [sic] thought that if Selassie would come to the island and deny his divinity, the burgeoning Rasta movement would be defused and all the foolish talk about going back to Africa would stop.

> (Simon and Davis, 1992: 76)

Instead, Rastafarians were emboldened by the Emperor's visit, which, in their eyes, validated the subject and personification of their faith. This spiritual steadfastness created a backlash of intensified victimisation against Rastafari by the state authorities, especially the police (Simon and Davis, 1992: 77). But this policy also failed to achieve its desired goals, as the political/police persecution only had the long-term effect of reinforcing the *Rastafari discourse* of African identity and resistance. This toughened discourse on African identity and cultural resistance, in turn, provided an uncompromising medium through which to confront the dominant power structures. Dreadlocked hair was defiantly symbolic of this resistance. Inevitably, this rebellious stance created a climate of consternation and fear at the state and institutional levels as well as in the society at large. In the following observation, Nettleford effectively captures both the fervour and scope of spiritual, cultural and political resistance that Rastafari represents.

> Needless to say, their bold, 'dread' and defiant exterior masks an organic protest against the Caribbean's 'sufferation' from the centuries-old crimes committed against our people. But this dread exterior also conceals a firm inner commitment to peace, love and a quiet determination to guard their own and mankind's self-respect and dignity.

> (Nettleford, 1978: 187)

Adherents of the *Livity* posit that the pronoun for the first person singular, the I (the Eye), or the Self, constitutes the singular and plural as the indivisible I, or *I-and-I (I & I)*, thus repudiating the divisiveness embedded in the hierarchical binary opposition of the pronouns you and me. In the same way that two eyes represent the single function of seeing, there should, according to this cosmology, be synchronicity in the intentions of social actors in order to realise the ideal of Peace and Love. This is the philosophical essence of the Rastafari mindset. And this is the mindset that undermines and counterbalances the partisan politics and violence that continues to rub the raw wounds that have been historically inflicted on the urban poor living below the poverty line. Thus, within the inner-city communities, Rastafari are popular role models, creating the foil for the *carte blanche* prominence of the *Rude Boy* or inner-city *Don*.

Figure 4.5: Youth smoking marijuana-loaded chalice. The motorcycle suggest the identity of Rude Boy while the chillum pipe that is being smoked is didactic of Rastafari influence on everyday street practices in the inner-city.

Besides using *Patwah*, as the local Jamaican Creole is called, Rastafari has also created a language of their own in a semantic representation of African resistance to domination. Despite efforts by the upper classes to invalidate these verbal self-expressions, '*Rasta-talk*' facilitates identity reclamation through investment in the rich oral resources of the grassroots. The extensive Jamaican linguistic repertoire has long undermined the hegemony of standard English, the official medium of communication and, by extension, the power structure that it represents (Pollard, in *Caribbean Quarterly*, 1985: 40).

In more recent years, Reggae music has facilitated the development of the *Rastafari Livity* as well as other expressions of popular culture emerging from Jamaica. Rastafari therefore represent the proverbial voices of the poor, crying in the wilderness of subordination for the development of systems of equal rights and justice.[52] These cries have inspired others searching for viable alternatives to negative self-concepts and the attendant low-self esteem and lack of race pride that beset the majority of the poor in Jamaica.

> [B]y electing to lead a life based on the affirmation of being Black, without at the same time being racist, the Rastafari have seized hold of one of the mainsprings of national development, namely, a sense of national identity...[and] the harmony between the reality of being Black and the consciousness and confidence in that reality. This point must not be glossed over. Some commentators accuse Rastafari of being a form of "reverse racism," sometimes comparing it to the Nation of Islam. Nothing could be further from the truth.

> (Chevannes, in Murrell et al, (eds.), 1998: 62)

The Pull of Politics on the Rastafari Force Field

Throughout its two terms in office in the 1970s, the PNP used important symbols of the Rastafari livity to gain electoral support. This was convenient to do because the so-called Democratic Socialist ideas of the PNP found congruence with the *Peace and Love* sensibility of Rastafari. The fact that the Livity emerged as a significant domain of masculinist authority couched in ideological and spirituo-cultural terms also made it easy for the PNP leaders to appeal to politicised Rastafari males to assist the party in the public relations campaign to woo the grassroots electorate. Some critical grassroots observers at the time perceived this PNP manoeuvre as a betrayal of the trust of the people, who were promised much but who received very little by way of social recognition and material benefits.

Nevertheless, Manley gained legitimacy with the Rastafari community and grassroots sympathisers with his proclamation in the period preceding the 1972 general election, that he had received a '*Rod of Correction*' – a Rastafari/African symbol of authority – from Haile Selassie I, Emperor of Ethiopia. This was a particularly significant declaration because H.I.M. Haile Selassie I is the pre-eminent figure in Rastafari cosmology.[53] By deliberately associating himself with the Supreme Mystique of the *Livity*, Manley, the self-styled Joshua, had designed a strategy which proved that he truly knew how to win the hearts and minds of grassroots people. *Joshua* with the Rod of Correction evoked a culturally correct interpretation of masculine authority, linking the phallus to politics and (violent) sexuality.

The alliance of state/class power and local phallocratic regimes was exemplified in the association of the charismatic personae of the prime minister of the 1970s, Michael Manley, with popular Rastafari/Reggae artist Clancy Eccles. In the 1972 election campaign, it was Eccles' song 'Rod of Correction' which assigned the more powerful seal of grassroots approval, substantiating the Manley's appropriation of the supernatural

---

52   As Reggae expert Peter Tosh sang in a didactic interrogation of the Peace and Love emphasis in the Livity and in criticism of the peace treaty signed by politicians and inner-city gangsters, 'I don't want no peace, I need equal rights and justice!'

53   See *Chanting Down Babylon: The Rastafari Reader* (Murrell et al (eds.), 1998, for a comprehensive documentary on Rastafari ideology and practices.

leadership capabilities associated with the Biblical *Joshua*,[54] the evocative name that he chose to adopt as a very prudent political nickname. Unfortunately, instead of carrying the *Children of Israel* (Rastafari) across the *River Jordan* (Atlantic Sea) to the *Promised Land* (Ethiopia) as Joshua did, Manley kept them in Egypt/Babylon (Jamaica) where he whipped them with the 'Rod of Correction'.

Rod of Correction

I say Hail that Man! A So!
Lot wife turned a pillar of salt
Lot wife turned a pillar of salt
Lot wife turned a pillar of salt
Down in Sodom and Gomorrah
Burn them in Sodom and Gomorrah
Burn them in Sodom and Gomorrah
Burn them in Sodom and Gomorrah
Lot wife turned a pillar of salt
King Pharaoh army was drownded
King Pharaoh army was drownded
King Pharaoh army was drownded
Down there in the bottom of the ocean
Beat them with the Rod of Correction,
Father
Beat them with the Rod of Correction
Beat them wid the Rod of Correction
Lot wife turned a pillar of salt
I said Hail that Man! Cause a so!

By starting the song with 'Hail that Man!', Eccles was greeting Manley in the popular Rastafari idiom of the time, a discourse reserved for initiates and intimates. The dominant themes in Eccles' lyrics emphasise the phallocratic power invested in the Rod. Lot's infamous wife is seen as insufficiently submissive, thereby incurring God's wrath – such as befell her with a vengeance because she would not unquestioningly submit to the vision of her husband, but dared to look behind her, thereby being punished.

Furthermore, embedded in the repetitious ditty are references to the moral recourse – burn them – which is recommended for Sodom and Gomorrah,[55] the site of rampant homosexuality that Lot's wife seemingly yearned to return to. This speaks to the violent opposition that prevails in Jamaica to practices which transgress the heterosexual norm.

---

54 Joshua was the leader of the Children of Israel who were able to make the walls of Jericho crumble through their combined Voice. This provides a powerful metaphor for Manley's charismatic verbal authority as well as the more profound allusion to his authority to represent and voice the state as speaking in interests of The People, by claiming to represent their resistance struggles and identity interests. As the people eventually realised however, this claim was falsified by the fact that promised programmes of social rehabilitation did not go far enough to change the fundamental structures and discourses of power.

55 See Genesis 19 for an elaboration of the practices and destruction of the inhabitants of Sodom and Gomorrah from which the righteous man Lot narrowly escaped.

Figure 4.6: Album cover showing Manley and Eccles.

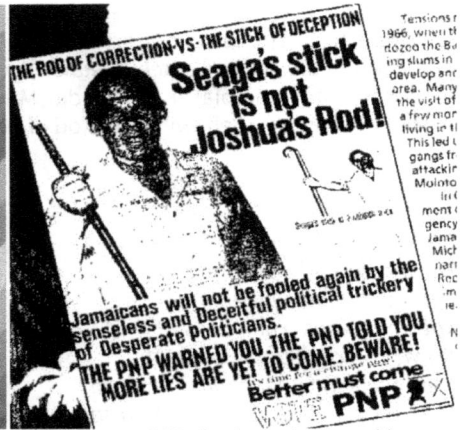

Figure 4.7: PNP electioneering pamphlet.

The campaign flier in Figure 4.7 represented Manley as the possessor of a big rod, the symbol of macho masculinity, and the Leader of the Opposition as wielder of a mere stick of deception, an invocation of the diminutive version of the heterosexual norm. The Leader of the Opposition, Edward Seaga is therefore parodied and portrayed as possessing an inferior *stick*. The metaphoric use of the *phallus* to define power demonstrates that sexuality and pseudo-sexual imagery provide the fulcrum for the cumulative shaping of power relations in all social spheres,

> Sexuality...is not a discrete sphere of interaction or feeling or sensation or behaviour in which pre-existing social divisions may or may not be played out. It is a pervasive dimension of social life, one that permeates the whole, a dimension along which gender occurs and through which gender is socially constituted; it is a dimension along which other social divisions, like race and class, partly play themselves out.

> (Mackinnon, in Nicholson (ed.), 1997: 160)

This propaganda campaign reified hegemonic masculinity as the norm of the gender order. Since, in addition to reinforcing the subordination of women, patriarchy delimits the power that some men have in the face of superior male power (Connell, 1995), this orchestration had its most momentous expression in the political propaganda card that the PNP played. Therefore, the portrayal of the national leader as possessing The Rod of Correction carried the underlying assumption that men and women of lesser power were being made into subordinate sexualised objects. This message politicised the theme of hegemonic masculinity in its most explicitly heterosexist definition, reinforcing the articulation of upper-class/state and grassroots patriarchies. This political manipulation of the *phallus* established the masculinist, political and cultural discourses of the body, as well as the social norms and sanctions arising from transgressions of these dominant registers.

Rastafari and Patriarchy

Rastafari have been outstanding for their critical commentary about the Babylon system. Yet their patriarchal practices have limited women's independent agency in the *Livity*, almost as much as in the wider society. In 1988, *Sistren Research* facilitated my own research on gender relations in Rastafari, a collaborative relationship that was itself a contradiction in terms.

> For brethren and sistren to be meeting at the headquarters of Sistren Theatre Collective (STC), the women's organisation concerned with the analysis of working women's lives, was unprecedented…STC supported the attempt by Rasta brethren and sistren to clarify issues related to ideology, sexuality, roles and image. And for Rastafari to be probing these issues within the space of a feminist organisation was doubly significant for the impact the process had on confronting stereotypes associated with women's struggle for the realisation for personal power.
>
> (Tafari-Ama, in Murrell et al (eds.), 1998: 90)

The development of a *feminist/womanist* consciousness in Jamaica, in the mature period of the modern women's movement, impacted gender relations in Rastafari as a matter of course. As a result, women's roles became more reflective of their self-conscious agency. In its deepest essence, the impetus to generate a discourse of woman's liberation within the *Livity* of Rastafari, indicated the Rasta *sistren's* commitment to the *Livity* itself, and not just to the Kingman with whom they might have been affiliated. It also represented the invocation of the strong tradition of resistance by African women in the Caribbean, generally, and in Jamaica, in particular.

There are strong parallels between practices of patriarchy in Rastafari ideology and those patriarchal practices that have been prevalent in the wider Jamaican society. French and Ford-Smith critiqued the gender biases in the Moyne Commission Report, which was established after the 1938 labour rebellion. They noted that this paternalistic, colonial institution targeted women as the most accessible category to provide a scapegoat for prevailing social ills and tried to make grassroots women take responsibility (negatively) for the project of sociopolitical transformation.

> 'The family' was to be the answer to the unemployment, the lack of wage work and the land hunger of the masses which the Moyne Commission identified as the main socioeconomic problems facing the island…If women were poor and families destitute, it was argued, it was because they did not have families with a man at the centre…The solution to female poverty, then, was not to pay women 'proper' wages for the work they did, but to deprive them of what little wages they had through the establishment of 'proper' families, and for the poor to establish the bourgeois family, without the bourgeois material base.
>
> (French and Ford-Smith, 1983-85: 293-294)

The state agents wanted to maintain the status quo by institutionalising the bourgeois family form at the grassroots level. Running parallel to this stream, Rastafari have appropriated the model of man as the head/breadwinner of the family. This can also be interpreted as an attempt to reclaim an idealised 'African' organisation of the household. Therefore, the ideology, language and practices within the institution of Rastafari can be attributed to,

> the African-style patriarchy among the Rastafari male. The man was the head of the house. He was the representative of His Imperial Majesty and therefore the "Kingman." The woman was his helpmate and, in the ideal family, occupied a place beside the Kingman in the same way that the empress remained beside His Majesty – silent and supportive in public but active, as we understood it, behind the scenes. This was not always the case in the movement. In some households...where the children were males, the women appeared to occupy a place below the children. However, this was not the rule.

> (Rowe, in Murrell et al (eds.), 1998: 83)

This emphasis on male dominance at the household level has been an attempt to re-instate the authority which African men lost during slavery. Nowadays, the classist and sexist construction of sex/gender role divisions in the household (hooks, 1981), re-inscribe the subordination of women across the board in the society, and therefore within the *Livity of Rastafari*. However, *womanist* resistance by sistren within the Livity, has also influenced significant changes in the patriarchal status quo.

> Without a doubt, Rastafari is a patriarchal movement. However, as with all social movements, Rastafari has, over the years, experienced dynamic shifts in gender power relations as a result of females revisiting their own self-definitions, juxtaposed against designations ascribed by males who created the movement.

> (Tafari-Ama, in Murrell et al (eds.), 1998: 89)

There has been a breakdown in this household arrangement (Rowe, in Murrell et al (eds.), 1998: 85) and as a consequence, Rastafari sistren have increasingly confronted the brethren's failure to uphold the very paradigm of masculinity that they advocate. Extra-partner unions in which some males engage assume a law of monogamy for the woman but not the man. Sisters who expected to be in monogamous unions have, needless to say, been chagrined by such developments which they see as challenges to their personal authority in the household.

What is curious is that many times, 'the other women' have been *Brownings* if not actual White women, whose body images are the antitheses of what is promoted as ideal in Rastafari, i.e. the Ebony/Black Queen. As a result, many Rastafari women have opted to move out of the household, raise their children on their own and in many cases, re-formulate relationships with non-Rastafari males rather than submit to the patriarchal dictates of Rastafari brethren. Thus, it is very clear that 'the contradictions of race, class, and gender distinctions operate as beguilingly in Rastafari as they do in the wider society' (Tafari-Ama, in Murrell et al (eds.), 1998: 104). Rowe suggests also that drug-taking compounds the domestic problems.

> Those [brethren] who fell victim of drug-taking are unable to guide the family...Those who have chosen non-Rastafari women have introduced a level of conflict in the home and in the movement that only the sistren seem willing to acknowledge...The sistren for their part, are now secure enough

in their persons to take a stand against what outrages them. An interesting element in this discussion is that of colour. As colour-conscious as Jamaica is, and in a movement as fiercely Black-conscious as Rastafari, many of these non-Rastafari women are not Black women.

(Rowe in Murrell et al (eds.), 1998: 85-86)

These are some of the domestic difficulties with which Rastafari have had to contend in the process of establishing the *Livity* as a strong sociopolitical force. Nevertheless, in the early years,

> family life flourished. Children were the unifying factor and much love and attention were given to them. Efforts were made to ensure that the children developed strong reasoning ability, an Afrocentric perspective, and a strong sense of self. In these responsibilities the male and female shared equally, though the male retained much of the authority. What authority the female gained in her relationship came to her through the role of mother.

(Rowe, op. cit. 82)

Many households have remained intact through the process of parenting and all the social relations surrounding attendant responsibilities. However, in several cases in the later years and up to the contemporary period, women have been the main movers and shapers of the household.

> The denuded Rastafari household has a committed Rasta woman as head; the father often maintains a visiting relationship with the children. But some families have been so broken that they do not keep in touch. In a few instances, children born and raised as Rastafarians in the early years are no longer being raised as Rastafarians, as the mother, in rebuilding her life, has totally rejected Rastafari.

(Rowe, op. cit.: 86)

Rastafari sistren have been primarily responsible for the persistence of the *Livity* in the so-called private sphere, which also influences the public maintenance of Rastafari as a viable social entity.

Colour-Coded Resistance

The paradox between the cultural efficacy of Rastafari and the problematic relations of gender is not unique to the *Livity*. On the contrary, these inconsistencies are also characteristic of other institutions of resistance in the Jamaican historical space. As the violence of the state authorities intensified between the late 1950s and the early 1960s, brethren sought to recover some of the dignity they lost at the hands of the police. This probably accounts for the increased patriarchal tendencies in the *Livity*. The Jamaican state authorities carried out several violent operations against sectors of the society that they considered threats to their hegemonic interests. Among the endeavours at which this response was directed was the alleged rebellion, in 1960, planned by revolutionary-minded Jamaicans and led by the Reverend Claudius Henry. This group called their organisation the African Reform Church.

Claudius Henry, like so many other Black Jamaicans – such as Claude McKay and Marcus Garvey – had gone to the USA to escape the racial discrimination of the educational system and to avail himself of opportunities for self-achievement. While training as a religious leader in New York Henry was exposed to the activities of the Ethiopian World Federation...and was present when Adam Clayton Powell paid a glowing tribute to Haile Selassie when he visited the US.

(Campbell, 1985: 103)

Claudius Henry spent some years in North America and returned to the island in 1957. He was impressed by the Rastafari's success in establishing a discursive climate of resistance on the foundations already laid by Marcus Garvey and other rebellious antecedents. He, therefore, proceeded to appropriate this energy to achieve his own politically motivated objectives. Calling himself 'the Repairer of the Breach', Henry capitalised on the rhetorical gains of the Garvey campaign by claiming that he could facilitate repatriation to Africa. He proceeded to sell 15,000 tickets at one shilling each to local Rastafari adherents (Campbell. 1985: 103). In 1959, thousands of expectant repatriators gathered in vain at the port of Kingston, finding it hard to believe that an opportunistic charlatan had duped them (see Murrell, in Murrell et al, 1998: 7).

Henry and his African Reform Church 'congregation', had many ambitious intentions. They were intent on transforming the Rastafari ideological confrontation with the *Babylon system*, into armed struggle, such as had been recently and successfully attempted in neighbouring Cuba (Campbell, 1985: 103). However, the brewing spirit of agitation did not escape the notice of the super-sensitive security forces, which had initially put this group under surveillance because of their connections to 'the First Africa Corps, an armed, militant Black group in New York' (Lacey, 1977: 82). In April 1960, the intelligence gathering by the security forces ascertained that members of the two groups were engaged in guerrilla warfare training in the Red Hills area overlooking Kingston. Quoting Leonard Barrett's account of this development, Murrell notes that when the security forces raided Henry's headquarters in 1959 they found

> 2,500 electrical detonators, 1,300 detonators, a shotgun, a calibre .32 revolver, a large quantity of machetes sharpened [on] both sides like swords and laced in sheaths, cartridges, several sticks of dynamite and other articles.

(Barrett, q. by Murrell, in Murrell et al (eds.), 1998: 8)

The law officers arrested Claudius Henry and some of his associates and charged them with treason. However, the activists, led by Claudius Henry's son, Ronald Henry, were still able to proceed with their attempt to stage a rebellion in the form of skirmishes between themselves and the security forces between April and June 1960.

> Henry's place in the history of Jamaica and of Rastafari was written in the blood of his son, Ronald Henry, who was murdered by the (British) Royal Hampshire Regiment subsequent to his call for Jamaicans to rise up against PNP/JLP manipulation. In 1960, this call by Ronald Henry and his followers, who had declared armed struggle in Jamaica one year after the Cuban revolution, was a call by a section of the Black population which wanted to move rapidly towards political and economic emancipation. But the revolt

of Ronald Henry, Gabidon and their supporters came to grief: the social conditions then did not lend themselves to a solution by armed struggles since the working poor had not yet exhausted all the possible gains by the bourgeois democratic struggle.

(Campbell, 1985: 104)

In the aftermath of the rebellion, the security forces and the mass media used Henry's association with Rastafari as a mechanism to undermine the social validity of the *Livity*. Ill-advised as it was, the attempt at armed rebellion indicates reflexivity on the part of the actors and their conscious choice to express resistance in this idiom in spite of the inevitability of the detrimental consequences. Surprising as it might seem, the small cadre of activists were convinced of the political value[56] that would be added to their community because they dared to attempt armed confrontation with the more heavily armed protectors of the state institution. The rebellion also set in motion a chain of events that reflected the growing attempts by Jamaica's Rastafari to translate spiritual vision into the kind of practical political action that would come to characterise the Rastafari involvement in the Grenada Revolution almost two decades later.

The Coral Gardens 'uprising' in Montego Bay in 1963 was another such conjuncture. The event was blown out of proportion by the security forces that were becoming more and more agitated by the fact and implications of the physical self-representation of Rastafari, as well as by their uncompromising cultural profile. However, upon reflection, the entire incident should have just been a storm in a teacup. While only a few Rastafari were directly involved in this incident, the entire community began to be subjected to severe forms of persecution by the security forces as well as by other civil society institutions, in the political backlash. As a result, up until a few years ago, the locks of Rastafari prisoners were automatically shorn once they were incarcerated in prison. It was only in the 1980s that Rastafari children were finally admitted into public schools. And, to this day, by social policy, which of course cannot be legally contested, Rastafari are generally denied employment in the public sector.

In 1965, a Black worker in a Chinese shop in Kingston was beaten following a dispute with the owner. This incident led to a week of riots during which a number of Chinese-owned shops were looted. Although this event did not in any way involve Rastafarians, it reflected the racial tensions of the day. The security forces reacted by shooting eight persons to death and arresting about 90. The anti-Chinese antagonism, which at its height involved hundreds of people, showed that poor Africans were venting anti-Brown sentiments against the most available group in this category. Chinese grocery shops were conveniently located mainly in the Kingston commercial district close to the spaces occupied by poor people. This eruption of community anger by poor/Black people was also the harbinger of the more disturbing gang violence that was to mushroom in the West Kingston area in the years that followed. Obviously, gender issues were not important factors in these particular incidents, although the overview in this chapter posits race resistance as a masculinist discourse.[57]

---

56   In an extensive footnote Horace Campbell records that '[a]fter Henry's release from prison in the late sixties he became an ardent supporter of Michael Manley and the People's National Party, endorsing the 1972 electoral campaign and in the process enlisting strong ecclesiastical discussion on the role of religion and politics in Jamaica' (Campbell, 1985: 104)

57   See Payne (1994) and Lacey (1977) for more detailed accounts of these events.

The Rodney Affair

A prevailing lack of gender analysis was evident in Walter Rodney's 'Groundings with (his) Brothers', as well as in the *Abeng* project, which linked grassroots activists with intellectual resistance. The so-called Rodney Affair of October 1968 is one of the most significant events in Jamaica's modern political history. It re-drew the battle lines in the quicksands separating elite- and lower-class interests. This confrontation amplified the racial hostilities seething below the surface of the class differences in a country that, as observed in the previous chapter, ironically declares its national motto to be, 'Out of Many, One People'. Born in Georgetown, Guyana, Rodney was a student at the Mona Campus of the University of the West Indies (UWI) in the early 1960s. He went on to Oxford University in England to pursue his PhD, after which he returned to join the History Department at the UWI.

Figure 4.8: Guyanese-born Pan-African activist/historian and UWI lecturer, Dr. Walter Rodney was banned from Jamaica in 1968 by the JLP Government for 'grounding with (his) brothers'.

Events came to a head after Rodney left Jamaica on October 14, 1968, on a visit to a Black Writers Conference in Canada (See Chevannes, in *Caribbean Quarterly*, 1990: 75, Payne, 1994: 23). On October 16, the JLP Government, led by Prime Minister Hugh Shearer, unsuccessfully attempted to manipulate then Chancellor of the University, Sir Philip Sherlock, to prevent Rodney from returning to his post on the campus. When this plan failed, the state authorities instead moved swiftly to ban him from re-entering the country. The security forces were subsequently given the mandate to use extreme force against the university students[58] and the community people who took to the streets to demonstrate their anger against the banning of the very popular

---

58 The students, who wore their university gowns in the process of registering their disapproval of the state's action, were, concurrently, also expressing their outrage at the violation of the sanctity of the university

Rodney. This event provided a significant opportunity for the oppressed and exploited to express their discontent about the intolerable socioeconomic conditions under which they lived in the urban grassroots. It also marked the turning of the political tide from the JLP, to the PNP, a mandate that the electorate established by a landslide when they went to the polls three years later in 1972.

One of Rodney's educational objectives was to raise the consciousness of those living in the inner-city communities, about the nature of the oppression and exploitation that they were experiencing. He saw this as a means of challenging the state and its apparatuses to develop a system of social justice to address these problems. To this end, he developed a practice of '*grounding*' or reasoning with his brothers in these communities. This initiative linked the intellectuals, politicised gang activists (Rude Boys), the urban poor and revolutionary-minded Rastafari in a *two-way interactive discourse* which, as Ken Post admitted,[59] was a connection that had previously been eschewed by the prominent political ideologues of the day. The response of the wider population also revealed the deep social cleavages that Rodney was determined to deconstruct.

> The Black Power movement in Jamaica was the work of the Guyanese Lecturer in African History at the University in 1968, Walter Rodney. Rodney formally launched a Black Power group on the campus and, more importantly, took his expertise...among the Rastafari, including the Claudius Henry Group...The "Rodney Riot"...had its causes in grave economic and social conditions...[which] saw unemployment double from 13% at the beginning to 25% at the close of the sixties, while all around were the signs of growing affluence.

(Chevannes, in *Caribbean Quarterly*, 1990: 75)

Rodney felt that, in addition to creating an educated elite, the role of the UWI was to facilitate the development of a political consciousness and a social-revolutionary spirit among the suffering masses. He was unapologetic in stating that the JLP regime refused to recognise that Jamaica belonged primarily to the African majority and instead, was devoted to serving the interests of the minority capitalist class[60] (Payne, 1994: 22). In an elaboration of the research methodology and the definition of discourse that I have been utilising, Rodney realised that he had to reason or ground with the actors themselves who experienced subordination and who were also engaged in discourses of resistance at the grassroots level. This is achieved

---

environment. As Post suggested, this has to be read as a contradictory display of the bourgeois biases, which were inherent to the university ethos in this era.

59 In a discussion with the author, Ken Post, who was a lecturer on the UWI campus at the time, recalled that he was actively involved in the production of *Abeng* as financier and writer. As I will discuss in the next section, most of the intellectuals and activists who participated in this project stopped short of direct interaction with people in the inner-city communities. However, students involved in the demonstration had connections with rude boys, and the discussion groups based on *Abeng* did involve grassroots activists.

60 Under the leadership of Hugh Shearer, the JLP banned the Black Power Movement and persecuted advocates of this ideology and practice. The party also banned any books pertaining to political discourse on Black identity from entering the country.

[b]y using words and significant gestures...[to] engage in interpersonal reflections...[and] show that a person is not an isolated cognizer or interpreter of the world but is engaged with others in practical, ceremonial, and communicative activities, constituting forms of life in...language.

(Harré and Gillett, 1994: 21)

Rodney therefore consulted with Rastafari and was impressed by their knowledge, language and social practices. He also reasoned with the politicised rude boys in the hope of stimulating them to critical consciousness. Rodney, thereby, hoped to counteract the destructive effects of the ideological hegemony. Harold, a resident of Southside, describes how that community experienced Rodney's intervention.

Walter Rodney was a man who was really genuine. He used to come to lecture us at 4 Stephen Lane. He told us that the political way was not the means by which we were going to get our rights. We have to go through different methods. The two party political system is to divide us. When we were dealing with him with the radical part, we were aligned with the Labour Party. My friend who was in the PNP asked "what kind of man did you bring here to lecture to us? You brought a reactionary!" We said, no, he is not a reactionary, he is a radical. He is not affiliated to any of the political parties. Soon after that, we heard that they had banned him out of the country.

When we heard that they had banned him, people started to march and things got violent! I went back to the same fellow and said, you see! You were cursing me before but now you are marching for the same man. He replied, "I never really knew that, that man was a radical." I said, yes man! He is a radical. A radical is someone who speaks the truth, does right, advocates justice for the poor. That's being a radical. Rodney told us that as Black people we have to get our rights through the (pause) well you know? Through a revolution. He thought that our rights must come through the gun.

He never really came back to us after they banned him out of the country. Now nothing is happening for the poorer class; we live hand to mouth. We are not educated and school fees are going up. We can't reach a certain mark. When you have the ghetto and people live like this, we must have war, you see? It's just like that.

(Harold, Old Man's Bridge)

Rodney's political activism had a profound impact on the tradition of resistance in Jamaica, which is based on race and class-consciousness. He left indelible footsteps in the environment of change in which other like-minded intellectuals and activists were soon to tread. However, he, too, failed to recognise the vital need to ground with his sisters. Had he paid more attention to the gender dimensions of subordination and resistance, Rodney would have been able to develop an even more balanced view of what constitutes knowledge and power. His patriarchal bias reflects a typical shortcoming of many male activists, who emphasise race as their resistance agenda.

In order to properly balance my critique, however, I must note that Rodney did touch on gender issues, if only fleetingly, in his classic book *How Europe Underdeveloped Africa*, in which he stated that:

> A realistic assessment of the role of women in independent pre-colonial Africa shows two contrasting but combined tendencies. In the first place women were exploited by men through polygamous arrangements designed to capture the labour power of women…Nevertheless, there was a countertendency to insure the dignity of women to greater or lesser degree in all African societies. Mother-right was a prevalent feature of African societies, and particular women held a variety of privileges…exercised through religion or directly within the politico-constitutional apparatus… The most frequently encountered role of importance played by women was that of 'Queen-Mother' or 'Queen-Sister'. In practice, that post was filled by a female of royal blood, who might be a mother, sister, or aunt of the reigning king in places such as Mali, Asante, and Buganda. Her influence was considerable, and there were occasions when the 'Queen-Mother' was the real power and the male king a mere puppet.

(Rodney, 1983: 247–48)

It should also be noted that Brother Wally, as Rodney was affectionately called, exhibited some amount of gender appreciation on a personal level. He did not marry a light-skinned woman with straightened hair as was usual for a university lecturer of his status; his dark-skinned wife, Pat, wore her hair in a low Afro and dressed in African print wraps. In addition, Pat, herself an activist, accompanied her husband on many of his trips abroad.

The Abeng Interlude

It was fitting for a group of Jamaican political activists to name their newspaper the *Abeng*.[61] *Abeng* was the name given to a cow horn that the Maroons fashioned into a medium of mass communication. During their struggles against the British militia and the plantocracy, the Maroon guerrillas of Queen Nanny's time used this instrument to blow messages of war strategy over the Blue Mountains or within the Cockpit Country. This method of communication derived from an African tradition, which persisted, despite the oppositional forces arrayed against such practices of cultural retention. The *Abeng* newspaper was, fittingly, used to channel discourses of Black Power resistance to local and international audiences.

The *Abeng* brought together intellectuals teaching at the UWI during the 1960s, with other activists who had been politicised by their involvement in the *Rastafari Livity*, and in the case of the rude boys, by party political affiliation. This politically unprecedented coalition followed directly on the work of Rodney, and not only reflected the absence of a gender analysis of resistance to dominant power structures, but actually deepened that absence.

---

61 This newspaper has always maintained a right-wing line and thus favoured JLP politics.

According to Barry Chevannes, the Rodney Riot was the event that inspired intellectuals at the UWI to develop working relationships with grassroots agents who enunciated popular discourses of resistance. Chevannes also notes that this momentary collaboration of intellectual and grassroots activists around the issue of race, aroused distress among middle-class conservatives.

> The riot once again did violence to middle class consciousness by raising the question of racial identity. But this time, thought found expression in action, as a group of intellectuals formed the 'Abeng' movement...[I]ts significance is to be found in the organic link it sought to establish, in the Rodney tradition, between the middle and working classes. It became a partisan voice of the poor.
>
> (Chevannes, in *Caribbean Quarterly*, 1990: 75)

The *Abeng* coalition and the newspaper it produced, also demonstrated the impact that Rastafari had made on the political, ideological and symbolic landscapes. The articles in the publication appealed to Black Nationalist sensibilities through the evocative, Rastafari-inspired grassroots language in which many of the messages were conveyed. This radical innovation found widespread appeal locally and internationally.

> It rapidly achieved a circulation of over 10,000 copies, reached a circulation of about 20,000 during the Gleaner58 strike of April-May 1969, was still circulating 14,000 copies in June 1968, lost two printing presses as a result of a fire and ceased production in October 1969. The Abeng was clearly associated with some groups which were revolutionary but was not a revolutionary paper. The Abeng provided the opportunity for serious revolutionaries to agitate for overthrow of the political system, but in retrospect also provided a vehicle that greatly assisted the PNP victory in the 1972 General Election.
>
> (Lacey, 1977: 59-60)

The combination of energies represented by the *Abeng* coalition demonstrates the dynamic possibilities opened up by combining various strands of radical sentiment in the construction of a discourse of resistance. Unfortunately, however, this tripartite political venture did not last long enough to pose a serious threat to the status quo. Nevertheless, while it lasted, the literary blowing of the *Abeng* had a profound impact on the growing ethos of political consciousness around the issue of African identity. Articulating the basic tenets of Black Power in one issue of the *Abeng*, Garvey's son, Marcus Garvey Junior, emphasised that it was erroneous to think that Blackness was valorised in Jamaica just because the country had a Black prime minister and a Black governor general. He underscored the low status of Blackness in the political arena by declaring further that

> we have a social and economic structure in which the White man is at the top, immediately below is the yellow man, then the brown man, and finally the Black man at the bottom. Where you have the Black mass submerged in inferiority, like the hidden portion of an iceberg, it is obvious that Black Power is not only relevant but an absolute necessity for such people.
>
> (*Abeng*, Vol. 1, No. 5, March 1, 1969: 3)

Garvey Jr.'s statement underscores the distinctions between the state/elite class and the African majority of the Jamaican population. However, his gender blindness is another indicator of the strong patriarchal force that runs through the resistance movement in Jamaica. He, too, failed to acknowledge that in the Jamaican society, poor Black women and children have always been the most disadvantaged. Thus, the glaring gender contradictions in the society were only superficially pursued by the *Abeng* coalition. Again, this oversight reflected the gender-blind perspective from which Black Power resistance was being enunciated.

While this gender myopia was conspicuous in the general outlook of the group, an unnamed writer did make a token attempt to address this lapse. In an article entitled 'Women', the writer declared that '*Abeng* stands for complete liberation of the female in our society.' This piece went on to detail the specific areas of sexuality, labour and civil liberties in which the rights of women should be recognised and protected (*Abeng*, Vol. 1, No. 5, March 1, 1969: 2). Despite this, Ken Post, who was a behind-the-scenes participant in this project, conceded that this lofty rhetoric was not matched by actual practice.

Figure 4.9: Rastafari Elder Sistren, Mama Farika Birhan, now a veteran journalist, poet and educator, was once the secretary and typesetter for the radical *Abeng* newspaper.

Veteran Rastafari journalist, poetess and author, Farika Birhan (formerly Norma Hamilton), who played pivotal roles in the production of the *Abeng* as typesetter and general gofer, was, nevertheless, rendered invisible by the gender blindness practised by the men who were central to the daily running of the newspaper. These activists included Dr. Robert Hill, Dr. George Beckford, Dennis Daley, Arnold 'Scree' Bertram, Dr. Rupert Lewis, Prof. C.Y. Thomas, Hugh Small and his brother Richard Small, Dennis Sloley, Dr. D.K. Duncan, and the brothers Paul and Carl Miller. There were other well-known persons, particularly from the Rastafari community, who were associated with the publication. Noted among these activists was Robin 'Jerry' Small, brother to Richard and Hugh, who was not as prominent as his siblings, perhaps because of his Rastafari identification. Other behind-the-scenes personalities were advisors, distributors, writers etc.

The gender myopia exhibited by the *Abeng* activists meant that Sister Farika's skills were totally overlooked by the male-dominated coalition, despite the fact that the government-owned Jamaica Information Service and later the *Gleaner* newspaper, concurrently employed her as a journalist. Farika recalls some of the harsher outcomes of her sojourn at *Abeng*.

> At one time, I was the only female in the inner circles of Abeng. I used to take the minutes at all their meetings and I was the typesetter. I also served as the anchorperson until Robert Hill and I shared that position. At first, I was the only paid person at the paper because I had to be there all day. I left my assignment at the Jamaica Information Service to typeset and stabilise the *Abeng*. When Robert Hill was put on pay, it split the very basic salary so I returned to working at JIS. Although I was a journalist, I was never asked to write an article or to do anything aside from typesetting the newspaper, answering the telephone etc.

> I once edited an article under the urging of Hugh Small. I put the headline that the choice between the two parties was like choosing between "Black Dawg and Monkey." It created an uproar with Scree Bertram. He accused me of not understanding the political weight of Socialism and his Marxist-Leninist theory etc. The opinion was divided among the cadres so I left off trying my hand at editing.

Among others, Arnold Bertram advised Ms. Birhan to 'stop writing [fiction] and [to] work for the revolution'. As she also recalls, they said, 'the revolution had no time for fiction writers' like herself. This veteran female journalist remembers that Dr. Hill and the 'rabid radicals' had many differences, and that she, herself, as a young activist, was also uncomfortable with the political tenor of the protagonists of the *Abeng* coalition.

> I questioned many things, especially Dr. Duncan's speeches and philosophy. I also noted that the group did not address class/colour/caste and women issues. I thought it was because I was a Black woman that my talents were not being appreciated by the group, especially when I noted what most of their wives looked like.

This testimony graphically demonstrates the extent to which the sociopolitical contradictions of the Jamaican society were enacted in the nexus of gender-identity-embodiment, which was played out in the patriarchal division of power and labour deployed in this 'radical' project. It is also interesting, as Lacey noted earlier, that in contra-distinction to the stated 'radical' objectives of African liberation by the *Abeng* federation, the PNP was able to hijack the energies stimulated by this resistance initiative for their own partisan politrickal gains. The electorate was seduced by the PNP's projection of race consciousness, embedded in the slogan of *Power to the People*. However, while purporting to support the Rastafari-inspired grassroots activists, the politicians, once they gained the allegiance of some of the more prominent activists, actually managed to dilute the resistance discourse.

CHAPTER 5

REBEL MUSIC:
REVOLUTIONARY OR REACTIONARY?

Wonder, should I sing another Love Song?
Till I truly understand what's going on
What, if we decide not to sing another line,
Would the people come together?
Stand in Love with one another?

~Beres Hammond & Marcia Griffiths
('Should I Sing' – Harmony House)

The Evolution of Rebel Music

Tourists come to Jamaica for more than just sex, sea and sun. They also come to the island for its world-renown Blue Mountain Coffee, its world-class marijuana and most of all for its world famous Reggae music. More than any other factor, it has been the music which has put Jamaica on the map as far as many foreigners are concerned. Hundreds of thousands of visitors have attended festivals like Reggae Sunsplash and Reggae Sumfest over the past few decades. Reggae Reggae music has also without doubt been primarily instrumental in widely disseminating *discourses of Rastafari resistance* and liberation/revolution to both local and international audiences. But, unfortunately, some forms of this rhythmic and melodious medium of cultural transmission also express reactionary male-centred messages which sexually objectify women. Thus, from the Black womanist viewpoint, even this popular music form needs to be critically and analytically deconstructed, in order to fully understand the varying social dynamics that may fuel this cultural expression.

The legendary Prince Buster is symbolic of the plethora of elements and binary oppositions that converge in the topic under discussion in this chapter. Prince Buster is one of the original rude boy/don archetype from 1960s downtown Kingston. While becoming a genuine superstar on the Jamaican sound system/music scene, Buster became friends with Mohammed Ali and was the first prominent Jamaican to embrace the US-based Nation of Islam in the 1960s and to publicly identify himself as a 'Black Muslim'. This was, of course, a highly controversial step to take in neo-colonial Jamaica, but in the Black Power days of the mid-1960s, it made Prince Buster a hero among the island's Black consciousness activists and other politically progressive or radical groups. Prince Buster clearly had made the transition from being a rude boy and a pawn of local political puppet masters into being a Black revolutionary with a broader worldview, even before the days when the music changed from rocksteady, which had evolved from the popular music genre of the early 1960s, ska, into Reggae. As a pro-Black community leader and businessman (he ran a record store), Buster was rubbing shoulders with all the major players in Jamaican politics, business and the music industry, and by the mid 1960s was already well on his way to permanently transcending his inner-city/ghetto origins.

In many ways, therefore, Black conscious lyrics and rebel music/message music in Jamaica started with people like Prince Buster. Songs like his ska classic, 'Judge Dread', put the rude boys on trial for their crimes against society. However, after being contractually betrayed and double-crossed in the mid-1960s by some of these same major political/music industry players in Jamaica, Buster's attempt to internationalise his Jamaican star status was blocked and his career began to stagnate.

This might explain why, by 1969 into 1970, the very same once conscious and progressive Prince Buster became equally infamous for the most popular song on the streets and in Dancehalls at the time (although it was deemed vulgar, banned and never played on the radio). That song, 'Wreck A Pum Pum', was the first big-time 'slackness' tune in Jamaica's modern music history. In its explicit sexuality and implied violence to the specific female organ of desire, the pum pum, it outdid even the Heptones' very suggestive lines 'I need a fat girl tonight…I'm in the mood' from their big rocksteady era hit, 'Fatty Fatty'. That degree of raw and open sexuality would not return to the fore in Jamaican music until the 1980s.

Although Jamaica's first two homegrown musical superstars, Prince Buster and Jimmy Cliff (star of both stage and screen), took the 'Black Muslim' route into message music, most of the younger singers/musicians who followed after took the more overtly African and pro-Garveyite avenue of Rastafari. Thus, Reggae Reggae lyrics as social commentary derive in large part from the messages that grew from Rastafari and earlier rude boy experiences, which are both cultural expressions that challenge prevailing structures of power.

Early signs of cultural self-identification and social commentary that were evident in ska became even more pronounced when the fast-paced ska tempo slowed down into the classic rocksteady heartbeat rhythms. The urban rebels of the day, the now legendary rude boys, still ruled the streets outside while the musicians were transforming the music inside the studios to reflect the outdoor mood of the times. Thus the rhythms and the lyrics of the protest music that was popular on the streets of Kingston during the 1960s, were in conscious rebellion against the neo-colonial status quo ruling the former slave plantation island. This is how and why late ska and early rocksteady era Jamaican music first acquired the nickname, *rebel music*.

The more upbeat Reggae tempo started taking centre stage from the slower, sensuous rhythms of rocksteady in 1968, with the production of 'Do the Reggay' by the Maytals, and the subsequent emergence of songs with a similar rhythm from studios like Beverly Records. As Reggae researcher Stephen Davis reminisced:

I once asked Toots Hibbert, lead singer of the Maytals and composer of "Do the Reggay," to tell me what the word meant, and his answer is as satisfactory a definition of Reggae as you're likely to get: "Reggae means comin' from the people, y'know? Like a everyday thing. Like from the ghetto. From majority. Everyday thing that people use like food, we just put music to it and make a dance out of it. Reggae means regular people who are suffering, and don't have what they want."

(Davis and Simon, 1992: 17)

In contrast, the more ideologically hard-core Rastafarian activist type musicians like Peter Tosh, Bob Marley, Culture, etc., proclaimed the real meaning of Reggae to be 'Music to the King' or 'Kings Music'. This interpretation gained increasing credence as more and more Rastafarians became singers....Or as more singers grew dreadlocks and/or became Rastafarians. In any event, by the early 1970s, the rude boy influence and urban rebelliousness of the rocksteady days were swiftly being replaced by a Rastafarian-influenced spiritually and politically revolutionary creative mindset with global significance.

When Bob Marley sang 'Rebel Music' in the mid-1970s on his *Natty Dread* album, this showed that the rude boy in him still remembered Reggae's origins in rocksteady and that he was still singing protest music. Hence that same *Natty Dread* album also contained protest lyrics like: 'I feel like bombing a church, now that I know that the preacher is lying' and 'Never let a politician grant you a favour, they will always want to control you for ever'. And Peter Tosh singing 'No matter where you come from, as long as you're a Black man, you're an African' illustrates that these cutting-edge Reggae singers had successfully transformed themselves from rebels into revolutionaries and had outgrown the ghetto streets of western Kingston, just like Prince Buster and Jimmy Cliff before them. By then, the natural evolution of Jamaican popular music from Rebel Music to Revolutionary Music (some say, Rasta Music) was complete.

The Schools of Reggae

Reggae has developed as a complex indigenous multi-faceted artistic form, which records real-time social events-in-motion in the philosophical, humorous, satirical, sentimental and, increasingly, more commercial and technically experimental voice of the people. The medium is the metaphoric environment that represents the most modern expressions of grassroots resistance in the current idiom of popular culture – music. This nexus among Rastafari resistance, the urban grassroots and the musical expression of popular culture, provides a powerful motif that signifies the innate capacity of the disadvantaged to come to voice. As 'social, political, and spiritual concepts entered the lyrics more and more...the Reggae musicians became Jamaica's prophets, social commentators, shamans' (Davis and Simon, 1992: 17).

For our purposes, Reggae music may be divided into four principal categories or schools. Firstly, there is traditional old school, roots & culture, message music-type Reggae. The rhythmic root of this kind of rub-a-dub Reggae is in the *heartbeat* pulse of the drum beat which is represented by the Nyahbinghi Order, one of the many Houses of Rastafari.[62] At Nyahbinghi ceremonial gatherings, the 'one-two' heartbeat rhythm of the drumming is the fundamental musical expression, which is complemented by the up-tempo beats of the lead *funde* and *akete* drums.[63]

Figure 5.1: Hon. Robert Nesta 'Bob' Marley, O.M., Rastafari Reggae musician. He is the quintessential embodiment of *we little but we tallawah*, which as I said before, means 'we might be small but we are strong'. This theme is vividly captured in extract from 'Small Axe', which follows.

The Wailers – Bob Marley, Peter Tosh and Bunny Wailer – are the archetypal folk heroes, and provide some of the most effective oral mechanisms to interrogate the political economy of identity in the Jamaican experience. They sang in the genre of *message music*, which is old school Reggae that is lyrically designed to raise consciousness and promote social change. The tensions that have historically existed between the haves and the have-nots because of the subordination and exploitation of the latter by the former are, therefore, pivotal to the revolutionary political messages of Bob Marley and the Wailers in both incarnations of the group.

Thus his 'Small Axe' composition captures the resistance consciousness embedded in his critique of domination through the experiential lens of subordinated subjects.

Small Axe

Why boastest thyself oh evil man
playing smart and not being clever
I say you're working iniquity
to achieve vanity

---

62 Although I did not elaborate on this differentiation in the previous discussion on Rastafari, it is important to note here that although Rastafari Mansions are unified by the recognition of the Divinity of His Imperial Majesty, Haile Selassie I, the Livity is characterised by internal ideological differences. This has resulted in the construction of a number of different Mansions or Houses, the most notable of which are the Nyabinghi Order, the Boboshanti Order and the Twelve Tribes of Israel. In addition, some Rastafari are members of the Ethiopian Orthodox Church while still others eschew organised groupings.

63 The emphasis on drums in the Rastafari livity demonstrates the extent to which the discourse of spiritual resistance and communication, which was nurtured on the plantations as a retention of an African ethos, has persisted to the present day.

but the goodness of Jah Jah
idureth forever
so if you are the big tree
we are the small axe
ready to cut you down, (well sharp)
to cut you down
These are the words of my master
Telling me this
no weak-heart shall prosper
and whosoever diggeth a pit
shall fall in it and
whosoever diggeth a pit
shall fall in it
shall bury in it

By utilising popular discourses as a tool of resistance, the Wailers, as the proverbially sharp *small axe*, affirmed the cultural integrity of Africans and the social legitimacy of the poor. They also epitomised the spirit of revolutionary resistance that has historically counteracted the *big tree* type power structures and discourses of domination. Bob Marley and the Wailers therefore represent the collective voice of the disproportionately dispossessed, subordinated and exploited African population, with an appeal, which as their songs demonstrate, also has universal application. Many other similar examples could be given using other old school, roots & culture singers and groups including Bob Andy, Prince Lincoln & the Royal Rasses, I. Jahman Levi, the Abyssinians, the Mighty Diamonds, Black Uhuru, Culture, Burning Spear, Third World and Steel Pulse, who are only a few of a host of other singers and players.

Next, there is the *lovers rock* school of Reggae, which characterises a branch of Jamaican roots music that has always had a prominent place on the Jamaican Hit Parade since the former ska and rocksteady Dancehall days until the present Reggae Dancehall era. Love songs, all the way from Jamaican re-makes of American R&B classics to indigenous and original compositions praising womanhood or manhood, have always received heavy airplay and exposure in Jamaica. Over the decades, such songs have been popularised by artistes including Slim Smith, Pat Kelly, Ken Boothe, Alton Ellis and his sister Hortense Ellis, Delroy Wilson, the Heptones, the Paragons, Marcia Griffiths, Judy Mowatt, Jennifer Lara, Dennis Brown, Gregory Isaacs, Sugar Minott, Beres Hammond, Pam Hall and J.C. Lodge in Jamaica, and by the likes of Winston Reedy, Aswad, Janet Kay and Sylvia Tella among others in England.

Songs falling into the category of *lovers rock*, tend to focus more on issues of sexuality, primarily from a romantic love perspective. *Lovers rock* is the primary school of Reggae music that captures the emotional and erotic experiences and fantasies of the gendered body, replaying them in sexy lyrics over the sensuously modulated beats that are characteristic of this genre. However, this discourse is set in a heterosexist framework and usually re-inscribes the stereotype of woman as the object of the male conquest and pleasure, thus becoming another potential mechanism for robbing women of their agency.

While, admittedly, celebrating the sensuality with which everyday life is infused, problematic themes of patriarchy are also embedded in these songs, in which men assume the texture of women's sexual 'needs'. This can also be read as the sexual objectification of women because men are in control of the medium of the Reggae music industry, as well as of many of the messages conveyed in this medium. In the following excerpt, John Holt reinforces the message of the masculinist values, which predominate in this musical mirror of the prevailing gender order in the wider society.

She Want it – John Holt

She want it she want it she want it
You better give her when she want it
....some say that she's a greedy girl,
*I just say she's a **needy** girl...*

As already noted, the political and sexual are intrinsically intertwined (MacKinnon, in Nicholson (ed.), 1997). So, while women in Jamaica do have and express sexual desires, these desires are contoured by patriarchal interpretations of sexual performance and expressed mainly through heterosexual codes.

Next we turn to *dub music*. As any of the many American and European enthusiasts can attest, *dub music* is a whole genre or school of **Reggae** by itself. A *dub* is instrumental music played with only occasional vocal interruptions. This hypnotic combination of a drum and bass foundation periodically overlaid with various other instruments and audio effects provides a rhythmic expression of self-affirmation and an insistent challenge to anything that is spiritually impure and materially unjust. In practice, the dub version was originally the flip side to the single (45 rpm) recording, or the extended instrumental bonus track on the 12-inch recording, on which elements of the artiste's voice emerged occasionally from the thick fog of the entrancing and hypnotic instrumental potpourri, to enhance the spell of the raw rhythms.

The legendary King Tubby and his trend-setting King Tubby's HiFi sound system have already gone down in Jamaican music history as the leading pioneer and innovator who turned mere B-side instrumental versions into full-fledged orchestrated dubs worthy of being plated (stamped) on metal discs rather than wax, hence, dub plate. The all-star Skatellites Big Band and the accomplished musicians of that era put out innumerable instrumental recordings. Then, coming out of the 1960s and the rocksteady days, a number of musicians like Jackie Mittoo and Ansel Collins also put out instrumental albums and singles, as did producers like Lee 'Scratch' Perry. But, by the time Reggae was in its full stride in the mid-1970s, audibly intriguing and sophisticated full-scale *dub* albums and productions were being engineered by King Tubby and his protégé Yabby U, the super creative and eccentric Lee Perry, and Niney The Observer, among many others.

The establishment of dub plates as an integral part of each sound system's musical arsenal gave more scope to the toasters to showcase their talents over the dub versions and to become high-profile DJs/MCs in the Dancehalls. This eventually led to the advent of 'specials', as in dub plates featuring name-brand DJs bigging up the particular sound system and crew for whom the premium recording is being made. *Dubs* and instrumentals also provided a perfect backdrop for another kind of artiste other than the usual singers and DJs – the *dub* poet.

Dub poetry first hit the streets of Kingston in the mid 1970s, and within ten years the art form had successfully established itself as one of the distinct and bona fide schools of roots Reggae music. *Dub poetry* consists of the enunciation and performance-presentation of poetry to the accompaniment of *dub music*, a unique combination of word, sound and power. Just like the works of American spoken-word trailblazers like Gil Scott Heron and The Last Poets, *dub poetry* is one of the most hard-hitting weapons of political and cultural resistance, both in its artistic form and lyrical content. This Jamaican form of word sound and power was originally popularised by artistes such as Oku Onuora, Mutabaruka, Malachi Smith (and Poets In Unity), Jean Breeze, Mikey Smith, as well as by Linton Kewsi Johnson and Benjamin Zephaniah in the UK. Later on, other strong poetical talents from Jamaica like Yasus Afari, Cherry Natural and Jabez have also gained prominence internationally.

Dancehall Reggae

As a medium of mass communication, Reggae has another major and immensely popular expression known as *Dancehall*, which alludes to the musical genre that spawned the DJ culture. Although the primary purpose of going to Dancehalls in the 1950s and 60s was for men and women to dance with the opposite sex and enjoy themselves, sometimes beer bottles were thrown and ratchet knives brandished, usually as men fought over women, and occasionally because of clashes between rival men from different areas. Originally, therefore, Dancehalls constituted the social spaces reserved for dancing, directed by the music selected by sound system experts as well as DJs, who were/are celebrated for their affirmation of the cultural legitimacy of the subordinated. Thus, the current new school manifestation of Dancehall has its antecedent in the *toasting* tradition, a practice which held sway from the late 1960s to the early 1970s. Artistes like King Stitt, U-Roy, I-Roy, Prince Jazzbo and Scotty were the leading protagonists of note in that early period.

> The dance hall is not so much a place as a state of mind, a spontaneous happening that occurs when hundreds of people get together in a building or yard or field or parking lot and tap into thousands of watts of raw Reggae power, crisp treble, strong midrange and a low end so potent that it feels like an earthquake.

> (Copyright © 1994 Thomas J. Weber: *Reggae Island: Jamaican Music in the Digital Age*).

The musical medium cum social space of Dancehall has long been the arena for using the voice as the instrument on which the words are played. So in fact, although it is seldom admitted, *Dancehall deejaying* or *toasting* gave birth to the rapping tradition, which found popularity in North America. The poor have utilised this medium to create their own stage, write their own scripts and perform their own social commentary dramas, through rapidly enunciated and cleverly concocted lyrics. The source materials for these compositions are the subjective experiences and viewpoints of the artistes, which, therefore, are best conceptualised as a tapestry into which the micro-practices of the poor are woven. During the 1970s the Reggae Dancehall DJs reflected the cultural consciousness of the times and DJs with generally positive sociopolitical messages like Big Youth, Brigadier Jerry, I-Roy, Michigan & Smiley, Super Cat, Cutty Ranks, Josey Wales and Charlie Chap-lin, all made their names.

The focus of Reggae music began changing (or was being changed) in the early 1980s concurrently with the passing of Reggae maestro Bob Marley. Soon after, the controversial albino DJ known colourfully as 'Yellowman' was being hailed as the new king of Dancehall Reggae. Yellowman was infamous for his penchant for slackness (sexually explicit) lyrics and he paved the way for the eventual crowning of Shabba 'Mr. Loverman' Ranks as king of Dancehall Reggae. During the 1980s and on into the 1990s, therefore, many disadvantaged inner-city youths came to see deejaying as an attractive way out of their situation and as a way to duplicate the fame achieved by Yellow and Shabba through their use of sexually oriented lyrics.

Interestingly, though, the advent of slackness lyrics was followed very quickly by a corresponding upsurge in musical gun-talk and violent lyrics. Clearly, sexual chauvinism and violence go hand in hand. Thus began the mass 'hustling' of the Reggae music business by one and all. In its current incarnation, therefore, the Dancehall provides the youth with an avenue through which they can *legally* express their creativity as well as achieve material advantage and upward social mobility. The oppositional ethos of the Dancehall space is hypnotic for many inner-city youth, who dream of *bussing it*, or succeeding as performers. The expression *bussing* it also means firing a gun, a coincidence of the significations of success, which are intricately and implicitly embedded in the inner-city *discourse* of masculinity and sexuality, and which are exhibited even overseas by the posses and the *yardies*.

However, the aspiration towards stardom and material wealth rarely come to fruition for the majority of talented young men. Economic success is even rarer for women. In addition, the emphasis on violence as a trope for expressing phallic identity shows the extent to which this particular construction of gender power has been imprinted on the cultural tableau. In fact, it is remarkable that a similar dialectic predominates in the *discourse of violence* that has developed in the inner-city experience.

> Overall, cultural celebration of Black male phallocentrism takes the form of commodifying these expressions of "cool" in ways that glamorise and seduce...Many Black men have a profound investment in the perpetuation and maintenance of rape culture...[T]hese brothers are not about to surrender their "dick-thing" masculinity.
>
> (hooks, 1994: 110)

The predominance of men in the music industry reflects the intersection of patriarchal interests, especially in this genre. Rastafari, the industry's production and distribution sector, as well as the rude boy elements whose identities are reflected in this artistic setting, all embody the misogynistic proclivity that permeates all social relations in the society. In addition, since most female artistes are also mothers, the primary responsibility for family support precludes the possibility for full-time artistic involvement for the majority of women in show business. Only a few women[64] can afford the luxury of investing the enormous sums of money and time required for pursuing this fantasy road to success.

Many of the new school Dancehall Reggae artistes also display an inordinate anxiety to prescribe 'normal' and 'taboo' sexual practices of the body, which reinforces heterosexuality while outlawing 'other' practices of embodied pleasure which do not conform to this norm. The binary opposition represented by this taboo is a typical characteristic of the practice of hegemonic masculinity in this environment (Connell, 1995).

See a batty boy him haffa run and go hide
Gunshot take off him headside
Fuck gal you live and if you fuck man you dead
Gun shot a take off him head.
Gay killer till me die
Haffi shoot a batty boy between the eye
No ask me why

'Elimination' by Ghetto Max

Carolyn Cooper agrees with critics of the violent male chauvinism in some of the songs produced in this genre. She argues that the DJ's obsession with 'slackness' in the 1980s is a metaphorical *double entendre* that treats women as sexual objects, an obsession for which the artistes have to be constantly interrogated. She also suggests, however, that their refusal to be bridled by the bit of political and socioeconomic domination reflects an oppositional feistiness that subverts the conservative order of structural power (Cooper, 1993: 141). This debate relates directly to the political sociology of Southside because one very culturally significant subtext of the embodied performances in the Dancehall environment is the recapturing of an African aesthetic.

This spirit of resistance was outlawed during slavery and has subsequently been reduced to something akin to 'social rubbish' by those who occupy the upper echelons of society. However, African traditions embodying resistance were subversively preserved in environments like the church, the workspace, the traditional wake and celebratory ceremonial gatherings. The call and response techniques of these rituals that were performed in the milieu of collective participation, constantly transformed the same spaces of subordination into sites of discursive resistance. Thus the DJ, who enunciates the discourses of the Dancehall, epitomises a master of this ceremonial practice of self-preservation.

> [T]he DJ's verbal art originates in an inclusivist neo-African folk aesthetic – a carnivalesque fusion of word, music and movement around the centre pole, and on the common ground of the dance floor. The DJ's original function of *livelin up* dance sessions made him a kind of praise poet for his sound system...

> (Cooper, 1993: 139)

---

64 Many of the women who succeed in the Reggae music business have often had a male patron with whom they also have a sexual relationship, which leaves this practice open to criticism as another mechanism of reinforcing stereotypes of dominant masculinity and subordinate femininity.

The Dancehall space thus provides hope for many inner-city youth that they can *buss it* or succeed in life through this exposition of their creative talents. The popular dances also enable the sound systems to compete against each other to output the heaviest session of heart-throbbing music and to develop the most outstanding reputations for people-centred entertainment.[65] The dance(hall) has, therefore, developed into an important psychosocial survival institution in the inner city. It appeals to the people's sense of self-esteem building and involves a chain of consumption and production enterprises – a whole industry – including body preparation[66] and the vending of food, drink and other consumer items. In this way, the dance provides a metaphoric mirror to reflect and refract the *daily discourses* of everyday life.

These days, violence and sexism converge in the lyrics of some popular DJs who suggest that these themes are more marketable than consciousness-raising lyrics.[67]

> [s]exuality...is not a discrete sphere of interaction or feeling or sensation or behaviour in which pre-existing social divisions may or may not be played out. It is a pervasive dimension of social life, one that permeates the whole, a dimension along which gender occurs and through which gender is socially constituted...*Dominance eroticised defines the imperatives of its masculinity, (while) submission eroticised defines its femininity.*
>
> (Mackinnon in Nicholson (ed.), 1997: 160, emphasis added)

Cooper says further that the DJ's preoccupation with slackness (i.e. sexually explicit lyrics degrading and exploiting womanhood), promotes a problematic view of gender power in an already patriarchal cultural context. But she also insists that the DJ's artistic creations should be regarded as metaphors of political opposition.

> [T]hough DJ slackness...is conceived as politically conservative, it can be seen to represent in part a radical, underground confrontation with the patriarchal gender ideology and the pious morality of fundamentalist Jamaican society. In its invariant coupling with Culture, Slackness is potentially a politics of subversion. For Slackness is not mere sexual looseness – though it certainly is that. Slackness is a metaphorical revolt against law and order; an undermining of consensual standards of decency. It is the antithesis of Culture.
>
> (Cooper, 1993: 141)

According to Cooper, while lambasting the artistes for promoting a less than complimentary view of womanhood, we should also consider that prevailing norms of class and race/colour hierarchies are also being undermined by the DJs. She notes that they defy bourgeois norms of morality and sexuality, and refuse to be imprisoned in a view of sexuality that does not include public discussions of this so-called private domain.

---

65 Stone Love, Kilimanjaro, Metromedia and Money Cologne are some of the outstanding Sound Systems.

66 People invariably treat themselves or are treated to complete outfits, hairdos, manicures and pedicures as part of the process of preparing for the dance.

67 Shabba Ranks is a noted example of an artiste expressing this sentiment.

Women as Dancehall DJs

As we have seen, the Reggae Dancehall idiom overflows with various binary oppositions and stark contradictions. Nowhere is this truer than as it relates to the women of today's Dancehall Reggae. The role of DJ/toaster on a sound system in a Dancehall, or recording in a studio, was an almost exclusive domain for men for years before the arrival in the mid-1980s of the most commercially successful crew of Dancehall DJ – the Shang Records crew that included Shabba Ranks, Mad Cobra and the young and dynamically vivacious Patra, who would be crowned if only briefly as 'Queen of the Pack'. Patra, as queen of Reggae/Dancehall enjoyed frequent appearances on MTV and VH1 and seemed well on her way to success in her own right irrespective of Shabba, before she suddenly disappeared from the entertainment business in the early 1990s. Nevertheless, before leaving the scene, Patra did open the door and became a prototype of the kind of success that is now possible for female Reggae/Dancehall artistes.

Other female DJs of the roots and culture genre like Sister Nancy, Lady G, Angie Angel and especially Sister Carol, have made names for themselves in the business as old-school-type DJs. But the old and entrenched male/female stereotypes did not start turning on their heads until the 1990s advent of the new-school-type of female Dancehall DJs like Shelly Thunder, who started turning patriarchal norms around and created waves by singing that 'sometimes a man fi get kuff' (i.e. sometimes a man should be slapped in the head). But once again, even these positive examples of independent agency by such female DJs are clearly fraught with contradictions and ironic reinforcements of the already prevailing violence-prone gender order.

That applies to another controversial female DJ, Tanya Stephens, who has always been a vocal supporter of women's rights, and who picked up in a similarly assertive vein to Shelly Thunder. However, Tanya's outspokenness against the attitude of some men does not mean that she is anti-man. Although she does make the seemingly chauvinistic statement in the track of the same name, that 'Man Fi Rule', she is equally adamant that 'No fool nah go rule Tanya'. Stephens first became known in Jamaican Dancehall circles for her suggestive late '90s hits 'Yuh Nuh Ready (Fi Dis Yet)', 'Goggle and Handle The Ride', songs that poked fun at the sexual inadequacies of macho men. In 2003, Tanya took the Dancehall world by storm with the underground hit, 'It's A Pity', promoted as a provocative anthem for a lust-driven society.

These days, Tanya Stephens, reportedly, says she thinks of herself more as a singer/ songwriter and producer rather than just as a mere female Dancehall DJ, and she has expressed her desire to break away from the pervasive sexual themes associated with Dancehall/Reggae music. Her 2004 album *Gangsta Blues* was one of the first releases on her Tarantula Records production label. The album chronicles the travails of a thinking woman in a male-dominated culture and in the male-dominated genre of Dancehall/Reggae, where the female viewpoint is seldom heard.

Ce'Cile is another of the few women in the Dancehall business who has transformed herself from being just a DJ/performer into a respected songwriter and producer. She first entered the Dancehall scene in the mid-1990s with the single 'Girls Fi Get Love' and became a regular fixture after that. Her biggest hit, 'Changez', made fun of her male Dancehall peers and gave reasons why she would not make love to any of them. Another of her singles with sexual undertones, 'Can U Do Di Wuk' along with 2004 Reggae Grammy winner Sean Paul, enjoyed a wave of popularity after being included on Paul's Grammy winning album *Dutty Rock*. And yet another of Ce'Cile's singles, 'Do It To Me', set tongues wagging (pun unintended) in Jamaican social circles because it glorifies a particular sexual act that is severely criticised and restricted by popular discourse.

By far the most successful and the most controversial of all the female Dancehall DJs is Marion Hall, aka Lady Saw, who presents another case study in cultural contradictions. Lady Saw is the undisputed diva of Dancehall and has a visually explicit and raunchy stage show and memorably/unforgettably vulgar lyrics, which the masses of ordinary Jamaicans clearly love. To many observers, it is a shame how many women in Dancehall get exploited as sex objects. But, rather than stumble into that trap, Lady Saw jumped in headfirst, lustily turning the tables on the self-proclaimed 'bedroom bullies'. When Saw gets raw, as is usual, as on her sure-shot crowd pleaser 'Stab Out The Meat', she can stand with any of the X-rated male DJs from General Echo to Yellowman to Shabba. So although slackness is hardly her only mode, her sexual frankness and verbal support of the prevailing heterosexual status quo does get results and wins her fans with both the men and, most tellingly, with the women too.

Although she ranked consistently as Dancehall's top female DJ for many years, Saw continually refused to be typecast as just a Dancehall artist. Her *Give Me The Reason* album includes credible country singing and she has dabbled in soca and rap, and even gospel. But these talents are all eclipsed by the performance she puts on in her ragamuffin mode with the hardcore tracks like 'Back Shot', 'Good Wuk', 'Hice It Up' and 'No Long Talking'. She has been quoted as saying 'I don't care about people who love to talk negative about me being lewd. I want to know if I see you jumping and screaming.'

Over the years, Lady Saw has run into trouble and has been banned from events like Reggae Sunsplash and Reggae Sumfest, due to her heavily X-rated material, even though equally slack male artistes continue to get stage time and airplay. Her solution for such censorship and setbacks has been writing songs that deal with the hypocritical double standards. Paradoxically, Saw's uncompromising lyrics are both her damnation and her salvation. Saw tells many social truths that Dancehall's testosterone dons typically overlook. But she does it in a provocative way that severely irks the sensibilities of the more 'proper' segments of society. And so they love to hate her. Nevertheless, she has more than earned her stripes in the male-dominated field of Dancehall, using her sharp wit, great charm and unique looks. She has been described as 'a male fantasy and a female champion'. Deliberately playing to the patriarchal whims and sexual fancies (fantasies) of the prevailing gender order has made Lady Saw a star and a financially independent woman. But the question remains: is she the best example and role model for women seeking true liberation from the dominant hegemonic masculinities that contour their lives?

Clearly, Lady Saw is herself a walking enigma. As Marion Hall, she is a quiet woman from St. Mary who initially tried to be a culture DJ, but received no props and no ray

ray from critical Jamaican music fans. But when she transformed herself into a loud, catty and sensually provocative performer with sexually explicit lyrics, her career took off like a rocket and there has been no looking back for her ever since. So strange and fictional as it may seem, the fact remains that today, Lady Saw, with all her alleged outrageousness and vulgarity, is the most commercially and artistically successful female DJ ever to rise in Dancehall music. In many ways, therefore, and especially in her verbal discourse, body language and stage act, Lady Saw has come to represent the voice of the inner-city and working-class Black woman.

What exactly Lady Saw's stage persona says about ordinary Black women in Jamaica is debatable. During a Reggae Sunsplash Festival appearance in the early 1980s, Yellowman asked the audience what they wanted to hear, culture or slackness. The crowd, especially the young females, roared back the reply: 'slackness!' Lady Saw has come to embody that slackness on stage and her teenaged, female fans in the audience have mimicked her sexualised body language to the extreme and without any shame. These days, therefore, even community street dances like the popular Passa Passa in West Kingston, often feature lewd and lascivious dance moves by the young girls who frequent such events in their see-through outfits. With photographers and video cameramen catching the action live from all angles, panty-less females gyrate and spin on their heads with their naked crotches spread wide open and their legs in the air. Or they may hike up already skimpy skirts to reveal their nude genitalia to the glare of video camera lights. It's like 'girls gone wild', Jamaican style.

In the meantime, the rise and success of female Dancehall DJs like Lady Saw, Ce'Cile and Tanya Stephens, as well as the economic and social motivation of the bashment girls of the Dancehall/street dance, are both subjects that are worthy of future study.

Music and Hegemonic Masculinity

Despite the international stature of veteran female singers like Rita Marley, Marcia Griffiths and Judy Mowatt and the recent progress of the Dancehall divas, the lyrical emphases placed on slackness, the *bigging up the status of the gunmen* and the censoring of homosexuality,[68] all emphasise hegemonic masculinity as the dominant discourse of power in the subaltern environment. Of course, such hegemonic masculinity prevails in an asymmetrical relationship to subordinate femininity. As Connell emphasises, these representations of embodied power are dynamic and therefore, adjust to the historical moments of their production as necessary. Therefore, 'to recognise masculinity and femininity as historical…is not to suggest they are flimsy or trivial. It is to locate them firmly in the world of social agency' (Connell, 1995: 81-82).

While, admittedly, posing a tremendous challenge to bourgeois discourses of power, some of the DJs and musical rude boys still represent a clear and present danger to

---

68   The common lyrical practice of the DJs in many dances that I have attended, is to command the audience to 'show the gun fingers or light up the lighters' as a signal of agreement to misogynistic discourses that are amplified with impunity in this space. There is, invariably, wholehearted compliance with this command, reflecting either fear of censorship for refraining from participating in this discourse or else, widespread complicity (Connell, 1995: 79) as a strategy of self-preservation from the violence of the dominant gender order.

the agency of those subjects in the immediate community who do not conform to the norms of embodiment that they prescribe. In fact, the DJs appear to be unconscious of the extent to which they actually reinforce the same dominant structures of power which simultaneously serve to marginalise them.

Some DJs perform as the artistic extensions of the street-wise rude boys, bigging up the status of the gunman in the lyrics of many songs. To be a *top shotter* or gunman is a vaunted self-concept in the genre of today's Dancehall Reggae music. Sexuality is another strong theme. For commercial and cultural reasons, women's bodies are the inscription sites for this emphasis. In 'Girls Wine' for example, Shabba Ranks commands women to '*wine*' for the voyeuristic pleasure of males like himself.

Girls Wine

Shabba style…make world o girls wine
All the girls must can wine to man at all time
Girls, you can't wine? You losing down the line
I'm the girl's psychiatrist…hear this now!
You better can wine, wine,
American girls come wine, wine
English girls come wine, wine
Canadian girls come wine wine
Jamaican girls can wine wine
Remember this? Big like P!
Remember this? Holler for the P!
Jump around if you man can wU.K. (work)
Remember this? A man want it,
make him pay down on it…
Wine up your body…
let them know that you're full up of winery…
Remember this? Hard and stiff
Remember this? Bad man a wicked in bed
Remember, it can't done, it can't done
Oh yes, Shabba Ranks make the girls have fun
Remember this? The girls are live blankets…
All woman! Wine up your body
Make your man know that you hold him steady…

The DJ names his many hit tunes which portray sex as a commodity for which women should unapologetically demand payment. Their wining[69] or displays of simulated sexual prowess, enacted through exaggerated gyrations of the pelvis, is the magical quality that arouses male attention. Men, who dominate the music industry,[70]

---

69   This theme will recur when I analyse the traditional wake as a discourse of resistance at the end of this chapter.

70   The prevalence of men in this arena is due to the fact that records cost a great deal of money to produce, and since women are more preoccupied with household responsibilities, their capacity to explore their

strategically use the medium of Dancehall music to lyrically exploit women's sexuality in order to gain materially. The *discourse of violence*, which pervades the inner-city environment, is also implicated in the norms that are reinforced by the popular culture. These regulations ensure that 'male power takes the form of what men as a gender want sexually, which centres on power itself, as socially defined' (Mackinnon in Nicholson (ed.), 1997: 161).

The diabolical question is whether the 'wining' women are being submissive and should the men be seen as oppressors? Given their meagre resources, the women can also be seen to be exercising some degree of agency. Carolyn Cooper acknowledges that the DJ's preoccupation with slackness, which treats women as sexual objects,[71] promotes a problematic view of gender power in a context that is marked by sharp phallocratic ideological and practical power mechanisms.

On the other hand, however, as noted before, Cooper also insists that the DJ's artistic creations should be regarded as metaphors of political opposition. As Cooper contends, the prevailing norms of class and race/colour hierarchies are also being undermined by the DJ's defiance of bourgeois norms of morality and sexuality. By encouraging women to join him in an international rhapsody of a sexualised (i.e. *wining*) public dance, Shabba Ranks refuses to be confined to binary restraints, which imprison discussions of sexuality to the private domain.

In another song, 'Roots and Culture', Shabba Ranks tries to justify his penchant for slackness or treating women as sexual objects by suggesting that in the competitive world of the music business, this is the popular genre of lyrical delivery which ensures commercial success for the usually destitute artiste. Shabba also declares that the masculinist power that he symbolically wields over women's bodies is compensated for by the fact that he also expresses himself in terms of cultural consciousness. This enunciation of resistance bears out Cooper's point that one should not homogenise the DJs. Their strategic discourses of cultural dissonance are specific to a reading of embodiment that is fundamentally different from bourgeois representations of the body.

Roots and Culture

United we stand and divided we fall,
Black man know yourself before your back is against the wall
A so you stay! You are only thinking one way
But I'm not a one-way deejay...
Shabba Ranking, Reggae people's calling out,
People from east, west, north and south
Say, all the emcees with the nasty mouths, they feel that
it's only slackness I can talk about
I know my roots and culture

talents in this realm is limited. However, I refer to productions by women artists elsewhere.

71   This practice, as Mackinnon (1997) argues, gives the pornography industry its raison d'être and promotes rape as a practice of gender power.

Who is the root? Robert Nesta
And Bunny Wailer follow after
It is music me charged for
Look how the world a suffer!
What have Black people under pressure!
Some talk this and some talk that
That everything from Shabba's mouth is slack
I love roots and reality straight to the max
Because I am a heartical ilabash
I love my roots and culture, to teach all the youngsters
Honour your mother and father,
So that your days will be longer…
A lot of them are fighting against slackness lyrics
But you have to please John Public
When you're dealing with the reggae music
Shabba Ranking you're a murderer
And it's music you're charged for
Got to be a musical ambassador
I'm going to teach all the youngsters
Some are bawling that they want culture
And they want people to be vulgar
I'd rather stick to my culture
Than to be a dirty character…
It's a new page I've turned over
teach them just like a teacher
just listen to me, like a pastor

Shabba Ranks embodies the dual DJ identity – the preacher and the bad man. It is Shabba as the pastor/teacher who sets the agenda for representations of popular culture, and also the real-man-as-bad-man persona. Although undoubtedly providing the means of countervailing the harshness of social disadvantages, we also have to question the ways in which the street-wise artists have strengthened (violent) masculinist power. Other artistes try to inspire the youth to avoid the badness so they don't have to tangle with the police, as the number of police killings in the inner city is so dangerously high. Shaggy, another very popular international Reggae artist, musically explains this dilemma in the following song.

John Doe

Let's do this one positive!
This one goes out to the misled
to preserve all the youths of tomorrow
Cause it's time to stop the unnecessary bloodshed
The life of a gangster is not sweet
I'm coming to you straight from the streets
This could be a story about anybody
But let's call him John Doe

Chorus
A Rude boy get Murder!
Cops were quicker on the draw
Another youth get Murder!
A victim of the law
A Rude boy get Murder!
(Voices make the blum! blum! Sound of gunshots)
Cops were quicker on the draw
Another youth get Murder!
A victim of the law

Johnny was wicked ragamuffin and raw
Pulled off a robbery but the cops he never saw
He got surrounded and they crushed him like a straw
John Doe went out like that!

(Chorus)

He heard them coming but he didn't get to flee
Wanted by the cops was living like a refugee
Do no evil think no evil try it and you will see
Bad boy and lawman don't 'gree

(Chorus)

Wicked around the microphone
That's where I get my vibes
Try to hustle and make a dollar
Ain't got no nine to five
Watching my back and going home
And trying to stay alive
Got to strive, got to strive got to strive

Shaggy emphasises the social anonymity of the real-man-bad-man and the desensitisation of the wider society to the monotonous regularity with which they are murdered. This syndrome of abandonment is typical of what takes place in similar communities the world over, the shantytowns of Brazil being a case in point.

> It is the anonymity and the routinisation of it all that strikes the naïve reader as so terrifying. Who are all these desaparecidos – the unknown and the "disappeared" – both the poor souls with plucked eyes and exposed mutilated genitals lying in a ditch and those unidentifiable men in uniform standing over the ditches with guns in their hands? It is the contradiction of wartime crimes against ordinary peacetime citizens that is so appalling... After the fall, after the aberration, we expect a return to the normative, to peacetime sobriety, to notions of civil society, human rights, the sanctity of the person...habeas corpus, and the inalienable rights to the ownership of one's body.
>
> (Scheper-Hughes, 1992: 219)

Thus, as they are trained to be brutal, it is an obvious non sequitur to expect the security forces not to display that vicious side of their sociopolitical construction. Shaggy's song is an allegory for the rude boys' encounters with the security forces. These clashes tell us all too clearly that, historically, the security forces have represented the interests of the upper class while by and large, acting aggressively against the mass of the population. When security personnel come upon suspected criminals – who are really doing what they think they have to do under their disadvantaged circumstances – empathy is not usually the first reaction.

> Here we can begin to see the workings of a hegemonic discourse on criminality/deviance/marginality and on the "appropriateness" of police and state violence in which all segments of the population participate and to which they acquiesce, often contrary to their own class or race interests.

(Scheper-Hughes, 1992: 225)

Hence the urgency of Shaggy's appeal to the youth to seek a different means of claiming selfhood other than picking up the gun. He recognises however, that many of the youth are sucked into the vortex of this masculinist survival and power discourse, because they, too, want to personify the power of the *wicked* or powerful man. Shaggy suggests instead that they should explore *striving* through music or some other creative endeavour, rather than pursuing the destructive pathways of violence, which are inevitably, and literally, dead ends.

The Wake as a Discourse of Resistance

The embroiled representations of embodiment are clearly enunciated in the *wake*, an institution that as applied in Southside, acts as a system of psychosocial reinforcement, albeit with strong patriarchal elements.

> It is really to cheer up the bereaved families that I do it. Sometimes I have to try and help out at three wakes for a night. Almost every day people are dying. If they don't die of natural cause, they are killed. It has become a really violent community with all the shooting, raping and robbing and things like that. Nowadays, the young people have no manners at all to elder people. When I was young, we had to go to Sunday school, YMCA youth club and square dance. When you asked a young lady for a dance, you said 'please', and 'thank you' when you take her back to the position where she was. You don't see anything like that nowadays.

Uncle Reff, 61, Shepherd of the Wake

The *wake* is enacted for specific periods after a person dies.[72] As an institution of both rural and urban life, demonstrating strong African retentions, the wake not only encodes meanings of spiritual resistance but also provides a psychosocial coping

---

72 This practice has African roots, as evidenced by the call-and-response patterns of communication in the singing, the rhythmic dance movements, the heavy reliance on the drum and other musical instruments such as bottles, graters, tambourines etc. The subtext of the practice is the belief that the spirit of the deceased will not rest if a 'singing' does not take place for specified periods. This belief is related to the African cosmological outlook of a unity among past, present and future. However, it also has absorbed Christian influences, as indicated by the use of the *Sankey* hymnbook.

mechanism for people who experience the death of loved ones. It is also a space of socialisation; in addition to seeing family members and friends who only come together on such occasions, eating fried fish and harddough bread, drinking coffee and chocolate tea, drinking alcoholic beverages and smoking marijuana, are some of the highly anticipated benefits of participation.

To have a *good singing* is even more important. Harmonising is therefore a key aspect of the renditions and if the singing is off-key it has to be corrected. At the end, there is a sense of satisfaction if the ritual had gone on until the wee hours of morning. The departed soul should have been satisfied at the outpouring of energy, which would have sustained the singing mourners throughout the night. This demonstrates the fact that micro-practices of power and the subjugated knowledges of the subordinated do indeed extend into the realms of the metaphysical and spiritual, allowing for the transcending of materially determined norms of structural power.

The wake, symbolically, shows that power is *produced* rather than possessed and that power is best understood as emanating from the micro-levels of society upwards, rather than as only being applied in a hierarchical direction from top to bottom. This tradition – the wake – might have died out as a cultural practice if it was not for the pervasiveness of violent deaths.

Figure 5.2: I share a pleasant moment with Uncle Reff, the Shepherd who leads the traditional wake, which is a ritual that is performed when someone dies. The individual Shepherd and the performance combine cultural, linguistic and symbolic capital and act as a social institution of community cooperation. This is ironic since it also underscores the tragic frequency of violent deaths.

According to Uncle Reff, the Shepherd of the wake, the persistence of this tradition in an urban setting[73] speaks to the dimensions of the crisis that it reflects. He thinks that what he is doing is 'strong', since the area has been systematically weakened by

73   This practice is enacted in other communities but the scale on which it is performed in Southside seems unique.

the lack of respect displayed by some of the youth through the perpetuation of the discourse of violence. As he emphasised,

> in the sixties was when the behaviour started to change, with the manners and the young people especially. I don't really like the behaviour of the people to tell you the truth. And I would like the violence to change. Everybody is cross, everybody wants to win. They want to win in the conversation or anything at all that you are having. Nobody backs down. I don't have a solution to the behaviour of these young people. The worst thing is the uncalled-for killings. Uncalled for because they are rebelling without a cause.[74] You ask them to tell you what they are fighting for and they don't know why. Nobody knows why. They just get up and kill one another for no special reason. You wake up to gunshots every day.

People die so frequently in Southside, as Uncle Reff told me, that the ceremonies have been made into an almost professional preoccupation for at least 40 people in his group and many more people in the community at large. The wake reflects the main agenda that is observed for nine nights[75] when someone dies. As I will show, the wake may be seen as a counter-discourse of resistance, notwithstanding its internal gender power contradictions.

The Shepherd noted that he usually has a singing on the third night after the deceased passes on; the other major event is the nine-night, the singing that is held nine nights after the death. If the body stays much longer, a singing is held on the eve of the burial and if required, also on the fortieth night after the date of death.

The linguistic content of the songs make repeated references to values of sexuality and gendered power and therefore justify an in-depth exploration of this experience. This focus is informed by my earlier explanation of body language, and the ways in which what is said about the body constitutes identities and social practices, even as it reflects social reality. The songs also speak to the longevity of the spiritual power of the dead, as well as to a gender differentiation in the rituals that are performed for female or male deceased.

The enactment of the wake is also marked by practices of gender and age power as the Shepherd explained

> I have four secretaries around the table to do the readings and to track the songs. On the table I require a glass of plain tap water. This is a traditional emblem of purification. Then you have one spoon of sugar and one spoon of salt; that is to just clear your throat. I operate with a whistle as a means of controlling the people, to stop the singing or if I have an important announcement to make.

Uncle Reff performs the role of the griot who, in African tradition, preserves the memories and therefore the knowledge of intergenerational experiences.

74 This view supports analyses from Molly, Clive and Heights Man.
75 As Uncle Reff elaborated, the nine-night is also extended to longer periods, which have special significance.

Clearly, disadvantaged people have to devise alternative discourses to the harsh reality of everyday life. This capability prevents people who have been exposed to systematised forms of trauma, from all becoming mental-health cases. This capacity for maintaining *sanity* also reflects the madness of the contradictory construction of their identities and social realities. This existential/material dilemma is eloquently captured in the Paul Lawrence Dunbar poem entitled 'We wear the Mask':[76]

We wear the mask that grins and lies,
It hides our cheeks and shades our eyes, –
This debt we pay to human guile;
With torn and bleeding hearts we smile
And mouth with myriad subtleties.
Why should the world be over-wise
In counting all our tears and smiles
Nay, let them only see us, while
We wear the mask.

We smile, but, O great Christ, our cries
To thee from tortured souls arise.
We sing, but oh the clay is vile
Beneath our feet, and long the mile;
But let the world dream otherwise,
We wear the mask

Although Winston James argues that among migrants to the US, Jamaicans were most accustomed to 'frontal struggles and open modes of encounter with Whites' (1998: 114), he also concedes that

> [i]t is not that they never wore masks; they did, as does everyone at one time or another...The difference between the migrants and their Afro-American counterparts was that in the Caribbean, at least in the post-emancipation period, they had not the need to wear the racial mask with the same degree of frequency and facility that Black people in America did.

> (James, 1998: 114)

However, James' definition of 'racial' as a Black/White binary, fails to acknowledge the nuances of racism in Jamaica, which is applied along a continuum of colour. On the other hand, while admitting that, 'the Caribbean does not constitute a homogeneous whole' (James, 1998: 114), he ends up presenting a homogenised perspective on the types of resistance enacted in various social spaces in the region and within countries.

James therefore fails to account for the variation in forms of struggle in which the subordinated sector of the population in Jamaica have been engaged. Further, by claiming a safe space in which to come to voice (Collins, 1990), subordinate subjects also circumvent the super-structural frameworks of domination. So, although it is true that these everyday performances might only provide temporary relief from constant

---

76 Dunbar (1872-1906), q. in James (1998: 113-14).

disadvantage, exercising agency in their own terms of reference certainly provides significant meaning at the ground level. This process of knowledge production is also directly linked to the Black feminist standpoint. As Patricia Hill Collins (1990: 34) affirms in this regard, 'the primary responsibility for defining one's own reality lies with the people who live that reality, who actually have those experiences'.

The language and practices inherent to the wake substantiate patriarchally defined binary oppositions. However, actors in this domain of social exclusion also demonstrate how gender norms are reshaped to reflect the ongoing production of resistance strategies. Uncle Reff said that both hymns and choruses are important texts for expressing comfort for the bereaved who experience the loss of loved ones with alarming frequency in the inner-city context. He sang a popular chorus, which I will unpack for the gender power discourses that are embedded in the lyrics.

When gal[77] lives at her mother-in-law's yard oh!
all the washing, she has to do it
When gal lives at her mother-in-law's yard oh
All the scrubbing she has to do it

Come, come, come and let us reason,
Reason, reason
Come, come, coffee and let us reason, reason
Thus saith the Lord
When boy lives at his girlfriend's yard oh
All the bills he has to pay them
When boy lives at his girlfriend's yard oh
All the bills he has to pay.
He said, better days are coming by and by
Better days are coming, in the sky,
Sorrow will be over; joy will come at last, better
Days are coming, by and by.

When gal lives at her boyfriend's yard o
All the wining[78] she has to do it
When a gal lives at her boyfriend yard o
All the wining she has to do it.

The messages embedded in this song reflect the predominance of patriarchy in the culture generally and specifically in relation to roles that women and men are expected to perform in the household. If a woman enters a man's house, she is obliged to have *all of the sex* (wining) desired and demanded by the male. Her domestic capabilities are also conscripted as part of this bargain. Thus

---

77 A woman is commonly referred to derogatorily as a gal, whereas it is intolerable to refer to a man by the equally derogatory reference, boy.

78 Wining here describes movements and rotations of the hips indulged in during sexual intercourse.

[h]ierarchic sexuality...derive[s] from the domination of sexual labour-power, not in some abstract way but in the material relation of bodies... Men's control of such sexual labour-power produces women as adjuncts of men, in relationships and in language.

(Hearn, 1987: 91)

The power dramaturgy that women and men enact in Southside also extends to the traditional tensions that exist between mothers- and daughters-in-law, which are expressed in Jamaican society as much as anywhere else in the world. In the song, the addition of the line 'Thus saith the Lord' in reference to the subservient domestic role that woman should play in relation to the mother-in law, emphasises the ways in which the institution of religiosity is invoked to reinforce women's oppression and exploitation. Again, this demonstrates the influence of institutional discourses on the female body, discourses which work to produce prescriptive notions of identity.

It should be very clear by now that patriarchy not only defines masculinities in relation to femininities, but also impinges on definitions of femininities *per se*. Thus, women often relate to each other in ways that support the prevailing gender hierarchies across class categories. As the song suggests, the mother-in-law has a stake in collaborating with her son to appropriate the quiescent daughter-in-law's labour within the household. Ironically, she enhances her status as matriarch by strategically capitulating to the patriarchal norm. This paradox suggests that power arrangements are not fixed, but can indeed be changed in much the same manner as they were constructed in the first place.

Since she is younger, the daughter-in-law submits; she does not want to upset her partner. She also has to be strategic with revealing her true feelings because she needs the financial support he can provide. If she was truly independent, she would not have to be caught in such a power trap (Holton, 1992: 172). When the equation is reversed and, as the song says, the man is living in the woman's house, he has to demonstrate appropriate masculinity by paying the bills. Women sometimes strategically negotiate with the patriarchal construction of gender relationships because,

[t]hese patriarchal bargains exert a powerful influence on the shaping of women's gendered subjectivity and determine the nature of gender ideology in different contexts. Moreover, patriarchal bargains are not timeless or immutable entities, but are susceptible to historical transformations that open up new areas of struggle and renegotiation of the relations between women and men.

(Kandiyoti, in Lorber and Farrell (eds.), 1991: 104)

Thus, in the male dominated space of the wake, 76–year-old Marva Coombs has persevered as a secretary in Uncle Reff's crew. Ms. Coombs assertively claims the role of tracker of the Sankey,[79] a task she performed even without the aid of eyeglasses and in defiance of the disapproval of some men in this space. Yet she also embodies the paradoxical fact that such autonomy is not a panacea.

---

79 This role refers to the person who calls out the lines from the hymnbook, which enables the gathering to respond in a chorus.

CHAPTER 6

DYING FOR A PIECE OF THE PIE

So I returned, and considered all the oppressions that are done under the sun; and, behold, the tears of such as were oppressed, and they had no comforter; and on the side of the oppressors there was power, but they had no comforter. Wherefore I praised the dead who are already dead more than the living who are yet alive. Yea, better is he (sic) than both they who hath not yet been, who hath not yet seen the evil work that is done under the sun.

(Ecclesiastes 4: 1-3, Scofield Reference Bible, 1967:698)

[I]f you want to get your outcasts out of sight, first you need a ghetto and then you need a prison to take the pressure off the ghetto. The fact that it does not make financial sense is not the point. Short-term terror and revulsion are more powerful than long-term wisdom or self-interest. That's why corrections is one of the few growth industries in New York City right now.

(Kozol, 1995: 142)

You are programmed to function a certain way, due to the system, due to needs and wants, and the fact that if you don't go along with the programme you will get wasted.[80] It's as if you are living in prison right in your community.

(Benjie, 19, former resident)

Defining the Pie

The 'pie' we are referring to here represents decent housing, sustained employment, social services and other community amenities. Politicians, who control the restricted access to these scarce resources, are usually trying to keep as many slices of the economic pie to themselves as they can. Periodically, crumbs from the pie are thrown grudgingly into poor communities and for which residents are programmed to compete. Those who prove themselves to be the most loyal, or the most mercenary, are rewarded with more and bigger crumbs. It is a hard if not impossible choice: many face dying without access to any of the pie, or risk dying trying to get a slice.[81]

---

80 This expression, which means to be killed, indicates the tenuousness of people's hold on life, in both material and symbolic terms of reference.

81 It is no accident of language that on the streets, 'to eat a man's food' means 'to kill someone'.

Enculturing Political Clientilism

One of the four assumptions on which this participatory research is based is that 'because of the political economy of Jamaica, people living in the so-called *ghetto* or inner-city areas of Kingston, have been constructed in the context of a discourse of violence, which is gendered in its myriad expressions.' This is proposition one. The research data provided adequate evidence to substantiate this proposition. The residents of Southside see poverty (and its attendant features) and violence (and its multiplier effects) as fundamental problems in their lives. The deliberate, politically motivated prolonging of the existing complex combination of disadvantages in the inner city, has led to deep psychosocial trauma for residents. This lifestyle is what we mean by a culture of political clientilism, and such a culture is now entrenched and endemic to Jamaican inner-city communities.

The political powers-that-be have a vested interest in enculturing and encouraging residents to become and remain dependent clients of their patronage. Popular discourses in the wider society blame the self-same victims in the inner city for the conditions of degradation that are their unfortunate lot in life.

Thus, any project of social transformation has to consider that the wounds are deep and might take as long a time to heal as they took to be inflicted. And, although the more serious side effects of this painful situation are being felt in the present, their roots are deeply embedded in the past. The positive view to take, however, is that because structures of power are social constructions, as Jacques Derrida suggests, they can also change and be changed.

> Indeed, the very idea of historical inevitability is anathema to the deconstructive programme...Derrida places us firmly in the realm of practice, telling us that this is where we are now, that we as social subjects are supports of the very structures that seem to repress.

(Boyne, 1990: 128-129)

When people in Southside talk about the causes of the current crisis they lay the blame squarely at the doors of the politicians who have encouraged this climate of dependency below the poverty line. So although the hard-core rude boys are seen as responsible for the endgame of violence, people also finger those who run the state and opposition institutions as being equally criminal for having issued guns to inner-city youths. Politicians have a vested interest in maintaining poverty and dependency because it gives them the ability to encourage partisan warfare in exchange for scarce benefits and other spoils of 'war'. The political economy is intrinsically intertwined in the prevailing *discourse of violence*. And, while not all men and boys subscribe to this power mechanism, they still implicitly benefit by virtue of being male (Connell, 1995).

It is rare for women to be involved in the gang wars between men, although two outstanding cases of such involvement were mentioned to me. Wars are also fought with gender-defined weapons. Men generally use guns and knives with deadly emphases to address conflicts and to protect turf and reputation. Women invariably engage in sexuality-defined wars, fought with implements such as ice picks, machetes, acid, and their bodies.

Underlying all of this is the combination of poverty and the stigma that prevents the poor from accessing opportunities for social advancement, which results in extreme levels of frustration for citizens in the inner-city. It is ironic that this syndrome of neglect is the norm considering that inner-city residents contribute the most votes to the political parties.

Figure 6.1: Molly.

This topic came up for discussion in Molly's *Southpole* bar on Tower Street. Patrons openly discussed the bogus voting that served to persuade politicians of the loyalty of their subaltern subjects. Beneath the patronage mentality, though, lurked a stinging cynicism that could be the harbinger of change in the way people view their forced insertion into the political system.

> I have stopped voting because I do not see any leader to lead me right now. But I used to make dozens of Xs for politicians. I just took a pack of ballots and voted because I supported a party and I wanted that party to win. I knew that what I was doing was wrong but several people were doing it – the opponents were doing it – so we couldn't just sit back and make them win. We had to fight back.

> (Donovan, Fleet Street)

Of course, election rigging is not peculiar to Jamaica but is a very commonplace feature of the organised deployment of so-called democracy, even in the United States of America. What is rare is to enlarge the skeletons behind the scenes of the disappeared ballot boxes, election intimidation tactics and superfluous voters' lists. Molly opened a door to vicious memories of hegemonic manipulation that pitted community members against each other.

In 1980, JLP took over from PNP; you call that switch. We *roped out* people
– mashed up their furniture, turned them out of their homes and the
community. They left and did not come back because they were PNP. Every
time that you have an election in my community that's what happens. The
people throw words, get vex with you and things like that. The politics is a
folly-tricks – the politicians – Mr. Patterson and Mr. Seaga – sit and drink
champagne and laugh at us down here in the ghetto. When I was much
younger, I used to give votes – even making some votes that you know...
(meaningful pause indicating the practice of illegal voting)...this is ghetto
talk and it is coming from the bottom of the grassroots...

Men have the most direct access to this culture of political clientilism although Molly's
testimony shows that some women break through this pattern too. Patriarchal
alliances are formed across class interests to make this power dynamic work,
weakening the possibility for people living in the urban grassroots to develop the kind
of class solidarity that could pose an effective challenge to this subtle system of divide
and rule. I will present several tragic and well-known situations in Jamaica's recent
political history in which inner-city men, pawns of the politicians, were manipulated
into literally dying for a piece of the pie.

The Green Bay Killing

The explosive Green Bay affair stripped the façade off patronage-packaged political
practices, revealing the canker eating away at the core of the artificially created
underclass.

It took place 1978 on the fifth of January, Thursday morning, before day.
They were Rasta Man[82] Natty Dreadlocks, with no work. Well, Guttu was
Santos' footballer and Guttu was my baby father; I had a son for him. So he
was also called Norman Thompson, playing for Santos; he was Jamaica's
links man. Norman Thompson now, and Glenroy Richards, he sang the
Green Bay music. One was Gold Eye and one was Gargo, one was Howard
Hamilton, one is Saddlehead. There were more men, ten in all. Five died
and five came back alive. We had to go to Spanish Town hospital to identify
them. They had this range down where the soldiers went for target practice;
they called it Green Bay. It was there that they told them that they were
going to carry them on a training mission. You had this girl called Susan
Hinds from the Forum Hotel, she and this individual guy, met and they took
back all the information.

The morning they came for the men with an ambulance, I believe and a van,
cars and everything. I had my baby father in it you know and I will never

---

82   The use of 'men' is an oxymoron within a Rastafari framework generally and in a grassroots environment
in particular. As said before, it is a term that means homosexual and is a taboo reference. However, for
conventions of English use, I use men to denote the plural of man that is usually rendered 'man and man' in
the local expression to linguistically emphasise the reified heterosexual norm of masculinity. In the previous
chapter, which explicates my culturally grounded definition of discourse analysis, I have already detailed the
impact that a Rastafari interrogation of language as a site of oppression and resistance has had on cultural
discourses in the wider society.

forget it. They searched the men and said that they should come *clean*[83] because they were going to teach them how to fire guns. It's a pity that they never knew, what was behind it. When they went down there, one man said he wanted to use the bathroom and he went in the bush.

They attracted the men with one box of gunshots. One box of shot and they got the gathering of the people. When the men were looking at the gunshots, that is when they were crowded up together, that was when the soldiers started shooting. Glen died, on the spot. Guttu, (Norman Thompson), Gold Eye, Gargo and Saddle-head...five dead and five alive out of those ten man. Ruddy Nesbeth is here,[84] Anthony Spencer is alive, in America. Bugga, he is in America, Ian Brown was in America but he is here. Jadda Griffiths had escaped the Green Bay death scene by jumping off a cliff onto a rock in the shark-infested sea. He is now a walking dead.[85]

That was **history** in Southside; honestly. From that time, I don't trust politics because it was a political affair. After the incident, they said that the men were trying to overthrow the government. At that time, I read and they said...it was Dudley Thompson who said that 'no angels were at Green Bay.' Then you didn't hear anything else about it. No, they weren't perfect but I didn't see why they had to kill off those men. I don't know of them killing anybody at that time. They only needed jobs. Guttu was playing ball all the time for Santos and he only needed to get some dollars because football wasn't doing anything that time. Football is making money now. If Guttu was alive and playing ball, he would be all right. He could afford to take care of his kids. **Yes, from that, people on a whole in the community say we don't trust anybody.**

Here is the experience; fighting your brother and sister, not for a bag of gold, not for a house – you can't even see what you are going to achieve, except a casket or a coffin or an unfound body. A man loses his life. You cannot be fighting for that when you should be fighting for strength, survival and power. I can't understand how you can be born and raised in a community where you have brothers, sisters, cousins and friends and then you turn around your gun and start to shoot your brethren, with whom you went to school. People with whom you sat together in the same class. With whom you lived side by side and used to eat together. That is what is happening in my community now, you know. Few business places are operating. Everything is just upside down; people are afraid and nobody wants to come here and spend anything and those who are inside, are not spending.

(Molly, Ladd Lane)

It was relatively easy for the manipulators to lure the unsuspecting victims into a death trap. Needs and wants created by extreme poverty have made the poor,

---

83 This expression in inner-city parlance means 'unarmed'; the soldiers were ensuring that the men would not have the possibility to rebuff the assassination plot that the soldier wing of the security forces (acting on behalf of the state) had designed.

84 Nesbeth was murdered during my period of research (February 1, 1999) and so were two of his sons in the subsequent round of reprisal killings.

85 The term used to describe someone who is hooked on cocaine.

even a nationally known and well-liked dreadlocked footballer like Norman Guttu Thompson, into grist for the politicians' mills. Instead of delivering the 'goods' of guns as promised, the middle men delivered bullets into the bodies of some of the duped local party supporters, leaving innocent blood crying out for justice. Without a doubt, those who control the state and their security arm will go to great lengths in order to consolidate their positions of power.

In the aftermath of this, the government conducted a public enquiry into the killing of the five men by the soldiers. The PNP's Minister of National Security and Justice at the time, Dudley Thompson, is infamous for trying to justify the criminal culpability of the state by saying, 'no angels were killed at Green Bay'. In the latter half of 1999, this can of worms was re-opened by justice seekers calling for the acknowledgement of the guilt of those state officials who were involved to be recognised and demanding that they should be brought to justice. However, no one has yet been held criminally responsible for the murders.

The ten men were, like so many alienated youth, in search of an identity that would compensate for the multiple forms of need that defined and shaped their lives. They sought material advantage – a piece of the pie – to offset experiences of systematic social exclusion. However, the Green Bay Massacre showed that attempting to gain materiality through sexist clientilism, ultimately has devastating effects in terms of blood, bullets and bodies on those who exercise agency in this vernacular. Considering that subordinated subjects perform the hegemonic project under the delusion that they are acting in their own interests (Lukes, 1986), it is useful to reflect on another watershed event in the evolution of violence in Southside.

The Gold Street Massacre

In the run-up to the 1980 general elections, the infamous Gold Street Massacre sent shock waves through the city. A motorcade led by Michael Manley, who at the time was member of parliament for Central Kingston and prime minister of the PNP Government, came under stone-throwing attacks by political activists of the predominantly JLP Southside community. This incident was followed on the same night by a violent repartee, so sophisticated in its style and content that the shock waves still ripple across the memories of people with whom I spoke. As one woman recalled, the attack on the community featured an unusual display of high-powered weaponry that left blood, bullets and bodies everywhere.

> I was in my house the night when we heard the shots. I had a window in the lane that was open. I said to my mother, it looked as if police came in on the men. In that time, gang affairs were common. I heard someone underneath the window in the yard. How I realised that it was not police but bad man, I heard one man say, "Down that yard is where Bugsie lives." Bugsie was a Labourite man, at the corner of Tower Street and Maiden Lane. I became afraid then. They were firing a lot of shots; my mother was in her room at first and then she bawled out "Lord God!" when she realised that Delroy was not in the house. I tried my best to quiet her, knowing that it was a good thing that I did not push my head out of the window because the men would

have seen me. I then heard when Grant said "Iyah[86] don't buss any shots here; remember that we are going to Gold Street."

The firing continued. A woman who lived next door to my yard, Yvonne, ran to her house shouting "Mama, mama! I have been shot!" Someone came into my yard, knocking on the door, saying "Fatty! Help me. It's me, Sixy, the one Sixy in South." I opened the door with a heavy heart. When Six Fingers came in, you could see where she had the gun pellets in her stomach. I had to make her keep quiet, moving her from the children's bed to my bed. There was a lot of blood all over the house but I didn't mind because I saved a life. When everything cooled down, they took the injured to hospital.

You have to take bad things and make laugh;[87] they fired shots at the police and they locked up the station and went to hide. One man hid underneath a man's bed upstairs.

(Ms. Williams, 55, Gold Street)

The attackers were dressed as soldiers and so masked their arrival in the community, worming their way to Gold Street where a dance was being held. Because the dance only had one entrance/exit – in the carryover of the housing style encouraged for Africans under colonialism – it was easy for the attackers to cordon off this escape route while they proceeded to open fire on the dance patrons. Several persons were injured and eight people died. What is frightening is that this misuse of authority is carried out under the aegis of the postcolonial state's peculiar practice of bourgeois democracy.

Politically, post-war Jamaica has been characterised by the existence of one of the tightest, most impermeable and consistent two-party systems in the hemisphere. There have been twelve general elections, eleven of them seriously contested by both parties...The system was underwritten by a number of features, including clientilism, extreme Westminster centralisation of power, and the absence of a strong, independent civil society. *Its success and relative longevity can be said to have derived from a series of unwritten pacts and compromises between the largely brown-skinned and educated upper middle classes who actually controlled state power, and the Black working and lower classes who voted for them and occasionally engaged in internecine warfare in the rank and file of either party.*

(Meeks, 1996: 127, emphasis added)

Patronage clients rationalise their recourse to criminal activity as inevitable to their attempts to survive. From the gruesome example of what happened at Gold Street however, such illusions have detrimental social consequences for their social security.

---

86   Rastafari expression for another person, the indivisible I(yah). This concept is central to Rastafari who eschew usage of the divisive you and me in preference for a generic I.

87   This is a Jamaican proverb that speaks eloquently to a characteristic survival strategy. By laughing at one's calamity, it is possible to devise some way to overcome it.

The crisis has many dimensions and takes different forms. In desperation some people turn to crime. Burglaries, robberies, larceny, drug dealing are all on the increase. In response, the police resort to brutality and frequent killings; in 1989, 180 Jamaicans were killed by the police. The fastest growing economic sectors in Jamaica are now drugs – and the security industry. Domestic violence, child abuse and drug-dependency are all serious problems.

(Kirton, 1992: 5)

The Arrest of A Don

An analysis of the poverty and violence experienced by residents of the Southside community cannot be undertaken in a vacuum. Fundamental to such an enquiry is an interrogation of the state/elite-class alliance, the dependent national economy and the neo-liberal monetarist policies that have been emphasised by successive governments. It is important to ask whether the prevailing discourse of violence would have taken root if chronic poverty was not also a part of the sociopolitical equation. The immediate response is that the social actors who occupy the more affluent sectors of the society have not been as susceptible to political manipulation, presumably because their healthier material circumstances allow them the space to maintain a safe distance from such tactics. On rare occasions, however, the trouble spills over the social boundaries, as happened in the huge drama surrounding the arrest of Zeeks, an area don from Matthews Lane.

During the week ending September 26, 1998, the City of Kingston experienced a dramatic 'Crisis in the City', as reported by the local *Observer* newspaper, which left four people dead and eight persons injured. The incident was sparked by the arrest of Zeeks, an area don from the PNP-dominated area of Matthews Lane, the community that adjoins Southside on the west. He is reputed to be the man who *runs the place*, and who, in this role, has replaced the upper-class politician in commanding authority through gun power and his own style of community patronage. It is alleged that his substantial financial resources are derived from protection money paid by business owners who operate in the downtown Kingston area.

Donald 'Zeeks' Phipps was arrested on charges of attempted murder and possession of an illegal firearm, which incited a massive demonstration staged by his supporters outside of the Central Police Station in downtown Kingston where he was detained. The case was legally compromised when the police brought the captive man onto the balcony of the station to prove to the irate crowd that he was unharmed. This action was unprecedented because Zeeks had not yet faced an identification parade. People from rival as well as supporting communities, including Southside (which is traditionally in conflict with Matthews Lane), reacted in strong protest against the arrest of the don; many people demonstrated by blocking roads. The security forces responded with gunfire, to which the gunmen in the affected communities did not hesitate to reply. Everyday life was disrupted as schools and business places were forced to close.

The *Jamaica Observer* newspaper quoted then general secretary of the ruling People's National Party, Maxine Henry-Wilson, as saying that 'the state may have given up critical aspects of its role which may have resulted in erosion of some institutions and could have contributed to this week's violent demonstrations in Kingston.' Henry-Wilson also said that she 'was concerned about the perceived power of the 'non-mainstream' leaders…' She emphasised that her 'government's role was to bring those persons back into the mainstream of society,' emphasizing that this was the state's 'greatest challenge.' Significantly, this challenge is a long-recognised one, which has not been correlated with the action necessary to give it a concrete solution.

On Sunday, September 27, 1998, on the local CVM television channel, the Cliff Hughes-hosted discussion programme voiced a number of interesting viewpoints. These perspectives also spoke to the importance of engaging in the discourses of the day, in order to gather the clues for addressing the political economy of the discourse of inner-city violence. Delroy Chuck, JLP member of parliament for North East St. Andrew, said that 'inner-city communities are not a social problem; they are an economic problem and until we get our economics right, we are not going to solve the problem'. On one hand, he is oh so right. On the other hand, there are several indicators that Chuck's comment is only half of the truth; the social aspects of the problems are too glaring to be denied and neither can the political precedents.

Further, the paucity of government support for inner-city communities has been structural as well as social. The local don, therefore, fills the resulting power vacuum, a phenomenon to which the panel gave considered attention. One panellist commented that since 'MPs can't control their communities', the don has acquired tremendous economic muscle. Chuck suggested that as a don, 'if you are not asking for protection money, like Zeeks; you ask businessmen for money to send children to school. He gets it.'

However, the legal vice grip on the don tightened a few years later. According to press reports published on May 22, 2005, Zeeks was arrested once again after some $18 million in cash was found in an uptown Havendale house owned by the Matthews Lane strongman. The police found the local and foreign currency in a safe in the St. Andrew house and the Financial Investigative Division put the amounts at J$10 million, US$100,000, and £9,000.

The Transshipment of Poverty

The United States of America includes four Caribbean nations – Jamaica, The Bahamas, Haiti and the Dominican Republic – on their list of major illegal drug-producing countries. In Jamaica's case, beyond the failure of the local political parties to address what is clearly a complex political and economic problem, the island's strategic location between North and South America, poses another tremendous 'problem'. The Reggae island is slap bang in the middle of a tourism and foreign-capital-dependent region and is much more than just a marijuana-producing nation. The relatively new but constant demand for cocaine and crack in Jamaica's inner-city communities is directly connected to a similar, but more long-standing, demand in both the inner-city and suburban communities of America, Canada and England.

So, in effect, North America imports cocaine and exports crime in the form of guns, while South America exports crime in the form of cocaine and imports guns. The dons on the South American continent supply the drugs for North America and Europe, while the demand for weapons of war in South America is filled from the controversially booming North American arms industry. Jamaica, like other Caribbean islands, is, therefore, also a transshipment zone for these debilitating, poverty-enhancing import-export transactions. In the process of all this, the Caribbean region, and especially Jamaica, naturally absorbs some of the deadliest ballistic and drug residue of these deals (Gunst, 1995).

The *Sunday Gleaner* of January 23, 2000, proclaimed the seriousness of the situation with the headline, 'Colombians take control of local cocaine trade'. The text of the report noted that

> the International narcotics Control Strategy Report first spotted the trend and reported it in March 1999 that based on information derived from U.S. and Jamaican law enforcement sources "there is an increased presence in Jamaica of Colombian traffickers involved in the transhipment of multi-kilogram loads of cocaine through Jamaica...Jamaica is the largest producer of ganja (marijuana) in the Caribbean and a major transhipment point for cocaine from Latin America, bound for the U.S. and Europe.

> (Lloyd Williams, senior associate editor, *The Sunday Gleaner*, January 23, 2000, pp. 1 and 3A)

The sad fact is that the Colombians are now in control of much more than just the local cocaine trade inside of Jamaica. Unbelievably, and for some still unfathomable reason, local dealers and drug dons at all levels have literally given control and full knowledge of the ins and outs of the domestic ganja trade to these South Americans. Such a voluntary abdication of responsibility over local territorial integrity and the transferring of such control to foreigners with their own vested interests is puzzling to say the least. As a result, Colombians are now also included in the matrix of violence which is exploding on Jamaican streets. This is a troubling occurrence, to say the least, and is one which is scarcely being accounted for presently by local sociologists and/or criminologists. It is a development which could well come back to haunt Jamaica and Jamaicans in the near future.

Meanwhile, because of intense eradication campaigns, Jamaica along with Belize, now produces a mere 0.5 percent of the ganja/marijuana in the region, with the remaining 99.5 percent of the herb grown in the *region* being produced in the US and Mexico.[88] On the other hand, the criminalisation of ganja and its users also has political implications. During the 1930s, the USA instigated the legal and social prohibition against the *herb*,[89] based mostly on extensive behind-the-scenes lobbying by pharmaceutical/

---

88 These facts emerged in a study in which I evaluated the impact of the Integrated Demand Reduction (IDER) Programme of the National Council on Drug Abuse in Jamaica in 1993.

89 A task force reporting to the Jamaican government on this issue in the summer of 2001 has recommended the decriminalisation of the private use of limited quantities of marijuana.

medical, chemical and lumber big-business magnates, and also partly by inconclusive apprehensions that were propagandised about its use and users.

Contradictorily, much of the ganja produced in the countries where the herb has been declared illegal ends up in areas like Holland and some USA states where marijuana has been legalised for medical and/or recreational use. By sleight of hand and through a sophisticated system of surveillance, the USA state officials are actually manipulating the terms and conditions of control of the drug trade to the benefit of America.

> Each March, Jamaica (as well as other countries) is certified by the President of the U.S. under the Foreign Assistance Act of 1961 as having in the previous year co-operated fully with the U.S. or had taken steps on its own to achieve full compliance with the goals and objectives of the 1988 United Nations Convention against Illicit Traffic in Narcotic Drugs and Psychotropic Substances.

> (Lloyd Williams, Senior Associate Editor, *The Sunday Gleaner*, January 23, 2000, p. 3A)

By linking economic assistance with drug enforcement policy, the USA has for four decades effectively implemented its own brand of international patronage politics. The acquiescence of countries like Jamaica to this power arrangement speaks eloquently of their dependent status in the world capitalist system. Particularly ominous is the impact that this new triangular trade has on the social ethos of the inner-city communities. The bottom line and end result of marijuana eradication policies and the transshipment of cocaine and guns through Jamaica and its waters, is even more poverty, coke-heads and violent crime, especially those inner-city residents living below the poverty line. And more of the pie, in terms of more drugs, more foreign currency, more power and more high-powered guns for the politically and/or criminally well-connected dons with overseas links to the so-called posses and *yardies* in the USA, Canada and the UK.

Jamaica, like most developing countries, is a dumping ground for surplus American products. Guns, ammunition and other ballistic accessories are a $6 billion a year bonanza business for big American companies like Remington Arms, Smith & Wesson, Bushmaster, Colt, and GLOCK Inc., USA/Canada. With retail gun stores open to the general public all over North America, it is no wonder that there are an estimated 200 million guns in civilian hands. Nor is it is a big surprise to know that some 88 people per day still die of gunshot wounds in America, even though that 2004 figure is down from what it recently used to be. Apart from the occasional 'pye-pye' (i.e. homemade gun), Jamaicans do not make guns and rifles. Jamaica does not manufacture the M-16, the AK-47, nor the Bushmaster. So when we lament about Jamaica being awash with guns, let us also remember where many, if not most, of these guns originated: the United States of America. Maybe Jamaica should bring an international class-action lawsuit against American gun manufacturers for the violent deaths and social mayhem caused by the purposely negligent distribution of their surplus products. And maybe also against British, German, Belgian, Austrian, Russian and Israeli gun manufacturers too.

Inner-City Origins of Jamaican Posses

When I interviewed[90] Chubby Dread[91], one of the traditionally high-ranking political leaders, this 'influential man' called himself an 'elder' rather than a don. A once-powerful figure, he had lost a considerable amount of his authority to the new breed of young gang leaders and was shot and killed just before this book went to print. This community leader described a time line, which illustrates the power transition from elders to youths.

> In the sixties we used to fight with fists and knives. Then in the seventies, it got **wickeder** and so did the eighties. In fact every decade it seems to get wickeder and wickeder and this is not only in this community but all over the inner city.

The pattern of men competing with other men for power is a recurrent motif within the inner-city space. The current spate of gang-warfare, which undermines the social health of the community, has its genesis in feuding related to party politics. However, a clear distinction is made in the collective memories, between the previous era of party political violence and the current conflicted climate, which is characterised by a power struggle for the respect that guarantees control of criminal turf. The present generation has been spawned in the womb of internalised violence (Fanon, 1967).

> It started out in 1983 as a struggle between the Laws Street (Tel Aviv) and Pow (Water Lane) gangs, for who would run[92] the community. There was always a conflict between the two leaders, Nesbeth and Chubby, for who would run things. The conflict that is happening now has a long history but I can't believe the Renkers crew would be against the Laws Street gang because they were the only ones who used to defend them at one time.

(Donald, 30, Fleet Street)

Since the late 1960s, the Southside community has been affiliated with the Jamaica Labour Party; Chubby Dread had been the prominent area leader. On the other hand, the adjoining Tel Aviv community has, over the years, been affiliated with the People's National Party. The power struggles among the men from these rival areas have had deadly consequences, both for those who have been directly involved in the war, as well as for those who have been victims of its inimical effects. This pattern of leadership accounts for the politicisation of crime in the inner-city communities.

> [T]he levels of organisation of the gangs have become more complex particularly those involved in international drug trafficking. *Their success is largely related to their linkages to the formal business sector (particularly in entertainment and other hospitality services), the state and party system,*

---

90 I interviewed this elder for one of the three video documentaries that I produced to share the data with the community in popular form. In addition, he was also a participant on the inner-city community radio station Roots 96.1 FM, on which I worked as a producer/presenter in fulfilment of my objective to contribute to the self-esteem building of the subjects by the politicisation of their voices.

91 This elder was brutally murdered one night in 2005 as he left the popular Asylum club in New Kingston.

92 The term 'to run the place' means to be in charge of the community. This is a commonly used expression within inner-city discourse denoting the man who speaks from the position of most authority as far as gun power and therefore being able to control other residents inside and outside of the community.

a significant measure of public approval, and the material resources (and social capital) with which to buy immunity from the law.

(Harriott, 2000: 18, emphasis added)

Although the Rae Town area is contiguous with Southside, it has political connections with Tel Aviv[93] through affiliation-identity with the PNP. The high-rise 'site' building, which resulted from the distribution of contract work and access to the housing facilities by supporters of the PNP, created a political tension within the community. Those gangsters who control this location have had an ongoing conflict with the Gully Massive gang, which is located on McWhinney Street, an allegedly JLP-affiliated area in the Rae Town community. South Camp Road separates this section of the area from Southside. However, the '(building) site' area has had a PNP identity and a relation of co-operation with the feared Renkers Crew located at Fleet Street, which is also one of the corners directly affiliated with gangs in New York.

> The Renkers gang, though vicious, was nothing like some of the other Jamaican posses – bigger syndicates like the Shower killed many more people – but in the pantheon of New York street gangs the Renkers were unusually violent.

(Gunst, 1995: 140)

In spite of the political machinations of the US Government, there is an unmistakable nexus among politics violence and drug dealing in Jamaica. Even a number of Jamaican government officials and policemen are implicated in this racket, which also involves, as Gunst's analysis shows, a coalition between offshore Jamaican gangs, especially in the US, and inner-city community *influentials*. In fact, as Anthony Harriott observes,

> [t]he highest levels of organisation and best articulated structures are to be found in the drug trade...Drug trading and protection rackets...are the two most stable sources of income. In 1993 the assets of one of the better organised gangs, the Shower Posse was valued by the US Drug Enforcement Administration (DEA) at US$300 million...Another gang, the Gully Posse, was valued at US$100 million...[E]ven if grossly overestimated, the resources at the disposal of these gangs are still vast. Moreover...[I]n some instances, even state agencies were forced to pay protection money to these gangs in the form of handsome "security contracts."

(Harriott, 2000: 18)

Harriott explains the success of the Jamaican posse gangsters as being the outcome of their connections to international criminal networks. In addition to their well known, local political connections, this transnational element in the power dynamics of local gangs was

---

93 Various names become locally ascribed to corners based on association with both internationally and locally significant events. The naming of Tel Aviv, the community to the north of Southside, which is separated by the border of East Queen Street, alludes to the ongoing war in the Middle East. A section of Southside is called Vietnam, another example of the appropriation of a dominant discourse of war to didactically explain the social temperature of that area. As Ras Carlie explained in Chapter 3, the political machinery also contributed to the internal constructions of the meanings those controlling an area confer onto the bearers of this discourse in that space.

facilitated by the illegal immigration of Jamaican criminals to North American and European cities. The quality of the integration into the global narcotics trade is reflected in the level of local earnings from cannabis exports...By 1990 Jamaican criminals had garnered some 8 percent of the US$8.8 billion cocaine and cocaine derivatives market. All these inconsistent overestimates have as their source the DEA, but they nevertheless indicate a qualitative transformation of the Jamaican underground.

(Harriott, 2000: 19)

The strange but true story of the notorious *Shower Posse* was what prompted White American author Laurie Gunst to spend a decade moving with and researching Jamaican gang members from Kingston, to Brooklyn, to Miami. Gunst eventually published a book, *Born Fi Dead*, in which she gave her own, firsthand account of the Jamaican gangsters that rode the crack wave of the 1980s and took over the streets of cities like New York, Houston, Miami, Toronto, London, Birmingham and Bristol. More recently, the BBC and ITN as well as various Canadian news organisations have also sent camera crews to Kingston in search of the inner-city origins of the now infamous *Posse*, which is also known and feared as the *yardies* in England and Canada. A number of people were subsequently shot and killed both in America and Jamaica because of names that were called and things which were printed and published by Gunst in *Born Fi Dead*. In their thirst for fame and their love of hype, many of the gangsters interviewed by the BBC in *Yardies* and by City TV in *From Trench Town to Toronto*, not only incriminated themselves, but implicated their associates too. If nothing else, they certainly have given the Scotland Yard police deployed to Jamaica some concrete leads to follow up.

The Leadership Vacuum

Leadership struggles have been a contentious feature of Southside's political evolution. Chubby Dread owned a bar on the 'Pow' corner at Water Lane. Over the years this space was also the venue of many entertaining community dances. The symbolism in the images on the wall are indicative of the identity politics that are invoked in the subaltern environment.

There was an early political alliance between Renkers and Pow (Fleet Street and Water Lane), especially because Chubby Dread, then Pow leader, originated from Fleet Street. However, over time, this relationship turned sour. In fact, the loss of community trust is so profound, that at the end of my research engagement in June 1999, the Rae Town area (namely, Thompson Avenue, McWhinney Street and Stephen Lane) was an area 'fighting against itself', as one man described it. As always, the reason proffered for the conflict is a power struggle for control or rule of the area. According to one woman, 'as soon as someone shows signs of leadership, he is killed.'

[Figure 6.2: POW Corner: To the extreme left is a representation of His Imperial Majesty, Emperor Haile Selassie I, the spiritual icon for Rastafari. Next in line are posters announcing dances. The juxtaposing of the almost naked body of a woman with popular DJ Shabba Ranks doubly denotes objectification of the female body for the pleasure of the male gaze. Shabba is infamous for his manipulation of female sexuality in the marketing of his music. However, he is also noted for the uncompromising political statements of his artistic confrontation of the privileged sectors of society.

Herman explained further how community violence and the style of politics practised by the parties have exacerbated the disadvantages of those living in the Southside.

> It started from politics, and with the fliction[94] you know, you have borders. You can't go there because PNP [supporters] live there and JLP live there and even before that, you had a little gang war with Southside and Telaville.[95] It started from there. That is from the seventies come down to the eighties. It is the same power struggle that I have been telling you about. All of them were friends, you know. The power struggle started from the gun thing. All of us were friends and what happened to me was that I had a gun and I loaned it to someone who did not want to give me back, claiming that I have too much, yeah! That's how it goes.

(Herman 45, Harbour Street)

The fragmented pattern of leadership in Southside is somewhat different from what obtains in many other urban grassroots areas like Tivoli Gardens where a more centralised system of men in authority is the norm. When I asked Herman to assess the current local leadership situation in light of his own past involvement with criminal activity, he made a clear distinction between the past, which he cast in relatively innocent terms, and what was currently happening in Southside. He explained that the struggle between the elders and youth as well as among the youth gangs was all about power.

> The young gunmen who are running the place now want help; without help, there can be no future. For them, power is a gun; they just know gun power.

---

94 Patwah word meaning conflict.

95 Tel Aviv is sometimes pronounced Telaville.

I don't even know what is going to happen to them. Some get their guns by whatever means and some buy it. I can tell you though; it is a power thing. The man with the most guns and the biggest gun, he feels that he is supposed to rule. Just because they have the most guns and the biggest guns they think on a different angle. You can have it, yes and you rule and nobody even has to know that you have it. That's how we used to run it: with money. Man used to wait until they saw other man going to look for some food out there. When everyone came in, they saw to it that everybody got something, even the older heads. That's how we used to deal with it. But these youths have no time, because they don't have the brains to deal with it.

Despite the crisis conditions under which Southside's residents live, they, like other inner-city residents, face even more mortal danger if they should voice their concerns too loudly inside their community, or worse, if they should communicate what they know to outsiders, particularly security forces. Violation of accepted codes of silence or informing therefore deserves critical examination as it has tremendous implications for citizen security.

See and Blind, Hear and Deaf

Life in the Ghetto

My mother's death was a big tragedy.
She was friendly with a woman
Who they said was a police informer
And the men came in the night and shot her.
They killed the lady before they came
To shoot up my mother because they said
that she was involved too. I was 19 and I felt
that I was going mad!
I ran to the police station and told them that
I was going to become an officer and kill off
the gunmen.
I have lived with this for years now
and although it has passed and gone and
the police killed them off, I still feel it.

In this environment, the act of informing is seen as a challenge to the authority of the local dons. Communicating knowledge of their activities to the security forces or other institutional bodies is an act that immediately endangers the lives of anyone committing such an offence. When he was a child, Johnny witnessed his mother being murdered because she was accused of being a police informer. As the preceding 'Life in the Ghetto' passage illustrates, the experience left this 27 year old man deeply scarred[96] and propelled him to the brink of retaliating in kind.

Johnny's experience shows that the gunman commands the greatest capacity to speak and sets the symbolic and material boundaries of this power domain. Those men, women or children who transgress this behavioural code virtually sign their own death warrants because 'the gunmen...serve further as enforcers who keep the dissidents and troublemakers in the community in line by methods varying from banishment, beatings, and threats to actual murder' (Stone, 1986: 57).

This masculinist power regime has to be linked to other discourses of domination. As Jeff Hearn suggests in this regard,

> there remains a case for retaining the concept of patriarchy that is fundamentally social structural. In particular it can be of analytical, and possibly political, use in focusing on the social structuring of gender relations, of the variety of forms of social relation and oppression between men and women. It can prompt the understanding of possible social structures underlying both institutional inequalities and everyday action.
>
> (Hearn, 1987: 43)

The discourse of power that prevents social actors from speaking freely exemplifies 'a differential knowledge incapable of unanimity which owes its force only to the harshness with which it is opposed by everything surrounding it' (Foucault, in Gordon (ed.), 1980: 82). In other words, the systematic process of silencing suggests that claiming access to voice (Collins, 1990; hooks, 1989) is the counter-discourse that the oppressed and exploited have to employ in coming to consciousness. Miss Dor summarised the dilemma when she said,

> When I talk to some people, some others say I am an informer but some appreciate me because when I talk to them, they know what they are doing is wrong. On my little corner, sometimes I don't even talk to the little boys because when they see people and interfere with them and I say they should not trouble them they will say cho! *You talk too much.*

Not all those who refuse to speak are succumbing to the dominant discourse of domination. Some, having considered the consequences of doing otherwise opt to comply with the prevailing norm as a social security strategy. The children in the discussion on Ladd Lane described the gruesome killing of a woman and her child who were eliminated because it was felt that she was the one who told the police where the guns were hidden. I gathered from the children that sharing the information with me was also fraught with danger but they also seemed relieved at being able to share the burden of this knowledge.

Well, a woman lived up the road

---

96 As I emphasised in the previous chapter, the severe psychosocial dimensions of the experiences of subjects in Southside is one of the most problematic aspects of the disadvantages faced by people who have been politically constructed as the underclass (Wacquant, 1994). I have to reiterate that any project of social transformation has to tackle this arena of the dynamic experience of subordination in order to begin what, as the historical trajectory has shown, is a healing process that is centuries overdue.

With two sons and one daughter.
I do not know what she did…
She talked!
Yes, she informed on them
And gunmen came in and
Shot out the whole of her teeth
Out of her head
And her son who was
Six years old chucked[97]
Underneath the bed
And her daughter
Jumped through the window.
Her little baby son
Got shot up and her
Big son grabbed him
And threw him in
The barrel and went
Underneath the bed.
When the gunmen left,
She was saying over and over,
'Ian, Theo, Tina,' her children's names
The last name she called was Ian.
The little boy got six shots
But he did not die immediately.
In the morning when we went to look,
We saw blood and we saw teeth.
Babsy Grange [the JLP Caretaker] helped to bury her.
And her son's head was swollen.

Informing brings deadly consequences; on the other hand, keeping silent protects the perpetrators of violence. This enforced silence foments fear and frustration and makes people wonder in despair if they will ever be able to enjoy the kind of peace that uptown people take for granted. Yet 'in their daily lives many…do not experience themselves as oppressed and, indeed, they exercise an amount of power and influence over other individuals' (McNay, 1992: 67).

Matey Wars

While 'the war' generally refers to gun violence in which strictly men are involved, some women, desperate for 'possession' of scarce men who can provide them with materiality – their 'piece of the pie' – often fight each other in a bid to stave off the ever-encroaching spectre of poverty and its attendant social ills. Women use various weapons including language, acid, knives, machetes, broken bottles, ice picks and their bodies in the aggressive encounters. These crews as well as individual women

---

97 Dived.

attack each other in order to have a relationship with the man of their common desire. These encounters are called *matey wars*. The adversary of the woman who is perceived to be the first choice of the man in question, is designated the mate – hence matey. Children as well as adults, tell of choosing sides for winners when these women clash, as this spectacle is seen as public entertainment.

The uncompromising tenor of the matey contests is captured in the slogan painted on the wall at the corner of Higholborn and Barry Streets, which the group of women who bear this identity have marked as their space.

Figure 6.3: 'Teka gal man' is Patwah for *take a woman's man*, a didactic statement of the *raison d'être* of the crew calling themselves by that name.

The rivalry between mateys is expressed in violent competitions where the objective is to outfight one's rival, dress more expensively and dance more creatively, especially in a sexually explicit fashion suggestive of who through superior sexual expertise, is more capable of capturing the man who might be the object of competition.

Earlier in the book, I referred to two women who said they would defend themselves if another woman attacked them, but that they would not take the initiative to fight over a man because it was a man's prerogative to pursue a woman and not the other way around. This opinion clearly reflected the internalisation of a patriarchal perspective on gender relationships, which prescribes specific roles for women and men. This value system is exacerbated by the discourse of violence; the rude boy, defined as sexy and powerful, has a premium on wooing and winning women. One woman in the group who had a man's name tattooed on her arm confessed that the owner of the name had been a gunman and had been shot and killed by the police. The grim irony of her being branded for life by the virtual ownership claim of a dead man was not lost on me.

Thus, the prevailing discourse of violence has not only incorporated men in a specific identity project, but also conditions how women define themselves and relate to each other. This has far-reaching ideological, political and material underpinnings. The women who adopt this gendered behaviour pattern are reflecting what Connell refers to as 'emphasised femininity' (1987: 185). This means that in some cases, women comply with the norm of hegemonic masculinity. However, in other instances, this acquiescence may actually constitute 'strategies of resistance' (ibid.) which women employ to circumvent the unequal relations of power that they have to negotiate in their daily lives. Life is indeed full of strange ironies.

Children – Living What They Learn

Although not addressing the taproot of their experiences of symbolic and social exclusion, the power gained in the matey competitions enhances some women's reputations in the community. In other cases, such notoriety enables them to gain some material advantage from their prize men. At the end of the day though, the violence in Southside has had deleterious effects on women and children alike. Just as women are not passive victims in this scenario, children also 'socialise others as well, including their own parents. It is misleading therefore, to conceive of socialisation as being a one-way process from adults to children' (Chevannes, 1999: 24).

Be that as it may, many children are subjected to corporal punishment, one of the main methods through which parents in Southside, particularly mothers, enact violence against children. And while there are several other experiences that children have which are pleasant, because violence is an expression of gender power, it is important to consider how children experience the more challenging features of their social construction.

Afoloshade, a member of the Sistren Theatre Collective, was one of the facilitators in the month-long summer workshop that I organised for a total of 75 children. In one session where we focused on patterns of socialisation, she asked a group of boys and girls to explain the ways in which parents can/should exercise power when dealing with their children who have misbehaved. The youth demonstrated that they have their own perspectives on how parental violence affects them, as well as about the implications of the widespread community discourse of violence for the construction of family relations.

The initial response was that beating is the most common form of power that adults used in their encounters with children. After some discussion, they suggested various other forms of punishment that would be preferable to being beaten. These included withdrawing benefits like television watching and talking to other children, giving them extra duties and cutting down on their playtime. They said that these would be more effective forms of punishment.

Some of the children said, however, that their own perspectives are generally not taken into consideration when punishment is being administered. Mothers, being the principal authority figures in the household, were identified the main ones to administer punishment. The children said women have major responsibility for child-rearing and, therefore, for disciplining them.

My mother beat me
my mother breaks me up
my mother burst my head
my mother punishes me when I am rude
my mother boxed me and kicked me
my mother can step up in my back
my mother can do me everything
my mother flung a nail board at me
my mother hit me with

the high heeled shoes in my face
my father never beat me yet
my mother said if my father ever touched me
she would report him at police station
my father is a cokehead so he does not care about me
my father is a mad man
I listen to my mother more because
I know what my mother will do to me
my mother does me worse things
if my father ever hit me I would kill him
if I were a mother I would put the children
under the bed or tie them up in an ants' nest
I have no feelings for my father
as for me I see when my mother and father are fighting
I feel good about my dad
you say you love your father yet he is so cruel to you
we know how badly he beats you
my father is dead and I don't want to talk about it
my dad makes me happy
when I was little I went out with my father
but he went to foreign and I have not seen him for a long time
a lot of times my father curses me
and then tries to cheer me up
my father is dead too
my father is in prison.
I want the war to stop
I'm not calling any names
but everywhere
you go inside the area
is at war.

Children are bearers of the culture of inner-city underdevelopment. The absence of fathers from many households is not only due to their being in jail or dead, but also directly related to their financial insolvency. Mothers are thus more likely to take out the frustrations that they have from lack of baby father support, on children. Although several women with whom I spoke expressed their satisfaction with being independent, several others said that they would like to have a partner in the household, particularly to help with the disciplining of children.

Girl children are most disadvantaged in this scenario because they have to take more responsibility for domestic chores than boy children, who are allowed more freedom to play. Girls are also more likely to be punished for exploring their sexuality. More often than not, girls are targets of parental power, which acts as negative reinforcement for rebellion rather than producing the desired result of discipline. This system of socialisation means that children also tend to use violence to resolve conflicts among their own peers. Then a 13-year-old girl, Tiffany, gave a graphic example of some of the causes and effects of antagonistic encounters among her age group.

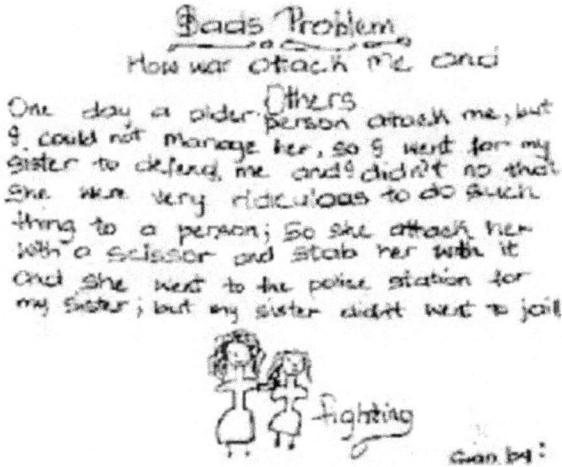

Bads Problem
How war attack me and Others

One day a older person attack me, but I could not manage her, so I went for my sister to defend me and I didn't no that she was very ridiculous to do such thing to a person; So she attack her with a scissor and stab her with it and she went to the police station for my sister; but my sister didn't went to jail

Fighting

Gion by:

Figure 6.4: Tiffany's story of violence among girls.

Tiffany's story suggests that from an early age girls are able to negotiate the games of authority, which are threaded into patterns of survival in the inner-city environment. Ultimately, episodes of violence in the community have a direct impact on the children, some of whom have lost fathers and other relatives. In a community of 6,000 residents, children cannot escape being directly affected by these traumatic events. One boy in the poem cited above refused to talk about the experience of losing his father through violence, even though we tried to get him to expand on his feelings about this loss. This refusal to speak is also a rejection of objectification under the gaze of the outsider/ researcher. Children use silence as a site of resistance even though they have been taught to be 'seen and not heard'. In the same way that those who run the place enforce silence as a gender power tactic, children appropriate and reverse the very discourse that has been used to rob them of agency.

Psychosocial Effects

Figure 6.5: All the headlines on this page of the *Xtra News* newspaper
testify to the widespread nature of the violent crisis.

Silence might provide temporary insulation against pain but is also an indicator of psychosocially crippling distress. Children know that 'informing' has deadly consequences in the inner-city environment and they are careful not to transgress this power boundary. But they suffer in this process of growing up in an environment of such extreme sociopolitical challenges. Even those children who might not have experienced violence as a form of punishment are affected by the far-reaching impact of its ripple effects.

> Jamaica seems to have settled into a profile of violence with over 1,500 violent deaths annually – 950 from murder, 400 from road accidents, 100 from police shootings, plus suicides and other accidental or domestic fatalities. This is one of the highest rates in the world. Northern Ireland with 3,000 deaths over the past two decades was regarded as being at war...A large body of opinion has the view that the widespread screening of violence on television is one of the major causes of the problem.

(Johnson, *Gleaner*, September 30, 1999)

It is inevitable that people experiencing such trauma will display signs of psychosocial disorder. I was on Fleet Street one day chatting with Clive, a community leader, who expressed strong feelings against the political culture that set in motion the internecine conflicts that citizens are now calling the 'no-cause war'.

> I am not really into the war but I become a victim due to where I live and the people I associate with. I become a victim of circumstances; that hinders me and stems my movements in my community. I know I have to be careful about who I see, who I talk to, who I associate with, where I go and where I stop. All the time, I have to keep looking out. The fear that you develop in yourself is just being cautious, because you know what it is. You don't need anybody to tell you that you can't go over there. So it becomes a culture of fear. It keeps you on your toes. You have to be on cue at all times. *But you only become controlled when you allow yourself to be controlled. It is not that you want to be controlled but because of how things are, you have to live by*

the rules. Rules are what counts. You can't step over the line and feel like yow! This is me.

It revolves and causes a chain reaction: *people start to get confused; people become violent against each other, not because they want to be violent but because they want things and they can't get them.* Then some guy comes along and says to you "those guys over there are fighters and you might want to get rid of them." So he issues some guns. In the meantime, someone else arms Tom and Harry over there. So now, they have two sets of man from both sides, properly armed. Then the politicians just stepped out of the middle of it, leaving us to fight it out, and they are out of the country. Out of the country versus inner city. We have no alternatives because we started to fire shots on Tom and Tom is firing at Harry James. Harry James' friend dies; Tom's friend dies. And so it goes on and on and on and on and on till it becomes an in-bred thing.

Clive, Higholborn Street

In Southside, the effects of the stagnant political economy are widely felt and have ravaged people's self-concepts and capacity to trust and build countervailing networks. The psychosocial well-being of those who are unfortunate enough to be caught in this matrix is definitely under threat. In this regard, Oscar Lewis suggests that, over time, the disadvantages that slum dwellers experience create within them a greater capacity for coping with the vagaries of their existence. These strategies, however, are not sustainable in the long term.

[S]ome of the adaptive mechanisms in the culture of poverty – for example, the low aspiration level helps to reduce frustration, the legitimisation of short-range hedonism makes possible spontaneity and enjoyment. However, on the whole, it seems to me that it is a relatively thin culture. There is a great deal of pathos, suffering and emptiness among those who live in the culture of poverty. It does not provide much support or long-range satisfaction and its encouragement of *mistrust tends to magnify helplessness and isolation.* Indeed, the poverty of culture is one of the crucial aspects of the culture of poverty.

(1967: xlvii, emphasis added)

While I agree with Lewis' argument that the syndrome of instant gratification is a positive survival skill developed by those who experience systematic social exclusion, I disagree that poverty of culture is fundamental to their existence. He is correct, however, in his observation that the generation of mistrust which is an inevitable outcome of the hegemonic machinery, engenders tremendous psychosocial suffering. However, this reality has notable caveats. The artefacts of resistance produced by the oppressed and exploited in Jamaica provide evidence of this creativity. This is so because

the experience of power and control may as readily generate a culture of resistance as a culture of submission. This argument focuses attention both on bodies of ideas or values, and on institutions embodying such values, as key elements in the dominance of powerful economic interests'.

(Holton, 1992: 158, emphasis added)

Chi Chi Bad Men

The extreme nature of the inner-city environment and the grotesque psychosocial mutations that these conditions spawn are graphically illustrated by a frightening and relatively recent development in the ghettos of Kingston. Over the past few years, a new and extreme phenomenon has appeared – the chi chi bad man. As far as I can tell at this stage, without any scientific research, this new inner-city personality is basically a bad man or bad boy who has assumed the lifestyles and behaviour of the despised chi chi man. In effect, they have become lower-class, male prostitutes who service upper-class gay men for top dollars. These downtown bad boys are mainly young gunmen from the city who have become the hired sex toys of rich uptown males. So they pretty themselves up in order to go to uptown suburbs at night to fulfil their well-paid but socially scorned jobs. They are handsomely repaid with rewarding slices of the economic pie for their time.

In most every way, these chi chi bad men or bad chi chi men, are the ultimate binary opposition to emerge from the concrete jungles of Kingston's urban slums. They are a bizarre contradiction and illogical end product of their own economically deprived and severely conflicted inner-city environment. This is one of the most unthinkable and unfathomable occurrences. No sociologist was able to predict that the product of the most violently antagonistic and consistently anti-homosexual discourse in the ghetto – the bad boy gunmen – who are supposedly the very antithesis of anything queer, gay or *funny*, would suddenly and voluntarily switch their sexual orientation to become the very kind of persons that they had previously hated so passionately – batty men. It is a classic case of the 'normalisation of pathological behaviour' by victims who adopt maladaptive lifestyles as their own. With *politrickal* patronage not being what it used to be, and with the drug trade under pressure, these gunmen have resorted to selling the use of their bodies and their sexuality – to men – all for pieces of the pie. It is a practice usually resorted to by inner-city females, not the males. In this case, however, rich men seemingly pay the poor inner-city young males more handsomely than women are willing to.

Figure 6.6: This *Xnews* headline tells a similar tale of homosexual 'bad boys' on the prowl in tourist capital Montego Bay.

And, make no mistake about it, these new inner-city chi chi boys are not your ordinary tame and domesticated/sophisticated kind of homosexuals. These are not the poor, defenceless and victimised Jamaican homos whose cause the British gay group Outrage! champions. No, these bad man chi chi boys are tough young killers who can defend themselves and who will not hesitate to shoot or cut up anyone trying to criticise or mock them for their decision to embrace this, still disdained, *lifestyle*. As a result, a known group of such gay gunmen has been brazenly coexisting in the slums of Kingston for some time without any known serious physical threats to their well being. Almost the same thing is happening in Montego Bay.

It does not take a cryptologist to decipher the signs given off by the garish hair colour and styles, the loud earrings, the extravagantly designed and coloured clothing, and by the effeminate style of dancing and modelling of certain prominent Dancehall DJs and male dancers. They are gay, or at least bisexual. But it does not end there. The story gets even stranger. Just like in American Hip-Hop, there is now even a well known but 'down-low', local sub-culture of prominent chi chi bad men producers and managers in Dancehall Reggae. These 'reducers' and 'damagers', as Peter Tosh would call them, interact mostly with the younger and more vulnerable artists, some of whom will do literally anything to succeed.

The international music business and the entertainment industry, in general, are already run and controlled by gay and gay-friendly executives. Slowly and quietly, gay-tolerant chi chi bad men are also extending their influence in the Reggae/Dancehall music business. As a result, younger and newer Jamaican DJ's moving in the wrong circles are now at serious risk of being propositioned for gay sex, or even raped. Yes, the situation is, allegedly, that serious. This may be one of the reasons for the lyrical fixation on homosexuality by many Dancehall DJs. They may have been confronted with a lot of secret gay activity in the music business; may have been victimised or solicited into secret taboo relationships; and may be covering up their dual identity by verbally lashing out against gays in general. Or they could be just verbally retaliating against a sexual trend in society and the industry that they do not like.

According to a few more perceptive observers, this antagonistic situation concerning sexual lifestyles and identity could have a lot to do with the controversial output of a number of overtly and explicitly sexual songs by the unofficial 'high priest' of the present youth generation – Sizzla Kolonji. Many elder Rastafari and other roots music fans have criticised Sizzla and questioned why he feels it necessary to produce such 'slackness' and gun-talk music considering his undoubted prior success with roots and culture recordings and the respect that this has brought him. However, according to some commentators, Sizzla, as a product of the ghetto himself, may be responding in the only way he knows how, or the only safe way he can, to the implicit and explicit threats from the bad boy chi chi men – both in and out of the studio. In other words, instead of having to personally face off against the gay gunmen, producers and managers and berate their lifestyle, Sizzla may be using music to 'throw words' instead.

Thus, Sizzla could be going out of his way to aggressively sing the praises of pussy/pum pum and to publicly advocate the 'ramming' and 'jamming' and loving of females, as a subtle yet vocally overt rejection of what he sees as the dangerous same-sex inroads being cut into the ghetto community and music industry by the new breed of young, violent and openly gay gunmen and producers. Thus in his song 'Pump Up', Sizzla says:

Step up inna front line
Fat, sexy girls Kalonji grind
Step up inna front line
Fire fi de man dem whey go ride man behind
The woman sey
Pump up her pum pum
She want me ram it up
Rooom!

The prevailing view on the streets is that 'bad man nuh par inna chi chi man gang' (i.e. real bad men don't associate with gay men). It thus remains to be seen just how long those practising this chi chi bad man lifestyle will be allowed to flourish before more traditional gunmen or other elements in the ghetto take direct steps to physically eliminate them, giving new meaning to the term 'homo-cide'. The inner city is already sufficiently conflicted with various desperate people competing for a piece of the pie. Now, however, there is an additional cause for yet another future ghetto war and such an eventuality has a very high probability of taking place in the not too distant future because this time, the gays under attack may be rich, well armed and dangerous.

Tivoli Gardens: 'Model' Garrison Community

As the prototype political garrison and the most independent urban political enclave in Jamaica, Tivoli Gardens is West Kingston's ultimate political paradox and social challenge. It symbolises both the beginning and the ending of criminal activities in Jamaica. Built on the bulldozed ruins of the former urban 'Shanty Town', the housing project was named Tivoli Gardens after one of Europe's most outstanding music and dance theatres. The housing scheme was the brainchild and pet project of now retired JLP leader Edward Seaga, who assumed parliamentary responsibility for the area and was virtually worshipped by its inhabitants. The new project was strategically located near to Newport West, which became the main waterfront wharf in place of Newport East, which was nearer to Southside and other parts of central Kingston. In time, this prime location gave an unparalleled advantage to the underworld members of Tivoli, who dominate and/or are major players in the smuggling of guns, drugs, people and other contraband items in and out of the island by way of the West Kingston wharves. Ironically and/or conveniently, Tivoli Gardens is also located adjacent to Kingston's biggest burial ground, the old May Pen Cemetery which adds to the garrison's deadly image and reputation.

The ramshackle buildings of the former 'Dungle' were replaced by modern, high-rise buildings with modern amenities and the loyal politicised residents received regular slices of the economic pie. Firmly under 'Mas' Eddie' Seaga's leadership for over 30 years, Tivoli Gardens became the national political hub and safe haven of the Jamaica Labour Party and its supporters. Accordingly, Tivoli Gardens residents are almost a 100 percent pro JLP and, collectively, they account for more than 50 percent of the total voting population in the volatile constituency of West Kingston. The urban housing scheme was and is the perfect environment in which to implement political clientilism as a policy and to practice *politrickal* puppetry as a tactic.

Tivoli Gardens was the early pacesetter in what would become the don-controlled garrison communities of Jamaica. The charismatic Claudie 'Jack' Massop emerged first as a community leader. Later, as the area's biggest don, he became a folk hero in Tivoli Gardens. His political inclination or commitment was never in doubt. He was literally the JLP's 'biggest gun' during the 1970s. Massop's lieutenants included Carl 'Bya' Mitchell, Lester 'Jim Brown' Coke and Alvin 'Micky' Gordon, and this quartet basically held sway in Tivoli for a time. Tivoli Gardens rapidly acquired a reputation for inflicting swift and terminal 'justice' on those who stepped out of line, and Massop and his crew of enforcers became some of the most feared men anywhere in Jamaica. Tivoli was the breeding ground and these political dons were the patrons of the younger gunmen who, wanted by police, eventually fled the island and formed the hard-core of the criminal gang that would later become infamous in the United States as the feared Shower Posse.

Since then, many people, including the police, see the Tivoli area as a prime source and safe haven for the criminal gunmen whose criminal activities in search of their own piece of the elusive pie, threaten public peace and safety and have fatal impact far beyond their own West Kingston constituency. The police say that there is strong evidence that criminality exported from Tivoli Gardens was at an all-time high in 2005. That is why it is said that Tivoli is the 'beginning of crime'. At the same time, however, although it is alleged to be a 'dangerous place', Tivoli Gardens itself has a very low street crime rate and is often one of the safest places to be, unless you are a known member of the opposing political party (PNP) or a member of a security force operation. People can usually visit the nearby Coronation (produce) Market or attend the party at Passa Passa, the weekly Dancehall street event, without undue fear of harassment or abuse. This is why, on the other hand, Tivoli can also be seen as a place where crime comes to an end: at least, even temporarily, or periodically.

The police themselves agree that Tivoli experiences one of the lowest crime rates in the island. This is surprising since the police do no police work inside of Tivoli, only around it. Short of using heavy artillery or helicopter gun ships and inflicting heavy 'collateral damage', the Jamaican policemen and Jamaica Defence Force soldiers literally have no way of shooting their way into the community without huge loss of life for the security forces. So even though the Denham Town Police Station is located across the street from Tivoli, the officers generally stay out of that garrison. On a number of occasions, combined police-soldier task forces attempting to deploy into Tivoli have been held at bay in running gun battles lasting two to three days, ultimately withdrawing in the face of withering and lethal gunfire.

There are, indeed, a very large number of illegal, high-powered weapons in Tivoli Gardens and with its trademark high-rise buildings to use as sniper nests and lookout posts, gunmen barricaded in the community have a wide and deadly field of fire. It is believed that there are all kinds of tunnels and dry-weather waterways in Tivoli which are used by criminal gunmen as escape routes towards the nearby sea coast. So, while using superior firepower to keep police and military patrols from their area, the political gunmen resident in Tivoli also do an effective job of policing their community. They succeed in 'ending crime' by executing swift and brutal street justice, including capital punishment, to anyone deemed to be a transgressor of any kind.

Bruce Golding, former Prime Minister and Member of Parliament of Tivoli Gardens, dubbed 'the mother of all garrisons', suffered the ignominy of having to resign following his clumsy handling of the extradition request from the USA for Tivoli Gardens strongman Christopher 'Dudus' Coke, then accused and now convicted of international drug and gun running, which resulted in the unprecedented yearlong standoff between Washington and Kingston over Golding-led stalling tactics. Golding's prevarication was compounded by his triple role-playing as Prime Minister, head of the JLP and MP for Tivoli Gardens, run by the de facto leader, Don Dudus. The JLP vainly attempted to lobby the USA government to drop their extradition request, made public by a probing Peter Phillips, then Spokesman on National Security, while the PNP was in Opposition. The subsequent public enquiry into these irregularities revealed the political machinations and subterfuge, at the end of which, Golding opted to sign the extradition order.

What followed remains a painful saga for the Tivoli Gardens community and Jamaica at large because the May 2010 storming of the Tivoli Gardens community by soldiers and police resulted in the official death toll of 73, a figure contested by community members who lost their loved ones. Despite decisive recommendations from Earl Witter, then Public Defender, for residents to receive recompense from the state, a class-specific public enquiry into the incursion and massacre by the then PNP government failed to assuage the psychosocial wounds.

Since then, wave after bloody wave of indiscriminate violence (which, ironically, had been held in check while Don Dudus held sway), has washed over the beleaguered Tivoli Gardens community, despite the determined efforts of the security forces to stem the tide of the human haemorrhage. However, there is a pervasive public perception that these agents of the state compound rather than are capable of solving the entrenched problems of social dysfunction because of their historical mandate (rooted in their 1865 introduction in Jamaica by British colonisers following the Morant Bay revolt by the disenfranchised Africans), to protect the rich from the poor, a charter to which they seem to have remained unswervingly faithful.

Nevertheless, Tivoli Gardens remains the most self-sufficient and the best-organised inner-city community in Jamaica. It, arguably, has the best urban landscape, is by far the cleanest inner-city community in Kingston, and has more and better maintained state-of-the-art educational and recreational facilities than any other garrison community. Tivoli has been very active in schoolboy soccer and sports generally as well as in various cultural events. The community has won the National Premier League football competition, and has a highly rated dance group and a prominent marching band. Most importantly, its citizens seem to have greater access to many more of the social benefits (pieces of the pie) than do their other urban peers.

Not surprisingly, therefore, residents of Tivoli have an even more fanatical community pride and party political loyalty than citizens from other areas, and in many ways the Gardens are often a model for what inner-city communities should be like. At other times, however, being in Tivoli is like being in Beirut or Belfast back in the days of the Lebanese civil war and the sectarian violence in Northern Ireland. In the best of times, average citizens may be less likely to be assaulted and robbed or raped in Tivoli than in neighbouring areas, but in the worst of times, citizens fear getting caught in the deadly crossfire between the security forces and the resident gunmen So, as a serious security threat, as an extreme social paradox, and as a baffling binary opposition of conflicting community traits, Tivoli Gardens continues to perplex police detectives, intrigue the wider society, and be defended by its most vocal, most partisan and most well-armed representatives.

While the foregoing discussion might cause one to despair due to the overwhelming evidence of compromised citizen security, it is timely to introduce an example of social capital, which demonstrates that efforts are being made to offer an alternative route to young men who may be inclined to seek their piece of the pie through violence. In the following treatment coach Percival 'Heights Man' Cordwell explains how he uses sport of football to instil positive values and attitudes in the youth.

Football as Social Therapy

Jamaica is well known and respected in virtually all spheres of the international sporting world. Activities like track and field athletics, cricket, boxing, netball, table tennis, basketball to a lesser extent, and of course football/soccer, have allowed poor but talented Black/Afro-Jamaicans to excel and shine on the world stage for many decades. This small island has consistently produced a remarkable number of world-class athletes of both sexes, and Jamaicans in general, male and female, are avid and very well-informed fans of those and all sports. However, the sport that is by far the most popular and widespread game in Jamaica is undoubtedly football.

Football is part of a social trinity of regular social activities or cultural practices participated in to varying degrees by a large percentage of ordinary Jamaicans: Reggae music, football and herb (ganja/marijuana). Most Jamaicans, rich and poor, Black, Brown or White, PNP, JLP or no-P, are certainly into Reggae and football to some degree, and maybe even the herb too. And the Rastafari and other grassroots users as well as rich/well-to-do users of the cannabis herb are definitely among the front-row fans of both musical events and football games, so the triune social nexus is self-evident. Even at JLP and PNP political street meetings, there is herb and music. Usually therefore, at most big Reggae concerts, football matches or political meetings especially, the police turn a studied blind eye to the culturally widespread and very public use of ganja/marijuana. That explains why vacationing tourists have to be constantly reminded that in Jamaica, marijuana is still illegal.

So, where there is music, there is more often than not also marijuana and sometimes even a football or two as well. And anywhere there is football, marijuana and music naturally follow. And where Rastafari youth are gathered socially and at leisure, there will also usually be marijuana, a ball and Reggae music. This is why the great love of football by Rasta/Reggae stars like Bob Marley and Bunny Wailer for example, is evident and well known in Jamaica, and has been well documented with photos, film and video by the foreign press and electronic media.

The deep importance of football to the national psyche and identity and its place in the grassroots culture, was seen clearly when Jamaica completed the CONCACAF 'Road to France' and qualified for the World Cup Final playoffs for the first time ever in 1998. Although knocked out in the preliminary rounds of the finals, the progress and achievements of the Jamaican National Football team, tellingly dubbed the 'Reggae Boyz' by the overseas press, was the cause of an unprecedented national euphoria and patriotism in the island. Local Jamaican team members even started getting relatively decent pay as (semi) professional players for the first time in history. As a result of the spotlight placed on Jamaica, professional football has now become another credible avenue like music, by which poorer Black Jamaicans from the inner-city or rural areas can escape the poverty of the island. More players are now being contracted to clubs in the English League and the MLS in the United States.

The Jamaican World Cup football team spurred widespread patriotism previously unseen in modern Jamaica. This patriotism was across racial, religious, class, age, political and gender boundaries, earning the team a lot of commercial sponsorship from the local business community and positive front-page and lead-story coverage from the Jamaican print and electronic media. Qualifying home games at the National Stadium in Kingston started with scheduled live mini concerts featuring the most popular Reggae/Dancehall artistes before the feature match. And even overseas, the previous international popularity of Reggae and the global familiarity with the Jamaican Rastafari/marijuana connection, automatically conferred a certain celebrity status to the so-called 'Reggae Boyz'. Names like Ricardo Gardner, Ian 'Pepe' Goodison, Theodore Whitmore, Onandi Lowe and even the controversial Walter 'Blacka' Boyd became household names. The euphoria even extended to Jamaica's National Women's Football team too, which was correspondingly dubbed the 'Reggae Girlz'. Thus, for an all too brief period, the game of football brought a high level of unity, positive self-identification and economic benefit to Jamaica.

Unfortunately, just like everything else we have looked at so far, football and the social/cultural infrastructure around it is rife with many contradictions and binary oppositions. All too soon, René Simoes, the ace Brazilian coach who led the 'Reggae Boyz' to the 1998 World Cup, left (to return with much promise in 2008), forced out by petty jealousy from Jamaican football administrators and coaches and by frequent and unnecessary threats from inner-city dons who wanted to see their favourite players make the team. So although football does indeed encourage health and fitness and is supposed to teach teamwork and discipline, local football games frequently erupt in confusion and chaos because of bad sportsmanship and indiscipline from the players, and threats, abuse and gunshots from unruly and violent supporting fans in the stands. In contrast, netball has no accompanying violence to speak of and therefore provides a much more stable avenue of social advancement for young girls than does football for young boys.

The reality is, therefore, that although football as a sport does have the propensity to be socially, economically and culturally therapeutic in the Jamaican context, and has been at times, at other times and more often than not, it is the administrators, coaches, players and fans themselves who are primarily responsible for sabotaging this eventuality. Some veteran sports and entertainment commentators even point to Alan 'Skill' Cole, Jamaica's own Pelé, as the best example of unfulfilled creative potential in this regard. Cole became a nationally known, football prodigy from his high school days, and received high praise and adulation from Brazilian experts while training and playing in Brazil for a while. A former star of Jamaica's Santos FC, he is widely considered to be Jamaica's best and most talented/skilful football player ever.

Cole gained further prominence when, as a close friend of Bob Marley, he became producer/manager for the Wailers in the early days of the Tuff Gong label, although some of the football star's business practices and his precise utility to the Wailers have increasingly been called into question. 'Skill' subsequently became a well known member of the Rastafarian Mansion known as the 12 Tribes of Israel in the mid-1970s. However, some observers fault Cole not only with not fulfilling his own potential as a professional soccer star, but also with failing to take adequate advantage of various opportunities to help develop and implement a national football programme in urban and rural Jamaica geared at discovering and nurturing the abundant natural talent possessed by Jamaican youth.

Not surprisingly, therefore, the level of competence and the standard of play in the Manning, DaCosta and Walker Cup schoolboy football competitions has deteriorated to such low levels that the issue has now become of major concern to older observers. It is clear that the enormous potential benefits of utilising the generally gender-specific aspects of football as positive social therapy in Jamaica is not being consistently realised at this time. A lot more can and needs to be done in this regard in the future.

Finally, a word about football as it relates to Southside. In order to counter the dominant theme of violence, Coach Percival 'Heights Man' Cordwell has used football to provide boys with an alternative method of expressing masculinity. Many youngsters to whom I spoke said that their principal ambition was to become professional footballers as a means of overcoming the disadvantages of the inner-city environment.

Figure 6.7: Playing football in the streets, even at night, is a major pastime for the youths of most inner-city communities.

Heights Man lamented the low level of material investment in the young footballers. 'The big sponsorship is for the major league competition,' he said. 'The youngsters are awarded trophies and medals and that's the extent of the recognition they are extended.'

Heights Man has served as coach for Santos and Rae Town, teams for which he played some years ago. He has ensured that successive teams keep Southside's Holy Family Primary School's sports name aloft among their football-kicking peers. The coach uses sports as a preventative measure against the magnetic pull of criminal activities, dictated by the 'needs and wants' generated by the perennial scourge of poverty that plagues the urban grassroots population. He also sees the sport as a mechanism of maintaining the discipline, which is so urgently needed to combat the violence, which haunts the community, even in 'peacetime'.

Changing young men's perceptions of what it means to be a man is a very difficult process because of the challenging material situation and also because '[g]ender transformation is a process involving subtle changes in gender relationships, taking place over long stretches of time, often remaining relatively unnoticed' (Risseew, in Davis et al (eds.), 1991: 154).

Figure 6.8: This picture, which was drawn by a boy in a focus group discussion, illustrates that football may be regarded as one of the institutions of rehabilitation in the Southside community.

The obvious limitation of this initiative is that football is geared at changing general perceptions of (violent) masculinity rather than addressing the more generalised norms of patriarchy that are institutionally reinforced in the society. A much more integrated approach to applying this vital development strategy should take into consideration prevailing power mechanisms that act as obstacles to the cultural development of the poor in general, and women in particular. Such a perspective should also consider how some women contribute to their own and to their children's oppression. In far too many cases, the violence enacted by women is inspired by contestations over men. But it is the children who often bear the brunt of women's exercise of power in the household, over which they, the women, have primary control. These considerations obviously need to be incorporated into any expanded programme aimed at using netball as a corresponding gender-based tool of social therapy.

CHAPTER 7

HEGEMONIC MASCULINITIES, SUBORDINATE FEMININITIES

> ..."hegemony" designates a process wherein cultural authority is negotiated and contested. It presupposes that societies contain a plurality of discourses and discursive sites, a plurality of positions and perspectives from which to speak. Of course, not all of these have equal authority. Yet conflict and contestation are part of the story.
>
> (Fraser, in Nicholson (ed.), 1997: 381)

Gender Power

Over the next three chapters, we will move into the core of this factual story that is proving to be stranger than fiction: female bodies for sale or hire, sexualised bodies ransomed for pleasure and power, and Black bodies bloodied and splattered by bullets. In the preceding chapters, we set the stage for this more detailed eyewitness examination of the *Sexual Politics* – the politically and economically influenced sexual intrigue – taking place below Jamaica's poverty line. The gender identities and expected gender roles of the sexualised body – male and female – form the social underpinnings of the existing real-world power equations that are at play in the ongoing life-and-death struggle for survival in Kingston's inner-city environment.

So far, we have seen that hegemonic manifestations of the *real man as bad man* syndrome and its corollary, the subordination of women, are located firmly in the political economy and in the various ways in which daily *discourses of domination* shape embodiment and identity constructions. In other words, everyday body actions, dialogue, speech and even music reflect and shape community ideals and anti-ideals about gender – that is, about what it means to be a man or to be a woman. As a result, performances of gender roles (Butler, in Nicholson, (ed.), 1997) in the Southside community reflect the prevailing power regime, which naturally contours gender definitions of both masculinity and femininity to conform to its own specific sociopolitical circumstances.

From this follows our second assumption – Proposition Two –that in Southside, gender power is expressed in terms of *dominant masculinities* and stereotypes of *subordinate femininities*, in tandem with other identities that defy these norms, in spite of prevailing sanctions. However, having made that proposition, it must also be noted that although 'concepts of power...may build on gender, [they] are not always literally about gender itself' (Scott, in Scott (ed.), 1996: 169–170). In other words, gender norms and sanctions are often metaphorical indicators of the wider structural organisation of power, with gender only providing a lever for the achievement of the ultimate goal of political, social and economic domination.

A word about representation is in order at this juncture because 'the politics of representation has been crucial for colonised groups globally in their struggle for self-determination' (hooks, 1990: 72). Entrenched White supremacist stereotypes depict Black men as prone to acts of violence without placing these in the context of the historical disadvantages in which such men are locked. The objective of this discussion, on the other hand, is to establish the linkage between the political economy and a particular *discourse* of masculinity. This correlation will enable us to uproot some primary development problems and avoid erroneously generalising about all men who live in inner-city communities like Southside.

Phallic State Power & Popular Culture

As noted earlier in the book, throughout both election campaigns in the 1970s, Michael Manley's PNP used symbols of the *Rastafari Livity* to gain electoral support. It just so happened that the Democratic Socialist ideas of the PNP matched the '*Peace and Love*' sensibility of Rastafari sufficiently to be flagged for a strategic electioneering alliance. The fact that the *Livity* was emerging as a significant domain of masculinist authority couched in ideological and spirituo-cultural terms, also made it easy for the PNP leaders to appeal to politicised Rastafari males to assist the party in successfully wooing the grassroots sector of the electorate.

Even more crucial for Manley's new-found, supposed legitimacy with the Rastafari community and grassroots sympathisers, was his astounding proclamation that he had received a so-called *Rod of Correction*, a Rastafari/African symbol of authority, from Ethiopian Emperor Haile Selassie I himself. This was a particularly significant declaration because the Rastafari proclaim the Divinity of H.I.M. Haile Selassie I. Manley was also proclaimed (or proclaimed himself) to be '*Joshua*', who had been sent to Jamaica to bring his people (the Children of Israel) to the Promised Land (Africa/Ethiopia). These Biblical connotations and associations implied that Manley had been imbued with divine powers, a truly deft political public relations move that proved to be an effective election strategy. This association also enabled the PNP leader to incorporate the powerful forces of class/state authority, with popular spiritual culture, as well as with norms of *phallic* power in his political embodiment.

By conjuring up these identities for his populist campaign, Manley claimed a legitimacy that was unprecedented in Jamaica.[98] The use of the *phallic* symbol of the African rod was evocative, because many Rastafari males extend the power of their presence with similar rods – elaborately carved shafts, which are treated as a sacred support of

---

98 Manley's legitimacy was also reinforced by his introduction of social reforms such as the introduction of free education for all, designed to empower the subordinated suffering the vagaries of living below the poverty line. These social reforms angered the Brown middle- and upper-class sectors, members of which did not hesitate to make their displeasure felt by the withholding of their economic resources at a time when the country could ill afford it.

spiritual identity.[99] Despite the PNP's manipulative political use of this didactic symbol, the electorate was not completely fooled and expressed their cultural sympathies for Rastafari rather than for Manley and his chauvinistic ploy.

> Poll figures of the late, highly respected political scientist, Carl Stone... showed that identification with the Rastafari movement was proportionately greater than with the rod. More new voters (68 percent PNP and 38 percent JLP) expressed sympathy toward the Rastafari than expressed identification with the rod (60 percent PNP and 12 percent JLP). The new voters were mainly youths who had reached the voting age of twenty-one between the 1967 and 1972 elections.

> (Chevannes, in Murrell et al (eds.), 1998: 66)

As a matter of survival, those who hold structural power are always pursuing *new discourses* as part of their ongoing strategy to maintain control over subordinate constituencies (Braidotti, 1994). Not surprisingly, they appropriate institutions of popular culture as a mechanism of gaining political legitimacy. Democracy is also a particularly effective instrument that the elite class uses to maintain political power. When the state purports to represent the interests of the people (Spivak, 1993), what emerges is the end of attempts by the disadvantaged to realise the elusive ideal of equal rights and justice, which attempts instead become subsumed in the reproduction of hegemonic interests.

Manley's project reflects what Schumpeter suggests – that democracy in its modern applications really amounts to little more than the upper class acting in their own interests. However, he concedes that sometimes, 'elites function not only in their own interest but also in the interests of society as a whole – an inevitable concomitant of the functional elitism now prevalent' (Cox et al, 1985: 95). This assumption is reflected in the uneven relationship between what successive governments have claimed to be performances in the public interest and the paltry benefits that actually trickle down to the poor.

Over-Sexualised Identities

At the grassroots level on the other hand, the power of the gun has produced a pervasive atmosphere of fear in inner-city Kingston, where the many exist in the thraldom of the few. The first time that I heard a Southside resident say, 'the biggest gun gives you the most power,' I was shocked. It was a theme that was to become quite familiar by the end of my fieldwork. On this occasion of initiation, I was sitting on the Stallag 17 corner with Luddy who was expanding on some of the nuanced meanings

---

99 When females carry the rod, the archetypal statement of masculinist authority, they are perceived as transgressing patriarchal boundaries. Nevertheless, viewed in an affirmative light, this sharing of authority celebrates the cooperative power of Rastafari man and woman as King Alpha and Queen Omega, the complementary conceptualisation of divinity. On the other hand, the carrying of the rod by women is also an indication that some females strategically appropriate patriarchal norms in the process of expressing their own power. Some critical observers see this rebelliousness as a power which, if not contained by a male hierarchy, could lead to dire consequences.

of the masculinity-identity-embodiment nexus, which are characteristic of practical definitions of power in the community.

Luddy explained the connections that are drawn between masculinity, identity and the body and the structures and *discourses of power* inherent to the society, which are characteristic to the inner-city space. In the course of this and other discussions, I gathered that the symbolism of verbal expression transcends the metaphorical realm to inform the everyday experiences of people living at the grassroots.

When men seek power through the use of violence, rather than being an authentic indication of authority, they are actually expressing a crisis in masculinity and, by extension, a crisis in the world system that gives it legitimacy (Connell, 1995: 84-85). In fact, 'ascendancy of one group of men over another achieved at the point of a gun… is not hegemony' (Connell, 1987: 184). Force *per se*, does not prove the existence of a hegemonic order. Rather, the prevalence of the use of violence to express masculinity illustrates the ideological influences underpinning this discourse, which as the political example above demonstrates, are institutionally reinforced to establish such a power apparatus.

Luddy went on to explain how rude boys, who are nowadays also known as shotters '*get their stripes*'.

> It is a figure of speech. What really happens, is if a man wastes[100] a badder[101] man than himself, they say that they get their stripes off that. So that is how they get their power.

Figure 7.1: Luddy.

100 Kills.
101 More powerful.

178

The war conditions under which identities are constructed in the inner-city communities of Jamaica, bear a direct parallel to the following example from the United States of America, which also demonstrates that this *phallic* ritual of violence is the basis on which war efforts world-wide are perpetuated.

> The dominance of the military by men was even more complete in the past. The United States armed forces, for instance, were 99 per cent men in 1960, 1965 and 1970. The percentage of women began to creep up in the early 1970s, with a formal policy of expanding women's role in the military starting in 1973. In most armies, nevertheless, women are forbidden to have a combat role. In anti-aircraft units in Britain during World War II women were allowed to do every job, including aiming the guns at the German planes – but not to pull the trigger.
>
> (Connell, 1987: 14)

Sammo, another young man from the case-study community, pushed this discussion further by explaining how the political economy influences the power definitions that are configured in competitions among the men in the community who are actively engaged in the discourse of violence.

> Once upon a time, you used to be able to make a little money easy. Keep a dance and it would be full. Nowadays, when you keep a dance, people don't buy more than two boxes of liquor because nobody really comes to your dance unless it is the same little man around here. Most of them come because they want something free. They had to close down the cinema up the road because every man is a shotter; *every man wants to go in free. It is the same with work around here. If you are not a shotter, you can't get work, you know.*

This conflation of socioeconomic authority with the violent *phallocratic* identity of the *Shotter*, speaks volumes to the presence in Southside of 'a patriarchal dividend' (Connell, 1995: 82). The power that the *Shotters* enjoy brings not only material and political rewards, but most crucially, the psychosocial benefits of *person/man/hood*. The tragic consequence of the ongoing, amorphous war is that there is now a direct correlation between the systematic erosion of human dignity by the overwhelmingly challenging material circumstances that characterise inner-city life, and the reinforcement of masculinity through the dialogue and enactment of violence.

Connell's analysis of this problem also shows that even men who are not directly involved in explicit practices of patriarchy or violence, may nevertheless benefit from the prevailing system and, therefore, offer tacit support to the normative gender order by their uncritical silence or strategic complicity. There is thus a contradiction between unconscious practice – in the sense that Giddens explains it – and strategic appropriation of the *discourse of violence*, as resistance against material disadvantage or social/citizen insecurity. According to Giddens, this dichotomy constitutes

> the *mutual knowledge* incorporated in encounters [which] is not directly accessible to the consciousness of actors. Most such knowledge is practical in character: it is inherent to the capability to 'go on' within the routines of social life.
>
> (Giddens in Cassell, 1993: 91, emphasis in original)

Have Gun Will Travel

In Kingston's inner city, rival men communicate by making their guns 'talk' to, or 'bark' at, their enemies. To the outsider it is incomprehensible that so many young men set out in relentless pursuit of the extremely vicious mode of violence as their preferred medium of self-expression. It does not seem plausible, either, that they are unaware of the inimical consequences of their actions. However, their lack of remorse is simply the result of the routine application of the reflexive rationality to which Giddens refers. It is a micro-expression of what happens on a grander scale in the arena of world politics. Things may seem magnified when viewed at the local level, but should be placed in the context of expediency. In the knowledge repertoire of violent individuals, acts of violence are not analytically assessed as morally indefensible; they are simply regarded as practical mechanisms of acquiring power. In this scenario therefore,

> [t]he line between discursive and practical consciousness is fluctuating and permeable, both in the experience of the individual agent and as regards comparisons between actors in different contexts of social activity. There is no bar between these, however, as there is between the unconscious and discursive consciousness. The unconscious includes those forms of cognition and impulsion which are either wholly repressed from consciousness or appear in consciousness in distorted form. Unconscious motivational components of action, as psychoanalytic theory suggests, have an internal hierarchy of their own, a hierarchy which expresses the 'depth' of the life history of the individual actor.
>
> (Giddens, in Cassell, 1993: 91-92)

Therefore, those who are seeking solutions to the dilemma of inner-city violence should consider that the psychosocial contradictions attending this phenomenon are the most challenging dimension of the complex problem. Most crucial, the men who '*run the place*', speak and act with the greatest authority, commanding pragmatic deference, even of those not beguiled by this interpretation of identity and power.

In addition, some women admire the ruthlessness or 'wickedness' in the shotter or rude boy as a sign of sexual prowess. His penis/gun power places him in the *desirable* category of being able to provide social protection and/or agony, the local expression for sexual satisfaction. These women openly compete for the *wicked* man's favours in an effort to gain the ascendant position as the number one spouse, thereby reinforcing the binary opposition of *hegemonic masculinity/subordinate femininity*. This gender power dynamic works because both men and women reap dividends from their strategic investments in this discourse.

Many people in the wider community are so paralysed by fear of the consequences of critical confrontation with those men who perpetuate the discourse of violence that they choose instead to comply with the shotter status quo. This *discourse* is also so deeply entrenched in the political economy of the community that it is difficult to confront and contest (see Scott in Scott (ed.), 1996: 168). Whenever I raised the issue of the crime situation, fingers inevitably pointed to the stagnant economy as a primary cause of this problem. It was also suggested that other manifestations of violence in the society, particularly in the domestic arena, are rooted in the frustrations induced by material lack and social exclusion.

> The trivial nature of the incidents which led to family murders or the murder of an acquaintance implied both that frustration was always near the surface in many family and personal situations and that the underlying social and economic reasons for this frustration related mostly to the family pattern in a particular economic context...[E]conomic pressure was the underlying factor which produced a family conflict, and the authoritarian family structure was unable to resolve the conflict without violence.
>
> (Lacey, 1977: 77)

Figure 7.2: Sammo.

Sammo agreed with this view, emphasising that the push factors which impel young men into the discourse of violence are not only related to identity construction (although that is significant), but are fundamentally political and socioeconomic. Therefore, as he said, the challenge to survive in the inner city is so great that

> sometimes you want to *touch the road*, but as a young youth, you do not have to touch the road for everything that you want. To touch the road is to go out there and look for it. Either you steal or beg it. You have other ways you can get your bread[102] too. I chose the way that around here is likely to make them call you a coward or a fool, but I am not into the corner war thing or the upfront gunshot thing. There are two basic roads that are available to youths growing up in the area.

---

102 Money.

I asked him to explain further what he meant by *touch the road*. He elaborated that it is so hard to achieve anything in the ghetto because of the paucity of available options and choices and the odds that are effectively arrayed against even the strongest survivor, that many so-called providers have no recourse but to become involved in criminal activities.

This young man also said that in the inner-city environment, community space was an indicator of male power; guarding turf is therefore a man's business, which is taken very seriously.

> You can't live somewhere and make them call you a *punk*[103] because round here, if they call you a punk, everybody just wants to come and lean on you as if you are a weak fence.[104] So I leave it alone; I just kick back,[105] me and my brethren next door, burn my weed, smoke our chalice, play a game of basketball or dominoes, that's it. You just have to hold your turf because this is our turf. You can't make anybody chase you out of your yard, or come and take over.

Political Puppet Masters

Even those who are not directly involved in the war are at risk if they should transgress the boundaries of the fiercely guarded turf. This anxiety syndrome indicates one of the most tragic consequences of inner-city warfare. The protection of personal territory is emphasised because

> violence becomes important in gender politics among men. Most episodes of major violence…are transactions among men. Terror is used as a means of drawing boundaries and making exclusions…This is an explosive process when an oppressed group gains the means of violence – as witness the levels of violence among Black men in contemporary South Africa, [Jamaica] and the United States.

> (Connell, 1995: 83)

While this is a critically important observation for assessing how the *discourse of violence* is played out at the subordinate level, Connell also emphasises that those who occupy positions of privilege, also use violence as a means of perpetuating their overriding power. In this case therefore, the state representatives responsible for instigating the *discourse of subaltern violence* are even more culpable than those who perpetuate the actual discourse in the inner-city communities. It was the political manipulation of their local party supporters in the first place, that set in motion the now out-of-control wheels of social disintegration.

Elite power brokers benefit from the fact that responsibility for the problem is projected onto the gun-talking inner-city rude boys. The gunmen pull the triggers, yes,

---

103 Weak person.

104 Graphic metaphor that likens the vulnerable to the fragile structures which inadequately secure the homes in the urban grassroots, many of which have been temporary dwellings for so long that some people have given up active hopes of removing.

105 Relax.

and that brings its own reaction, but those political puppet masters pulling the strings of the triggermen, get off without a scratch. They refuse, point-blank, to address the factors that promote violently opposed gender differences as a fundamental avenue to domination. More troubling, conflicts in the inner cities are not nationally acknowledged and analysed as a war, even though the hostilities are identified as such in the inner-city lexicon and local dialogue.

The alarming and extreme violence in Jamaica's inner-city communities, which is proving extremely difficult to unravel as it grows uncontrollably, is thus the product of multiple factors. These elements are part and parcel of a 'lower quality of life and a degeneration of our values as our society has become more urban, more materially developed, more modernised, more affluent and more competitive' (Stone, 1989: 113). In this scenario, the notion of being *the Man*, includes ideological and symbolic meanings of identity as well as embodied references to the normative characteristics of masculinity. This *discourse* therefore reflects the patriarchal apparatuses of power that constitute the gender-identity-embodiment nexus. We therefore need to remember that

> [d]iscourse analysis differs metatheoretically from other forms of qualitative analysis in its view of experience as fundamentally constituted in discourse. The two involve different assumptions and the use of language as a resource...discourse analysis focuses on the discourse itself, not on internal structures or previous events to which the discourse is seen as a route.
>
> (Wood and Kroger, 2000: 28)

The Gun As A Sex Symbol

What is said about manhood is also an indication of how gender will be performed by the social actors in question (Butler, in Nicholson (ed.), 1997). Sammo noted that he had identified his turf and refused to allow others, perceived as more authoritative, to gain ascendancy over him in any way. This assertiveness marked his social identity as a *real man*, with agency in the idiom of inner-city understandings of power, as being intrinsically tied to his gender and embodiment.

> I was never really tempted to be a press-button,[106] because I always wanted to be the man[107] himself. Anything that I am doing, I always like to be the upper hand. To be an upper hand you have to go through the hills and the valleys. I just hold my turf; if I am to be the man, I will be the man of my own speed, because you can't rush anything nowadays. When you are the man, you are the shot-caller. Everybody respects you, you drive a nice car; everything is legit for you, you don't have to work or anything of the sort. Your links deal with you fine. If I can't be the man, I want no part of any organisation. That means that they can't fool me.
>
> (Sammo)

---

106 Seen as someone who can be easily influenced and led astray. To 'take programme' is a similar expression.

107 The don who speaks with most authority and commands the kind of respect which will ensure that he is able to programme the 'sprats' or small fish to carry out his orders, no matter how or especially if, dangerous.

This exposition recalls the debate between those who define identities in essentialist terms and those who attribute the values and behaviours of the individual to processes of social construction. Being *the man* indicates a direct link between biological identification and social expectations of how gender performances are reproduced by the embodied individual, and contoured by the social expectations of authoritative identity. When the body is as heavily implicated in the definitions and practices of the self as it is in this case, it is clear that 'social constructionists do not escape the pull of essentialism, that indeed essentialism subtends the very idea of constructionism' (Fuss, 1990: 5). Thus in so many words, the *phallus* is the man is the *phallus*; a vicious chicken-and-egg cycle seemingly without beginning or end.

> The gun has become a sort of language among the young people. The most common gesture of a young male in an angry exchange is a hand tensed in the shape of a pistol and an arm pivoting in symbolic intent...The so-called inner-city don is a role model not only because of his ability to command and dispense largesse, but also because he is a living source of power – the power over life and over death, the ultimate man. Among the youth, a common name for the penis was rifle...In inner-city communities, the dream of many a young boy is to be able to own a gun, preferably for himself but jointly with the crew if necessary.

> (Chevannes, 1999: 31)

Discussing Foucault's linking of power to the body, Lois McNay sheds more light on the aspiration previously expressed by Sammo to be the man or the don, in local parlance. She observes that '[p]ower and sexuality are not ontologically distinct, rather sexuality is the result of a productive "bio power" which focuses on human bodies, inciting and extorting various effects' (McNay, 1992: 29). In an attempt to ascertain the effects of the acquisition of the bio power of being the man, and how this identity is translated into material and symbolic benefits, I asked Sammo to explain why a man would choose to be a *shotter*. He was incisive in his response.

> When you are a shotter, you get everything free. You can go out at the Arcade[108] and say I am a shotter from Southside and you get what you are to get. If you want a pair of sneakers, you get your sneakers. Here they respect you in the ways how they deal with you. They say "yes Sir" even though you are a little youth. It's just mostly about respect. I would say that 85 per cent of the youths want to be a shotter and about 70 per cent achieve it. Some of them, their family takes them out before them really *buss way*[109] big time. You probably shot a one man and your family abroad sends for you. If you are a big time shotter, you run business places. You are the main man. The man who presses their buzzer could even be outside of the island. The shotters are upset when it is peacetime.

> (Sammo)

Luddy also elaborated on the sexualised meanings that are inherent to the prevailing gender power regime in Southside, which are incorporated in the popular expression 'the man with the biggest gun has the most power'. In perusing his analysis, it is important to bear in mind that '[d]iscourse analysis does make a move to treating

---

108 This is a market place downtown Kingston where imported consumer goods are sold.

109 Get too deeply involved.

utterances in terms of actions...the critical point [being] that this sort of categorisation must be shown to be an activity of participants' (Wood and Kroger, 2000: 29). Speaking of the *shotters*, Luddy explained that

> because they want the *ratings* and they are in a massive,[110] and among their friends they can say this man is a killer and that man is a killer, so they want be a killer too. You have some men who have some *firepower*, which makes him control some soldiers. That man can just come and accumulate back his things. So a lot of these youths who you see firing guns don't actually own them. A man gives them the tool and presses their buttons. The massive gives them the vibes that make them feel like... (giving the fist sign for strength). *It's full time for the wickedness to stop.*

(Luddy)

The politics of recognition and admission that Luddy addresses have relegated poor Black men to a miserable life on the periphery of the society.

> Significantly, admittance here operates...in the sense of letting enter; second, in the sense of validation and acknowledgement...The existential burden that weighs on the Black man is...that even if he has acquired all the rightful permits of entry into the White world – by education, for instance – he does not feel that he is acknowledged as an equal.

(Chow, in Alessandrini (ed.), 1999: 37)

Thus *the man*, is a contradictory combination of class powerlessness and embodied (gun) power. Like Bigger Thomas, the protagonist in Richard Wright's novel, *Native Son*, the young men in Southside are products of a system that constructs them as *others* based on the various identities that they embody. The political psychology of their existence is predicated on their social exclusion and invisibility. In trying to rationalise his feelings about murdering a White and a Black woman to Max, his lawyer, Bigger sums up this predicament as follows:

> For a little while I was free. I was doing something. It was wrong, but I was feeling all right. Maybe God'll get me for it. If He do, all right. But I ain't worried. I killed 'em cause I was scared and mad. But I been scared and mad all my life and after I killed that first woman I wasn't scared no more for a little while...I wanted to do things. *But everything I wanted to do I couldn't...I just lived from day to day...*

(Wright, 1995: 392, emphasis added)

A group of youths on Ladd Lane echoed Bigger Thomas' exhilarated frustration. They were also very explicit about what inspires youths to become *shotters*. One 14-year-old explained that some boys become gunmen

> because when they see that their friends die, they don't care anymore. And they just go on and on after that. Some youth say they are *shotters*, so they have to prove, and man tell them to go and pop corn[111] and mask[112] gun and when they do it now, they become big up in it.

---

110 Big group.

111 Fire shots.

112 Hide.

This recurrent theme of proving oneself among peers suggests that the youths are impelled by their unemployed status to seek material and symbolic power by becoming shotters. Once they achieve this identity, they often have to choose (Gramsci, 1957; Giddens, 1993) to maintain it by doing more and more daring and devious deeds in order not to be seen as weak and ineffectual in the institutional context of the gang.

Domineering Masculinities

Prisoners at the General Penitentiary were among others who said that there is no remorse on the part of the *shotters*. The inmates were also in agreement with the community residents who maintain that it is difficult to interrupt the inexorable cycles of violence because the *shotters* tend to justify their crimes by citing their disadvantaged circumstances as the cause of the crisis. Richard, my research assistant, further clarified the social meanings of authoritative hegemonic masculinity that are embodied in the rude boy and why these elements tend to desensitise this archetypal hero to the impact and repercussions of his devious deeds...

> Rude Boy is the terminology which is commonly used to refer to youths that live in the ghetto but it does not necessarily mean the youths who are "bussing it" or firing guns but those youths *who have knowledge* of such activities. The expression is used in everyday language as a greeting or a casual reference to any man. Other expressions we use are King, Killer, Dads, My Youth, and Hardcore.

Figure 7.3: Richard Samuda, Personal Assistant.

> *You can tell from his appearance or how he moves. He doesn't have to be killing anybody but from you see a man, you can know the difference.* If you live in certain circles and deal with certain people, you will see the difference. You don't know if he is a bait or what, to how he approaches you. But he can be a Rude Boy, meaning that even if he is not bussing it, he has a form of flexing or behaviour and appreciation and knowledge of certain things so

that you can understand that he is a serious youth. You can't fully explain it but you can pick up clues from his type of dressing...but it is truly hard to define because you cannot see a man's deeds on his face or even what he is capable of doing. It would probably take a change of place to prevent him from getting involved because from the moment that he is flexing with certain friends he can't avoid it.

It is worse if there is a gang war going on. As a rude boy, he has to get involved, automatically. This is simply because you can't pass on the next street and tell man on the other side that you are not involved and you come from the other side that they are warring with. If you were involved in the war before and you decide for instance, to become a decent working man, it is the moment when your guard is down, when the war is on, that you are likely to be killed. People don't forget things; you might have fired a shot at someone ten years ago and even if you have changed since then, their family is not likely to forgive you or to forget. So if you were once a rude boy, the only chance you have is to move out.

When someone calls you a Rude Boy it is also a form of respect.

The last phrase in this quotation, which focuses on respect, is worthwhile emphasising because it explains what makes the rude boys participate in *discourses of violence*. Because of the denial of the fundamental human right to respect (see Levy, 1997), it is inevitable that those so disenfranchised will display colossal features of alienation. This combination of factors creates

the dog-eat-dog world where you do what you gotta do to make it, even if it means fucking over folks and taking them out. In this world view killing is necessary for survival. Significantly, the logic here is a crude expression of the logic of White supremacist capitalist patriarchy.

(hooks, 1994: 117, emphasis added)

The recurring motif of (lack of) recognition and a resort to violence to fill this void in the identity repertoire, points to the direct relationships between violent *hegemonic masculinity*, psychosocial identity and embodiment. Paradoxically, the men in the inner city who appropriate this definition of embodied identity and gender authority, end up reinforcing their own oppression and social exclusion by virtue of the heinousness of the criminal acts that they commit. Gender differences are therefore not just a question of mere inequalities in social relationships between women and men. Such inequalities are also inherent to the political demarcations between those who control the state and those minions who enact the hegemonic project, which in turn, contours the power relationships between men and women in the same social environment and between men and women from different social categorisations. Ultimately then,

[g]ender has been employed...in political theory to justify or to criticise the reign of monarchs and to express the relationship between ruler and ruled...[I]t seems important to note that changes in gender relationships can be set off by views of the needs of the state.

(Scott in Scott (ed.), 1996: 171)

Clearly, the state guardians have a stake in the perpetuation of gender power differences between specific social categories; such manipulation of differences reinforces their power base. As Richard's testimony also indicated, an integral component of the gender order is the outlawing of versions of masculinity that do not conform to culturally constructed norms of *macho* heterosexual manhood.[113] Socially acceptable body language (i.e. language about and by the body), reinforces norms of power in terms of *hegemonic masculinity*. This discourse consequently projects stereotypes of *subordinate femininity* on 'aberrant' men. For example, a man who is perceived as weak, is popularly called 'a pussy' and is said to 'behave like a girl'. The following photograph graphically expresses this sentiment, which is part of a mural on a Fleet Street wall.

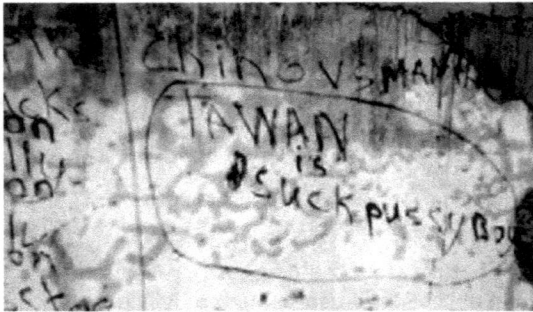

Figure 7.4: The proclamation written on this wall 'Tawan is a suck pussy boy' is the penultimate condemnation of Tawan. Only an accusation of homosexuality could be more damaging. Whether he actually performed cunnilingus is immaterial. The more detrimental consideration is that once so identified, this male has been certified as socially undesirable and even expendable.

The implicit innuendo is that a man who does not subscribe to the dominant gender order of over-emphasised *macho* heterosexuality, is symbolically or latently homosexual.

Figure 7.5: The term pussy, seen here as part of the graffiti of subaltern discourses, used to denote the vagina as the gravitational centrepiece of embodied power plays. On the other hand, the term is used to denote a weak man. This was a recurrent motif in several discussions. This linguistic reversal is one example of how women's sexuality is devalued in the patriarchal project of power attribution.

113 This tendency was epitomised by the Manley election campaign and is amply present in the contemporary rhetoric of the JLP electioneers.

The taboo attributed to performing one's gender in the homosexual mode underlines the importance of *body language* in establishing identities in *discourse*. However, although

> [g]ay masculinity is the most conspicuous…it is not the only subordinated masculinity. Some heterosexual men and boys too are expelled from the circle of legitimacy. The process is marked by a rich vocabulary of abuse: wimp, milksop, nerd, turkey, sissy, lily liver…Here too the symbolic blurring with femininity is obvious.

(Connell, 1995: 79)

The suspected sexual preference of former Jamaican Prime Minister P.J. Patterson has been a propaganda hobbyhorse of the opposition JLP and, indeed, of the general public for some time now. Even so, some people were astounded when the national leader found it necessary to make a public statement defending his heterosexual identity. Political analyst Stephen Vasciannie described this unprecedented development as 'gutter level politics'.

In the pecking order of patriarchy, men who are socially marginalised try to exercise power over other men, women and children by proscribing the boundaries of their sexual behaviours (Connell, 1995: 83). This deployment of patriarchy reflects the prevailing political economy of power, which pervades practices of social inclusion and exclusion. Not surprisingly therefore, homosexuality is still an illegal practice in Jamaica and is deemed to be socially immoral as a result of proscriptions promoted by institutions of religion, education, family socialisation and popular culture. The violent anxiety about homosexuality and concurrently, protection of heterosexuality, suggests that sexual violence is already implicated by the valorisation of masculinity as heterosexual (Woodward, in Woodward (ed.), 1997: 208). The violence in the language itself is indicative of a transmutation of the desire to perform an act of actual violence, into linguistic abuse instead.

Let me say at this point that I am neither condoning nor condemning any particular sexual orientation. The fact that I am heterosexual and am not actively promoting homosexuality, does not mean that I am going to 'fire bu'n' all *batty men* (i.e. call hell fire down on all gays), because as Bob Marley himself said, 'every man got a right to decide his own destiny'. Therefore, at this juncture, I am leaving all judgement to the conscience of each, in terms of their own definition of right and wrong. 'Live and let live' is my philosophy, for we need to arrive at a place where we respect differences – whatever they are. Then, the energies we currently spend projecting our normalising value systems onto 'others', thereby making victims out of them, would be more productively utilised in creating peace and productivity, which doesn't always have all that much to do with who's zooming whom in whose bedroom.

By the same token, I am also not trying to legitimise so-called 'alternative (homosexual, bisexual, transvestite or transgender) lifestyles', which all have their own inherent contradictions and risks. So while I am not advocating by any means a lack or absence of boundaries or rules and laws, at the same time, such laws should still protect human rights across the board. Thus, I am deconstructing sexual preferences here, mainly to show how society's normalising value systems serve to marginalise and 'otherwise' those who do not fall neatly in line. This includes women, children, the poor, Blacks, inner-city residents, Rastafari, as well as gays – like it or not – who all fall into the same kind of marginalised category. This same contradictory marginalisation process self-perpetuates the flourishing of *discourses of domination*.

Thus, although the medium of Reggae music is important for channelling *discourses of resistance*, it also has been used to reinforce normative stereotypes of the gender-identity-embodiment nexus, which reinforces the binary opposition of *hegemonic masculinities* and *subordinate femininities*. The emphasis placed on the *phallus* in this genre is also symbolised by the almost devotional allegiance to the array of high-powered gun weaponry that some (gun)men unabashedly tote, often in full view of other citizens or even police officers.

> For a lot of the *shotters*, it is *just a proving thing*. A man is proving that he can do this, because he has some heavier arms. Some men gain respect because they had a strong voice. But without *firepower, nobody recognises them. That is how a lot of them get recognition around here.* They will then say, 'it was John who killed Tom Brown. Because Tom Brown was a *Diego* [i.e. strong person] who was dealing with *certain things* and John killed him, John just got Tom Brown's stripes. So every man is just saying, John, John. And yet, John just came out of his yard the other day.[114]
>
> (Luddy, Ladd Lane)

The gun and a penis are symbolic representations of the *phallus*. Both are called a tool, piece and machine, among other nouns, and in the ghetto, both are the weapons with which males prove their manhood most effectively. Bobby explained how violent masculinity has come to mean real manhood in the inner-city community of Southside.

> The *shotters* are shooting each other for power. They want power to run the community and power to just set certain things between themselves and their friends. The youths are not saying anything conscious, they are only preaching violence. This one is saying that he is the Don, that one is saying that he rules and this then causes a conflict among them. So you have power struggles between men on the different corners. The youths are hungry and they are not hungry for work. They are hungry for power; they just want to know that they have a gun in their hands. That is power for them, to do anything that they feel like doing. As long as you have a gun, it is as if you have the whole world in your hands. Nobody can talk to you then and you can do anything that you feel like doing. So you have it among man and man on the same corner and then you have one corner fighting against a next corner. It is like this: up here is fighting against down there because each corner wants to run the whole community – Pow, Renkers, every area. It is a power thing.
>
> These youth nowadays though, you can't talk to them. *All you have to do is just, see and blind, hear and deaf and just go through because what is happening will not stop and it can't be changed.*[115]
>
> (Bobby, Higholborn Street)

---

114 Meaning, recently emerged in his identity as a criminal generally and a killer in particular.

115 This was a commonly repeated phrase, which accurately describes the outcome of the culture of fear that prevails due to the situation that this young man describes.

Rape as a Tool of Hegemonic Masculinity

The linkages among discursive violence, gun violence and sexual violence are unmistakable. For example, there is a direct correlation between war practices and the fact that women are often proxy victims of this hegemonic order. Similarly, the prevalence of violence in discourses about the body desensitises the society to the rising incidences of sexual violence in the society. The routinisation of these forms of violence reinforces the dichotomies that have been constructed among various constituencies. Women are invariably, losers in this charade.

Rape as Routine Ritual

The news was on the television
A woman was raped
and there was a demonstration
but all this is background noise
for the nation which has become
desensitised to violence
and so absorbs the ravages
as part of the everyday script
It's all part of the technology
Of virtual reality
you see violence on TV
and it is deemed to be meant
for your entertainment
so when the real life version
hits the screen
it can be seen
to be part of that contrived reality
that you can avoid easily
because you don't have
to turn on the news
or cross the social
boundaries of Cross Roads or
Half Way Tree
to feel the pains
of the inner-city

© **imani tafari-ama**

The *real man* as *bad man* syndrome has had damaging effects not only on the men who are subordinated by this gender power regime, but also on women, who are particularly disadvantaged as a direct result of this gendered definition of sociocultural authority. This theme of women bearing the brunt of the violent conflicts that are enacted between men was also a quite prominent feature of the 1994 Rwandan genocide, a notorious war scenario, where, '[w]omen [were] targeted partly because of their ethnicity but mainly because of their gender and their bodies are used as the figurative and literal sites of combat' (Twagiramariya and Turshen, 1998: 103).

Hilary Nicholson, a member of the local activist network *Women's Media Watch*, wrote an article assessing the escalation in incidents of sexual violence against women in Jamaica, which was published in Jamaica's *Daily Gleaner*. She reported that

> in 1998, there were 1,552 reported crimes against women and girls (murder, rape, incest, carnal abuse), including 880 cases of rape. Studies, she said, have shown that between 36 per cent and 62 per cent of sexual assault victims are age 15 or less. It is estimated, however, that...crimes against women, especially sexual assault and domestic violence, are underreported. It is estimated that only one in 50 of these crimes is reported.
>
> (*The Gleaner*, April 14, 1999)

Like soldiers from ancient history to the present day, some men in Southside have violated women's bodies as a naked expression of hegemonic masculinity associated with their territorial conquest (Brownmiller, 1975: 31). Or, the women may be proxy targets for men with whom other men have a dispute. Legally, 'rape entered the law through the back door; as it were, of a property crime of man against man. Woman, of course, was viewed as the property' (Brownmiller, 1975: 18). Women are dehumanised in the war effort, not only for men's sexual pleasure, but in order to prove the superiority of the marauding males over their more impotent foes. Analysing the World War II context of Europe, Brownmiller observes that

> war provides men with the perfect psychological backdrop to give vent to their contempt for women...To take a life looms more significant than to make a life, and the gun in the hand is power. A certain number of soldiers must prove their newly won superiority – prove it to a woman, to themselves, to other men. In the name of victory and the power of the gun, war provides men with a tacit license to rape. In the act and in the excuse, rape in war reveals the male psyche in its boldest form, without the veneer of "chivalry" or civilisation.
>
> (Brownmiller, 1975d: 32-33)

During slavery, rape of female slaves was taken for granted because 'sexual abuse of Black women was not classified as rape and therefore was not legally actionable, nor did rapes committed by White men lead to prosecution' (Stoler, in Lancaster and di Leonardo (eds.), 1997: 20). Nowadays, rape is sometimes directly related to the war; others blame the victims for their predicament.

> Rape was not common in my time because if a man even did it, he would be lashed, plus getting a sentence. When he came back, if he was living in this community, he would have to run away. Even his family would abandon him. But you still have to ask yourself, when a woman has on a pair of shorts, which is cut in the shape of certain panties, walking on the streets, what do you expect? Especially when you know that so many of the ghetto youths are taking drugs. Many of the women need more moral decency; they need to respect God and themselves to make other people also respect them.
>
> (Ms. Patsy, New Road Park)

This elderly woman has internalised dominant meanings of masculinity and femininity, which penalise women whose garments (or lack thereof) are so provocative that men are driven to rape. This outlook only serves to perpetuate the prevailing violent expression of patriarchal power against women, and also shows how great is the influence of the *dominant discourses* which have permeated the people's everyday practices and definitions of gender norms and taboos (Scott, 1996: 169).

> There is, therefore, a logic to such paradoxes as the gross exaggeration of difference by the social practices of dress, adornment and the like. They are part of a continuing effort to sustain the definition of gender, an effort that is necessary precisely *because the biological logic*, and the inert practice that responds to it, *cannot sustain the gender categories*.

> (Connell, 1987: 81, emphasis in original)

Ms. Patsy was even more disparaging of young girls' style of dress, which, she said, also contributes to the sexual abuse of women by men.

> Some of the things that I see young children are wearing now! In my days, it couldn't happen. You had a law for that; they called it 'indecent exposure'. I remember when I was a girl, that the nylon material became popular. If you dared to put on something made out of *nylon without* having something underneath it like a blouse and go out on the street in only a brassiere, police would arrest you for indecent exposure. If you did not even respect your body, they would force you to respect it because your body is the temple of Allah. In those days, it was very seldom that you would see a woman dressed in anything that reached above her knee.

> (Ms. Patsy)

Figure 7.6: Ms. Patsy's comments could very well be directed at these girls who were some of the children who participated in the summer workshop at the Fitzgerald Fun Centre, summer 1999. The sexist stereotypes embedded in her arguments reflect the gender norms that are specific to their social space.

Despite her location in an inner-city community, Ms. Patsy's views reflect values of bourgeois morality which she uses as the yardstick to denounce women's self-presentations in Southside. Other institutions of socialisation including the mass media, the family, school and peer groups, reinforce the value-loaded recipes for moral conduct, which are then multiplied as everyday norms. Such values, which are again bourgeois in origin, set the parameters for practices of the body and become the standard by which progress in society is judged.

A loss of moral direction is what is seen by some social thinkers as the root cause of the current social tensions in Jamaica, and women's embodied identities are somehow implicated in such thinking.

> Morality has to do with human needs, interests and purposes in terms of the wider community. These needs, interests and purposes are related to human responsibility and accountability, individually and corporately. They are a necessary condition for human well being. *What this means is that morality, humanity and community go hand in hand.*

> (Taylor, 1992: 16, emphasis added)

Taylor assumes that moral standards are self-evident and value free. Yet, in reality, such standards have been formulated within the Judaeo-Christian Ethic and are institutionally reinforced in the interest of privileged classes and patriarchal authority. At the other end of the continuum, the rapist transgresses all moral boundaries, as a mixed gender group of children on Ladd Lane explained, 'They run a *Duracell* (battery) on women,'[116] some boys said. Murvin from Foster Lane also suggested that if the women will not 'let off'[117] during the peace, then 'they have to get taken' during war. In other words, if they won't willingly have sex in peace time, they have to be forced to do so in war time.

Tom, a youth from Fleet Street said that, 'the other thing that has become prevalent from the other day is raping. About five women had been raped since this war thing started up again[118] and is the men from that area involved.'

Although some persons suggested that the men who rape came mainly from the McWhinney Street area, others disagreed, suggesting that the violators are dispersed within the community. Kay from Ladd Lane, a woman in her early thirties, corroborated the report, saying that there was one young woman, 17 years old, who had been 'batteried' by 15 men.

> The next day she was walking like nothing had happened; she is one of those loose girls. What was she doing on the road at one o'clock in the morning dressed in a punny squeezer?[119]

We had a vigorous discussion about the issues raised by this question. We debated long and passionately about the meanings of dress and the gender implications that

---

116   i.e. gang rape. Gang rape is also termed 'battery' hence the brand name of multiple rape, 'Duracell', the brand name for a strong battery.

117   Have sex freely.

118   This was in May 1998. The number has increased since this discussion took place.

119   A tight-fitting pair of pants which accentuates the contours of the crotch.

are attributed to how women represent themselves in public. Kay insisted that the women only have themselves to blame for being raped if they choose to wear clothes that emphasise or expose their vaginas, breasts and other body parts. I suggested that this line of argument emphasises women's powerlessness, while suggesting that men have power over public spaces and that women should not enjoy equal freedom.

'The things these women wear nowadays!' Kay insisted. 'The fact that she was on the street practically naked and she knows how the place runs, she was asking for it.' I responded that this line of argument denies women their right to act as free agents. We both realised that our debate would not have an immediate resolution because we were arguing from opposite ends of the embodiment continuum.

What is irrefutable is that rape incidents were becoming more and more gruesome. In two cases that came to my attention, gangs of men are alleged to have forced their female victims to perform oral sex on all of them. This demand is significant in light of the fact that even when it occurs between lovers, this sexual practice is the subject of severe social stigmatisation and is part of the taboo repertoire of 'bowing', on which I will elaborate in the next chapter.

Sharon Marcus suggests that rape is an 'act' which 'is not only scripted – it also scripts' (Marcus, in Butler and Scott (eds.), 1992: 391). She cautions, however, against seeing rape as a pre-given relationship between rapist as actor and the woman being raped as victim and suggests that the act should be seen as a 'process of sexist gendering which we can attempt to disrupt' (Marcus, in Butler and Scott, (eds.), 1992: 391). Marcus recommends that women should undermine the rape script by refusing to perform in the passive role demanded by the rapist, whose power is ensured by the powerlessness that women display to the attack. She also says that women are constructed into a psychology of fear in a way that men are not, a fear which is so powerful that it results in 'a complete identification of a vulnerable, sexualised body with the self...[W]e...come to equate rape with death, the obliteration of the self, but see no way we can draw on our selves to save that self and stave off rape' (Marcus, in Butler and Scott, (eds.), 1992: 394).

What this author does not adequately address is the strategic element in women's passive response to rape. The forms of resistance that Marcus recommends (such as using a viable weapon to fight back or else attacking the rapist at vulnerable points like the testicles) would be practically suicidal. To try to re-write the rape script in the process of the debacle is a creative conceptual luxury not practical for people subject to such indignity.

When women are raped in this environment, they may also be threatened with murder as they are threatened at gunpoint. Guns are symbolic as extensions of penises, holding women at a double disadvantage. Marcus clearly does not understand what really happens on the ground, but then that's how armchair theorists operate. She would sing another tune if she had to dance around the power dynamics of some of the more violent rape situations that some women in Southside have to negotiate.

Furthermore, when men force women to perform fellatio at gunpoint, this has gender power, class and moral implications because in the *grassroots discourses*, this practice is not recommended for 'decent' women. Joan French's analysis of the social construction and relations of power inherent to rape, which is based on the contradictory experiences of women in situations similar to those that I am addressing, provides complementary material for this discussion. Her article cites the testimony of a woman who frequently observed rapists as they violated women next door to her house, a situation she was powerless to avert.

> Dem have these boys in my area. All the time them coming behind my house wid some young girl. One take her, use her, go out, den another one come, and so on. Sometimes dem even ask me for newspaper and I have to give dem. I can't say nothing because dem have gun and knife. One time one a de little girls mek up her face – she didn't want to whine,[120] she just stand up stiff, so de boy jus tek out him knife and start flashing it on either side of her face and tell her 'whine, a seh, yu better whine,' and de poor likkle girl start whining an she crying at de same time saying is her mother sen her to shop.

(French, *No to Sexual Violence*: 5)

A similar incident created a furore during May 1999, just before I concluded my research. A woman was *battered* in apparent response to a clash between a male relative of hers from a nearby community and some men in Southside. Although the number of men involved in the crime was disputed, the details of violation closely resembled other incidents in which women were forced at gunpoint to perform the highly taboo act of fellatio. As Hanif also emphasised in her own research, rape reinforces the real man as bad man mode of power, within which women are defined as subordinate through the interpretation of their bodies as vessels of violation. In Hanif's work, Tula, reported that, she had suffered sexual abuse by a former lover.

> One day him come inside a me house and him hold on pon me and make himself forward. Me say no, and me push him way and him hold me down and rape me. Me fight him, but him strong and him box me in me face and kick me. Me cry and me go a police and dem take statement and him hear that me carry report pon him.

(Hanif, 1995: 1)

Unpacking the experience of Tula, Hanif concludes, '[h]er gender was central to this act of violence' (Hanif, 1995: 1). The myriad ways in which women's bodies are sexually objectified, such as in the mass media, which blatantly treat women's bodies as commodities, are implicated in the act of rape.

> Violence against women is embedded in systems and beliefs whose premise is that women are not equal to men. As a result, women are discriminated against not only in matters like equal pay for equal work…but in matters of their physical well being and sexual safety. The litany of abuse taken by women is unending but true, and the advent for feminism – the radical idea that women are fully human – has become therefore essential.

(Hanif, 1995: 1-2)

In Southside, Lissome also shared her experiences with me, which address some of the deep personal issues related to the political economy of rape. I spoke to her along

---

120 A colloquial expression, which means to rotate the hips in a sexually suggestive movement, a derivative from wind as in the motions, made in winding a clock.

with some of the members of her immediate family. Because the power relations entailed in the rape experience usually manifest themselves in residual feelings of guilt and blame in female victims, I asked her to share her emotions in the wake of being sexually violated by her boyfriend.

> I felt bad. Him draw mi inna di yard an tear off mi clothes. I was the only girl who had one boyfriend because he was my first boyfriend. I did not have more than one boyfriend like other girls. They used to tease me saying, wha you have dat so different from fi we? To be able to deal wid it I just say to myself that it happened a'ready so I am not looking back. If it happens tomorrow I know that I can soon say it happened yesterday.[121] Sometimes I think about it and those things burn you when you think about it but when you know that the past is the past, you are free. When I meet somebody new the first thing I always start with is 'Shower,[122] I have been raped already you know...' I tell them what are the bad things about me.

> (Lissome)

This woman has internalised her rape experience as one of the *bad things about herself*, which is a common response of women who are sexually abused. Unfortunately, the syndrome of guilt and blame is usually taken for granted as the norm by many victims/survivors. The act of rape thus becomes something that the victim owns, since she cannot escape from the memory of the act and the repercussions of its recurrence on her psychosocial agenda through the passage of time.

> The police may never find the "brother" who raped me, and I may never get him to read the seven-foot scroll detailing *all* I have suffered since he slithered into my life.

> (Rushing in James and Busia, (eds.), 1993: 137, emphasis in original)

Lissome refused to go to the police because she did not feel confident that she would get social justice through the system.

> I decided not to press the charges because he should live...and suffer. I know who it is. He even has a one-year-old daughter who will soon be two, and they can't even look after her. And when he sees me, he has to walk and hold down his head and I walk and hold up my head.

She did not press charges and does her best to rationalise away the fear knowing that her family could pay terrible consequences if she dared to voice her pain. She felt morally justified because her ex-boyfriend has had fallen on hard times. Her arrogance was contrived to cope with the knowledge that she was powerless in the face of the strength of his reputation as a Rude Boy. These feelings of helplessness are also addressed by Rushing in her analysis of the lingering effects of her own rape experience.

---

121 This psychological coping mechanism suggests that people who have to live with violence do find ways of codifying their lives in order to survive the ravages of the abusive experiences.

122 Shower is a pseudonym, which is used conversationally in JLP communities. Slogans popularised by the two major political parties are Shower (JLP) and Power (PNP). The national Democratic Movement, which was hatched in the womb of the JLP, has not yet matured to the sloganeering stage and is still without such a mark of distinction.

Now, as it did when I was actually being raped, my mind scrabbles for a safe place and, finding none, tries to shut off, but the strategy is no more effective than it was that gruesome night...Peer blinking as I did the rape night, into the living room. Tense, heart racing, afraid.

(Rushing, in James and Busia (eds.), 1993: 135)

The power machinery embedded in these rape episodes exemplifies the hierarchical gender binary of hegemonic masculinity and subordinate femininity. This confirms the proposition that informs this chapter. Namely, that women who are already socially excluded because of their class and race/colour, are being exploited by men living in similar social circumstances, a clear case of multiple marginalisation. Meanwhile, the men in question earn their 'ratings' by the extent to which they create fear and violate females on the basis of their gender and embodied identities.

Subordinated Femininities

Although the circumstances of power enactment are sometimes beyond the control of women, females should still not be seen merely as docile bodies experiencing patriarchal power like hapless victims. On the contrary, even in performances of passivity, women experience their embodiment as agents (Benson, in Woodward (ed.), 1997: 130). In fact, as the second part of the proposition indicates, some people's behaviours challenge this stereotype of performing true to gender identities. Ironically, some women also use violence to exercise agency; Precious confronted her partner with a degree of fierceness that he was unable to cope with and thereby curtailed his abusive attacks.

He tried it with me; that is how I got to stab him. He had to ease off or I was really going to kill him. I told him point blank that I would kill him. I had a dozen glasses in my buffet and I smashed them on him. I even went to the police station but I did not get any support there to take revenge so I came back. I only recently put down my knife you know. I am cautious every time I have a knife because I say that any time that I draw it, I am going to use it. My friends are always warning me to be careful that I don't end up in prison. My mother always says, think on the last son that you have. That thought made me get afraid to even pull it. But all I know, no man is going to hit my body and get away with it because I have been beaten too many times already.

(Precious)

Women who use violence as a form of resistance are actually appropriating a mechanism of oppression in order to overturn it. They are also reinforcing the prevailing gender pecking order. Precious' response reflects the extent to which her own identity construction has been influenced by the dominant *discourse of violence*.

Once these mental representations are in place, the dominated group and its members will tend to act in the interest of the dominant group 'out of their own free will'. The dominated group may lack the knowledge or the education to provide alternatives, or it may accept that the dominance of the dominant group is natural or inevitable and resistance pointless or even unthinkable.

(van Dijk, 1998: 162)

But Precious' reaction is an aberration – Fay, Maxine and Errol all agreed that in the late 1960s and early 1970s, it was more commonplace for men to be beating up women even on the streets. 'Some of the women liked it,' Maxine said, 'because they used to tease the men and provoke them into getting angry so that they could get their beating. One woman called her Black Eye, her trademark.' She explained that several women held on to the perception that their partner was demonstrating optimal love when they beat them.

These examples of the intersection of gender power and the deployment of sexuality were also referred to in at least two other discussions. Some of the male youths in a group of ten on Foster Lane, suggested that women do not respect men unless the men beat them. 'If you do not beat them,' one man said, 'they think that they can sit down in your face and call you a pussy.'[123] Again, I was struck by the linking of a weak man to the female sex organ, and the parallel drawn between this taboo representation of manhood and the practices of violence against women.

The competitive fights between women over men, which I mentioned earlier is also an example of women's enactment of the *discourse of violence* among themselves, as an adjunct of the binary of *hegemonic masculinity* and *subordinate femininity*. In other words, men benefit directly from violent rivalry among women, which implicitly reinforces their status as the Man. Two young men admitted that they felt good when women fight over them and one explained that 'no girl wants to go with you if you have only one girl. They want to have something to war and fight over so that one can say they won you.'

Molly was telling me one of her life stories one day and as I shared her memory I was struck anew by the paradox between oppression and agency in her everyday survival strategies.

> Too much pressure was at home and I wasn't getting any attention. I did not really care whether I lived or died because I was tired of it. So I started to stand on the corners, go to friends' yards, sometimes I would stay on Fleet Street. Sometimes I would not even come home. I did not care; I just wanted to get away. I got involved with a man who had a baby mother and two kids…I had no-one to defend me and I had my knife. One day I got into a fight with the woman. I stabbed her with the kitchen bitch – that's what we call a big knife. First stab I gave her was in her neck. I stabbed her all over. But the more I stabbed her, the more she came back at me. I danced, skipped round her. She was pregnant and I did not even know.
>
> She said, "Are you going to kill me?" I said yes! I am going to kill you! I stabbed her, stabbed her, stabbed her…so much, that I cut myself.
>
> I told my brother to light the torch [Molotov cocktail bomb] and throw it away immediately towards the woman I was fighting. But he did not do that; he lit it and held it while threatening them and it caught my aunt. She was the one who got burnt. Eventually the woman's baby father confronted me and told me that he liked me and at the age of 15 that was it. Although

---

123   Oral sex is an extremely taboo issue; this man says that unless women fear/respect men, who are capable of being violent with them, they assume that they can reduce him to having oral sex with them. This practice would only earn the man the dubious qualification of being a pussy or a weak man.

I feared him because he was a known bad man, I went to him. He never abused me or anything. All he did was love me. What he did is what my mother should have done. She couldn't have sex with me but she could have loved me.

(Molly)

Molly's expression of embodied violence both disturbs and reinforces the normative gender power regime. While defying the prevailing gender stereotype, she also *re-inscribes* violence as the norm for expressing personal power and resolving conflicts, thereby subscribing to the kind of gender performance that denotes *hegemonic masculinity* in the Southside community. Even as one is able to acknowledge the pathos of the dysfunctional family situation against which she was rebelling, the brutality of the attack on her rival is undeniably vicious. She ultimately capitulates to the power of a Rude Boy, whose control over her was interpreted as the most adequate substitute for the maternal love which she had been denied. In the final analysis therefore, her rebellion is a farcical one; her attempt to make creative alterations to the subordinate conventions into which women have been constructed, actually results in its accentuation.

Bad Man, Sexy Man

The picture she paints
of the loving thug
is the most crucial break point yet;
when all she wanted was a mother's hug
she took his love
she was fifteen
fit to smash it into his net
for the real man was a bad man
and
the bad man was sexy
The dichotomy
of hegemonic masculinity
and subordinate femininity
stood on its head top
did a bad-ass whine
and threw up the trope of sexuality
as the element of identity
providing space to exercise agency
defying norms and prevailing sanctions
yet coming to a conclusion
of myriad contradictions

© **imani tafari-ama**

CHAPTER 8

THE SOCIALLY INSCRIBED BODY

In the discursive type of account, self-location within discourse is the key to understanding constructs and through them personality. People adopt or commit themselves to certain positions in the discourse that they then and there inhabit.

(Harré and Gillett, 1994: 140)

The Body – Bridging Culture & The Individual

The third assumption of *Blood, Bullets and Bodies*, Proposition Three, suggests that *body language* reveals the complex identity contradictions that poor people negotiate in everyday life. Such problems are directly related to class, race/colour, gender, sexuality, social location and age. These cultural factors are the entrenched indicators of power in the Jamaican society and are more graphically expressed by *body language* the further one goes below the poverty line. In the inner city, therefore, the prevailing political economy of cultural embodiment has established ideal bodily types of femininity and masculinity, which are explicitly expressed in hierarchical values of social and sexual desirability. This cultural construction of individual subjectivity derives from the 'dominant value systems' of the prevailing social environment (Grosz in Gunew, 1990: 71).

In other words, the subjective cultural values and psychology of individual bodies (persons) are constructed and shaped by the social values and economic conditions that prevail in the wider society. To guarantee that this system works, 'state apparatuses ensure that there is harmony between the requirements of a socioeconomic system and the subjects it therefore produces' (ibid.). These dominant and domineering cultural values are in effect programmed or *socially inscribed* into individual bodies, or, more specifically, into their minds/brains. Thus, the general bodily behaviour of people living in any given situation is most often an unconscious reflection and representation of the predominant (ruling) cultural value system existing in that society or community. In this respect, the human body symbolises a bridge or physical interface between the culture of the surrounding macro-world and the internal micro-world inside the body/head of that individual. This is how culture impacts the body, and influences the psychosocial state of individuals in a community.

On the other side of the coin, the human body also provides an important resource, or weapon, for socially excluded citizens like those living in communities such as Southside. The body is like a slate on which the owner writes and expresses their own *counter-discourses of resistance* to the material, gender and other symbolic forms of domination that the Black body faces daily. Therefore, individuals who so choose, may instead engage in various *discourses* expressing independent agency: such as revolutionary or rebellious verbal dialogue; such as dressing in and wearing non status quo attire; such as displaying a non-traditional physical appearance in terms of hairstyle and grooming; or, such as dancing in provocative and sensational ways designed to showcase their belief that their bodies are hot commodities which should be desired and that are worth top dollar.

Obviously then, it is possible for human bodies to be personally and independently *self-inscribed* by their owners, but only to the extent to which such individuals are self-motivated, self-conscious, independent minded, free thinkers. Otherwise, their bodies would be as *socially inscribed* and culturally programmed as the average inner-city resident.

The Political Economy Of Desire

The class-specific construction of the Jamaican society renders White men the most powerful category in political, social, economic and embodied terms. Although (rich) White women also share this class and race advantage, patriarchy intervenes to lessen their cultural authority. By the same token, Brown males and females are the second most influential social grouping. Consequently, in this colour/class-specific paradigm of subjectivity, Black women, men and children are at the bottom of the social ladder. Black men emerge as considerably disadvantaged in political, economic and social terms vis-à-vis their White/socially White counterparts. By this measure, the White man, then the White woman, followed by the Brown (socially White) man and the Brown woman, represent the ranking in terms of desirability for marriage or sexual liaisons or other social intercourse.

Furthermore, in Jamaica's historical experience of racism, Black men bore the brunt of White male anxieties, which have been played out in vicious mechanisms of psychosocial, material and sexual control.

> [S]kin colour and unemployment...are important features of social relationships in urban Jamaica. Colour reflects the continuing, though diminishing impact of racial differences on the social relationships within the non-White majority of the urban population. It derives from the plantation origin of the society which made clear status and prestige differences between Blacks and Browns.

> (Stone, 1973: 119)

One outcome of this antagonism, a common feature of the African Diaspora, has been the propagation of the notion that Black men had no recourse but to dominate Black women in order to compensate for their subordination by White men. This argument suggested that Black women's strength of character posed a danger to Black men's self-realisation. In the United States of America, for example, this dilemma was fortified by *The Moynihan Report*. The racist and sexist conclusions drawn by the author of this document sparked a vitriolic debate, summed up in the following extract.

A question that might arise from these observations was why men, rather than women, seemed less able to fulfil family obligations under the pressure of racism and discrimination. The answer, Moynihan speculated, was that although all Blacks suffered, men suffered more: "It was the Negro male who was the most humiliated…Segregation and the submissiveness it exacts, is surely more destructive to the male than the female personality." The reason for this evidently had to do with the inherent nature of the species: "The very essence of the male animal, from the bantam rooster to the four-star general, is to strut," was his scientific conclusion.

(Giddings, 1984: 326)

Similar essentialist ideas run through stereotypes of gender identities and relationships between Black women and men in Jamaica, as well as other power relations in the wider society. This tendency to use racist determinism to account for the embodied identities of *the other*, has also resulted in the representation of Black men as sexually insatiable. This attribution of a lack of control over sexual desire, carries the subtext of the Black men's (supposed) proclivity for rape, which fails to differentiate between the minority who subscribe to this mode of expressing power, and the majority that does not (Giddings, 1994: 322).

Racist discourses have stereotyped Black men as brutally sexual, due to overrated assumptions about the size of their penises (Bordo, 1994), thereby rationalising the need for the symbolic and material castration of Black men by the White power brokers who control the realms of domination. The reinforcement of the stereotype of the Black man as rapist, has been historically constructed in order to perpetrate the notion of the White woman as the embattled symbol of purity. The ultimate obsession of the White man within this configuration, is to protect the so-called, 'frail' White lady (Giddings, 1994: 321), from the perceived danger of the sexually marauding and promiscuous Black male. You know the archetypical story, the good Christian White knight in shining armour who rescues the fair (i.e. 'blond') damsel in distress from the evil Black Knight.

However, while 'Black men's Blackness penalises them…because they are men, their self-definitions are not as heavily dependent on their physical attractiveness, as are those of all women' (Collins, 1990: 79-80). Be that as it may, by internalising and practising the myth of exaggerated sexuality, some Black men demonstrate not only their capitulation to the ideological referents of structural power, but also their active role in perpetuating that cycle of racist and sexist domination. Yet in the view of the dominant cultural value system in Jamaica, Black men should be the least desirable individuals to women in general because of their black complexion and because they are assumed to be poor.

Meanwhile, the neo-colonial cultural construction of the ideal type of woman as being White/Brown has been designed with a default that configures Black women as *the other*, and encourages them to negate and look down on the attributes of their own embodiment. This is particularly detrimental to the Black woman's self-esteem precisely because women are by nature more heavily dependent than men are on having a positive image of their own physical attractiveness.

Externally defined standards of beauty...claim that no matter how intelligent, educated or "beautiful" a Black woman may be, those Black women whose features and skin colour are most African must "git back." Blue-eyed, blond, thin White women could not be considered beautiful without the Other – Black women with classical African features of dark skin, broad noses, full lips, and kinky hair.

(Collins, 1990: 79).

In general, therefore, African identities have been constituted within a contradictory aesthetic of race/class/gender/sexuality by so-called dominant ones who thereby designate Africans, as *the Other* (Collins, 1990: 79). Thus, the terrain of physical embodiment has to be seen as a complex politicised sphere of crisscrossing power interests. Since poor Black women also experience subordination in their relationships with Black men, it is again evident that patriarchy is a significant intervening variable in the matrix of domination, which is eloquently expressed in the production of discourses about the body.

The body is then an interface, a threshold, a field of intersecting material and symbolic forces. The body is a surface where multiple codes (race, sex, class, age etc.) are inscribed; it is a linguistic construction that capitalises on energies of a heterogeneous, discontinuous, and unconscious nature. The body...is now seen as a situated self, as an embodied positioning of the self.

(Braidotti, 1994 : 169)

As we have seen, the human body, and by extension the human mind, can be conceived of as an ideological/political construct, whose materiality is contingent on normative notions of race, class, gender and sexuality, which are culturally produced and reproduced. Therefore, performances of the body have to be read in the context of this discursive constitution.

[D]iscourses, significations, subjectivities and positionings...*actually* exist... The idea that the mind [and body] is, in some sense, a social construction is true in that our concepts arise from our discourse and shape the way we think. This goes for the concepts that concern what is around us and also for the concepts that concern our own mental lives. Therefore the way we conceptualise the mind (or anything else) is a product of the concepts available within our discourse.

(Harré and Gillett, 1994: 22, emphasis in original)

In Jamaica, *discourses* about the body determine identity constructions and shape the sexual desires of social subjects.

The resulting reality is much more complex than one of an external White society objectifying Black women...Instead...[Black] women find themselves in a web of cross-cutting relationships, each presenting varying combinations of controlling images and Black women's self-definitions.

(Collins, 1990: 96)

Some of the meanings *inscribed* on the Black woman's body are clearly expressed in the following Jamaican proverb.

Black Betty a bun, but choo im culla yu naw seet. [Patwah]

Black Betty is burning but because of her colour you can't see it [English]
Some people endure much pain and suffering without exposing their true feelings [Idiomatic Meaning].

(Morris-Brown, 1993: 159)

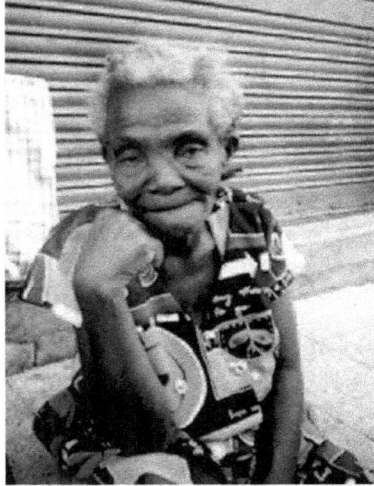

Figure 8.1: A type of Black Betty, this woman possesses the capacity to survive despite the myriad disadvantages she faces as an inner-city resident.

One of the chief elements of oppression – the colour of her skin – is also the main symbolic and material resource of resistance that is available to Black Betty. She is able to use the covering of her body to disguise her responses to disadvantage, a pain which she exposes only when she thinks that she is in a safe space to do so (Collins, 1990).

By reclaiming the features of physical embodiment that have been used as signs of oppression, and by transforming them into stepping stones of survival, the subordinated have created *counter-discourses* to pervasive power mechanisms. Since the all-pervading elements of domination have been discursively constructed, they can also be neutralised through *counter-discourses*, although as we know by now, many contradictions are embedded in such resistance efforts.

By reclaiming the features of physical embodiment that have been used as signs of oppression, and by transforming them into stepping stones of survival, the subordinated have created *counter-discourses* to pervasive power mechanisms. Since the all-pervading elements of domination have been discursively constructed, they can also be neutralised through *counter-discourses*, although as we know by now, many contradictions are embedded in such resistance efforts.

Nevertheless, it is a tremendous challenge to come to such self-consciousness in a space like Southside where material conditions are so harsh. The capacity of the people in question to act on that consciousness is also limited by their survival challenges. Once self-consciousness is acquired however, Black Betty (and the multiply fractured constituency that she metaphorically represents) is able to recognise that skin colour, gender, sexuality, age and social space are sites of oppression, exploitation and exclusion. But Betty also acts to transform these sites of oppression into opportunities for self-advancement. However, we should not go to the extreme of glorifying the survival impetus that drives the disadvantaged to the doors of success. Unless the entrenched power structures are tackled in fundamental ways, such resistance tactics only take the subordinated subjects one step forward, but relentlessly slide them two steps backwards.

The interlocking of gender, embodiment and identity in the agency/resistance dynamic of Black Betty's Janus-faced everyday existence shows that

> our bodies are not merely possessions that we use and enjoy; nor are they simply extensions of ourselves. Our bodies are integral components of who we are, how we see ourselves in the world, and the way we interact with others…Emphasising embodiment draws attention to the sex and gender of persons in civil society. Issues of sexuality, pregnancy, and childbirth are thus no longer confined to a private sphere. Instead, they are fundamental themes for society as a whole.

(Dean, 1996: 92)

It is a truism that one can only have social self-confidence if one is free from fears of threats to the body. The ability to develop and project positive images of the self is also an asset. However, the organisation of social life in the wider society creates boundaries that prevent inner-city residents from realising their full potential. The public/private dichotomisation of the labour force also mirrors the gendered biases that undergird the state structure and its institutional apparatuses.

> Rather than occupying an empty place, power in a democracy is embodied in a particularly masculine body. This masculine body mediates between an outside that has been moved into civil society itself – the private, familial, and domestic sphere to which women are confined – and the inside world of political action. As citizens, men are inside, within the public sphere of debate and competition. As heads of families, their power appears to stem from a realm outside of this discursive public. Since women remain excluded and "other," the masculine form can be constituted as the "one," a form in which women cannot recognise themselves.

(Dean, 1996: 78)

Clearly, the categories of man and woman are not homogeneous, but are further fragmented by race, colour/class, sexual preference and other social indicators of embodiment, which carry their own contradictory meanings of power. It is evident therefore, that the bodies of women and men are constructed differently in a particular cultural context. Therefore, notions about physical embodiment transcend the material realm to reside in ideological notions about the body. At the same time, the various subtle meanings ascribed to the physical body and its various component parts also have direct relevance for an understanding of the gender-identity-embodiment drama.

In North America and Britain, the moral breakdown of society has been attributed to the embodied performances of teenage mothers[124] and violent young men. However, such views do not pay adequate attention to the structures of power which leave the subordinated little recourse but to exercise agency through such gender performances.

> Right-wing ideologues, conservative politicians and anti-feminists lay much of the blame for the perpetuation of the underclass through lone motherhood on the agency exercised by women…Whilst we would not wish to suggest that women living in inner city 'ghettos' can choose to escape 'structural poverty'…we do believe there are women living in situations of structural poverty who are exercising agency and consciously deciding to have children without depending on a male partner.
>
> (Mann and Roseneil, in G. Jagger and C. Wright, (eds.), 1999: 112-113)

Cultural values about fertility contribute to the construction of a political economy of embodiment and also define an elaborate repertoire of taboos and sanctions for certain embodied performances. In more ways than most people probably realise, women's identities are intrinsically tied to the generalised *discourses* about their sexuality. For example, a barren woman is regarded as a social failure.

Thus, from an early age, there is a general scramble for young women to prove their social competence through the practice of child bearing.

Therefore, what is said about the body of anyone in social spaces like Southside is as politically loaded as the cultural/social institutions that generate and facilitate such gendered expressions. Describing someone as 'Black and ugly' or, conversely, 'Brown and pretty' reveals value-loaded and race-specific connotations of social and sexual desirability. It is the same thing for 'coarse kinky hair' compared to 'straight good hair'. Guess which racial type has which?! And before – and maybe even despite – the present popularity of dreadlocks, guess which type of texture hair a good percentage of Jamaicans would most desire? 'Straight good hair' of course! Not the 'coarse kinky hair' which actually forms better and stronger locks. Such sentiments are a direct indication of the political economy that shapes the subconscious desires of Southside residents.

---

124 Since I extensively address the concept of parenting as the central theme of Chapter 9, I confine myself to a superficial introduction of this practice at this juncture. Nevertheless, as I will explore, deterministic views only serve to highlight the extent to which the political construction of popular gender stereotypes reify and reinforce the very identity contradictions that denote the defects in the various power hierarchies that I have been analysing. Therefore, in this identity contestation, matrices of domination and resistance crisscross each other in an ongoing orgy of power contestations.

The 'Boom Bye Bye' Mentality

Nowadays, the theme of heterosexism is one of the most prominent features of the obsessive references to the body in the popular culture and music of Jamaica. To a very large degree, the promotion of this heterosexism is expressed in terms of an overwhelming anti-homosexual rhetoric targeted at the much despised batty man/ chi chi man.

Because of this stance, popular culture in Jamaica as represented by the Reggae music industry in general and Reggae Dancehall in particular, has been on an inevitable collision course with the international pro-gay-and-lesbian lobby for many years. Whether it is traditional Rastafari-influenced *Old School* Reggae, or today's more commercially acceptable *Dancehall* genre of Reggae, the same strong aversion to homosexuality is clearly evident in Jamaican music. Therefore, the glut of gay-bashing lyrics in Reggae/Dancehall is indicative of the equally pervasive rejection of gay lifestyles in both mainstream and urban inner-city Jamaican society.

On October 2, 2002, England's *Guardian* newspaper published the following headline: 'Reggae Fans Attack Gay Rights Protest'. The paper reported that 'Gay rights protesters were beaten, kicked, and spat at by a crowd of up to 250 rap (sic) fans as they demonstrated against the homophobic lyrics of three singers nominated for Music of Black Origin awards.' The *Guardian* reported that a small number of members of the gay-rights group called OutRage! was set on when they hoisted placards outside the awards ceremony at the London Arena, and had to be rescued by police and security staff. According to the newspaper, the protesters were objecting to the nomination of three top Jamaican Reggae/Dancehall stars, Capelton, Elephant Man, and TOK, some of whose songs, allegedly, advocate the murder and incineration of gay people.

The reporter said the attack was led by 25 teenagers shouting 'Kill the batty boy' and 'Kill chi chi men', which she called 'Caribbean slang-abuse for homosexuals'. Security staff dragged the five protesters to safety, and police had to throw a cordon around them and evacuated them from the area as the crowd tried to break through. Peter Tatchell, the gay protest leader, was quoted saying that 'This was one of the scariest moments in my 30 years of campaigning…Our lives were threatened several times, particularly by two men who claimed to have knives…Beer cans, coins and cigarette lighters were thrown at us. The mood of the whole crowd was very ugly, not just the group who were actually violent.' There were no arrests at that time.

However, a year later in October 2003, news surfaced that the same Tatchell was demanding the arrest of Beenie Man, Elephant Man and Bounty Killer, claiming that British law allows officials to prosecute singers who encourage violence against homosexuals. According to the OutRage! leader, 'These Reggae bigots are fuelling anti-gay hatred and violence. The main victims are Black lesbians and gay men, both here and in Jamaica.' Tatchell said that British authorities have an obligation to arrest the Dancehall artists under violations of the Offences Against the Person Act.

In my view, the inordinate amount of attention that is devoted to the homosexual aspect of the *body language discourse* only serves to highlight the fragility of the identities of the rude boys who characterise the portrayal of *hegemonic masculinity* in the prevailing discourse of violence.

A lot of people also consider that some rude boys are homosexuals in the closet. Some of them will not go near their women. *They will kill you if you call them that yet know that they are not totally against it.* But because of the taboo issue and the prototype that is typical of the ghetto he has to maintain the image of toughness and badness. That is why you see that a lot of them brutalise their girlfriends but can't stop them from going to have sex with a next man down the lane. Then when she is seeing her period, he is going to say that he doesn't want her to cook for him. So if she meets a man who is loving and is going to treat her tender in those times, she is bound to be unfaithful.

(Richard, Personal Assistant)

On one occasion in the late 1990s, when members of the Jamaican gay and lesbian community proposed a march through Half-Way Tree (a major Kingston/St. Andrew intersection) to lobby for the right to social recognition, the *oppositional discourses* were profoundly preventative. After one such outburst, when the radio talk shows were inundated for weeks with this discussion, the gay activists were forced to review and cancel their plans. They realised that they were under the threat of serious physical violence that men and women in *civil society* promised to visit on those damned as deviant and brazen enough to flaunt and promote their same-sex preferences in public. These objectors, who emerged from all classes and genders, drew upon institutional references like the Judaeo-Christian Ethic, public morality prescriptions and family values, to justify condemnation of these dissident gay statements of sexuality.

This marginalisation of non-heterosexual identities (Connell, 1995) bears out Foucault's argument that the body is 'a key site of disciplinary practices, and also a site of resistance to such practices' (Segal, in Woodward (ed.), 1997: 210). The practices that are most threatening to heterosexual male identities have, on several occasions, caused offenders to lose their lives. During my research, it was alleged that a man, Andy Bowers, was killed because he *bowed* by having oral sex. In a group discussion, some young men threatened that they would kill any youth that was said to have engaged in oral sex, a transgression deemed to be more deadly than even habitual coke (cocaine) taking.

These reactions serve to underline what Connell refers to as 'crisis tendencies', which 'provoke attempts to restore a *dominant masculinity*' (1995: 84). As a group of women and two men confirmed, homosexuality is an aberration in a space where the norm is being 'straight' (Butler, in Nicholson (ed.), 1997: 308).

An important observation needs to be made at this point. In recent years, more and more attention has been paid to the need for anthropological researchers who study the sexualities of *others* to exercise ethical responsibility in their representation of the realities they encounter, as well as of their own sexual identities (see Kulick and Wilson (eds.), 1995). Critics suggest that such research often masquerades as intellectual production but amounts to little more than voyeuristic and masturbatory pastimes (ibid.: 2).

I wholeheartedly agree that it is important to interrogate myself as critically as I questioned the subjects who enabled us to gather information about their sexual experiences for the advancement of our academic careers. I was therefore very open during the research process to responding to questions from the participants, especially because of the quality of the friendships that we shared. However, even more ethical questions arise about the implications of disclosing these conversations in this book. Thus, 'race, gender and other social relations no longer function within solely ideological structures…[but] operate always within a field of power, and their particularities typically take the form of hegemonic struggles' (Fiske, 1993: 254).

Since sexual identities are linked to class, gender, age and social location, I asked a group of women if homosexuals live in Southside and if so, what are people's attitudes towards them. Due to the sensitivity of the issues and the dangers such disclosures entail, I have changed the names of the participants in this discussion.[125]

Lee: I know a man who rented a room from my mother and he is a batty man…

Merl: Two live at George's Lane.

Tanya: I know some lesbians who live at Ladd Lane. The man one wears pants and the woman one wears skirts. Once, two fat ones were out on the lane doing their thing till the wee hours of the morning. I don't call their names to harm me[126] but Peaches and Cream are sodomites. Big, *tapanaris*[127] sodomites, walking with cellular phone. Their Queen sodomite give them a cellular and a car, bleached out their faces and gave them the latest batty rider and the latest lick.[128]

Merl: One time it was not as popular as now. I can't tell you how it happened but some of the women say woman love is sweeter than man love. They say the right thing is when somebody sucks their pussy.

Tanya: Listen to what they say. They say woman to woman better than woman to man but if any woman ever tries that with me, I would stab out their eyeball.

Susie: Yes homosexuality is definitely here.

In Southside, taboo practices of sexuality or *bowing* are seen as reprehensible personality defects. They are thought to be damaging to the character of the transgressors as well as to the reputation of the wider community. Prohibited practices include prostitution, oral sex, lesbianism, bisexuality, masturbation, abortion and homosexuality. Demarcation of these embodied boundaries indicates how 'power

125 In most cases, where this kind of danger does not attend the knowledge sharing, I have an agreement with the participants to identify them. This is part of the process of validating their power and contributing to the political process of self-esteem building in the face of the systematic social exclusion that they have experienced. As we also discussed, this process is also an important part of the project of social transformation.

126 This is a phrase that is commonly used if the name of a dead person is called. The linguistic expression suggests that homosexuals are regarded with abhorrence in public discourses.

127 A local expression, which denotes someone who possesses tremendous authority.

128 A batty rider is a very brief pair of shorts, which is cut in the shape of panties, leaving part of the buttocks exposed. The latest lick is an appropriate pun with obvious sexual practice inference. The more subtle reference is to the outfit being à la mode or the latest designer wear.

establishes technologies that direct themselves towards the bodies and behaviours of subjects' (Grosz, in Gunew (ed.), 1990: 89). Institutions of socialisation reinforce these regulations, thereby producing *docile bodies* as the prototypical mechanism of exercising power (Foucault, 1980). Sexuality prohibitions are, therefore, inundated with

> gender ideology [which] is a disciplinary discourse running parallel to and reinforcing state power...An important feature of the gender discourse (as well as of other disciplinary discourses) is its assimilation by the actors involved. Both women and men internalise the gender discourse.
>
> (Delsing in Davis et al (eds.), 1991: 135)

It is culturally correct for so-called real men not to bow and to verbally '*blood and fire*' and threaten to 'boom bye bye' (i.e. shoot) those who do. Jamaica and Jamaican music are notorious for the verbal and physical violence directed against homosexuals. Penile penetration of the vagina is perceived as the all-time and only normal way to have sex. This outlook is also institutionally reinforced, because in Jamaica, the predominant Judaeo-Christian ethic influences many other institutions of socialisation such as the education system, the family and popular culture. These institutions are therefore important channels for the transmission of the ideology and practices of heterosexism.

Woman To Woman

In spite of the real risks involved, some individuals challenge the dominant embodiment proscriptions. Molly described her aunt as 'a lesbian' who 'wore only pants and shirts'. Looking rueful, she said it was 'very rare for you to see her in a dress.' Nobody really bothered her because, interestingly enough, the violent surveillance of embodied practices is more stringently directed at men than it is against women. The fact that such a woman openly defied the prevailing cultural norm suggests that, '[w]hile domination may be inevitable as a social fact, it is unlikely to be hegemonic as an ideology within that social space where Black women speak freely. This realm of relatively safe discourse, however narrow, is a necessary condition for Black women's resistance' (Collins, 1990: 95).

The women whom I quote here trusted me enough to share some of their most intimate thoughts on issues related to sexuality – woman to woman. Therefore, disclosing this data with a wider audience also has problematic ethical implications. However, the participants were also aware that I would be translating their confidential stories into material for the public gaze and they agreed to this use of their experiential knowledges. That said, questions still have to be raised about the power relations on which such manipulation of the researched and their knowledges by the researcher, is predicated.

> The disturbing dimension of our discourse about sex is crucial to bear in mind when considering any aspect of Western sexuality, particularly anthropological interest in other people's sex lives. One of the reasons why sex has always been of concern to anthropologists is because, in addition

to being fetchingly risqué, the sexual behaviour of other people has been widely understood to be a point of irreconcilable difference between 'us' and 'them'.

(Kulick in Kulick and Willson, 1995: 4)

By delving into the arena of sexuality and linking this theme to the political economy, my aim is to demonstrate that sexual desire is in many respects a social construction and directly related to the power mechanisms that abound in the wider society. In addition, this analysis is also designed to demystify gendered notions of secrecy that surround the domain of sexuality and in the process, substantiate the knowledges and power of the socially stigmatised and excluded subjects of Southside. Moreover, this data is not peculiar to the women concerned, but also has implications for a more general treatment of sexuality in other wider social contexts. Therefore, I maintain that this process of interrogating the 'forbidden' subjects of the discussions is a valid part of the process of deconstructing the hierarchical binary oppositions, which establish power mechanisms of defining, confining and delimiting embodied practices.

It was in this context and with the foregoing in mind that I, as a woman, also asked the other women to explain to me, woman-to-woman, the community's response to the individuals who were known to be same-sex lovers.

Tanya: From people know that you are a sodomite, *you have to leave us*. We don't want you near us so leave! We will get rid of you. Either you go to the country[129] or uptown because...

Merl: Because most of it is uptown.

Tanya: Most of this sodomite thing is uptown because those are the kind of people who tolerate those kinds of things.[130] Most of the whores and the batty man are uptown.

Lee: Most people say how can that be right when my pussy was made to be fucked?[131]

The violence implicit in these responses as well as the persistent denials of the presence of homosexuals in the community, which contradict the previous admissions, illustrate what Connell refers to as the '*authorisation* of the hegemonic masculinity of the dominant group' (Connell, 1995: 81, emphasis in original).

As Lee's enquiry at the end of the interview quote illustrates, many women have also internalised the dominant heterosexist norms. In addition, it seems like the hegemonic gender order disqualifies women's capacity to supersede the socially constructed identities that have been projected onto them as a result of their biological sex. This tradition naturalises women's roles as 'mothers, sexual partners [of men] and housekeepers' (Delsing in Davis et al (eds.), 1991: 135).

---

129 To the rural areas.

130 In a significant reversal, poor people who are usually otherised for living below the social line of snobbery, have their own ways of ridiculing the would-be better-offs.

131 In dominant discourses, oral sex is taboo for men and women alike. However, when I probed into privately guarded sentiments, I discovered that these taboo practices were very much part of desire.

Yet a group of children on Maiden Lane said that in spite of the popular discursive norm of heterosexuality, homosexuals lived in the area. One boy explained, 'some girls don't want to be with men because they are sodomites. When they are dancing, they whine up on each other.' I had previously observed this pattern when the girls choreographed their own dances in the summer workshop. When I asked them about this practice, they said that they were copying what they saw 'big women do' at dances. While this act may not necessarily denote a sexual relationship, the boy's statement suggests that, in spite of the taboo discourses against this practice and the denials already mentioned, lesbians are present in the community.

The popular culture accepts closeness among women as non-threatening, an assumption which is perhaps also linked to the choice to deny the presence of lesbians in a heavily Christianised context.

> [T]he importance the Bible plays in Afro-Caribbean culture must be recognised in order to understand the historical and political context for the invisibility of lesbians...[who are known by] this dread word "sodomite" – its meaning, its implication, its history.

> (Silvera, in *Feminist Studies*, Fall, 1992: 523)

Every time I attended a dance, I asked patrons why the women dance up against each other. I was told that they are doing it to display enjoyment of the dance and to accentuate the social bonding among women in a crew. Thus, in this space, the homosocial intersects with the homoerotic, as well as with taboo assumptions about homosexuality. The homosocial is reflected in the display by Dancehall Queens[132] of intimate camaraderie through their dance movements, which some children mimic as part of their intra-gender bonding. These embodied enactments are loaded with homoerotic desires, which have to be masked because of the dangers that attend such embodied expressions.

However, this choreographed closeness could also be viewed as the creation of another 'safe space' in which oppressed women metaphorically 'find a voice'. Their embodied bonding is, therefore, a form of resistance.

> In some cases, such as friendships and family interactions, these relationships are informal, private dealings among individuals. In others, as was the case during slavery...in Black Churches...or in Black women's organisations...more formal organisational ties have nurtured powerful Black women's communities. As mothers, daughters, sisters, and friends to one another, African-American [and other Diasporean] women affirm one another.

> (Collins, 1990: 96)

And yet, these women's intimate interactions could also be seen as a performance for the male gaze, and as an extension of the transaction of exchanging sex for materiality. Whatever the explanation, these embodied expressions openly challenge hegemonic

---

132 In a later section, I will devote more attention to the women whose performances as Dancehall Queens serve to disrupt normative notions about the gender-identity-embodiment nexus.

heterosexist norms of morality and demonstrate as Collins also argues, that 'a distinctive, collective Black women's consciousness exists' (Collins, 1990: 92).

Not surprisingly, the women with whom I interacted eventually questioned my own sexuality even as I probed the intimate details of their lives. Such self-critical reflexivity is also a pre-requisite of Black womanist standpoint politics (hooks, 1990; Collins, 1990). I was therefore as frank with them as they were with me – woman to woman. I was asked during several discussions if I was having a sexual relationship with a man. When I initially said no, the women asked in unison how I deal with feelings of sexual desire. This was a question that I had avoided on a previous occasion, as I explained in my response.

> **Imani:** I was talking to a youth and he wanted to ask my business but in a diplomatic way. He said, so when you do all your research work and you cool off yourself, what you do? I kind of avoided answering because I felt embarrassed to tell him that I sometimes masturbate.

> **Merl:** What is that?

> **Susie:** Like when you lie down and think about sex and you feel yourself up.

> (Much laughter greeted this explanation).

> **Merl:** Not only women do it; a lot of men back their fists[133] too.

After discussing masturbation for a while, the conversation proceeded to oral sex. The women explained that oral sex is a highly disqualified sexual practice in Southside. This taboo is rationalised with references to the Bible and other institutionalised resources for *discourses* of heterosexuality. Popular beliefs suggest that oral sex practitioners symbolically transfer the defilement of their practices to unsuspecting victims when they share eating utensils, smoking material, and saliva fluids in kisses. If a rude boy should suspect that he has been implicated in this embodied taboo through social interaction, the offender could receive the most brutal reaction, or even death.

However, the women in the group also disclosed that they had private feelings about oral sex that definitely contravened the prevailing norms.

> **Tanya:** What happens if you meet a man, you have sex several times without it ever crossing your mind to have oral sex. You eat out of his mouth, you play with him. Then one day he tells you that he sucks pussy. Well, basically you bow too, you know, because since he *grounds*[134] down there, you grounds down there too.

> **Susie:** If you love him you will not leave him; you just have to keep it between you and him. I would just tell him to suck my own. People don't know that it is one of the cleanest ways to have sex.

> **Tanya:** But you see, if people brand you by saying that you bow you have to defend it. That's what my man had to do among his friends and clear his name when they were spreading a rumour that he sucked

---

133 A Patwah expression, which means male masturbation.
134 Patwah verb which means to be comfortable.

my front. But God doesn't think you sinned for that though. If you are multiplying, it doesn't matter how you want to have sex you know.[135]

Merl: Even doctors say that nothing is wrong with oral sex. I got an offer and I think that I am going to take it up. Somebody tells me that it is very nice so I have to try it. A big man told me that that is how a man makes love. A lot of people don't know that sex, fuck and making love are different things. When you fuck, a man just jumps on and comes off. He just does it very fast. It just looks like dogs fucking. Sex now, is not romantic, but it's a little bit better than the fuck. Lovemaking now, that is the thing that makes you feel really nice. There are some old men you know, who tell you that they kiss their women on their legs, and even their feet! A man told me that he kissed his woman all over her bottom.

Tanya: My boyfriend kisses me on my leg. He kissed me on my breasts, on my neck, down to my belly. He kissed me on my leg. But he did not bow to the pussy.

Merl: My man kisses me a little below the navel. People would say, that from the moment that he passes the navel he bows but not to me. He did not bow. He kissed me on my leg; he kissed me from my toes and came up. Susie, do you think that he bowed?

Lee: I don't think that he bowed; I think that was a showing of extra love.

Susie: Yes, I feel that by doing that, he is showing me that he loves me more than anything else in this world.

Tanya: Well, I can't call that bowing because when my man and I are making love and he kisses me on my toe? Jesus! Jesus! That's what gets me in the mood.

These disclosures display an erotic assertiveness, which enables the women to transcend *dominant discourses* of otherisation, exclusion and stigmatisation, through the exploration of their sexuality. Their sexual knowledges and the power that this capability engenders, result in the transformation of their bodies into sites of personal empowerment. In addition, although there is compliance to normative definitions of embodiment, these are also countervailed in the behind-the-scenes context of private practice and conversation. Analysing similar prejudices that characterise dominant attitudes and responses to the AIDS epidemic in the United States, Jeffrey Weeks concludes that

> we all too often confront this complexity with moral and political positions that assume we know what constitutes correct sexual behaviour, and with powerful interests which seek to enforce them. When faced with sex, we readily abandon respect for diversity and choice; we neglect any duty to understanding human motivation and potentialities, and fall back on

135 Reproduction, which is stylised as women's natural role, rationalises the performance of sexual taboos in this woman's view. I will elaborate further on this assumption in the next chapter.

received pieties, and authoritative methods. The result can be devastating for those forced to live on the margins of social acceptability – and inhibitive for those who do not.

(1985: 53)

Maintaining Theoretical Integrity

This hegemonic regime works to lock the power brokers who control the state and its apparatuses, as well as the social actors at various levels of the society, into a political economy of embodiment that is so rigorously amalgamated that it merits the use of the hybrid theoretical approach that I am employing to adequately deconstruct it. This rigorous reflexivity also entails '[p]roblematising this once self-confident figure [the researcher]…[and] subjecting it to scrutiny and criticism…dealing the death blow to the myth of anthropological objectivity' (Kulick, in Kulick and Willson (eds.), 1995: 2). Despite the attention I paid to maintaining an ethical standpoint (see Chapter 11), I am also keenly aware that leaving the space (perhaps never to return in any substantial way), and objectifying these intimate exchanges through this analysis, also has exploitative implications. Feminist partiality does not always amount to ethical responsibility, because there is a

> tendency in anthropology to think that problems of power, privilege, and perspective can be defused simply by inserting the self into one's accounts and proclaiming that dialogue has occurred. To the extent that this move leaves unchallenged the epistemological basis of anthropological knowledge, all it does is subsume the other into the project of the self'.

(Kulick, in Kulick and Willson (eds.), 1995: 16)

However, the fact that halfway through the research effort, I became involved in a relationship with a man from another inner-city community who was my cultural interpreter *par excellence*, afforded me the opportunity of sharing in other intimacies that enlarged my understanding of the meanings that I encountered in Southside. Jean Gearing, who had a similar experience, observes in this regard that,

> as anthropologists we typically use very subjective emotional reactions as well as so-called 'objective' intellectual criteria, to evaluate the success or failure of our research enquiries. Positive and negative emotional reactions to individuals or to situations guide what we pay attention to, and how we interpret the significance of our observations. As researchers, we must learn to take our emotions seriously, and not dismiss them as interfering with our objectivity.

(Gearing, in Kulick and Willson (eds.), 1995: 207)

I realise that my commitment to epistemological integrity could create a backlash of (unintended and unwelcome) security threats to the discourse participants and myself. However, my objective is that this analysis should be viewed as

> emerging from an oppositional, progressive, cultural politic that seeks to link theory and practice, that has as its most central agenda sharing

knowledge and information in ways that transform how we think about our social reality...[and linked to] concrete needs of marginalised groups.

(hooks, 1990: 6)

I trust that my commitment to this risky process of critical cultural engagement will not jeopardise the social security of the participants in this project. Going out on a limb is sometimes the only recourse when we consider that

> nothing in society will be changed if the mechanisms of power that function outside, below and alongside the state apparatuses, on a much more minute and everyday level are not also changed'.

(Foucault, 1980: 60)

Skin Bleaching And Idealised Sexuality

> The paradox of Caribbean life is that the more things change the more they remain the same. The vault-like ascent by the society from slavery into freedom and then from colonialism into constitutional independence is yet to be matched within the society by a corresponding progress from cultural inferiority of the vast majority to cultural self-confidence.

(Nettleford, 1978: 3)

In a severe expression of internalised racism, more and more poor Black women are bleaching their skin nowadays in a bizarre attempt to acquire the psychosocial status associated with brown or 'socially white' skin. This is a prominent example of how *racist discourses of inscribed embodiment*, which place particular emphasis on women's idealised sexual desirability, reflect the historical fracturing of Black identities. The physically and psychosocially damaging effects of this bleaching practice are another graphic example of the way in which institutionalised racism has become inscribed into the identity schema of disadvantaged social actors below the poverty line.

At the end of my research engagement in June 1999, the Pharmaceutical Society of Jamaica discontinued the distribution of bleaching agents which contain damaging amounts of hormones and steroids. They declared that this retraction was due to the destructive effects that these agents are known to cause to the body. However, the practice of *bleaching* persists among Jamaican women, especially poor Black women. While physiologists are commenting in consternation on the damaging effects of bleaching creams on Black skin, critical cultural activists like myself, are also trying to make sense of this phenomenon of sociological self-denial. Routine processing of so-called *resistant* hair to make it straight, is the corollary attempt by the socially disadvantaged to reconstruct themselves into the image of the idealised (Brown/White) subject.

This practice reiterates the fact that 'the factors shaping sexualities and identities are appropriated and created differently by females and males because of the way sexed bodies are culturally interpreted and defined' (Blackwood and Wieringa, in Blackwood and Wieringa (eds.), 1999: 48). It is as if the subordinated Black woman has to represent her main identity features (face and hair) in masquerade or muse,[136] in order to be valid. This performance of the body throws up the contradiction of treating essentialism as a site of political struggle and self-affirmation, and affirms on the constructionist side of the debate,

Figure 8.2: Black women with split personalities bleach their skin and straighten their hair in a vain attempt to look 'white' (Artist: Jabez).

that subjects who institute actions are themselves instituted effects of prior actions, and that the horizon in which we act is there as a constitutive possibility of our very capacity to act, not merely or exclusively as an exterior field or theatre of operations. But perhaps more significantly, the actions instituted via the subject are part of a chain of actions that can no longer be understood as unilinear in direction or predictable in their outcomes.

(Butler, in Butler and Scott (eds.), 1992: 10)

As I mentioned earlier, the ideological and material privileging of (socially) White femininity turned the entity of the White/Brown woman into the icon of sexual desirability in Jamaica. Some disadvantaged Black Betty-type women neurotically parody the bourgeois construction of the subject in a desperate self-realisation gambit.

The question of colour takes on particular significance in urban Jamaica because it relates to the salience of status factors in interpersonal relationships, in a society characterised by a history of rigid social hierarchies. *The rigidity of the class-colour hierarchy of stratification that evolved from the early plantation society of Jamaica during and immediately after slavery has left indelible marks on inter-personal relationships in the contemporary period.*

(Stone, 1973: 120, emphasis added)

---

136   As I will discuss in the next section of this chapter, the elaborately coloured wigs that are part of the Dancehall Queens' costume also typify the moment of contradiction. On the one hand, subordinated women attempt to subjectify themselves in the image of the idealised White woman. And on the other hand, by this practice of making a parody of their identities, these women demonstrate their extraordinary creativity in developing a mosaic for making body statements which contest bourgeois classifications of beauty. However, this dialectic also poses the thorny question of whether agency should be treated as given. Embodied enactments of resistance, which contain such eloquent identity paradoxes, have to be constantly questioned for their reflection and refraction of discourses of domination onto those who appropriate pejorative discourses in their efforts to come to self-realisation.

This stratification system demarcates social groups into upper, middle and lower classes, on the basis of historically constructed and embodied identity factors, and is further complicated by the *subaltern discourses* which, often subconsciously, reproduce and reinforce the abstract yet rigid definitions of femininity and masculinity (Grosz, 1990).

Figure 8.3: Pictured above are some of the members of an extended family who embody the wide range of skin colour shades that mark people as more or less s exually desirable in the inner city as well as in the wider society.

I conducted an interview with the extended family shown in the preceding photograph, which was taken in their yard on Maiden Lane. I later incorporated this discussion into a morning edition of *Groundings at the Grassroots*, the radio programme which I hosted on Roots 96.1 FM. In the following extract, Tamara describes how the subordinated value system privileges brown-skinned women over dark-skinned women in the inner city. This hierarchical constitution of embodiment is particularly significant in the inner-city social space where, as I will elaborate in the next chapter, sexuality is one of the few resources with which disadvantaged social actors can negotiate in order to gain material advantage.

> Once you are a Browning in the community, to me, you get more look-up-at. People look up at you because they are going to say wow! Browning! I see with my eyes that when you are Brown and you go to look for a job, you get through quicker than a Black person does. I had a friend who was working in a store; she is a Brown, good-looking girl.[137] When she was going to look for the work, she took a friend with her who is dark in complexion and they took on the Browning and told her friend that they had no more space. What was more was that in less than no time, she was further ahead than the Black people who were there working all the time. In this community, if you are not Brown, you are not saying anything and I don't think it should be that way.

The ongoing practice of skin bleaching graphically illustrates the internalisation of racist values of the ideal sexual identity as being whiter rather than darker (Freire, 1967; Collins, 1990). As Stone (1973) emphasises, the value system of embodiment

---

137 These associations are usually combined in a connotation of sexual desirability in the same way that describing someone as 'Black and ugly' is the prevalently used converse expression.

that obtained in colonial and postcolonial Jamaica persists to this day, ensuring that the codes of colour-class definitions of privilege still inform the social locations of the races occupying this island polity. These hierarchies are even more magnified in the urban grassroots, with value-loaded distinctions being made among shades of Black, even to the extent of the self-destruction of melanin-rich skin via bleaching agents. This practice represents both the result and the continuation of discriminatory definitions of racial embodiment, definitions that were constructed in plantation society.

Tamara also elaborated on how body and language constitute social actors and in turn circumscribe their own capacity to cross the boundaries demarcated by such *discourses*. It is therefore worthwhile quoting her again for further clarification of the associations drawn between skin-colour and social status, which pervade the entire body politic in Jamaica.

> Most of the women bleach because they figure that men will go after them when they will look like a Browning. A whole lot of them feel that bleaching makes them look good while some of them just follow fashion. Still, some of them do not realise that to be dark is to be a browning because you have many different shades of brown. Another reason women especially bleach is because they are not proud of their colour. Being Black is so beautiful more than being the bleaching colour that there is now. This goes for men too because you also have men who are bleaching.

> I think that the women who are bleaching should stop because the bleaching creams do not work well with the sun. When you bleach the skin, you thin out the layers so you can't take the sun as before and if you get a cut, it takes longer to heal. The sun is hot and the bleaching creams were designed for cooler climates so some men and women end up having two faces or two different types of skin complexion which make them look bad because everybody can see that it is not the true skin showing.

As this example shows, *embodiment* discourses are often politically and externally contrived and emphasise the hierarchical social value system that underpins the stratification of the Jamaican society. As I mentioned earlier, the practice of bleaching corresponds directly with the process of hair straightening. Housing facilities are so inadequate in the inner city that people claim the street as a social and public space of gendered power (Connell, 1987; Braidotti, 1994). In the following photograph, the street provides the space to show off the expertise of the *beautician* and the beauty *aspirant*, both of whom are engaged in the process of reproducing the much sought after image of the (socially) idealised subject, in the purposefully styled and fashioned embodiment of Black women.

Bleaching and creaming are routine body practices for some inner-city residents, who aspire to reduce the distance between the glamorous way they would like to see themselves and the harsh and chronic experiences of stigmatisation and exclusion they experience because of the way they actually look. Women even take so called 'fowl pills' in order to make their 'bumpers' (i.e. their bottoms) bigger and rounder. It is even understandable that such dissonance will be the cultural norm in an environment where skin colour and hair texture are such problematic indicators of social status. The tragedy, though, is that there is no evidence of strategic consciousness in this dissonant practice of status symbol acquisition. This elusive goal of acquired beauty is being pursued at the expense of the conception of a self-sustaining and socially transformative identity paradigm.

Figure: 8.4: In Southside, the street is a gendered institution of socialisation, gender identity establishment and social practices, which disrupt divisions between notions of public and private.

Still, some contradictory embodied actions – such as those performed by Dancehall Queens – can be interpreted as the exercising of agency. Many disadvantaged women have constructed an alternative aesthetic to the racist and sexist configurations that I have just discussed. However, their personification of embodied resistance has serious drawbacks because of its inevitable reproduction of pervasive norms of domination. I, therefore, interpret these women's embodied expressions of agency as archetypal expressions of the perennial tension between structure and agency (Giddens, 1993, Torfing, 1999: 137-138).

Dancehall Queens: As Bare as you Dare

> Sexuality is far more of a positive product of power than power was ever repression of sexuality.

> (Foucault, in Gordon (ed.), 1980: 120)

While not constituting a homogeneous group, Dancehall Queens personify subversive subaltern femininities, which unsettle bourgeois prescriptions of morality (Cooper, 1993; Meeks, 1996). They produce their own *embodied discourses* of power by centring their identities in such a way that, in a peculiar reversal, the 'uptown' subject of (socially) White femininity becomes reconstituted as *the other*. Like the so-called Black Betty, Dancehall Queens strategically use their bodies to refract hegemonic power and to produce their own *discourses of self-realisation*. However, because these gender-identity-embodiment reconstructions are also conjugated within dominant phallocratic norms, these self-definitions also have inherent problems in terms of issues dealing with real emancipation for women.

Regardless of those issues, the subjects of this identity odyssey definitely *big up their status* through their embodied performances. This *counter-discourse* has also shifted authority over the embodied cultural domain from hierarchical bourgeois prescriptions, to subaltern identity inscriptions of opposition (Cooper, 1993; Meeks, 1996). Therefore, although '[g]ender boundaries, like those of class, are drawn to serve a variety of political, economic, and social functions...[t]hese boundaries are often movable and negotiable' (Conway et al, in Conway et al (eds.), 1989: xxiii).

Figure 8.5: From the movie *Dancehall Queen*: Reggae Dancehall artiste Beenie man, whose lyrical and acting talents were featured in the film, is seen here juxtaposed against the typically sexually explicit self-representation of a queen of the Dancehall.

As an established social institution, the Jamaican Dancehall is an important environment for subordinated young men in the inner city to 'strive' or achieve a measure of self-realisation, as DJ Shaggy suggests. Paradoxically however, the heterosexist themes emphasised by many of today's Dancehall artistes only serve to objectify women and contribute further to the increasing incidents of sexual violence. The inordinate emphasis placed on physical embodiment through constant allusions to both sacred and profane performances of the body, speaks resoundingly to a high-power *phallocratic* investment in controlling the sexuality of women. Here again, we see the convergence of the political economy, class, gender and embodiment, which are all conveyed in the discourses of popular culture.

The cultural rebelliousness of the Dancehall Queen, who emerged from the inner-city environment, is symbolised by practices of elaborate *undressing*. Dancehall Queens defy bourgeois norms of morality by *daring to bare*[138] their bodies as a bold appropriation and transformation of stereotyped notions of the *exotic* African body as being primitive and/or vulgar in its nakedness. Reclaiming (near) nudity as a *subversive discourse* of dress in the Dancehall space has been an effective mechanism for these queens to proclaim the death of bourgeois ideological domination in the domain of self-representation. These queens therefore embody a disruptive regime of discursive power, which presents a direct challenge to class-specific structures of power.

Dancehall Queens recall the embodied traditions established by enslaved Africans on the plantations, which continued into the post-emancipation era and which form an

---

138 Dressing 'as bare as you dare' is a popular slogan for Dancehall events where women are encouraged to compete with each other to show off as much as their bodies as possible, a practice which has spawned a tremendous range of new fashion statements.

integral component of the continuum of resistance. Especially at Christmas time, the Set Girls who performed alongside the Jonkonnu revellers, paid meticulous attention to dress as well as artistic etiquette in their competitive performances.

> The key elements in the Set Girls' parades are clearly competition and display or, since the two elements are inseparable *competitive display*, setting against one other associations of women...Although much, perhaps most, of the money needed for the purchase or making of Christmas finery came from the slaves' own "alternative" economy, all observers stress the part played by contributions from slave owners or other Whites...
>
> (Burton, 1997: 74-75, emphasis in original)

The big difference between the Set Girls of the past and the contemporary Dancehall Queens, is that the former left the structures of power intact while the latter are definitely a disruptive force to reckon with.

> The slaves saluted and praised their masters and mistresses and received gifts in exchange. Blacks and Whites danced together to the most "African" of music. There was some mockery and satire from the slaves, which was expected and probably enjoyed by the Whites provided that it did not go beyond certain mutually understood limits...And that, on the surface of things, was that, as in due course the slaves moved out, either back to their village or on to another plantation to salute, serenade, and confront both its masters and its slaves.
>
> (Burton, 1997: 77)

On the other hand, the embodied performances of Dancehall Queens focus primarily on their own enjoyment. By claiming the socially disqualified space of the inner city as a locus of power production, the patrons of this space develop strategies of subjectivisation such as those created by Black women writers, who also struggle against discursive systems that relegate them to the role of *other*.

> The self-inscription of Black women requires disruption, rereading and rewriting the conventional and canonical stories, as well as revising the conventional generic forms that convey these stories. Through this interventionist, intertextual, and revisionary activity, Black women writers enter into dialogue with the discourse of the other(s). Disruption – the initial response to hegemonic and ambiguously (non)hegemonic discourse – and revision (rewriting or rereading) together suggest a model for reading Black and female literary expression.
>
> (Henderson in Butler and Scott (eds.), 1992: 156)

In the Dancehall, the competitions that ensue among women emphasise the ability to *wine* or to dance with exaggerated hip movements. The pathway for this embodied performance is charted by the ubiquitous DJ and elaborates a *discourse* of competitive power relations among women. This contradictory cultural matrix is directly related to the 'matey competitions' discussed in the previous chapter, in which women vie with each other to secure first place in a man's hierarchical organisation of partners.

The competitive pseudo-sexual displays provide an opportunity for collective female bonding and self-entertainment; these displays are enacted competitively *within* crews and *against* other crews. In former years, men retained the prerogative of asking women to dance; but nowadays it is very unusual for men and women to dance together. Amazingly, there is an invisible line drawn between the genders in the Dancehall space, which has specific inter- and intra-gender power implications.

Paradoxically, by performing (using) the body as a sexualised object, Dancehall Queens strategically ensure that their sexual availability is communicated to possible partners in a sex-for-materiality trade-off.[139] This recreation of self may also be read as individualistic performances of the body, which men may gaze at but not possess. By *re-inscribing* social subjectivity on their own bodies, these rebellious women have in fact shifted the paradigm of popular definitions of sexual desirability, which I critiqued at the beginning of this chapter.

> In terms of dress and popular fashion, the growing disparity in normative trends is again evident in the dance hall. Unconventional modes of dress, often involving colourful and daring cut-outs and highly unconventional patterns, suggest that the cues as to what is to be considered as high fashion are neither coming from the traditional middle classes nor, for that matter, from a purely North American context. Instead, they are being refracted and reinvented through the lens of the urban ghetto experience into something not only peculiar to that experience, but in an adversarial position to traditional fashion.

(Meeks, 1996: 132)

But although the Dancehall Queens' use of fashion as a site of struggle creates an alternative aesthetic within which to define their sexual desirability, there are problematic limitations to acknowledging this self-recognition within the confines of 'either/or dichotomous thinking' (Collins, 1990: 88). By positing their statements of resistance in the sexist discursive mode, the women also demonstrate the extent to which they have superseded the dichotomy of *hegemonic masculinity/subordinate femininity*, even as they enact the prescriptive cultural codes.

Figure 8.6: Although the Dancehall scene is a male-dominated one, it is the female, like a queen, who reigns supreme.

139 I will provide more detailed treatment of this transaction of resistance in the next chapter.

Some *man and man* suggested that if women did not dress in the brief fashion styles,[140] they would not be able to appreciate the contours of 'the merchandise' on which they were expected to spend their money. And although women with whom I interacted said that the brevity of their dresses is designed to reinforce their own self-esteem, this embodied practice of exercising agency is ambiguous. On the one hand, the apparent disregard for bourgeois values of dress by the Dancehall Queens may be seen as a celebration of the African women's bodies, which have been systematically subjected to *discourses of domination*. Thus, do *subordinated women* reclaim their physical embodiment as an asset that should be admired, rather than as an impediment of which they should be ashamed.

On the other hand, however, this practice also reinforces the hegemonic prescriptions of beauty and sexual desirability, which are reinforced in the popular culture. These matriculation requirements of embodiment treat women as objects for men's validation and pleasure. Therefore, the complicated project of creating structural and discursive change, which dismantles the racist and sexist political economy of embodiment, requires

> [c]reating an alternative feminist aesthetic [which] involves deconstructing and rejecting existing standards or ornamental beauty that objectify women and judge us by our physical appearance. Such an aesthetic would also reject standards of beauty that commodify women by measuring various quantities of beauty that women broker in the marital [sic][141] marketplace.

> (Collins, 1990: 88)

One could argue further that Dancehall Queens possess the incipient consciousness that is required to change prevailing structures and *discourses of domination*. Their reconstruction of their bodies into an artistic statement, in which the colour of the dress is matched by the colour of the wig and shoes, parodies bourgeois perceptions of fashion and body image. As Patricia Hill Collins suggests in relation to quilt production by women in the African Diaspora, this combining of colour in dress, creates a pattern of self-affirmation and elaborately reflects resistance to dominant notions of beauty in a most dramatic form.

> A strong colour may be juxtaposed with another strong colour, or with a weak one. Contrast is used to structure or organise. Overall, the symmetry in African-American quilts does not come from uniformity as it does in Euro-American quilts. Rather, symmetry comes through diversity.

> (1990: 89)

The outfits of the Dancehall Queens are expensive and elaborately reflect the positive self-concepts of the wearer. While some women might depend on men for financial

---

140　The 'hotti hotti' girls (as the women noted for the brevity of their clothing are called) dress in outfits like brief shorts – so-called batty-riders – because of the cuts that reveal as much of the buttocks as possible without leaving the woman completely naked. Other outfits include compositions of tights, transparent and/ or short dresses that leave little of the contours of their bodies to the imagination.

141　My disagreement with the use of the word marital in this context stems from the implication that it creates, of the non-legitimacy of conjugal relationships that are not sanctioned by marriage, and which is a value judgement that is moralising and class bound.

support, the Dancehall Queen also symbolises the capacity of oppressed women to resist social lack and express agency through financial independence.

> Our genuine dance hall women leaders who originate from downtown, typically, have a measure of economic power and independence. Some achieve this through lucrative activities as informal commercial importers. Some have become successful by way of dressmaking and other business concerns. These women can afford to buy themselves the most fabulous finery, successfully competing with the well kept women of the dons. They often go out by themselves, in posses, dressed in their garments of liberation. They can certainly afford to pay their own bar bills. This level of economic independence has implications for the man-woman relationship. It seems to me that the ongoing power struggle between man and woman has taken on some new dimensions in dance-hall culture.

> (Fairweather-Wilson, quoted in Meeks, 1996: 133)

Clearly then, in spite of their subordination, women in Southside do strategise to rescue a sense of self-identity through the deployment of sexuality, which as Foucault suggested, 'emerged...as a mechanism of new ways of organising knowledge' (Diamond and Quinby in Diamond and Quinby (eds.), 1988: xi). In Southside, this self-knowledge is also illustrated in the everyday practices of caring for the body, which has to repeatedly pass the muster of critical gazes from the competitive crews in the Dancehall environment. Nevertheless, these preoccupations also provide opportunities for women to connect with each other. For example, the manicuring of the nails, which takes hours to complete, affords women invaluable opportunities for relaxation and social interaction and provide one of the 'safe spaces' (Collins, 1990: 95) for creating subjectivities that explode the stereotypes of poor African women's social victimhood and sexual undesirability.

Thus, a culturally significant subtext of the Dancehall Queens' embodied performances is a recapturing of a self-centred aesthetic and embodied spirit of resistance. This capacity to exercise agency was outlawed during slavery and has subsequently been denied through the proverbial tossing of the socially disenfranchised onto the social rubbish heap of history/herstory by those who occupy the upper echelons of society. However, African traditions of socialisation and *cultural communication* have been preserved in the subaltern milieu of collective participation, thereby transforming the spaces of subordination into sites of discursive resistance.

The first time I got my nails 'done' with extensions and all, was when Molly insisted that she wanted to give me a present for helping her to build her own self-esteem by being involved in the process of critical consciousness (hooks, 1989), which characterised the research process. In the following photograph, Figure 8.7, I was the willing patron of the artist on the left, who is seen performing a manicure operation on the customer that I followed.

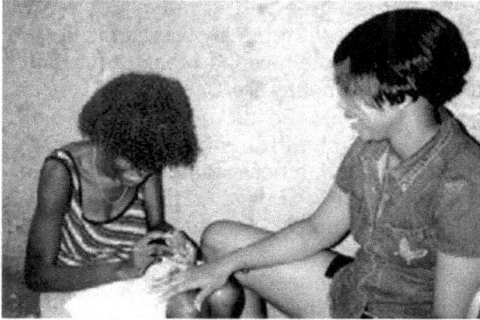

Figure 8.7: Taking care of self is an effective means of self-esteem building and also an important mechanism of bonding; the leisurely manicure process which in my case took three hours, provided an opportunity to talk to the women gathered in that space, about various issues affecting their lives. As they told me, this was a usual practice, which helped them to counteract the social difficulties with which they have to contend.

In summary therefore, Dancehall Queens who denude themselves in their body-celebrating and rebellious fashion genres, present a direct challenge to the bourgeois status quo through their unorthodox self-presentations. These embodied statements directly challenge what has been traditionally institutionalised as 'decency' with all the moralising considerations that this connotes. Undoubtedly, these practices are fraught with myriad contradictions. So, although women who embody the Dancehall idiom of rebelliousness, reconstruct their bodies to challenge norms of what constitutes beauty and decorum, they also reinforce patriarchal norms because of the sexualised meanings inherent to the gendered gazes of their audiences. Thus,

> femininity and masculinity are truly the mirror-image of each other, for while orthodox men's desire may "wither" under too powerfully defining a gaze, the "feminine" woman may require constant external "definition" (that she is attractive, desirable) from the gaze that [she believes] constitutes her.

(Bordo, 1994: 301)

A critical review of the definitions of femininity emphasised in the fashion statements and embodied practices of Dancehall Queens suggest an internalisation of patriarchal norms, which define so many aspects of how women should re-present themselves. In the Dancehall, I have heard DJs calling the gender power shots and ordering women to expose their various body parts... 'Mek me see all g-string now, c'mon ladies, it's your time' or 'all di gal dem wid di firm tittie, mek we see dem now!' Some women comply in a call and response rhythm so sensual it's as if they are having sex in public and we, like so many voyeurs watch in fascination as this ritual of unabashed interaction proceeds. The camaraderie of the moment suggests that like any other dance performance that is conveying any amount of themes, this celebration of sexuality is truly liberatory for people whose lives in the confined inner-city space demands some form of creative release. Make no mistake about it; you also have to be very skilled to do those dances. The children in the summer workshop implored me to 'make my body like rubber' to do some of the moves, because I was 'too stiff' in my efforts to imitate their flexible flaunting of their skills.

What I experienced makes me agree with Carolyn Cooper's (1993) assertion that attitudes to Dancehall politics are notoriously class specific and disrespectful of the ways in which disadvantaged people have had to contour their survival strategies to the specific circumstances in which they are located. This resistance dynamic includes how they enjoy themselves in dramatic idioms like dance, which reach back in time to traditions that Africans brought with them and which survived the holocaust of slavery. All of those factors make me hesitate to say that women like the Dancehall Queens are just trapped in a matrix of hegemonic imperatives. The women actually seem to enjoy baring breasts, g-strings, or whatever else the maestro commands them to do. But, then, that is why Gramsci's argument about how hegemony works is so persuasive. The manipulated do indeed perform the *dominant discourse* under the strong impression that they are acting autonomously.

In the genderised pecking order of this discourse, it is no coincidence that men usually hold the video cameras and record the graphic details of the women's pelvic gyrations. Gyrations offered with creative generosity and with all the graceful skills the dancers can muster. Men are also the protagonists in projecting and *inscribing* pornographic meanings onto the women's bodies through the meanings inferred from the enlarged images of the bodies that are filtered onto screens mounted at strategic points in the Dancehall. Videos of these events are reviewed with monotonous regularity on local cable channels.

So although the body is an important resource of resistance as far as poor people are concerned, structural social transformation has to take place to ensure that poor women have access to the resources that would give them more options to choose from. If more opportunities for social advancement were available to these disadvantaged inner-city citizens, they would not have to resort using their bodies to refract *discourses of domination* and to rewrite self-realisation survival strategies.

However, would they really want alternatives? Some women have actually *chosen* to exercise agency in the sex-for-materiality transaction mode and should be seen as active subjects in that sense. Still, we should not romanticise the *embodied resistance discourses*, especially when the material conditions of the inner city are as awful as Maxine described it in the Introduction. No one living above the dreaded poverty line would voluntarily move to live in Southside and the average resident in spaces like Southside, are themselves desperate to move out. So something must be wrong and, cliché or not, the grass is, indeed, always greener on the other side of the poverty line. But the prevailing intolerable socioeconomic conditions beg the question as to whether something urgent shouldn't be done by the powers-that-be, to alleviate the conditions that create the stage on which Dancehall Queens perform their highly sexualised and embodied resistance dramaturgy.

It should be remembered that the rebellious clothing designs of the Dancehall Queens merely mask the systemic exclusions and structural deficiencies *socially inscribed* all over the bodies of these Black Bettys (and their male counterparts) in communities like Southside. When they return to their inadequate housing conditions and take off the gaudy and glittering costumes, the naked truth of the social disenfranchisement of the Dancehall Queens, who are invariably heads of their households, is only too apparent once more. Thus, one has to interpret the power exercised by the Dancehall Queens as being strategic; '[t]he ability of a woman to control her femininity and be in charge of its social circulation is more important to her than the ideological meanings of femininity' (Fiske, 1993: 254).

Disciplinary Power in the Community Prison

> Because power can be conceptualised as an ever-changing grid with specific points of intensity and sites of greatest force, it can also be seen as a grid that necessarily generates points of resistance. This implies that knowledges, methods, procedures which at one time support forms of power, at another time or in a different context, can act as sites of resistance, struggle and change.

> (Grosz, in Gunew (ed.), 1990: 89)

Like their female counterparts, inner-city man and man also have to use their own bodies to broker some measure of agency. In this section, I have chosen to look at men who are in prison and who are, therefore, facing multiple risks, in order to explore the discursive contradictions that are *inscribed* on the Black man's physical body in the doubly restrictive realm of the inner-city prison. The General Penitentiary prison, 'GP', which is located on Tower Street in Southside, eastern Kingston, was built in the eighteenth century and was originally designed to hold 760 persons. Given its location, this ghetto prison has long been an inner-city Kingston institution, but it is now severely overcrowded, with a population that often goes up to 1,400.

Although their economic class is a marker of embodiment that marginalises grassroots Black men on inner-city streets, in the prison environment, those same men access other culturally defined attributes of power – such as violence and allegiance to the norm of heterosexuality (or homosexuality for that matter) – enabling some of them to achieve a measure of embodied authority. Life in the all-male prison is quite regimented; the inmates are released into the confined open space of the prison yard and surrounding rooms at 7 a.m. and locked up again in their cells at 3:45 p.m. Those who pass the required test are allowed to work in the nearby brickyard, while others may attend school or the skills training programmes in carpentry and welding. If anyone breaks any of the assigned rules, the wardens punish them by having their remissions denied or visitor allowances forfeited.

In the autumn of 1997, then Jamaican Police Commissioner, Francis Forbes, made the controversial recommendation that condom use should be promoted in prisons in order to encourage safe-sex practices. Objectors to this perspective within the prison populations as well as in the wider society, hotly debated the underlying assumption of the suggestion, that inmates and/or warders were engaging in homosexual relations. Simultaneous with this outraged response, there was an outbreak of violence within the General Penitentiary prison, which was alleged to be a direct response to the conflict over the implicit charges of homosexuality within its walls.

However, when I spoke with some inmates and their supervisor, it was suggested that the outbreak of violence at the institution, which claimed 19 lives, was the result of warfare between rival factions that had their power interests in gangs outside of the prison community. The prison authorities were initially overwhelmed by the vehemence of violent statements that the gang representatives made on a daily basis during the crisis period. They then responded with even greater force, to quell the insurgency. 'Marlon' put the course of events into perspective and spoke directly to the multi-level and varied applications of embodied power within this institution.

> The rioting did not stem from homosexuality. It is a privilege for everyone to do what they feel like.[142] It was really to do with gang warfare. Every man in here wants to rule. They want to prove something, like I am the don. They have to shoot and slaughter to get fame and be able to control girls and guys. Two separate gangs, one from Vivian Blake's gang and one from Bobby Reds' gang were fighting to rule. Bobby Reds is a drug man with resources but Vivian Blake only has minority support. During the sick out[143] Bobby Reds wanted to take full control. This conflict started before they came into prison; so the two sides started to fight. There were 500 on Bobby Reds' side and 100 on Vivian Blake's. If you and Vivian were friends, you knew that your life was in danger. It was caused from just that. Bobby Reds controlled the entire open area of the prison. Vivian Blake was in charge of H North block, which was the minority.

> Bobby Reds' gang started to *disrespect* Vivian's friends who were also in the open. They started to kill off Vivian's connections that lived in the open areas. Sixteen of those who died were all *big men*. I stood at my cell door and saw it all but I was not involved. Those who were remanded in custody joined the sentenced men so Bobby Reds' gang was at full force. They used knives and machetes most of which were thrown over the prison wall. Although some of us were neutral, we knew we couldn't stay down there because we did not know which day was going to be our destiny.

> So the gangs were just using the homosexuality hype as an excuse to fight, when the proposal came to use condoms.

The superintendent in charge of the area, who had been listening to the revelations up to this point, then made his contribution to the debate, taking the perspective that heterosexuality is the norm and that homosexual practices result from either genetic defects or else the practical inconvenience of incarceration.

> I believe that if a man was *living good with his wife* outside, and never mixed with homosexuals, his willpower and self-esteem should enable him not to lead himself into a homosexual situation. Here in the prison, we prove that men can live for months without having sex and he does not have to bow. However, another person without the will power will give in. *I don't think it is a question of power as some people say but willpower.* For some it is a genetic thing while others were interfered with as children. There are homosexuals in society who are the big money men who always find other men to use. Some of these men don't want children because they are not willing to share their wealth and power.

---

142 This assertion was nevertheless contradicted in a later disclosure that a man had been killed in his cell because his fellow inmates discovered that he had had a 'wet dream', which is perceived in this environment as an abnormal practice of manhood.

143 This sick-out was staged by the prison population in the General Penitentiary to protest the internal insecurity in the detention centre.

Taboos of the Male Body

Homosexuality arouses extreme disquiet in men in the Jamaican society. According to the warder, this deviation from the cultural norm of heterosexuality is due to a genetic defect rather than a social/sexual choice. But denied sexual access to women, the prisoners have developed an elaborate power dynamic around homosexuality, which is typical of such situations of confinement. The homophobic theme is also directly linked to the dominant regime of violent hegemonic masculinity. As Connell (1995) argues, under this gender power regime, sexualities that do not conform to the heterosexist paradigm are disqualified and outlawed.

The warder's assertion that imprisoned men have the capacity to restrain their sexuality if this norm cannot be satisfied is also problematic. This injunction can be interpreted as part and parcel of the regulatory mechanisms that operate through hierarchical binary oppositions in the wider society, to keep certain social constituencies (defined as Other) *in their place*. As Foucault suggests in this regard, 'the sexual body is both the principal instrument and effect of modern disciplinary power' (McNay, 1992: 31).

Although the dominant gender power regime of heterosexuality is intrinsically tied to other discursive domains of domination, this does not mean that heterosexuality is not also a legitimate source of pleasure and positive self-identification. On the contrary, as my discussion on parenting, in the next chapter, will show, heterosexual practices have been a major source of resistance for poor people who deploy their sexuality (Foucault, 1980) as a popular expression of agency. Thus, it is clear once again that various contradictory power regimes all converge around the human body, with the result that sexual desire cannot in most senses be regarded as simply *natural* and unproblematic. The gendered, sexed body is suffused with various investments of power and control, which all have tremendous political, material, social and symbolic meanings.

Furthermore, the violence that the subject of homosexuality evoked in the prison environment, and the gang violence sparked by this discontent, provided the justification for the security forces to apply their own brand of violence on the dissidents. This use of force opened up the pre-existing divide between the dominant and subordinate classes in the Jamaican society. The violence employed by the security forces, the executive arm of the state, is administered with impunity in the prison system in order to ensure that those who control power at the community level, do not transgress their boundaries in the wider hierarchical social arrangement.

Therefore, the social relations of power in the prison mirror the paradoxical systems of stratification present in the wider society. In GP, different versions of *hegemonic masculinity* have established clear boundaries for embodied behaviour. As the inmates suggested too, the violent contestations among the prisoners are intrinsic to the heterosexist *discourse of violence*, which has bloodied the psyches of victims as much as it has messed up the streets of communities like Southside. Thus, 'differentiation can be made between strategic elites, which may have power over society as a whole, and segmental elites...which are predominant or which vie for predominance in restricted fields' (Cox et al, 1985: 95). However, through institutional mechanisms like the prison, those who control the state and its apparatuses create other systems that regulate the level of agency that subordinates can exercise. Analysing this dilemma, Foucault argued that enforced prohibition is one of the practices of power used by various institutions to police sexual identities and by extension, to police the way people see themselves and relate to others. As he suggests,

> you have the system of surveillance, which...involves very little expense. There is no need for arms, physical violence, material constraints. Just a gaze. An inspecting gaze, a gaze which each individual under its weight will end by interiorising to the point that he [sic] is his own overseer, each individual thus exercising this surveillance over, and against, himself.

> (Foucault, in Gordon (ed.) 1980: 155)

The powerful interests vested in the institutional gaze and its function as a mechanism of social control, assures its longevity as a means of exercising power over the physical bodies of the subjects under surveillance. In this regard, Assistant Superintendent London observed that the situation in the General Penitentiary

> has a demoralising impact on the men, especially those who didn't do the crime they are accused of and end up being labelled and blamed. The worst aspect of being incarcerated is the fact that *the ones who are hard working cannot mind their families or provide security for their homes.*

When impoverished men are unable to fulfil the norm of the male breadwinner, it really damages their self-esteem (Chevannes, 1999). This dissonance is magnified when they are imprisoned. The officer said that the prisoners often express feelings of alienation especially when five of them on average are locked up in a room which only measures four feet by six or eight feet. Moreover, because the toilets are located outside of the locked cell area, they have to use the slop buckets during the night. However, practices like defecating in a slop bucket are included in the extensive array of '*bowing*', transgressions.

> If man drops his toothbrush or toothpaste, walks barefoot or is assigned to the isolated area, which is reserved for boys, they are said to bow. A big man is a man who does not do the things that homosexuals do. We are not denying that society breeds homosexuals and that this is the means of introducing this practice to others, which results in chaos and confusion.

> (Marlon, inmate)

The informal bowing bylaw in the penal institution is a metaphor for the pervasive prejudices entrenched in hegemonic state power, popular culture and subaltern authority regimes.

Isn't it ironic though, that poor blue-collar Black men are imprisoned in institutions like the General Penitentiary, while white-collar criminals from the upper class invariably escape such humiliating experiences. Therefore, institutions of correction definitely have class/ race-bound and gender biases in the way they operate. The White-collar criminals (like the politicians who instigated the *discourse of violence*)[144] are not even

---

144 At time of writing in the summer of 2003 – given that I had to convert the thesis into this book – blame is being cast at the door of weapons manufacturers for crises like what face the people in Iraq as a result of

indicted. Furthermore, male and female prisoners are treated differently; men are generally subjected to harsher treatment than the women are. In addition, the violence and taboos that are attributed to the body are more pronounced for men, both inside and outside of prison, than they are for women. This is because sexist practices, which result in the subordination of both men and women, have a greater stake in preserving '*dominant masculinity*' (Connell, 1995: 84). This form of power drama is most lethal when performed through the medium of violence.

Some men who go to prison construct a *discourse of hyper-badness*, which induces fear in those who are not so bold. Therefore, in a paradoxical reversal, when a *man* comes out of prison, he is seen in his own eyes and through the perspective of his peers, as more powerful and distinguished than he was before he went in. However, the general community practice is to remind him that he just left a space where he was likely to have had homosexual experiences as part of the alternative power practices that are performed in the prison. Even if this transgression of male embodiment was not actualised, such an accusation is sufficient to start a war, as the Rude Boy feels impelled to defend his reputation of heterosexuality.

As Connell argues in this regard, '[v]iolence can become a way of claiming or asserting masculinity in group struggles' (Connell, 1995: 83). The violent imperative to fulfil publicly prescribed heterosexual criteria of embodiment, also prevents the rude boy type of closet chi chi man from admitting that he entertains private (homo)sexual desires that deviate from normative notions of heterosexist manhood (Connell, 1995: 83).[145]

State/class interests intersect with the prevailing male-dominated power apparatus in the prison. This alliance constitutes a peculiar patriarchal project, which deserves to be unpacked as a part of any analysis of the political economy of embodiment. This discussion of the power relations in the General Penitentiary prison has also allowed me to confirm my third hypothetical assumption. The evidence shows that the construction of the subjectivity of subordinates in Southside is intrinsically tied to the hegemonic structures of societal power, which set the boundaries of performances of gender and the body. As I have shown, *body language* is the carrier of *hegemonic discourses of domination*. This articulation of expressions of power illustrates that

> [h]owever materially deprived or politically and socially repressed a... social formation may be, the one area of social life of which they can never be deprived and which they can always control is that of practice. Practice is what people do with systems and resources that, in their structural dimensions, are not theirs but are those of the dominant other...[However] *[t]he language that a society develops is always inscribed with the interests of that society's power bloc.*
>
> (Fiske, 1993: 211, emphasis added)

the US-led war.

145   Yet shockingly, during the week ending August 9, 2003, a lone gunman held up a 15-year-old schoolboy and sodomised him repeatedly.

For men as well as for women residing in communities like Southside, the body has become the primordial site for the working out of contradictory power contestations. The men who are the local wielders of power present an unmistakable challenge to the dominant structural order. Yet they fail to recognise the ways in which their bodies have already been compromised and incorporated into the overwhelmingly hegemonic state/class project. They are also curiously myopic about how their own regulations on alternative types of embodiment subvert efforts to achieve social transformation.

CHAPTER 9

THE BODY AS A RESOURCE FOR
EXERCISING AGENCY

[T]he field of political contestation is not restricted to the state or the workplace, but also includes the family, mass and popular culture, the sphere of sexuality and the terrain of the refused and forgotten.

(Giroux, 1992: 119)

If you as a man are trying to get a girl and can't wear a $6,000 crepe and a $2,000 shirt and jeans pants for $3,000; they don't want you, for they want *Name Brand Man*.

(Focus Group Discussion on Barry Street)

The Oldest Profession

Although people living below the poverty line in Southside have life hard, they are not hapless victims. Their various survival strategies speak volumes for people using incredible creativity – including the use of their physical bodies – to counteract the plethora of disadvantages that plague their lives. This explains why some people have no recourse but to engage in sexual transactions for material gain, simply because of the paucity of other opportunities for well-being and social advancement that are available to them. If this situation/solution has in fact existed since as far back as human memory and history go, then that says something about the innate nature of *Homo sapiens* and the social civilisations that they create as a group. There is therefore no need to unnecessarily stigmatise the people in general and the women especially that live in Southside, because of any observation that is made here. The situations they find themselves in, and the reflex response of their survival mode solutions, are both bigger forces than they are.

Thus, Proposition Four assumes that, despite their disadvantaged social position, Southside women, men, adolescents and children have survival strategies related to their use of sexual advantage for material gain, which they choose from the limited options available to them. Hence, various versions of the oldest profession in the world – *prostitution* – still serve as everyday survival strategies in particular for inner-city women whose severe experiences of social exclusion leave them little recourse to do otherwise. The human body is thus a primary every day resource in their socioeconomic power transactions.

At the same time, prostitution is also underwritten by 'tendencies implicit within capitalism...[which result in] the expansion of perceived sexual needs, particularly among men' (Weeks, 1985: 23). In other words, the contradictions of the patriarchal political economy actually preconditions women to become prostitutes in the first place. But that is only one side of the story. Individual women also consciously choose to 'sell some pussy' as one woman put it, as their way to make a way out of no-way.

This is the essence of our examination of the 'sexual economics' and 'sexual politics' at work below the poverty line: the whys and wherefores of the prevailing society that give poor disadvantaged women few other choices than to sell/rent their ripe bodies to the highest bidders; and the whats and the whens in their personal psychosocial motivation that cause such inner-city women to actively and willingly seek material gain and economic profit, sometimes even beyond their survival needs, from their political decision to put their Black female bodies on the free market as fresh meat in the 'sex exchange' (i.e. 'stock exchange/stock market'). These are the innate and off-shooting binary contradictions that exist between the social (the socially based whys and wherefores) on the one hand; and the individual (the psychological personality-driven whats and whens of individuals) on the other hand. This is the critical point at which all the elements in the mix – the people and the blood, the politics and the bullets, the sex and the bodies, the economics and the poverty line, the words and their implied meanings – all come together in the fiery crucible formed by the narrow streets of inner-city Kingston.

Of course, commercial sex, the selling of bodily services, is not just a business transaction but also a source of supreme pleasure. A woman and man validate self and each other in the course of this embodied physical interaction. Yet discursive meanings of power transcend the sexual act, as what is said about the body – body language – prescribe and proscribe behaviour. The roots of prostitution in Southside can be traced back to the days of slavery when downtown Kingston was the auction block on which Africans were sold as commodities for production and reproduction. And as today's elders recall, the early industrial years of Kingston's post-slavery development gave rise to flourishing prostitution enterprises in the seaport town. Again, we need to delve into the rich reservoirs of the living memory banks of Southside's residents, in order to uncover the wealth of intelligence about the contradictions inherent to these gender, race and class-specific transactions and embodied bodily exchanges.

The Body as a Commodity

Fleets used to come here
Sailors used to come into Jamaica
Yuh had di paddies
Di ones dat wore di
full khaki
and others
The Madam used to call us
as washerwomen
When we left our homes

we didn't return until
di boat had left the shore
and gone back to their homes.
Sometimes she would pay us
twopence-ha'penny for a shirt
dat she had been paid
seven shillings for
She used to take disadvantage
but in those days
I had no children
but I just loved to work
I did not sit down and depend on anybody[146]
I worked at Blue Mirror
which was another sporthouse[147]
run by a woman called Ivy Boothe
who is now dead
The whole of here used to be sporthouses.
From Hanover Street
right back to Ladd Lane
At the corner of Barry Street
and Ladd Lane
there also used to be a sporthouse
They used to get girls
from the country
and sell them out
to the sailors
We who worked
and got money
it did not help us
because they sold their bodies
for us to get paid
by the whore mistress[148]
So even if we bought
a piece of clothing
it eventually tore off
because they sold their bodies
to get the money
We worked in the
Whorehouses
cleaning up
washing sheets

146 She is speaking here to a deeply woven Caribbean tradition of female independence, which dates back to slavery and has evolved through the years of nation building.

147 Local word for a whorehouse.

148 This observation introduces a moral argument, which will be pursued further in the course of the analysis.

and renting rooms
to the sports.
It has stopped
some years now
since the man-o-wars stopped coming.
And that's a good thing
because a lot of the children
would be sailors' children
and we wouldn't know
who the fathers are.
I am glad it stopped too
because the young people
in schools
would only be wanting
to go and work
in the sporthouses
and catch the sailors.

(Miss Jenny, 65, Higholborn Street)

Today's elders in Southside remember that in the 1950s and 1960s, the Kingston Harbour provided a convenient entrance way for sailors whose business of commodity trading and other mercantile pursuits included the purchase of sexual services from women in the seaport town. Even at that time, prostitution provided the principal means for some poor women to countervail chronic socioeconomic lack. Molly recalls that when she was growing up on Ladd Lane, there was a 'sport house'[149] next door to where she lived. Her father, Mr. Malcolm elaborated that in the early 1960s, women would come from the rural areas to work in the many places where male patrons were mainly sailors from ships that would dock in the Kingston Harbour.

> In the fifties and sixties, Central Kingston here had a lot of whorehouses; even beside me, there was a whorehouse. The whole of Hanover Street from Harbour Street to Laws and East Queen Street, were all whorehouses. The whole place was *infested*, because you had regular Navy ships coming here. The majority of girls in those sport houses were girls from the country.[150] People used to go in the country and tell the young girls that they were going to give them a barmaid job. Then they would bring them here and get them into that way of life. Those days they knew nothing about AIDS; that time they had a thing called gonorrhoea and what they used to do was give the sailors preventatives before they came ashore.
>
> (Mr. Malcolm, early seventies, Ladd Lane)

---

149 Prostitutes are called 'sports' in a subtle rendition of the value judgement that the term invokes. The word 'sketel', which is currently applied to sex workers, carries even harsher overtones of critical evaluation of this form of employment.

150 Rural areas.

I asked Mr. Malcolm, to tell me what became of those prostitutes who became involved in the industry and he said that some of them had died while some were married.[151] He also had much to say about the political economy of prostitution.

> People of my age, some of them made good while some of them fell down. You used to have some prostitutes that didn't deal with Black men; they only dealt with White men, while you had some who only dealt with Black men. Like some you used to have on East Queen Street. That time though, you used to have more unity, but politics has mashed up the whole area; they unite to divide, you understand?

Prostitution: From Economic Necessity to Labour Choice

Out of economic desperation, some mothers actually use their offspring as commodities and encourage the sexual exploitation of their own daughters – usually by older men – as a material method of maintaining their families. Still other girls in the ghetto get involved in the sex-for-materiality trade-off as a way of escaping some of the harsher conditions of poverty. They are sometimes exposed to explicitly sexualised environments even before they have developed sufficient competence to negotiate the harsher terms and conditions of this territory (Ennew, 1986).

Figure 9.1: Molly and Mr. Malcolm, her father.

A number of boys on Maiden Lane told me that girls are often not interested in having sexual relationships with boys in their own age group because young boys usually do not have money or material things to offer. In the meantime, the taboos that surround infertility also provide a compelling push factor for the early explorations of sexuality by young girls. For all these reasons, the body is seen as a mere commodity, as a vessel to be used in any and all ways, and prostitution has become a taken-for-granted route to survival. For example, Catherine, like her mother before her, was a prostitute, a vocation she abandoned just before I met her. She had just had a baby, found religion and moved out of the community in the hope of improving her previously challenging life. Catherine said that her mother, who used to work both in sport houses and on ships, is now destitute and of unsound mind. One day as she lay on a sidewalk, she was attacked and wounded in her head by an unidentified assailant.

---

151   This observation suggests that they had evolved along a continuum of respectability, a value judgement that is revealing of the stigma which is attached to women who are practitioners of the sex trade.

As we can see then, although some women might go the prostitution route to exercise agency and counteract their disadvantageous social conditions, these efforts are insufficient to transform the entrenched structures that caused them to be in such desperate circumstances in the first place. Just like the mother's mugger, structures of power always deal the marginalised a proverbial head blow before too long. Given the severe limitations of their personal resources and the constraints imposed by the political economy, women in this community therefore straddle *discourses of domination* and *embodied resistance*, as both victims and agents. Despite legalised, high-priced, Cable-TV-promoted prostitution at places like the Bunny Ranch and the Wild Horse Adult Resort in Nevada, USA, many unpleasant images still come to mind when people think of 'sex work' and 'sex workers' – people who are forced to 'sell their bodies' as a means of economic survival. Thus, once again, some international context is necessary for a more balanced view of what is really going on in Jamaica.

Human Organs and Tissue Trade

And, sex is not the only commodity for sale. For instance, there is a huge hidden market and international trafficking in blood plasma, with poor people selling gallons of their blood over time. Poor people also sell their skin, kidneys and hair. In India, for example, many people cut their hair for religious reasons at temples which eventually sell the shorn hair on the international market where it is turned into wigs and extensions which are marketed as 'genuine human hair'. The label is right. It is!

Today, it is said that there are at least 50 surgical products made from human skin, bones, corneas and heart valves that are used in various procedures ranging from lip enhancements and eye surgery to repairing fractures. For sure, fresh skin is always needed for use on burn victims, while deceased bodies sometimes end up as crash-test dummies or may be used in other product-safety research.

This ongoing commodification of the human body simultaneously with the development of new methods of fertilisation and organ transplants, has forced modern society to confront many new and complex moral and legal dilemmas. Who owns someone's body? How relevant is bodily integrity? What moral/ethical issues are really involved in changing the sex (sexual identity) of a body?

Obviously, then, there is a pressing need to ask hard questions and to critically re-evaluate established norms and values in relation to the human body, sexuality, the family, and the definition of life and death. As a result, the ethics of practices from live-organ donation, to gender-reassignment operations, to legalised prostitution, have recently received considerable media attention in the US, where both the medical profession and the government have been addressing issues such as the scarcity of kidney donors for instance. Meanwhile, the University of California, Los Angeles, had to stop accepting donated cadavers (i.e. dead bodies) for a period during 2004, amid an internal probe into the alleged illegal sale of body parts at the University. And, in New York in early 2006, the owner of a biomedical firm, a mortician and two others were charged for body stealing and illegally harvesting bones, tissue and organs from hundreds of corpses at scores of New York funeral homes.

Furthermore, the US Government estimates that some 800,000 people are trafficked worldwide each year and 20,000 of those are being trafficked into the United States where many of them are forced into prostitution. Unfortunately, it's not usually the glamorous Bunny Ranch type of prostitution that makes good TV. In Thailand and some of those other places swamped by the killer 2004 tsunami, thousands of girls and even little boys are, reportedly, being used as sex slaves for North American and European tourists. Although tens of thousands of Albanian women and girls are thought to have been cheated, abducted and forced into prostitution, we won't get into that whole issue of the virtual enslavement and forced prostitution that thousands of Russian and Central and Eastern European women have been trapped in since the fall of the Soviet Union. Any way you cut it, therefore, the commodification and manipulation of the human body remains as a mega-profitable international business enterprise.

The point of all the detail in the foregoing paragraphs, is that while what is happening in Jamaica is by no means ideal or desirable, the decision of inner-city residents to use their bodies and its parts as commercial commodities is not at all different from similar decisions made by poor and not-so-poor people all over the world. Looked at in this way, Jamaican ghetto women who supposedly 'sell pussy' are not really *selling* their vaginas. They are renting, or sometimes leasing it. They are not actually selling their bodies, as in giving them away. Rather, they are hiring out their bodily assets, repeatedly, for short, temporary periods of time, thus empowering themselves by maintaining control and ownership of their most precious commodity: their physical assets.

Although the trafficking in separated body parts is not yet a major problem in Jamaica, the US State Department says that the island is now being used as a transit country for illegal migrants to North America, as well as a source country for children trafficked internationally for sexual exploitation. In recent times, there has been a significant increase in foreign exotic dancers, predominantly Russians, on the local entertainment circuit in Kingston, Montego Bay, Negril and Ocho Rios. Since the State Department report was made public, the Jamaican Government has pledged to take steps to remove the island from a list of 14 countries that could face sanctions over the issue. In the meantime, there just is no getting away from examples of the body being used as a commodity. Thus the body, alive or dead, sacred or profane, and what is done with it or with its parts, and what is said by it and about it, is clearly a complex and controversial issue that is going to be hotly debated for a long time to come, both in Jamaica and in the rest of the world.

Exceptions To The Rule

Since the survival strategies of subordinated women sometimes result from their unconscious actions (Giddens, in Cassell (ed.), 1993: 94), we have to be careful 'not to fall into a celebration of praxis per se [because] [t]he uncovering of a creative or imaginative substrate to action does not amount to a valorisation of agency...' (McNay, 2000: 22). We also have to bear in mind that people are not socially homogeneous in the inner city. On the contrary, everyone speaks of a hierarchy of paucity, ranging from *poor* to *poverty* to *poverty stricken*.[152] Some women feel that they have managed to

152 Differences in social status that were reflected in the hierarchical definitions of social lack: 'poor', 'poverty' and 'poverty stricken' being cited as indicators of the intensity of someone's relationship to the poverty line. Lack of access to opportunities for self-development like skills training was one definition of being poor; another was knowing where today's meal is coming from but not tomorrow's. The person who proffered this definition also said that the poor includes those who do not know where today's meal is coming from but find it somehow, e.g. through begging for the means to make a meal. Those who are poverty stricken

maintain some distance from abject poverty if they refrain from selling their bodies. Thus, Miss Williams proudly observed that, 'There are only two things that I never did – steal and sell my body.' This sentiment reflects the socially and morally flawed dimensions of the sex trade, as defined by some of the very same people living in the cultural context of the urban grassroots.

Forty-seven-year-old Sonia, also felt she was better off socially than the sex workers because she had not performed any act of prostitution in her entire life. She said she was independent and worked hard so that she did not have to depend on a man to support her. 'I am not really going to go out there and sell my body to get something,' she said adamantly. 'I prefer to take a basket and sell some things; I don't really put sex on my mind. *I would like to have something of my own that I live off of myself.*'

Sonia clearly recognised, even if just subconsciously, that the political economy of relationships between women and men presupposes sexist meanings of dependency and oppression. These psychosocial obstacles can only be circumvented if women manage not succumb to patriarchal ways of defining gender performance. However, prevailing structures of power restrict the capacity of *subordinated women* to exercise voluntary agency.

> At some level, of course, practices of the self are suggested or imposed on the individual by the wider social context and, in this respect, some practices are more imperative, or offer less scope for autonomous choice, than other practices. For example, it is much harder to stylise freely one's identity in the realm of sexuality – given the taboos and injunctions that operate around masculinity and femininity – than it is to stylise one's existence as a political citizen.

(McNay, 1992: 70-71)

No wonder, then, that the *everyday discourse* of current popular music remains staunchly against this method of survival for women. One of the new young Roots & Culture vocalists, I-Wayne, calls down 'flames and fire' on what he calls 'flesh sellers' in his 2005 hit song, 'Can't Satisfy Her', the lyrics of which include the following:

Seh she flirt with her boyfriend brethren
Him have money and bling, So she go bed with him
Catch disease, Now it starting spreading
She start to seek penicillin, She's dying
Mercy please, For life she begging
When she hear seh, To the morgue she heading
Seh she bruk out at the age of seven
She's dancing before she eleven

One man can't satisfy her
She needs more wood for the fire
Sex price getting higher
More money she require
House, car and land she desire

---

do not know where their meal is coming from, cannot find it and so end up eating out of garbage or doing without – today and tomorrow.

Embodied Agency

It should be emphasised here that the practice of trading sex for materiality is not only restricted to the commercial encounters represented by prostitution. This trade-off in sexuality is intrinsically tied to the prevailing political economy, and therefore permeates the transactions brokered in everyday relationships – like marriage. This range of practices reinforces the *dominant discourses*, especially about the female body, and are internalised and performed with and without consciousness or intended consequences (Giddens, in Cassell (ed.), 1993: 94). Thus, 'the social theoretical concern with power relations serves as a reminder that any theory of agency must be placed in the context of structural, institutional or inter subjective constraints' (McNay, 2000: 22-23). Yet again, we can see that embodied survival strategies are suffused with power ambiguities, as the sex-for-materiality syndrome shows once again that *discourses of domination* inevitably produce *counter-discourses* of resistance.

> Power relations depend on a multiplicity of points of resistance, which serve at once as adversary, target, support, foot hold. Just as there is no centre of power, there is no centre of revolt, from which secondary rebellions derive, no unified class that is the seat of rebellion. There is a plurality of resistances, each a special case, distributed in an irregular way in time and space.
>
> (Sheridan, 1980: 184-185)

Thus, experiences of protracted subordination enable social *objects of domination* to develop a knowledge base about their actions and the contexts that produce these actions and within which they are reproduced (Giddens, in Cassell (ed.), 1993). However, while saying that, Giddens' formulation still fails to address the importance of the physical body to the process of exercising agency. My introduction of the concept of embodiment into this analysis of entrenched power structures politicises the concept of agency. In addition, the concept of embodiment more soundly integrates the symbolic, material and inter-subjective elements involved in the process, and redeems the socially disadvantaged people under discussion from the passive determinism that is inherent to Giddens' dichotomous model of structure/actor.

> Feminists have [therefore] argued that the category of embodiment replaces dichotomous formulations of the relation between mind and body with monistic and more dialogical conceptions. The emphasis in praxeological or lived aspects of corporeal being suggests a more fluid relation between body and subjectivity than is available in dualist concepts. This monistic approach expresses a revised understanding of gender identity as not simply imposed through patriarchal structures, but as a set of norms that are lived and transformed in the embodied practices of men and women.
>
> (McNay, 2000: 13)

In this particular case study, women and men in Southside have developed a pragmatic transaction of survival, of embodied agency, whereby men provide women with money and in exchange, women give men sex. The concept of women giving men sex in exchange for material advantage, reinforces the *phallocentric* power arrangement by which 'the feminine is defined only in some relation to the masculine, and never autonomously in its own terms' (Grosz, in Gunew, (ed.), 1990: 60). However, one cannot overlook the definite element of deliberate agency in this transaction, because in the present Jamaican environment, inner-city women are reputed to have '*the wickedest slam*', or to be enthusiastic participants in doing sex, as opposed to merely having it done to them. Nevertheless, the hierarchical binary role expectations of performances of embodiment persist as an idealised register of gender power.

Double Standards

This commodification of the Black female body, and the glamorisation of its material expressions, depict the interaction of the capitalist political economy, which creates the conditions of poverty, and the reinforcement of disadvantage through the no-win choices that disadvantaged subjects are forced to make in their often futile efforts to circumvent the material and psychosocial impediments they face. This interaction of capitalism and embodied culture has created an all-pervading and very real double standard in the society's claimed values and its actual practices. For instance, women who choose to appropriate these ambiguous and contradictory *discourses* are also reinforcing their gender power by strategically subscribing to binary stereotypes of embodiment that may happen to operate in their interest at that particular moment. Social security is the most important resource that they acquire in this process. As Mr. Malcolm suggested, it is the men who are involved in the discourse of violence, who have the greatest capability of satisfying requirements for both materiality and social security.

> The young girls don't want a decent companion because he can't cope with their cost of living. So they take a gunman and when that gunman is killed, they take another one of them. The gunman will go out and rob and the money comes thicker and faster. They are not thinking and it is hard to curb them.

Once poor Black women trade their bodies as a way of getting money, they are stereotyped as mercenary. Their sexual practices and embodied lifestyle become a cause of hypocritical concern for institutions and people who are anxious to preserve bourgeois standards of public morality, regardless of whatever sexual lifestyles they themselves may subscribe to or engage in privately behind closed doors. Ironically, no such moral aspersions are cast on the embodied practices of men – who are equally active in the body/sex-for-materiality/ money transaction!

However, the women engaged in these performances do not have the luxury of indulging in these pretentious values. They are too preoccupied, physically and mentally, with demonstrating in unequivocal economic terms, their refusal to be victimised by their cumulative experiences of psychosocial and material disadvantage.

The Price of Pleasure

> Because our actions change the world from one in which we merely exist to one over which we have some control, they enable us to see everyday life as being in process and therefore amenable to change. By persisting in the journey toward self-definition we are changed, and this change empowers us. Perhaps this is why so many…women have managed to persist and "make a way out of no way." Perhaps they know the power of self-definition.
>
> (Collins, 1990: 113)

In a focus group discussion on Ladd Lane, Shacka explained that sexual 'enjoyment' is an important part of a relationship. However, for those living below the poverty line, indulging in such pleasure depends on the social profile of the man in question.

> A sexual relationship is more profitable with an older man who is able to provide financial as well as emotional support. I avoid di young man dem who can't give yuh nutten. You have to be two or three years older than me because I do not want a little baby. I am a baby, I have a baby, and therefore I do not want any more babies. When you are young, you want to wear hot clothes and the young boys can't bear the responsibility. Since I am 19, I would want a man who is 23, nothing under. We do not want giddy headed boys who, when a baby comes, they want to say it is not theirs. *If you have a big man with whom you are having a relationship, he can finance you.* When you are going to school – because as you know, some of them start young, he can help you; you are alright that way.

The material value of sexuality in the survival arsenal of grassroots women is, therefore, intrinsically linked to the wider political economy and reflects a perspective on power relations that does not conform to stereotypical binary concepts about the capacity of women to exercise power.

The schoolgirl in the group discussion said that her parents did not have the means to finance her education. So she traded sexual favours with an older man for financial support. On this score, Ann was of the view that, 'if you are having a man he has to be older because the young boys are unemployed. When babies become involved, they can't mind the baby and they can't even mind themselves.' In agreement, Shacka said that a woman should not have sex with a man unless she was receiving some material benefit in return.

> How can he want to fuck me and leave me to go hungry and not even have soap to wash up my vagina? A woman takes a man for help. The type of help that men want is your body, that's what mostly a man wants. What is a woman going to give their body in exchange for? They are looking for something; they are looking for help. Something for something.

Ann added that as a woman, she likes to be independent but that if she was not working, she was going to require support. Dean, the only man in the discussion asked, 'Can't you just see a man and like him for himself? You will not know if he has money or if he can take care of something if you don't give him a chance to prove himself.' Shacka responded that she was not being strictly materially prescriptive but insisted that,

> your man should help you. You go out, you go with him; he works you. When you come back, you are hungry. You go again and spend one or two nights and you come back; he does not give you a dime. Why are you having a relationship, having sex and so on and yet you can't buy a pack of biscuits, or a roll-on deodorant to fix up yourself? Can this be right?

The obvious conclusion from this instructive disclosure is that you should be paid for being '*worked*'. This truism actually has strong resonances of the bourgeois norm of 'man the breadwinner, woman the housewife', which is the bedrock of White/capitalist ideology.

This theme also resounds in the 'Girls Whine' composition of Dancehall artiste Shabba Ranks that I quoted earlier. As Shabba prescribes, 'if a man want it, mek him pay down pon it'. The advice reiterates the pragmatic strategies of survival to which some Southside residents have to resort. The exchange of sex for materiality can therefore be seen as a *discourse of resistance*; the tailoring of meanings of embodied sexual transactions to the tune of the cultural context. It is all about how socially impoverished people produce rich reservoirs of knowledge and resulting actions, which become the chief indicator of their personal power (Foucault, 1980).

> Mutual knowledge is applied in the form of *interpretative schemes* whereby contexts of communication are created and sustained in interaction... Mutual knowledge is 'background knowledge' in the sense that it is taken-for-granted and mostly remains unarticulated...[but] is never fully taken for granted, and the relevance of some particular element to an encounter may have to be 'demonstrated', and sometimes fought for, by the actor; it is not appropriated ready-made by actors, but is produced and reproduced anew by them as part of the continuity of their lives.
>
> (Giddens, in Cassell (ed.), 1993: 106, emphasis in original)

While some men assume that all women should make whatever sacrifices are necessary in order to demonstrate love, as the women in this discussion insisted, such recourse is usually more beneficial to the men concerned than the women. Therefore, when Dean suggested that 'many women take up with a man who has nothing and they even sleep at his house and in the morning, they drink tea and come home with nothing more,' Ann retorted that women who do that, '*have it already*.' However, for her part, she said, 'everybody thinks differently about it. I am definitely not going to take up with any man who not giving me anything.'

Susan further explained the strategic importance of being clear about the material requirements of the relationship from the outset, so as not to impair one's chances of gaining maximum advantage.

> If you build up a man who has nothing and then you see another man and say to him 'buy me a juice' he is going to tell you that you have your man. So why are you going to have a man if he is not going to find what you want him to give you, to prevent you from going to beg from another man?

Shacka was also adamant that she would not be relinquishing the pleasures of her body without the assurance that she would be materially compensated. The reflexivity of the research exchange was clear, when she asked me what my aim was when I had sex. I responded that I was 'usually motivated by love.' I asked in return whether this was sufficient cause for sexual involvement and she laughed derisively. 'It starts with *help*,' she said in between chuckles. 'It grows up to like, and then it grows up to love.'

Obviously, both the material and symbolic circumstances of her survival *needs and wants*, precluded the possibility of indulging in my kind of emotional extravagance without material reward. She also indicated that my choice was based on a class-specific option, since, according to her, I had 'lived uptown too long.' Lois McNay suggests that in assessing the type of agency expressed by disadvantaged women, one should not promote what she calls 'negative paradigms', as this implies that *resistance discourses* produced by subordinated people are just reactive. Rather, one should consider

> [a] generative theory of subjectification [which] provides a more dynamic theory of agency through which to examine how social actors may adapt and respond in an adaptive fashion to the uncertainties unleashed in an increasingly differentiated social order.

> (McNay, 2000: 161)

The lively group exchange of views continued for hours from afternoon into night. However, when the discussion turned to the enjoyment of sex, the heat was turned up on the passion with which opinions were expressed. As it came out, both women and men experience power in the pleasure portion of sexual encounters. Yet, this does not ultimately alter the fact that they are all multiply disadvantaged by the prevailing power structures and attendant discourses. The tragic consequence of their involvement in the domination matrix is that the identity markers of disadvantage have, in many cases, been internalised and reproduced in resistance strategies, notwithstanding the element of self-consciousness that informs these expressions of agency. The consequent syndrome of internalised oppression (Fanon, 1967) proves to be as challenging a problem as the *discourses* of structural power in any project of development and social transformation.

Boys As The Real Small Fry

> *The reflexive elaboration of frames of meaning is characteristically imbalanced in relation to the possession of power...* 'What passes for social reality' stands in immediate relation to the distribution of power; not only on the most mundane levels of everyday interaction, but also on the level of global cultures and ideologies, whose influence indeed may be felt in every corner of everyday social life itself.

> (Giddens, in Cassell (ed.), 1993: 112, emphasis in original)

When it comes to embodied strategies of survival in the ghetto, boys rather than girls are seen to be the real 'small fry' in every meaning of the term. I facilitated another focus group discussion on Maiden Lane with 14 boys whose ages ranged from 4 to 15 years. They discussed a number of issues related to sexuality, which revealed that they were as aware as adults were, of the value system that motivated the construction of embodied survival strategies. These boys expressed feelings of self-consciousness when they observed that girls prefer, for material reasons, to have relationships with older men. This implies that feelings of psychosocial inadequacy by adult men start with early experiences. When I asked the boys what they think the girls want in a relationship, a number of voices in unison echoed as one utterance, 'The girls want money!'

Boy 1: It would have to be a girl that really likes you, not for what you have, but for who you are.

Boy 2: Big man she wants; she doesn't want any little youths.

Boy 3: When they get the money and men tell them to cook, they don't want to cook.[153]

Boy 4: They are watching your name-brand shoes and they decide that they also want one.

Boy 5: Some of them laugh at you and say you are only wearing an imitation. But when you are in your *wicked*[154] shoes, they are running behind you and begging you money.

Boy 6: Some girls don't want you till you go to foreign and come back. After that, they run you down. And want to drive in your car and that kind of thing.

Boy 7: And boops[155] you out. When you don't go back to foreign,[156] they laugh at you.

For their part, girls learn at an early age how to negotiate with their bodies to gain the maximum material advantage. Boys are at a disadvantage in this power drama because of their material insolvency and the dominant heterosexist culture, which results in girls being targeted as sexual prey by men wishing to shoot their cupid

---

153 This comment was a reinforcement of gender roles; money given by men is often seen as in payment exchange for sex and domestic favours from women, a transaction with which women comply for material expediency and in fulfilment of stereotyped gender roles. This negotiation is reflected in the discussion held by the group on Ladd Lane to which I previously referred, where it was maintained that men were most valued for the material contributions that they made to women. The reinforcement of this role stereotyping in the environment of high male unemployment, serves to marginalise lower-class men, as described by Miller (1986), and indirectly maintain patterns of criminality, which provide the only recourse available to some of the youths as they strategise to survive.

154 A word which varies in meaning. Here it means something spectacular.

155 This expression denotes women bargaining with sexuality to gain an unfair advantage in material goods from a man who is usually several years her senior, in exchange for a minimal amount of sex.

156 Some of the men, and to a lesser extent women, who go abroad, are deported, usually because of criminal activities. As a consequence, they lose the power that they previously enjoyed because of their ability to access the material benefits and the attendant status these brought.

arrows. The prevailing homosexuality taboo makes the reverse a rare case. However, as discussed earlier, there is an increasing tendency for (violent) men from inner-city communities to be participants in the sex-for-materiality transaction.

Beyond the mundane dimension of sexuality, boys and girls are socialised early in life into opposing 'appropriate' gender identities. These identities enable them to survive, or result in them succumbing to *power discourses* that make them even more vulnerable or potentially dangerous in the volatile social environment in which they are trapped.

> The meaning of human sexuality is socially constructed and changes dramatically across cultures and throughout history. Children find themselves placed not only within an age hierarchy but also, however young and however innocent, they are part of the division of society according to sex. And it is biologically determined sex, not socially defined gender, which really makes the difference in the last instance, because all gender systems take their justification from observed physiological distinctions and from the consequences these can have in adult life.

(Ennew, 1986: 26)

With such complex layers of power confronting them, it is difficult for children to resist the overwhelming influence of the dominant norms of gender and embodied power transactions. And while social institutions sometimes act as restraining influences for adolescent girls, even their exposure to and awareness of the materiality associated with sexuality presents a challenging opportunity for the construction of self-hood. Exploring sexuality, however, entails opening another Pandora's Box of power, pleasure and potential pain. Immanent abuse hovers on the edge of every embodied encounter.

> Gender roles are inscribed in childhood through socialisation processes, although children are specifically excluded from both sexual and power aspects of gender that simply exist as promises for the adults they will become. Paradoxically, it is exclusion from both sex and power, that makes children vulnerable to adult abuse and exploitation – sexual or otherwise – whether they are male or female. The combination of innocence and powerlessness makes both boys and girls sexy.

(Ennew, in *Vena Journal*, 1994, 6 (2): 51)

Notions about the 'unknowing' child who should be seen and not heard are clearly class bound. The bourgeois assumption of childhood innocence takes no notice of the knowledge that disadvantaged children have to have in order to negotiate the terrain of the ghetto. Self-concept development in turn is directly related to their engendered pathways of survival. These differences call for analyses that are tailored to suit the cultural context where ultimately, childbearing is the embodied action that gives most weight to identity validation.

The Contradictions of Conception

The meaning of childbirth is interlocked with a society's attitudes towards women. Both reflect its economic system...One does not have to be a Marxist to understand these connections between motherhood and the economy.

(Oakley, in Jackson et al (eds.), 1993: 199)

Figure 9.2: The caption on this postcard photograph reiterates the Jamaican proverb, 'children are poor people's riches'.

In Jamaica, it is considered a truism that 'children are poor people's riches'. While providing pleasure in their own right, children also constitute the social capital in which many disadvantaged parents invest in the hope that they (the children) will actualise their parents' deferred hopes and aspirations. In the absence of a viable social security system, children are also regarded as future caregivers for parents when they are no longer capable of looking after themselves. Since children are able to gain upward social mobility, they provide a practical method for families to overcome the stigma of low-class location and the attendant social disadvantages (Shorey-Bryan, 1986: 70).

Consequently, motherhood is a practical way for women to exercise agency, although the cost of such actions are not always intended (Giddens, 1993). For residents in Southside, parenting is also a highly contradictory practice when assessed in relation to overriding and chronic material disadvantages. However, the culturally compelling reproductive imperative still provides the psychosocial space to compensate for some of the debilitating effects of poverty and social stigma. Young women, who are impelled at an early age to prove sexual maturity by childbearing, are motivated by cultural values which stigmatise the childless woman as a 'mule'. Tremendous shame is attached to the woman who has not 'succeeded' in the act of childbearing. This stigma can be traced all the way back to the Bible, an iconic reference in this predominantly Christian society. In the final analysis, chronic social lack consistently undermines the social effectiveness of this act of exercising agency.

The reclamation of parenting by women as a domain for exercising agency also suggests that gender identities are not fixed, but are adjusted to reflect the dynamics of cultural experiences. Although socio-historical, ideological, religious, material and symbolic forces all converge in the constitution of this practice as a necessary requirement for achieving self-hood, subordinated subjects also appropriate this discourse as an embodied expression of their *self-inscribed* social power.

Figure 9.3: As a mother, this woman has fulfilled what is
regarded as an intrinsic part of her Rastafari identity.

Here agency is seen as discursively produced in the social interactions
between culturally produced, contradictory subjects...Subjectivity and
agency are not, however, fixed prior to language and the discursive practices
in which individuals assume subjectivity. This is not to say, as some critics
have argued, that the material world ceases to exist and is replaced by
discourse. It is rather to insist that the meanings of the material world are
produced within discourse.

(Weedon, 1999: 107)

In reality, it is impossible to separate the tactical survival strategies of poor Black
women from the machinations of the wider political economy (Collins 1990: 166).
Moreover, the fact that parenting is linked to the wider political economy means that
women perform the dual roles of production and reproduction, in many cases without
any emotional, much less material, support from men.

Figure 9.4: The youthfulness of parents in Southside makes it unremarkable for the subjects in this
photograph to represent three generations. (L-R) mother Molly, two daughters and granddaughter.

This intergenerational picture of motherhood further illustrates the gendered
dimensions of power structures and subaltern expressions of agency, which construct
the social subjectivity of women in terms of their race, class, gender, age and sexuality.

> Motherhood is an identity which appears to mark women from men, but the problematic relationship between the biological and the social, between the prescriptions about motherhood and its psychic investments, suggest a more complex construction within different contemporary public discourses...The emphasis here is largely upon the analysis of representations and discourses which construct maternal identities.
>
> (Woodward in Woodward (ed.), 1997: 246)

Issues of power, gender and the body are all intricately intertwined in the inner-city environment of chronic poverty and violence, as all three are inherent to the construction of both identity and survival strategies. These elements are all eloquently reproduced in the practice of parenting. Young women like Susan consciously choose to have a relationship with an older man, because as she said, 'the older men take care of their responsibilities.' However, from her poetic reflections we can also detect the pain and confusion that too often confront young mothers.

The Period That Did Not Come

When I just found out
that I was pregnant,
I cried.
I always sat by myself
and thought over
what had happened.
I wouldn't have an abortion
because if people knew early that
I was pregnant
and the father knew
that he made me
pregnant
and that I threw it away,
people all around here would
tease me and
I would feel ashamed

The commanding effect of taboos against the termination of pregnancy constrained Susan in her attempts to decide whether or not to have the 'unexpected' child. Her situation also illustrates the layers of constraints facing disadvantaged women who are under severe pressure to conform to the dominant social value system, which valorises motherhood as the compelling norm. A common feature of the process of individuation by young people is often rebellion against behavioural prescriptions provided by parents and society and a search for independence (Lawler, 2000: 95). Some young girls feel that they are exercising agency when they become pregnant against their parents' better judgement. However, in many cases, bearing children puts a strain on young women's capacity for social self-determination.

Although she had a steady partner with whom she lived in an extended family household, Tamara had mixed feelings when she discovered her pregnancy. 'A thing just happened,' she said. However, she was committed to having the baby because she did not want to be accused of being a cemetery, as women who terminate pregnancies are called.

Lorna said that when she discovered that her last daughter, who was still in school at the time, was with child she felt frustrated by the fact that she could not encourage her to terminate the pregnancy because of the negative things that people would say. Instead, she resigned herself to again becoming a grandmother. The cultural taboo against abortion results in many young girls having children that they are not adequately prepared to raise.

Further, as the six people in the focus group discussion on Barry Street argued, there is a direct correlation between the youthful age of parents and the lack of discipline in children. Poor parenting is seen as one of the main push factors behind young men becoming involved in violence. 'Di madda dem a pickney demself,' one woman said. 'Dem a raise a generation a youth dat dem can't control, an a so come everybody life inna danger.'

Some girl children are leaving school prematurely because they become pregnant. Four persons in the group said that children usually become sexually active around age 12. They are often unaware of the long-term implications of their actions. But this knowledge is a skill that not many of them were taught to apply.

> Not only in terms of their daughters' sexuality, but in terms of their overall development into adult women, mothers of daughters face a series of contradictions. They are supposed to inculcate a self which is inner-controlled within the daughter, yet they must also be sure the daughter turns out 'well'; thus they are caught in the tension between guiding and advising, and leaving the daughter to her own devices...As a result, the daughter's failure to 'achieve' can be blamed, not on a social system which militates against her 'achievement', but on her mother.

> (Lawler, 2000: 99)

The issue of childbearing is, evidently, a very contested one, which is intertwined with identity and self-esteem issues that are negotiated every day by social actors generally, but 'especially by those who have been marginalised and excluded or whose identities have not been acknowledged' (Woodward, in Woodward (ed.), 1997: 242). In this scenario, women who come to self-realisation through parenting are just continuing a time-worn tradition that their ancestors carved out over time and across space.

> We must [therefore] distinguish between what has been said about subordinated groups in the dominant discourse, and what such groups might say about themselves...Personal narratives, autobiographical statements, poetry, fiction, and other personalised statements have all been used by women of colour to express self-defined standpoints on mothering and motherhood. Such knowledge reflects the authentic standpoint of subordinated groups.

> (Collins, in Glenn et al, 1994: 48-49)

Of course, pregnancy as an expression of agency is not a panacea for the social ills that are sharply accentuated by the parental responsibilities that inevitably accompany the practice. In fact, if one were to only assess this project of self-realisation in material terms, it might seem absurd that women have consistently resorted to childbearing as an opportunity for achieving social improvement. Apparently, however, the psychosocial benefits seem far outweigh the material challenges. Therefore, when development planners prescribe restrictions on poor women's reproductive capacities as a strategy of poverty reduction, they are blaming/punishing the victims for the conditions of their disadvantage, rather than attributing such difficulties to the prevailing power structures. But there are still a few good signs for the future despite all the problems.

According to reports published in the press in May 2003, Jamaica is ranked among the better places in the world to be a mother. This is according to the fourth annual Mothers' Index, published by Save the Children, a British-based international child aid organisation with offices in over 70 countries. Jamaica was ranked 28th out of 117 countries in the index, published in the May 2003 'State of the World's Mothers' report. The Mothers' Index reflects how individual countries compare in meeting the needs of mothers. The island also performed reasonably well in the indices which measured how much attention countries pay to the needs of women and children, tying with Trinidad and Tobago at position 26 in the children's index.

In the meantime, both men and women interrogated my own sexuality on a number of occasions because at the time of the research, I was nearly forty and had not given birth to a child. In one focus group discussion, the participants inverted the interrogation process by placing me on the other side of the microphone.

Tanya: Do you have a boyfriend?

Imani: No.

Merl: And you don't have any children?

Imani: Well, I can't get pregnant if I am not having sex with a man.

Lee: So how come you never breed?

Imani: Well, I did nothing to prevent it so my body probably does not want to deal with that.

Merl: Maybe you can still get pregnant.

Imani: Maybe. But if not, I will adopt or do without.

Tanya: A baby is a nice thing to have. A woman should never abort or give up her child because that could come to be her star child in life.

Lee: *A womb without a child is not a womb at all.*

The women insisted that I was 'lacking something' because I had not produced a child of *my own*. Sexuality, therefore, provides a profound resource for the (re)production of *discourses of power* and powerlessness. Before the project was over, I had experienced two miscarriages. These events enabled me to realise the extent to which I was my own tool of analysis as this process incorporated the very norms and taboos connected to women's bodies and the politics of sexuality that I was analysing in the study. I had to come to terms with the extent to which my own experiences reflected the combination of cultural identity, pleasure and pain, which are invested in the choice to exercise agency through motherhood. The fact that the process was prematurely albeit involuntarily terminated, was read by some significant others as social failure, which reflects the taboos which are invoked by infertility, miscarriage and/or abortion. These value judgements also reflect patriarchal definitions of femininity, which are internalised and reproduced by women.

Let us take a closer look at the cultural prohibitions against abortion, which is seen in the ghetto as tantamount to murder. Such cultural prohibitions are directly related to the prevailing power regime of heterosexist *hegemonic masculinity* and sets distinct boundaries for women's capacity to exercise independent embodied agency.

Abortion as Taboo

In inner-city communities like Southside, women who terminate pregnancies are called *cemeteries* because they have transgressed the normative boundaries of womanhood. Yet African women have long had a tradition of birth control that they practised during slavery, which was informed by what their continental ancestors used to do.

> Greater insight into the practice of abortion by slave women can...be gleaned from a cross-cultural analysis of the practice in African societies. Major abortifacients used by African women include infusions from herbs, leaves of special shrubs, plant roots and bark from certain trees. Common plants used include manioc, yam, papaya, mango, lime and frangipani. Mechanical means are less popular and rely, for instance, on the insertion of sharp sticks or stalks into the vaginal canal.

> (Bush, 1990: 140)

However, many people in Jamaica, particularly the Rastafari, believe that institutions of Planned Parenthood have genocidal intent. They cite examples from the slavery era of systematic annihilation of millions of Africans as just cause for their objections. The similarity of historical experiences in the Caribbean and North America also makes it worthwhile to refer to the African-American experience in order to emphasise the psychosocial impetus underlying patterns of resistance to fertility control in general and abortion in particular.

> In the USA...fears of depopulation produced...a pronatalist trend that had not previously existed. This trend also built into traditional Black values that conferred adult status on women who became biological mothers, the first significant step toward womanhood...The opposition to fertility control for African-American women in the 1920s came primarily from the Catholic Church for religious and political reasons...and from Black nationalist leaders like Marcus Garvey who believed that the continuation of the Black race demanded increasing, rather than decreasing, the African population as a defence against racial oppression.

> (Ross in James and Busia (eds.), 1993: 148)

Unfortunately, supporting repopulation as a form of resistance against cultural annihilation runs the risk of essentialising women's sexuality.[157] To answer the cultural question on terminations, we need to acknowledge, that 'every woman experiences many reproductive opportunities in her life, not all of which she wants to eventuate in a child' (Poovey, op.cit.: 252). Therefore, we can 'place abortion in the context of contraception, not murder' (Poovey, op.cit.: 252). This review would remove the burdens of shame, guilt and fear that women experience on this score.

Parenting is also an important cultural trope for establishing identity and therefore deserves special attention as an indicator of how poor people exercise agency through the strategic deployment of their sexuality by way of gender-specific and culturally normative behaviours.

Parenthood as a Discourse of Resistance

In Jamaica as elsewhere in the world, institutions of socialisation and law and order project sacred and profane meanings onto the surface of bodies of people living below the poverty line. As should be very clear by now, women are invariably at the bottom of this ladder of social injustice. It should also be obvious that female access to power is curtailed by widespread cultural values that serve to keep them in places of subordination. Women are still the lowest paid and the most unemployed in the lowest social development index. In order to compensate for their material lack, women live out the cliché that *children are poor people's riches*. Parenting is therefore another means by which inner-city women psychosocially compensate for material lack and in the process, come to self-realisation and exercise independent agency.

Since her mother had had only one child, Ms. Williams had six children because, as she said, she wanted 'to bring back the family'. Thus, in spite of the contradictions involved, *'the fact is that women themselves do want children'* (Senior, 1991: 67, emphasis added). But I cannot emphasise enough that parenting is not a panacea; the pleasures that undoubtedly result from reinforcing identities through practices of mothering do not always compensate for endemic social and material lack. As Miss Jenny a 65-year-old woman said, 'To be candid, the worst time of my life is since I had kids.' Miss Joyce, 68, was equally melancholy when she remembered her own experiences.

> Sometimes I sit by myself and I say, 'Father, what did I really do to my self?' If I didn't have them, I would be better off. My grand-children grew how I didn't want them to grow and they abuse me. I just have to give them prayer.

It is difficult for parents who are struggling to survive and to care for children to address their own needs for self-realisation. And while some fathers have always been willing and to some extent, able, to take responsibility for the care of their children, the social aspects of child-rearing have long been seen as primarily female prerogatives. However, the contracting economy makes it difficult for both women

---

157 As I argued in Chapter 2, although subordinated subjects sometimes strategically claim essentialism in their struggle to politicise identities that have been deemed pejorative by dominant discourses, one should also be aware of the ways in which it is possible to collude with these very dominant discourses, if the strategic element is not present in the assertion.

and men living below the poverty line to manage their responsibilities effectively. Meanwhile, groups like Fathers Incorporated have spearheaded consciousness-raising efforts to encourage men to become good fathers. While this was successful uptown, it has been difficult to achieve similar success below the poverty line and this had serious repercussions on social relations. In the Ladd Lane focus group discussion for example, Shacka questioned the value of men claiming the benefits of fatherhood if they were not also playing a material role in the childcare process.

> if I get pregnant for a man, what is the use for me to only look at him with the baby looking at me and we all not being able to do anything for one another?

Her question is particularly revealing of the contradictions inherent in the quest to exercise agency through embodied transactions like parenting. The query also shows that the cultural structural factors that construct (socially inscribe) the meanings of motherhood are often more compelling than the independent determination (*self-inscription*) by women to use this device to develop discourses of resistance. Many women will admit that they enter a union with the overt or covert intention of making a baby, which they hope, will guarantee long term loyalty and material support from the man. Therefore, sexuality provides an embodied resource with potential to transcend the confines of class and gender disadvantages, which have socially constructed such women as the *other*. Therefore,

> for women of colour, the subjective experience of mothering/motherhood is inextricably linked to the socio-cultural concern of racial ethnic communities – one does not exist without the other…The locus of conflict lies outside of the household, as women and their families engage in collective effort to create and maintain family life in the face of forces that undermine family integrity.

> (Collins, in Glenn et al (eds.), 1994: 47)

Therefore, whereas *subordinated women* exercise agency through a re-appropriation of embodiment, their limited economic options and social choices (Post, 1996), dictate that, paradoxically, their resistance strategies also reinforce the very ideological and cultural norms which they seek to undermine. But what of their male counterparts? We need also to look at how they manage to navigate the difficulties that life has thrown their way, in order to fully understand the gender power drama of inner-city identity politics.

Paradoxes of Fatherhood

'To be Poor is a Crime', as the popular Jamaican saying goes. That is what some fathers in the ghetto think at any rate. As much as they would want to look after their youths, many men find themselves unable to do so because of their chronic condition of unemployment. When a man gets children, he is seen as a real man. On the other hand, the sexuality of a man who has not fathered children is likely to be sharply questioned. In the script of popular culture, a man who has plenty children is seen as a strong man. A childless man is likely to be described as a *maama* man – a shade shy of an outright homosexual. When a man has children but does not provide financial support for those children, people do not stop to think about his fragile ego that is under pressure because of the stagnant economy. No; all kinds of judgement – including the *maama man* characterisation – are heaped upon him. As the ultimate scapegoat, this man has no recourse but to go out into the wilderness of the society and try, by fair means or foul, to make a life for himself.

This combination of factors has reinforced prevailing stereotypes of irresponsible fathers who engage in multiple relationships and equate biological parenting with the extent of the role that they should play in the 'family'. However, the validity of these stereotypes has been challenged by research undertaken by Barry Chevannes.

> In a national stratified random sample survey…I found that only fifty percent of the males interviewed acknowledged that they had more than one partner. However, many more indicated that they would have liked to have more, implying that lack of finance was the limiting factor…Less than a decade later…males made a clear distinction between love, which implied both sex and commitment, and sex, which implied sex but no commitment, and they confirmed that men were not averse to having sex with women who they did not respect. This was truer for adolescent and young adult males than for the older middle-class men in their thirties and forties, among whom an outside relationship tended to involve some commitment as well.

> (Chevannes, 1999: 6)

Despite the validity of these research findings, it is common knowledge at the grassroots level, that the practice of men having multiple relationships or 'gal inna bungle' as Beenie Man sang it, is a phenomenon that accentuates the rivalry between women. 'Tink about it!' Molly said. 'Dat man could have his personal woman and probably have four more girls round the corner that he has to look after. Some of the woman dem come on strong when they see the *material man* and don't know that it's not one woman that he has to deal wid.'

While they might not provide financial support, many poor men are actively involved in providing other forms of childcare. As Chevannes reported, '[c]hildren gave them a sense of being grown-up and responsible [and they] reported spending considerably more time with their children than popular opinion would have suggested' (Chevannes, 1999: 7). As I also observed, there are several men among the residents of Southside, who take the best care of not only their own children, but grandchildren and non-blood relations as well. For example, Donovan, 35, father of five children, endorsed the view that parenting has a sobering effect on men like him who used to 'touch the road'. Explaining the evolution from immature behaviours to manhood, he said,

> when you are a more childish youth, you do more childish things, you know? Yeah. And as time goes by, you are just growing and you are changing and tell yourself that because you have a woman now, you have responsibility. When you have a baby mother and rent to pay, you have to just start thinking manly and moving manly.

As explained here, and reflected in other men's experiences,[158] fatherhood is a domain for expressing gender power while also being a significant area for effecting personal as well as social transformation.

Below the poverty line, fatherhood presents its own peculiar challenges simply because many men do not make the necessary linkages between biological, social and material interpretations of this discourse of masculinity. Moreover, the distinctions that the men in Chevannes' research conveniently draw between sexual desire and material capability, imply that there is some measure of irresponsibility involved, especially when children are part of the equation. This gendered hierarchical binary mechanism does not easily accommodate the shifts in power relationships that are taking place in the society. Previously, normative gender roles have been transformed as more and more women are being acknowledged as independent providers for their own households.

Figure 9.5: Donovan and (now grown) sons symbolise the construction of responsible fatherhood as a counter-discourse to the stereotype of unstable fatherhood.

In light of this, when men who cannot fulfil the breadwinner stereotype draw a distinction between love and sex, one has to wonder if they do so because of material lack. To overcompensate, they try to maintain control over women in the domain of sexuality. Some men even become violent to express their frustration when women resist their attempts at control by being independent.

---

158 Although I only cite this man's experience, I also encountered several other fathers – such as Percival 'Heights Man' Cordwell, Errol, Taffa, Binghi, Clive, Luddy and Sammo – whose performances indicate that claiming this register can contribute to breaking the vicious cycle of the discourse of violence. Many concerned citizens described the youths caught up in outrageous acts of violence as 'a generation of vipers' who cannot change because the indicators of their construction are too deeply embedded in the political economy and their sense of personal power. This sense of inevitability is derived from the lack of consciousness with which these men operate. However, although I also recognise that fatherhood by itself will not bring about the desired goal of social transformation, the caring themes that are basic to this performance can help in the character-building and social-development processes that are so desperately needed in the community.

Even if individual men refrain from employing physical force against their partners, men as a class benefit from how women's lives are restricted and limited because of their fear of violence by their husbands and lovers as well as by strangers. Wife abuse or battering reinforces women's passivity and dependence as men exert their rights to authority and control. The reality of domination at the social level is the most crucial factor contributing to and maintaining wife abuse at the personal level.

(Bogard, in Jackson et al (eds.), 1993: 197)

Although both women and men living below the poverty line have appropriated parenting as a *discourse of resistance*, this practice is saturated with gender power contradictions. The violent backlash from marginalised men who cannot offer women material support when the culture defines this capacity as the norm, creates its own domino effect. Therefore, the psychosocial damage that has resulted from performances of violent hegemonic masculinity needs to be addressed as a fundamental component when developing strategies for social change. This is especially important because in the long run, viable performances of parenting are endangered by the prevailing patterns of violent hegemonic masculinity.

Growing up in the Shadow of Death

Below the poverty line, those trying to be responsible parents have to be consistently swimming against the tidal wave of the violence that threatens to swamp the inner city. Time and time again, residents of Southside spoke of the ways in which the deadly *discourse of violence* affects the capacity of women to be effective parents. On the other hand, some women who are primary caregivers, often turn a blind eye to the criminal activities of their children. They are bemused because they can gain material benefits from the illegal activities of their offspring. The following poem is a rephrasing of four testimonies about the negative impact of the *discourse of violence* on parenting and socialisation practices and the damaging effects that this expression of gender power has had on individual sensibilities. The recurring theme of psychosocial damage is starkly emphasised as a threat to strong community spirit.

Gunshots are my Neighbours

A gunshot connected to flesh
You know
The difference
A young man and mature woman
said
Because there is no echo
But a hollow thud
As flesh sucks up bullet
The frightened mother and children
Fly in practised motion
Under the bed

As a staccato volley
Answers the initial round
And they can hear the agonised wail
of the injured party
Mi get shot; di whole a
mi belly tear off! Mi get shot![159]
The little girl starts to whimper
and clutches the mother's breast
The little boy whispers fiercely
I want to be a gunman so that
I can kill police
The mother feels the silent tears
searing her cheeks in hot rivulets
As she remembers the fate of her children's father
Fatally wounded in a shootout with the police
She witnessed him with hands upheld
Being cut down in his prime
No angel to be sure because he
Had put it on[160]
a victim or more In his time
All of a sudden it seemed to be
A revolution of the cycle
Another bullet connected to flesh
Without echo
and they all shuddered

© imani tafari-ama

These revelations show that in communities like Southside the practices of bearing and raising children as acts of identity affirmation have glaring caveats. Children are unlikely to escape unscathed from the contradictory codes of gender behaviour that are emphasised in this social milieu. In view of the evidence of these experiences, I therefore question the validity of the arguments put forward by theorists who suggest that rather than 'victimising' children and adults alike who have intergenerationally experienced such psychosocial trauma, their knowledges should be distilled for their positive meanings. One such theorist says,

> [a]pparently dysfunctional behaviour patterns...can in practice be extremely effective strategies for survival in certain contexts. The social meanings given to violence and suffering may act as a resource for children and give them the resilience to cope.

> (Boyden, 1994: 261)

---

159 I got shot; the whole of my stomach has torn off. I am shot.
160 An expression that means to fire a gun. It also carries the connotation of having good sex.

No human being should have to suffer the indignities that are commonplace in the urban grassroots communities of Jamaica. And, although harsh experiences mark Southside's residents as remarkably resilient, this very capacity reinforces their *de facto* designation as marginalised *others*. Their identities are constructed as a function of prevailing power mechanisms that solidify the dichotomous distance in the Jamaican society between rich and poor. People who have no recourse but to live with the *discourse of violence* are unapologetically critical about the impact of chronic disadvantage on their lives. The following poetic summation captures some of the eloquence expressed by boys in the group discussion on Ladd Lane. These youths were particularly concerned about the connections that exist among problematic family and community relationships and discursive violence.

Survival

There is a lady,
Her son is a gunman and so
Anybody that they hold for them
They are going to kill them
They do not cater[161]
Family, or anybody, they lick them out[162]

The material and non-material benefits that some young women derive from sexual alliances with gunmen also demonstrate the extent to which everyday acts of exercising agency become inseparable from *discourses of domination*. These embodied contradictions emphasise the paradoxes of the structural dynamic, which both constitutes the subject as well as the very framework of the constraints within which s/he exercises agency.

> According to the notion of the duality of structure, rules and resources are drawn upon by actors in the production of interaction, but are thereby also reconstituted through such interaction. Structure is thus the mode in which the relation between moment and totality expresses itself in social reproduction.

> (Giddens, in Cassell, (ed.), 1993: 123)

The criminal activities of some young men and the prevalence of teenage parenthood are usually cited as the main problems that prevent people in inner-city communities from escaping from the confines of their social condition. However, these conclusions deflect attention away from the impact of prevailing power structures on these expressions of agency by social subjects and the extremely limited alternative options that are available to them. The scarcity of material capital gives greater impetus to embodied practices that enable the subordinated to acquire symbolic if not material power. This creates a vicious cycle, since the sex-for-materiality transactions, which

---

161 They do not make any concessions.
162 To 'lick out' means to eliminate or to kill.

reify phallocratic notions of resistance, only serve to consolidate the chronic conditions of social, material and gendered disadvantage.

This frightening and seemingly hopeless situation is what led Bounty Killer to pen the following lyrics, words for which he was roundly and soundly criticised by polite Jamaican society. However, a careful review of the words to 'Look Into My Eyes' make it clear that this is actually the most profound song Bounty will probably ever write. Rather than being a glorification of the 9 mm gun and the bad man lifestyle, the song is instead a desperate appeal on behalf of the poor for help to find an alternative way.

Look Into My Eyes

Chorus: *Look into my eyes, tell me what you see?*
Can you feel my pain? Am I your enemy?
Give us a better way, things are really bad,
The only friend I know is this gun I have.
Listen to my voice, this is not a threat
Now you see the Nine are you worried yet?
You've been talking 'bout you want the war to cease
But when you show us hope, we will show you peace.

Verse 1: *Look into my mind, can you see the wealth?*
Can you tell that I want to help myself?
But if it happen that I stick you for your ring
Don't be mad at me it's a survival ting.
Look into my heart, I can feel your fear
Take another look can you hold my stare?
Why are you afraid of my hungry face?
Or is it this thing bulging in my waist?....

Verse 2: *Look into my life, can you see my kids?*
Let me ask you this, do you know what hungry is?
Well in this part of town, survival is my will
For you to stay alive you've got to rob and kill.
Look into my house would you live in there?
Look me in the eyes and tell me that you care,
Well I've made up my mind to end up in the morgue
Right now I'd rather die, 'cause man a live like dog....

Verse 3: *Look down on my shoes, can you see my toes?*
The struggle that we live nobody really knows
Stop and ask yourself, would you live like that?
and if you had to then, wouldn't you bus gunshot?
Look into the schools, tell me how you feel?
You want the kids to learn without a proper meal
Den what you have in place to keep them out of wrong?
If they drop out of school dem a go bus dem gun.

~Bounty Killer ('Look Into My Eyes')

CHAPTER 10

MARKING TIME BELOW THE POVERTY LINE

Sierra Leonean Proverb:
Yu kohba smok sote, i mohs kohmoht

No matter how you try to cover up smoke, it must come out.
A person's bad character cannot be long hidden.

Sexualised Literature

As is being increasingly acknowledged in academic circles, there has been a serious lack of representations of sexuality in Caribbean literature. This lack exists despite the proliferation of sexual imagery in popular regional cultural music forms like Dancehall, Calypso and Soca. Indeed, it has been quaintly fashionable for so-called intellectuals to separate the sexual from the spiritual and the erotic from the economic. For instance, most researchers and writers completely fail to identify the common denominators of the dynamics linking political power with sexual 'pussy power'. However, life in Jamaica and the Caribbean is more than just sea and sun, and is much more sexually textured and sensuously contoured than such prim and proper writers or gender-conscious researchers would have us believe.

It seems clear, therefore, that in many, still unidentified, ways, centuries of enslavement and colonialism have negatively impacted our public discourse and the freedom and ability of Jamaican/Caribbean people to express any kind of serious sexuality and eroticism, whether in art or in literature. However, as Caribbean people carve out a new place in the sun for themselves in the 21st century, we must be able to freely discuss pleasure and desire of the flesh, or to use the erotic as a site for *poetic discourse*, or to use the sexual as a means of socio-political analysis. This is exactly what we have explicitly attempted to do in ***Blood Bullets and Bodies***, advance the body of politically influenced sexual literature, as we discussed the linguistics and nuances of sexual politics and *politricks* below the poverty line and its effects on crime and violence in '*Jamaica land we love*'.

In 2005, the *Gleaner* published the following story, highlighting how accurately we had named the problematic in the title and texture of this book.

Blood and Bullets –
Cops, thugs in hour-long gun battle

published: Sunday | March 13, 2005

(PHOTOS BY NORMAN GRINDLEY/DEPUTY CHIEF PHOTOGRAPHER)

Police officers stand guard on Bryden Street, as residents flee to safety after four persons were murdered in the community yesterday.

Robert Lalah and Rasbert Turner, Gleaner Writers

THE BELEAGUERED community of March Pen Road in Spanish Town, St. Catherine was yesterday plunged into a state of anarchy, as a heated hour-long gun battle between lawmen and armed thugs, sent residents scurrying and cowering in fear. Police reports are that about 8:30 a.m., they responded to calls about incessant gunfire coming from 76 March Pen Road, commonly known as Big Tree. The police party that went to the area was met by a group of about 20 scantily clad men, armed with several AK47 and M16 rifles. The gunmen fired on the police party and the fire was returned. As the gun battle proceeded, the lawmen found themselves overpowered and outnumbered, and were forced to call for back up. On the arrival of a police armoured personnel carrier, the gunmen retreated.

Residents say the perennial violence in the area, which involves persons with allegiances to rivalling political factions, has got particularly worse in recent weeks.

Distraught residents yesterday related a tale of savagery at its worst. They said two young children who dared to venture into enemy territory on their way to school on Friday, were sent running for their lives, after gunmen fired upon them with powerful artillery. The gunmen sent the children away with a simple message, "Nuh come back up yah so." The children were not harmed.

Hours after yesterday's gun battle, residents of the area slowly ventured from the relative safety of their homes with forlorn expressions on their faces. One woman with whom The Sunday Gleaner spoke, said she has been unable to leave the community for over a week. "Di man dem who control di exit nah go allow mi fi leave. Anyhow dem even see wi, dem ago kill we. Mi hungry from Tuesday and caan get nuh food. Di one shop down here a run out a food. It nuh nice roun' here," said the woman with an obvious note of despair in her voice…

We are now nearing the end of this all-too-true, bittersweet, sexualised saga of how and why blood, bullets and bodies have overflowed the politically demarcated poverty line in Jamaica's inner cities. We have provided graphic and tragic evidence of how and why fact is indeed stranger (more erotic and violent) than fiction in the Jamaican scenario. We have seen that many inner-city residents caught below the poverty line in the 'ghetto trap' are marking time, going nowhere except the cemetery, as life marches on around them. This is the beginning of the final summation, the section where we connect the beginning of this strange story to the end and rehash and re-summarise all of the main themes and issues raised during the preceding nine chapters. This is where the meanings of the body language we have analysed and the meanings of all the 'intellectual' sounding words we have used in this story all become crystal clear.

Marking Time

Jamaicans are very much like Californians: they are marking time and waiting for the feared 'big one' to happen. In Jamaica's case, it is not necessarily another killer earthquake like the one that swamped Port Royal in 1692, although a tsunami-like situation such as that is possible too. No, Jamaicans are waiting for a big explosion of out-of-control violence. Mini explosions of community violence break out periodically in various parts of the island, but, a big island-wide explosion of the volatile social powder keg that is Jamaica still lurks in the country's uncertain near future. Clearly, the average tourist kicked back with a fan sipping a rum and coke on a security-patrolled beach sees a different Jamaica, through his/her rose-coloured glasses, from the average Jamaican, marking time swatting flies and kicking his/her heels against the curb somewhere on a narrow and dangerous inner-city street. Paradoxically, sex-for-materiality transactions are also seen much differently in the tourist resorts of the north coast than they are in the urban ghettos of the south coast, just as naked White tourists are regarded differently than naked Black Dancehall Queens.

As we have graphically detailed, the life-and-death situation facing the *socially inscribed* and circumscribed African bodies living in *garrison communities* below the poverty line like Southside, is a very complex one. So complex, in fact, that it requires a multi-level approach to understand it, much more to try to change the prevailing ballistic conditions. Despite the millions of dollars that have been invested in crime-fighting measures through the years, inner-city violence has escalated and spilled over the poverty line into the mainstream of the Jamaican social landscape. Fear and frustration have down-spiralled into a pervasive feeling of despair as local citizens lose hope that the situation can be changed – for the better. This is because the root causes of the problem, as we have explored them, are not being systemically addressed. The dilemma of the 'ghetto trap' is compounded by the apparent lack of *political will* to address the material roots of the problem and to take the necessary measures that would lead to amelioration of the 'blood for blood' and 'fire for fire' mentality and situation. But while the politricksters are marking time and wasting opportunities for action, the lack of public security in inner-city Kingston[163] is only getting worse.

For far too long, the puppeteers who control the state and its apparatuses have used divide and rule power mechanisms to preserve their political interests. This has resulted in a value system that marks a Brown minority as privileged in material and

---

163 Spanish Town presents even graver challenges to the citizen security situation.

racial terms, while excluding the African majority of the population, particularly those in the urban poor areas, from access to the means of production and from slices (i.e. benefits) of the economic pie. These power practices have had deleterious effects at political, social and economic levels of the society. The prevailing *discourse of violence* in Southside provides a prism for examining the identity themes that are intricately intertwined in the deployment of this power mechanism, which is exactly what we have done.

Chapters 3–5, the historical background chapters, illustrated the myriad factors that have converged to produce such difficult socioeconomic circumstances for the urban poor in present-day Jamaica. These chapters clearly showed that the political economy, which has been unstable for some time, is symptomatic of the stark social inequalities that prevail in this island state inhabited by two and a half million people. The perennial *needs and wants* that plague both women and men in this environment also act as push factors for transactions of trading sex for material advantage as necessary strategies for their political and economic survival. The dos and don'ts of these sex-for-materiality transactions constitute '*sexual politics*' in its most nitty-gritty, down-to-earth form. However, while people living in Southside are psychosocially disadvantaged and dispossessed generally as a class, the patriarchal dimensions of social relationships result in women and girls experiencing super-exploitation because of their gender identities.

Chronic psychosocial lack has also made some inner-city residents grist for the mill of partisan political and gang warfare, with the result that violence has become one of the deadliest threats to citizen security in Jamaica. While young Black men are the main protagonists and victims of this complex configuration of structural, discursive and embodied power, women and children are also active players in this dramaturgy. The state is implicated in this configuration too. In an interview with Professor C.Y. Thomas that I conducted on Roots 96.1 FM radio, the eminent economist asserted that, 'poor people who live in Caribbean islands like Jamaica are penalised for the facts of their socio-historical origins'. He predicted that the economic and social-security woes which Jamaica has been experiencing for some time will not be alleviated until the *powers-that-be* make a concerted effort to address fundamental issues of poverty symbiotically associated with the African majority, which are clearly race/class determined and gender-specific.

The desperate situation involving crime and violence that exists in Southside is now common not only in other inner-city communities in east, west and central Kingston, but increasingly in other major urban areas like Spanish Town, Montego Bay and even Mandeville. Tragically, the fragile social situation in Jamaica also provides a metaphor for what has become an all-too-typical scenario in many far-flung urban parts of both the under-developed and developed worlds.

> The correlation between poverty and violence is well established…Poverty means not having enough money to maintain a satisfactory standard of living…Increasingly, being poor…means living in a devastated, crime-ridden neighbourhood. It often means growing up in a family without a father and going to schools where most students fail and most are expected to fail. It is hard to measure the exact impact of these phenomena on the homicide rate, but surely the impact is great.

> (Prothrow-Stith and Weissman, 1991: 17)

It is now time to sum up the main arguments on which this book is based. I will therefore review these assumptions and the extent to which the data supported or challenged these theoretical sketches.

Summary of Arguments: Proposition 1

Because of the political economy of Jamaica, people living in the so-called ghetto or inner-city areas of Kingston have been constructed in the interstices of a discourse of violence, which is gendered in its myriad expressions.

The complex factors that have produced the inner-city problem in communities like Southside are not new. In fact, the city of Kingston is rooted in the system of British colonialism and subsequently, the bourgeois definition of democracy that has been applied in this northern Caribbean island. A generation-span of just over 30 years has seen cataclysmic changes in the character of the socioeconomic landscape of the major city. From a situation of relative affluence, when middle-class Kingstonians inhabited this particular community, the face of the area has changed to one of dire poverty and burgeoning violence, as Black people of African descent replaced the Brown mixed-class residents, and violence became endemic to partisan politics.

The grossly unequal relations of capital, labour, production and trade in the world economic system in which Jamaica is inserted, and which are mirrored by the socioeconomic and political systems of the highly stratified Jamaican society, serve to subordinate the African majority as a class/race. These social contradictions were approached via an analysis of the political economy of identity, and elaborated through the routes of patriarchy, class, gender and sexuality. This led to a hybrid interpretation of the multifaceted manifestations of state power experienced by residents living in this subaltern enclave, Southside. In this scenario, the criminalisation of the gangsters who are constructed as the enemies of the state, has legitimised the use of extreme state violence by the security forces, not only against the gunmen in particular, but against inner-city residents in general. This strategy of containment and control now has the sinister connotation of ethnic cleansing.

However, Jamaica's history/herstory is rife with vivid examples of how systems of domination have always roused the oppressed to responses of creative struggle and resistance. In the 1960s and early 1970s, the grassroots' politicisation of race as a discourse of resistance and the ongoing reclamation of the Black body as a site of struggle and identity construction have provided significant avenues for the downtrodden to express agency. However, such instances of resistance are also suffused with gender power contradictions. Further, the tendency to separate the domains of race and gender as oppositional turf for men and women respectively, only serves to reinforce divide-and-rule power mechanisms. Maintaining such differences also occludes the possibilities for simultaneously synergising the masculine and feminine principles, which are all vital to processes of conception, identity, growth and development – in material, political, symbolic and metaphysical terms.

In this regard, and maybe to the surprise of some, the Rastafari have clearly made a strong and positive impression on the popular culture and feature prominently in leadership roles in both inner-city and rural communities of Jamaica. Therefore, any project of social transformation in Jamaica should pay attention to the concepts of *Peace and Love* that are central to the *Rastafari Livity*. Such efforts should also centralise the politicisation of race and gender as mechanisms for defusing the perennial conflicts in the urban enclaves, thereby providing alternative sources of subaltern empowerment.

In the meantime, we saw that patriarchy links privileged politicians and elite grassroots characters. The puppet masters employ violence as a *discourse* of political manipulation, while the rude boys/shotters appropriate the *violent discourse* as a means of resolving conflicts and expressing hegemonic masculinity. Thus, the violence, which is a direct reflection of the divide-and-rule pattern of patronage politics, has produced a traumatic legacy of systematic underdevelopment. All of this tragic social drama is acted out in an atmosphere of fear and silence, which are distinctive metaphors of the hegemonic masculinist gender order. Yet as we also explored, the prevailing silences and apparent lack of action are sometimes strategic forms of resistance, which are effectively appropriated by the subordinated in their efforts to deflect and counteract overt expressions of power (Scott, 1990).

This practice of adopting subversive identities in the face of domination characterises the strategic capitulation of women to sexist norms, often as a necessary survival strategy. Women's identities are also contoured and circumscribed by the normative *discourse of violence* experienced in their everyday lives.

Summary of Arguments: Proposition 2

In Southside, gender power is reified in terms of dominant masculinities and stereotypes of subordinate femininities, in tandem with identities which defy these norms in spite of prevailing sanctions.

During the decade of the 1970s the reproduction of the hegemonic discourse of *violence* created a vicious range of prohibitive identity registers, which delimited the capacity of the wider body of inner-city residents to challenge this gender power regime. The ominous tenor of the prevailing *discourse of violence* is most profoundly appreciated when one thinks of the development implications of this scenario, not only for Jamaica, but also for the many Caribbean and other countries where this phenomenon is a typical characteristic of the political economy.

Gang members' overdeveloped sense of personal pride is a reflection of the impoverishment of their environment – they have little to feel proud of except their reputation – and it is a reflection of their age-appropriate narcissism... '[W]hen someone "disrespects" or "disses" these kids, the consequences can be fatal' (Prothrow-Stith and Weissman, 1991: 109).

Although men and women exercise power in various public and private domains, in social spaces like Southside, men are the chief perpetrators of *the war*, which is the public expression of gender power. Accordingly, men are the primary targets of violence as well as the principal negotiators of peace treaties. However, antagonistic relations also erupt among women who demonstrate the internalisation of patriarchal norms of gender power by fighting each other, usually to secure male attention.

The mainly political warfare of the 1970s and 1980s has now evolved, or devolved, into gang warfare. Men, women and children who live in inner-city communities like Southside experience various versions of this patriarchal construction of identities. From the 1990s to the present, drug-related turfism has added an element of viciousness to these already contested social relations. Nowadays, gunmen and victims alike suggest that the politicians, who armed their supporters to fight against each other from the early 1970s, have to be identified as the architects of the project to keep the poor powerless through tribal warfare.

It is evident from the research data that male violence against women is directly correlated with the ongoing turf conflicts between men, as well as with the attendant discourse of homophobia that is intertwined with these expressions of hegemonic masculinity. The material and gender subordination of women is thus compounded by their vulnerability to domestic and social violence and sexual abuse. The (gang) rape of women, now an indictable war crime, is another sinister aspect of the current spate of urban conflicts.

Women living in Jamaica's urban grassroots communities, therefore, experience multiple embodied disadvantages compounded by the culture of fear and shame that is attached to the *possibility* of being a rape victim. Their disadvantaged situation is exacerbated by the emphasis placed on forced oral sex, an extremely taboo issue in dominant discourses of heterosexist-embodied practices. Although this is not the fate of all women, the likelihood of it happening automatically places them at risk. Women thus become receptacles of defilement because a few men manage, through their use of extreme force, to dictate the terms of what takes place in the social space, thereby dominating lives of other men, women and children alike.

On the other hand, the competitive *matey* wars that have become a routine feature of Southside and other communities, only serve to *re-inscribe* the sexist terms on which embodied identities are negotiated. Children also internalise this contradictory indicator of identity and power, which has become especially problematic for them in their encounters with parental, peer and social violence.

While we recognise that the men responsible for perpetrating the *discourse of violence* are desperately searching for ways to validate their personhood in the face of chronic social exclusions, they also have to be held accountable for visiting a high level of viciousness on their perceived enemies. Therefore, while one can justifiably attribute blame to the political manipulators, one cannot ignore the fact that the young men who choose to partake in the hegemonic enterprise, albeit from limited options, are still responsible for their own actions and, therefore, have to be held accountable.

This acknowledgement is a pre-requisite for the shifting of the status quo. Unfortunately, such a change is predicated on the challenging prospect of the gunmen suddenly recognising the senselessness of their actions. This is of course, a difficult task, given the low premium that is placed on peaceful practices of conflict resolution and the huge identity resources that are invested in the violent interpretation of masculinity. Yet, it is only by focusing on the theme of accountability under this regime of male power and thereby reducing violent expressions, that one can begin to contribute to the process of inner-city renewal for which social activists are so desperately clamouring. Most crucially, both elite and grassroots perpetrators of social injustice have to take responsibility or be indicted for revisiting the vicious *discourses of domination* on the inner-city areas.

This notion of renewal has become the political buzzword ever since the longest-serving prime minister of Jamaica, P.J. Patterson, assumed paternity for this process. He stepped into the social breach created by the increased fear of the threat posed by inner-city violence. He articulated the truism that this phenomenon is of concern not only to those directly affected. Rather, citizens of the wider society and those who control the state and apparatuses like the security forces which are determined to eliminate this subaltern power elite, all have an interest in inner-city life for one reason or another. All stakeholders watch nervously from opposite ends of the continuum – at one end, in the deplorable living conditions that characterise areas located below the poverty line; and at the other end uptown, behind the tenuous security of iron-grilled and security-saturated work and living spaces.

Summary of Arguments: Proposition 3

The embodied intergenerational discourses elucidate the complex identity issues of, and power discourses incorporated in, class, race/colour, gender power, sexuality, age and space, which are negotiated in everyday life, and which provide the major concepts for interrogating the institutional and social contradictions that inhere in the Jamaican society and are, therefore, expressed in Southside.

The configuration of the inner city in Jamaica is undoubtedly unique in its political and social evolution. Although other Caribbean countries share the colonial history that I have outlined, until very recently, no other had displayed the combination of oligarchic political practices and vicious manifestations and notions of masculinity that has come to characterise the Jamaican landscape. In addition, the comprador relations that obtain between the island's local bourgeoisie and the external foreign interests they represent exacerbate Jamaica's already dependent position in the shark-infested world economic system. Ultimately, this has deleterious effects on the urban poor. This client relationship finds a direct parallel in the patronage style of politics in which inner-city agents are incorporated.

Furthermore, the 'garrisonising' of the urban grassroots has also legitimised fatal conflicts between security forces and gunmen. This deadly dilemma only serves to accentuate the lethal dimensions of the class contradictions that undergird these examples of structural and discursive power. The hostilities reflect the contradictions inherent to the Jamaican political economy; the perennial demarcations between the rich and poor are politically conceived and deliberately maintained. Thus, the following observations that Rex Nettleford made about this phenomenon some decades ago, still have sharp resonance for the situation that exists today.

The fact remains that even today one is still able to have 'Whiteness' connote privilege, position and wealth and, of course, purity which is ingrained in Christian mythology. This attitude is particularly evident among many who form the large majority of the population and who happen to wear that colour of skin long associated with poverty, manual labour, low status and ignorance. The in-between-ness and half-identification resulting from these attitudes is probably one of the positively distinctive features of Caribbean communities emerging from a plantation and colonial system.

(Nettleford in Lowenthal and Comitas (eds.), 1973:38)

Despite the significant strides that Jamaica has made in its development as an independent nation, there remains a glaring contrast between the privileged status of the elite classes and the programmed poverty of the poor, especially the urban poor. The cynicism that was a recurring motif in many of the testimonies shared by subjects in Southside during the research process indicates that the people who experience the brunt of this divide and rule construction of nationhood are quite conscious about the political implications of their plight. However, it is apparent that this knowledge is not sufficiently motivational to result in consistent and wide-ranging individual or collective efforts to confront and challenge the structures of power. Nevertheless, precisely that kind of solidarity is vital for the development of policies and programmes which are designed to rationalise the distribution of the wealth of the country to reflect a system of sociopolitical justice. The need to de-stigmatise the citizens who occupy the space of the inner city and accord them access to the benefits of civil society should be an integral part of such a rationalised system and be mandatory for any long-term social effort to eliminate the causes of the problems that we have addressed.

Although as we have seen, the human body exemplifies the contradictory prejudices that characterise *discourses of domination*, it – the body – is also a source of expressing race pride and gender agency. In this regard, Dancehall Queens in Southside and other inner-city communities should be seen as legitimising an *oppositional discourse* of identity politics; their dress is an allegorical voicing of their embodied power in contrast to bourgeois notions of beauty and sexual desirability.[164]

Linda Boynton Arthur, who researched the gender/power significance of dress in Mennonite communities, suggests that

[n]egotiations about women's dress are also negotiations about gender and power...The social body is male. As women resist the dress code, they also restrict their otherness, their location on the margins of power.

(Arthur, in Fisher and Davis, 1993: 69)

On the other hand, the practice of sexually explicit dressing can also be read as a concession to the prevailing patriarchal norm that commodifies and objectifies women through representations of their bodies. Women might, therefore, appear to

---

164 It is interesting to note that Dance Hall Queen Carlene, a fashion model from an inner-city community who popularised fashionably skimpy outfits, gained popularity not so much for her strategic deployment of her sexuality for erotic and economic gain, but for the colour of her skin. Her light brown complexion makes her an acceptable model on the gangplank at posh hotel poolsides.

be acting autonomously in expressing their gender power but, like most men, they are also being manipulated by unseen hegemonic cultural norms. Therefore, without the attendant all-important component of self-consciousness, the socially disruptive and politically significant meanings of the Dancehall Queens' dress codes stop short of the mark of resistance. Such inadvertent compliance with *discourses of domination* corroborates Foucault's (1980) theorisation that social power is effected through discourses that circulate about sexuality and the deployment of sexuality in social practices.

Inasmuch as the baring of the body in an urban setting denotes an internalisation of sexist norms, this practice also indicates grassroots women's refusal to be confined to the codes of bourgeois morality (Cooper, 1993). Yet, as the discussions in Chapters 7 through 9 reveal, this is by no means a flat-surfaced phenomenon. On the contrary, there is a constant tension between embodied domination and resistance. So, whereas women who bleach their skin and straighten their hair claim that they are just doing what it takes to make them beautiful, their actions also reflect the extent to which they are succumbing to normative notions of sexual desirability, which are suffused with connotations of internalised racism. At the psychosocial level of identity construction, these practices only serve to accentuate the yawning class/race differentiations that permeate the Jamaican society.

However, it is also understandable that the subordinated would be susceptible to such cosmetic notions of valorised embodiment. The class arrangements and racial politics of embodiment that are reflected in images projected in the mass media of *popular discourse* as well as in the institutions of socialisation, all collude to privilege light skin over dark. The practices of self-mutilation masquerading as beauty treatments that result from this value system are mirrored in the notoriously high rates of un(der) employment and compounded by the pervasive *discourse of violence*. This volatile combination of lethal social conditions suggests that people in communities like Southside are, in effect, socially programmed by the convergence of hegemonic sociopolitical orders, to treat each other as enemies. Unmistakably, '[t]hese wounds cut deeply into the flesh of the Black community' (Prothrow-Stith and Weissman, 1991: 72).

There is also a tremendous extent to which taboo values about sexuality and, correspondingly, sexual preferences, intervene in the formation of normative behaviours in the public domain, although these are sometimes challenged by discourses that emerge in the security of private spaces (Collins, 1990). This, in turn, produces tremendous anxiety on the part of subalterns to conform to heterosexist norms that are reinforced in the popular culture, in order not to invoke the brutal sanctions that are applied with impunity to transgressors. Even the institutionally defined beliefs, and behaviours that are articulated in everyday interactions, speak eloquently to the social fact of the wider society being *inscribed* on the bodies and mentalities of social subjects, inasmuch as such subjects also dynamically contribute to the (re)production of the embodied culture that informs their self-concepts, social values, practices and aspirations. The identities of subalterns in Southside are therefore circumscribed by paradoxical experiences of class, gender, and age power.[165]

Although Africans in inner-city Jamaica embody contradictory identities of class, race, gender, sexuality and age, which locate them on the outer margins of a rigorously stratified society, there is still a lack of homogeneity within this class/race categorisation. Moreover, despite their experiences of disadvantage, the differentiated social actors in the garrison communities should not be seen as unmitigated victims. And yet, it must also be admitted that it is also extremely difficult for them to avoid being strongly influenced by the overriding power mechanisms that dictate the socioeconomic conditions and relations in their macro- and micro-environments.

Summary of Arguments: Proposition 4

Despite their disadvantaged social position, women, men, adolescents and children in Southside have survival strategies related to their use of sexual advantage for material gain, which they choose from the limited options that are available to them.

In Chapter 9, which focuses on the trade-off of sex for materiality between women and men, it becomes clear that because of the paucity of social options and choices (Post, 1996), the human body is a significant resource in the survival strategies that are enacted in the social space of Jamaica's inner city. This transaction is also directly linked to the norms and taboos that are associated with procreation. Parenting is, therefore, a complex practice of gender identity construction and negotiations. To some extent, this embodied practice provides symbolic and material satisfaction although the challenging socioeconomic circumstances undoubtedly militate against the full realisation of the benefits of this custom.

Parenthood, for both men and women, also indicates an overcoming of taboos that are attached to infertility, homosexuality, abortion and safe sex. In spite of the economic/health dangers attached to this expression of gendered sexuality, the opportunities for unprotected sex also provide men and women with a source of pleasure, directly linked to personal empowerment. Motherhood and fatherhood are, therefore, loaded with layers of identity meanings that are even more significant in an environment of material lack and social exclusion.

However, the attempts to resolve deeply entrenched political and economic inequalities with psychosocial and symbolic tactics only serve, in many cases, to exacerbate the already strained living conditions under which the socially disadvantaged subjects have no recourse but to struggle. In addition, both women and men suggested that

---

165 Differences in social status that were reflected in the hierarchical definitions of social lack: 'poor', 'poverty' and 'poverty stricken', being cited as indicators of the intensity of someone's relationship to the poverty line. Lack of access to opportunities for self development like skills training was one definition of being poor; another was knowing where today's meal is coming from but not tomorrow's. The person who proffered this definition also said that the poor includes those who do not know where today's meal is coming from but find it somehow e.g. through begging for the means to make a meal. Those who are poverty stricken do not know where their meal is coming from, cannot find it and so end up eating out of garbage or doing without.

in a situation where most men are chronically unemployed or at best, self-employed in the informal sector, males are obviously unable to fulfil the material expectations of many women. Yet, the dominant patriarchal ideology of 'man the breadwinner', is reinforced in the value systems that are reproduced through religious, educational and cultural institutions.

Subaltern men and women who play out the charade of nuclearity, which belies their socioeconomic reality, are also acting against the grain of a strong tradition of independence displayed by women, outlined in Chapter 3. Ironically, while there is an established cultural code that women should receive material support from men in exchange for sexual and domestic favours, many grassroots women have never had the luxury of enjoying even the material, much less the presumed psychosocial benefits of playing the dependent role.

Nevertheless, some disadvantaged women choose to appropriate the *dominant discourses* as a strategy of survival and persist in their expectations that men should be breadwinners. This contradictory convergence of norms impels many men into illegal activities, which enable them to fulfil their socially constructed roles and responsibilities as *men*. It is extremely important to emphasise however, that contrary to popular beliefs, not all inner-city men are criminals. Furthermore, as the examples of alternative survival strategies attest, there is also no linear relationship between poverty and crime. However, the push factors for 'touching the road' or seeking recourse for survival in criminal activities are compelling. This is so because those who control the state have failed miserably to make generalised material means of human-resource development available to this sector of the population. Scant if any, community-based infrastructure has been provided.

Further, some children and adults cited teenage parenting as problematic because '[o]ften young girls have babies because they want someone to love *them*. Indulging in the magic thinking that is typical of adolescents, they romanticise the emotional paybacks of parenthood, while not focusing on the expense and the sheer drudgery that caring for a small child entails' (Prothrow-Stith and Weissman, 1991: 77, emphasis in the original). Some of the youngsters suggested that they preferred older men who offer more social security than do youthful partners.

Teenage parents tend to be women; men start fathering usually in their early to mid-twenties. The domain of parenthood is, therefore, a gendered and age-specific one, over-determined by the norms of the cultural space. Moreover, parenthood is a *discourse* that is intrinsically connected to patriarchal definitions of female desirability; parenthood is also yet another mechanism that some men use to exercise control over a woman's sexuality.

In addition, as several persons also indicated, the position of dependency in which many teenage mothers find themselves makes them susceptible to domestic abuse. Teenage parenthood, which was identified as one of the most problematic development issues in the community is, contradictorily, also a vaunted *rite de passage* into womanhood and the acquisition of cultural legitimacy. However, one cannot ignore the perils that this practice poses to the social development of the women concerned as well as the wider community.

New mothers need empathy, the ability to put themselves in their squalling babies' place, to understand what their babies feel and to accurately imagine what they need in order to be safe and comfortable. Empathy is derailed by the adolescent's age-appropriate narcissism.

(Prothrow-Stith and Weissman, 1991: 77)

Furthermore, some desperate mothers encourage their daughters to enter into sexual unions with men of means in order to offset the effects of household poverty. Other mothers are stoutly against their children having offspring at an early age. The general sentiment expressed is a hope that the children would make better choices than they themselves (the mothers) had done. However, the push factors of social construction are unrelentingly strong; the dialectic evolves from satisfying pressing 'needs and wants', to making choices from the limited options to exchange material or psychosocial support for sex. In many cases, the ideal turns out to be an illusion; the material support may not be forthcoming because the income of many men is, at best, uncertain. This social incompetence is what usually triggers some men to resort to domestic violence, a tactic that is used to compensate for their loss of power in the material realm.

In the final analysis, the joys of motherhood and fatherhood cannot be denied. People, the poor in particular, realise a sense of empowerment from having children in whom they are able to invest their dreams and aspirations of psychosocial self-realisation. Yet the fact that some mothers in the inner city are supportive of their children's criminal activities demonstrates linkages between power attained through violence and parenting, another means by which the vicious cycle of violence is perpetuated. Older people complained that young parents are most culpable where this practice is concerned, riddling the parenting domain with contradictory themes of pain and pleasure.

Prospects for the Future

In searching for ways to bring about some positive outcomes to this strange but true story of 'sexual politics below Jamaica's poverty line', it is important to highlight the fact that power does not only move in a hierarchical direction. In fact, the production of discourses of power by people from the urban grassroots – in spite of the myriad disadvantages that they face – is clear proof that some good can yet come out of this apparent sea of hopelessness. Nevertheless, it is still obvious that structural changes are also required in order to introduce more equity in the distribution of material and psychosocial resources. It is appropriate here to quote Lucien Jones again:

the most noble ideals must be kept in sight. Not just the judicious use of power; not just the provision of scarce benefits; not just the proper management of the economy and the provision of social services, but rather the protection of the weak from the strong, and the practice of the art of the possible. Those should be the ideals of good government.

(Jones, 1995: 45)

This is indeed a beautiful dream and it is a dream whose time has come. Today's generation of Jamaican leaders can achieve true greatness by manifesting and embodying this dream, but only if they have the vision, the *will* and the courage to act in the best interest of the people. And, only if they have the *will* to change (prospects for) the future by championing the cause of the poor and needy, thereby creating history. Hopefully Jamaican leaders will be capable of achieving what, for now, remains as a deferred yet beautiful daydream. In the meantime, Jamaican citizens, particularly inner-city residents, continue to live a terrible nightmare of persistent poverty, chemically addictive drugs, rampant crime and vicious violence. So the question is: where do we go from here with the knowledge that we now possess? And, how do we move from here into the better future that we all dream of? A number of answers and suggestions – *options for development* – are coming next, in the final chapter.

Despite all the sex and political intrigue of the foregoing episodes, Chapter 11 may prove to be the most important section of this book because of the suggestions made, proposals proffered, and the yet unfinished work – the *options for development* – outlined there. First however, we need to refocus on sex and literature and on the subtle, yet critical, centrality of the spoken word and the embodied word in action that informs my recommendations. Following that focus, we will review my sociopolitical-activist perspective which, as you will see, is clearly influencing the conclusions and recommendations of this book. And, finally, in order to locate some specific areas that should be emphasised in drawing up a practical and workable plan for sustainable sociopolitical change, I am going to make my concluding remarks and suggestions in the context of:

- the role for the politicians;
- the role for the security forces (especially the police);
- the role for the tourism sector;
- the role for the community (especially the entertainers);
- a gender-sensitive approach to development;
- the role for the Women's Movement;
- validating children's voices;
- the role for the media;
- the role for Rastafari;
- ethical considerations;
- further research.

CHAPTER 11

OPTIONS FOR DEVELOPMENT

A politician will stand for what he thinks people will fall for.

~ Unknown

Words Sounds & Power

The preceding ten chapters of **Blood, Bullets and Bodies** have provided a tragi-comedy of social contradictions, all emanating from this dramatic story of sex for sale, vicious violence and political intrigue. And, as this strange but true story has unfolded, we have indeed discussed sex and *sexual politics* from a kaleidoscope of angles. As I warned in Chapter 1, the language used has sometimes been as raw as the bloody, bullet-riddled bodies, and as nakedly profane as the X-rated female bodies that are under discussion. However, just one more unavoidable dose of hardcore profanity is upcoming, as we put the finishing touches on the paradoxical issue of sexualised words, and sex and language. To paraphrase a popular old Tenor Saw song, 'you can't say I didn't warn you'.

Blood, Bullets and Bodies has amply illustrated how words can mean what we want them to mean at different times, and how language (verbally and bodily) has historically been used in an ongoing *patriarchal national discourse* that has culturally belittled and socially downpressed the Black majority in Jamaica. However, we have also seen the positive psychosocial benefits of the revolutionary *counter-discourse* of words sounds and power contained in the music, poetry, art and fashion produced by the dispossessed inner-city civilian objects of this Eurocentric domination. There is absolutely no doubt, therefore, that words do indeed have power, creative and destructive.

During a media interview, John Baugh, a Stanford University linguist, confirmed that manipulating language can certainly shape perceptions. Baugh noted, for instance, that in the US, conservatives changed American public opinion simply by referring to the 'inheritance tax' as the 'death tax' instead. But Baugh also warned that less powerful social groups who try to change the meanings of words face a higher hurdle. Usually, whether the usage will change permanently, or not, depends on whether it is in the interest of the mainstream culture to accept the change.

This explains why so many Rastafarian words and phrases have been accepted and incorporated into the Afrocentric-influenced Patois/Patwah speech patterns of the

Jamaican population – it is in the cultural best interest of the majority Black/African grassroots culture of Jamaica for that to happen. So it is that *Rasta Talk* has long provided better ways for young people to define themselves. Rastas think of and speak of young brothers as 'lions' and 'kings', and the sisters as 'lionesses', 'goddesses' and 'queens'; instead of using the now popular and, supposedly international, urban Black slang descriptions such as 'niggas', 'dogs' and 'gangsters' for men, and terms like 'bitches' and 'whores' for women. It is all a matter of proper and positive self-consciousness and self-identification.

Blood, Bullets and Bodies has, thus, been using *popular discourse* – words and their various perceived meanings – to examine what happens when violent masculinity meets sociopolitical chaos in circumstances of abject poverty, and the emerging big picture painted by this strange story is far from pretty. Just as a complexity theorist pulls seemingly disparate threads together, so too have I utilised my hybrid analysis to uncover the hidden connections between elements in Jamaica's everyday social life that appear to have no connection. The common denominator, or thread, tying all these disparate elements together on our literary tapestry is words, words in all their various stages of manifestation, and hence this section of relevant linguistic anthropology finally weaves all these threads together.

Most people think in their mother tongue, the language they speak. Therefore, the way a language is structured says a lot about how the society that created or uses (speaks and writes) it, thinks and behaves. Besides being virtually gender blind, practically speaking (which may be a defect in this instance), the English language uses semantically opposed ideas, while the syntax is based on a linear two-dimensional paradigm of yes/no, right/wrong, up/down, right/left etc. Jamaica's official language is English (the British/UK version, not US 'English'). Historically, therefore, English is the *'Language of Domination'*, which Rastas say predisposes Jamaicans to think, speak and act in a self-deprecatory and culturally conflicted manner. In essence, Afro-Jamaicans are thinking borrowed thoughts with contrived intellectual parameters, using words derived from a foreign language, a European language, which was deliberately imposed as the dominant tongue of enslavement in Jamaica by the island's British colonialists.

English, as a hybrid language itself, is one of the most innately contradictory mainstream languages to be found in Europe. It is a language in which words that sound the same are spelt differently and mean various or, sometimes, even opposite things. The words which most exhibit this kind of binary opposition are so-called 'bad words', the expletives otherwise known as 'oaths', 'swear words', 'curse words', profanity, obscenity or vulgarity. And, just what is an 'oath'? In one context, an 'oath' is a solemn, formal declaration, or promise to fulfil a pledge, often calling on God, or a sacred object as witness. But, in another context, an 'oath' is a curse or an irreverent or blasphemous use of the name of God or something held to be sacred. As in 'taking the Lord's Name in vain'. A curse is generally accepted religiously and socially as being a bad thing. 'Curse' is defined as an appeal or prayer (in word and thought) for evil or misfortune to befall someone or something. Usually when people curse in modern times, they are using 'bad words' or profane and obscene expressions, usually of surprise, irritation, disappointment or anger. 'Curse' is from the Old English 'curs', meaning to 'swear'. On the one hand, to 'swear' means to make a solemn declaration, promise, or vow, invoking a deity or a sacred person or thing, in confirmation of and in witness to the honesty or truth of such a declaration. On the other hand, 'swear' also means to use profane oaths or to curse using expletives or 'bad words'. So, is swearing a good or a bad thing, you may ask? That depends...on the context and meaning of the oaths.

In the same vein, an expletive is an exclamation or oath in a word or phrase, especially one that is profane, vulgar, or obscene. It is a word or phrase that sometimes may not contribute any extra meaning, but is added only to fill out a sentence or a metrical line. As for 'profanity', that is understood to be abusive, vulgar, or irreverent coarse language marked by contempt or irreverence for what is *sacred*. In regular everyday usage therefore, profanity, obscenity and vulgarity are pent-up emotions expressed as words, phrases, acts, or gestures that are held to be indecent, lewd, offensive or repulsive to the senses and/or social tastes. Confusingly, however, both the sacred and the profane are frequently represented by the very same words.

Soft-core British curse words like 'damn', 'hell', 'bollocks' and 'sod' (for sodomite), can all be found in any good English dictionary. So too can the word which is regarded as the most explicit and vulgar profanity of them all: 'fuck'. That same word, arguably the worst word in the English language, is known and understood by virtually everyone on Earth today, no matter what their mother tongue is. However, that same one 'bad word' is used variously as a noun, a verb, an adverb and an adjective depending on circumstances, making it probably one of the most used words in everyday conversation worldwide.

But what is the history of this controversial word that supposedly should not be spoken? The obscene word, *'fuck'*, is known to be a very olde (sic) word and seems to have been considered shocking for some unknown reason from it was first used. Despite its long and now universal use, it has only been over the past few decades that the word has been seen in print and heard in movies much more often and freely than in the past. Describing the word as 'vulgar slang', the Microsoft Word dictionary first defines 'fuck' by its original Olde English meaning, 'to have sexual intercourse with'. Thus, the word really means to procreate, and such 'mating' (i.e. trying to procreate) is taken to be a good thing. However, other definitions of 'fuck' include, to take advantage of, to betray, to cheat, to victimise, to interfere with, and a despised person; which are all taken to be bad things. So what we have is a situation in which the popular word describing the act of sexual intercourse – taken to be the most intimate and normal bodily expression of love between a man and a woman, a bodily activity that naturally produces children and starts families – that same word is also the most abominable and vulgar word in the English language and, simultaneously, means a whole lot of other bad things. Go figure!

In any case, 'fuck' is the ultimate and prime example of a sexualised word with multiple and consistently contradictory meanings. And this is the big paradox in a nutshell. Sex, as in having sex, having sexual intercourse or 'fucking', the bodily union of opposite sexes, is clearly a site of supreme conflict, with the physical/ bodily sexual act itself being deemed to be both sacred and profane at one and the same time. It is both pleasure and pain. And that is before further complicating and conflicting the sexual equation with same-sex and transgender sexual relations. Could this vulgar word be the linguistic representation of the conflicted guilt complex regarding sex that is peculiar to 'Christianised' European culture? A complex that sees sex and sexuality as being 'dirty'? That religious based guilt complex seems to have been spread to Europe's neo-colonial subjects worldwide, indicating that there is indeed a lot more important research work left to be done by experienced linguistic, cultural anthropologists and sex therapists.

Regardless, similar linguistic principles as those just described for English hold true and even more so in the case of Jamaican Patwah. The creative profanity of Jamaicans and the 'bad words' used on the island are now almost legendary, worldwide. Thus, in addition to the English profanities used on the island, Jamaicans have their own homegrown 'bad words' and employ non-English grammatical patterns of speaking. 'Raas' is one Patwah word which is used nationally as a noun, verb and adjective, and although it has a different meaning from 'fuck', it is used in multiple ways in much the same way as the infamous English 'four-letter word' is.

Curiously however, the most popular 'bad words' in Jamaica generally relate back to the female genitalia and/or to the female menstrual cycle and the associated paraphernalia. Hence, 'pussy-claat', 'blood-claat' and even 'bumbo-claat' all relate to the cloth/rag used as a tampon or pad to restrict or wipe up the vaginal blood of menstruating women. In addition, calling someone a 'pussy', especially a man, is one of the worst forms of verbal disrespect to a person's character and integrity. In Jamaica, men dis other men using that word, and even women also dis men using 'pussy' as a derogatory word meaning effeminate and weak-kneed. The British mean just the same thing when they call someone a 'cunt'. It is no different. And, speaking of the UK, why is 'bloody' regarded as a 'bad word' in English slang, when it is used in that particular way? Could that be related to female menstruation too?

Be that as it may, the Rastafari identify one of the causes of Jamaica's mental/linguistic cultural division and conflict as being the enforced use of the 'Queen's English' by the present descendants of the Africans who were formerly enslaved on the island. They suggest that the Willie Lynch philosophy/mentality has been encoded in (the alphabet and words of) a language – English. Thus, African people thinking, speaking and writing in this colonial language are in many ways historically predisposed to psychological contradictions and limitations. This is the reason that Rastas claim that English, and its inherent contradictions, is the linguistic source of the pathological psychology at the root of the widespread violence, and that this syndrome can be detected in the hybrid mix of sexually conflicted words that can be heard on Jamaica's inner-city and suburban streets. That same violent and conflicted mindset can also be seen in the *body language* of Black ghetto residents as much as in the *body language* of Jamaica's 'Brown' suburban residents.

In contrast to standard English speech, *Rasta Talk* specifically and Jamaican Creole/Patwah generally, both illustrate an attempt by Black/Africans in Jamaica to redress this cultural division in thought and tongue, as well as in word and in deed. The Rasta/Jamaican speech creation of a *'Language of Resistance'* is the epitome of the kind of cultural survival skills shown by African people worldwide. Such speech creation is also a way for Black people to return some much-needed holistic and multidimensional cultural perspectives to their every day vocabulary and thinking. It even allows African people to express thoughts and concepts for which there are no English words. Traditional African languages and all ancient languages were generally more holistic in their structure than standard English. Holistic thought and language means that a whole idea or an entire/complete concept is contained in one symbol, or one word, or one phrase, and that the very sound of that word or phrase is in tune, in harmony, with the precise meaning of the idea/concept.

Modern linguistic anthropologists now accept that spoken languages often develop nuances (i.e. new words) spontaneously at different times for different reasons. By any measure, the copious number of new words entered into the Rasta and Patwah lexicon annually in Jamaica, literally, speaks volumes to the high level of cultural resistance and linguistic creativity of the island's Black majority. According to the Rastas, this ability comes from a genetically intrinsic survival instinct embedded in the very fibre of the people with the Melanin hue. Some of these new words and phrases regularly end up becoming the names of popular new dance steps and dance moves that accompany the latest and hottest Reggae/Dancehall 'riddims'. Thus are *words of resistance* expressed in musical *body language*.

All this explains why the spoken word and *discourse* in all its myriad forms has been such a flexible and useful tool in the Jamaican context, and has been the main nexus/matrix interconnecting all the various elements that we have analysed. Words are indeed sounds that embody social power, sometimes creative and sometimes destructive. Clearly, our first social responsibility is to commit to doing our best in transforming destructive discourse into creative cultural expressions, and elevating merely profane words into truly *sacred speech*. And, as idealistic as this may sound at first, the need for transforming our words and their meanings may, in fact, prove to be a very practical necessity in the long run. In the meantime, Jamaicans have to do more to transform their words into physical deeds that feed and meet their bodily needs. As it is said, bodily 'actions speak louder than words'.

Perspectives In Activism

The data presented during the course of the book has confirmed that 'perspective is everything' and that socialisation and choices define our identities – who we say we are – and influence how we construct meaning, and shape how each and every one of us acts in society. This, in turn, informs our *verbal discourse* and *body language* (embodied words in action), either reinforcing structures of patriarchal, racial, class and gender domination, or reinforcing opposing socially revolutionary structures. Accordingly, my perspective in **Blood, Bullets and Bodies** has been deliberately culture specific, politically non-partisan and has been very much influenced by my *Rastafari identity*. As I intimated in the Introduction, I was able to cross forbidden political, territorial and confidential personal boundaries in order to conduct this study, primarily because of my overt Rastafari self-identification and also because I am a woman. This almost automatic conferral of special status to me was directly linked to the leadership and peacemaking roles fulfilled in the community by people who live a *Rastafari Livity or Way of Life*.

Clearly, then, I do not speak in a vacuum or from that nebulous and fictitious nothingness called an 'objective' perspective. On the contrary, the way I view the world in general is influenced by my subjective politics. Thus, my perspective has also been influenced by the *Womanist* or *Black Feminist* standpoint politics that I advocate. I am a cultural activist for women's rights because in a world dominated by patriarchal power systems, women have special problems that demand special political attention. By extension, I also support the struggles for self-realisation and social justice by all disadvantaged constituencies including the poor, the aged, children, ethnic minorities, the physically challenged, and so on.

From an activist perspective, I want to use *cultural journalism* to enable subjects in inner-city communities like Southside, who have experienced social exclusion and subordination, to reflect critically on their lives and in the process achieve some form of empowerment. My intellectual aim in writing this book is to contribute to the process of social transformation by my literary deconstruction of some of the binary oppositions that have been used in the politically motivated construction of social relations and individual identities in Jamaica. By necessity, this process entails using *cultural communications* as a consciousness-raising and development engine.

Cultural communications involves the use of media like music, dance, theatre, poetry etc., as teaching tools on an individual level and, ultimately, as essential tools for community-wide mobilisation. In optimising this interpretation, I also used *cultural communications* as a tool to gather the relevant research data and then return the final products of that investigation in multimedia formats to the same individuals and/or community. This reflexivity was observed in fulfilment of the ethical responsibilities required of feminist ethnographers. My use of *cultural communications* is also relevant for addressing similar problems to those I tackled in this strange story, similar problems which have taken root in other urban parts of the world.

Having produced a community radio programme, a number of video documentaries and a CD-ROM among other replicable products, I have reaffirmed that the mass media in general and individual media practitioners like myself in particular, have a crucial part to play in the socioeconomic development process. Media resources enable those disenfranchised by the various discourses of domination to give voice to the various issues that challenge their cultural development. Audiovisual media, in particular, are effective tools in promoting the self-esteem building that is fundamental to redressing the decades of psychosocial trauma that Southside's citizens have experienced. I will continue to use these methods to raise consciousness about the power matrices into which inner-city citizens like those in Southside are embedded. We will return to this process later on in the chapter.

In her controversial 1970 book, *Sexual Politics*, well-known American feminist scholar, Kate Millett, raised the question, 'Can the relationship between the sexes be viewed in a political light at all?' The answer depends on how one defines politics. According to Millett's definition, the term 'politics' refers to power-structured relationships. That is, arrangements by which one group of persons is controlled by another. Speaking about the sexual act of intercourse, specifically, she explained that,

> Coitus can scarcely be said to take place in a vacuum; although of itself it appears a biological and physical activity, it is set so deeply within the larger context of human affairs that it serves as a charged microcosm of the variety of attitudes and values to which culture subscribes. Among other things, it may serve as a model of sexual politics on an individual or personal level.

(1970: 23)

Millett seems to use the word 'politics' when speaking of the sexes, primarily because the word is eminently useful in outlining the real nature of the relative status of the genders, historically and at the present. She further identifies patriarchy as a socially conditioned belief system masquerading as nature and demonstrates, in detail, how patriarchal attitudes and systems have penetrated mainstream literature, philosophy, psychology and politics. Deemed an incendiary work, *Sexual Politics* illustrated how *cultural discourse* subtly reflects a systematised subjugation and exploitation of women. In this Jamaican case study, I have also used **Blood, Bullets and Bodies** to deconstruct what is said about the human body (especially the female body), and its sexuality in particular, in order to show how such verbal discourses become culturally normalised and institutionalised on the one hand and, conversely on the other hand, how transgressors are demonised and endangered. This discussion also revealed a persistent political interest by the Jamaican powers-that-be in the maintenance of a patriarchal gender order dominated by violence.

I have argued that practices like exchanging sex for materiality and the taken-for-granted act of parenting are really primordial self-realisation and survival mechanisms. Some subjects have little recourse to do otherwise in the face of the various meanings of oppression and exploitation that are i*nscribed*/written/carved onto their bodies. And, while females are certainly not a homogeneous category, women in general are particularly disadvantaged in inner-city scenarios like Southside, due to the prevailing *discourses* of racism, sexism and elite classism which saturate the social fabric. Thus, women's bodies are literal battlefields in either the reproduction or, conversely, the eradication of structural, discursive and gender power dynamics.

We have now come full circle in telling this strange story of sex for sale and vitriolic violence below Jamaica's poverty line, and in examining how and why a Caribbean tourist paradise has been turned into a living hell for its inner-city residents. We have highlighted most of the facts about '*sexual politics*' and exposed much of the fiction about patriarchy, and separated these facts from the fiction, all in an effort to help save '*Jamaica land we love*'. Now it is time for us to seek and hopefully find some enduring real-time solutions that will help reduce the distressing flood of blood, bullets and bodies that is threatening to overwhelm the inner-city streets of Kingston. I trust that by my clarification of the facts and exposure of the fiction, this book will be a catalyst in motivating the political and community *willpower* that is necessary to implement the upcoming suggested real-time solutions and *options for development*.

The Role for The Politicians

The leaders ah let the people down
Have them ah hold on to straw
When them ah drown...
Have the people dem ah wear a frown

~Capleton

Jamaica, a land of sea, sand, sun and sex – a popular tourist destination no less – is also a prime example of the complex and crippling effects of economic globalisation on the world's developing countries. The political reality in Jamaica is that the streams of racial and class oppression that flowed in plantation-based, colonial society have, seemingly, crossed barriers of time into the contemporary wage-labour-based New World Order era. Past systems of injustice have been exacerbated by the development of a present-day *discourse* of bourgeois democracy, liberally tainted by a local discourse of violence, and deliberately contaminated by imported 'samfie' policies for economic development, policies which have only led to economic stagnation and social disintegration instead. The catastrophic result is that 'the lot of the mass of the people, *almost one-third of whom live below the poverty line*, has not changed significantly' (Jones, 1995: 29, emphasis added). Without a doubt, this unique literary project, **Blood, Bullets and Bodies**, serves as a major indictment of the old guard of politicians who have fomented the discourse of violence in Jamaica's inner-city communities through the practice of patronage politics as a mechanism of colonising voter support for their parties.

In this practice of partisan power, patriarchy links privileged politicians and so-called grassroots dons in a devious drama of nepotism and intrigue, which has had dire consequences. While the politicians encouraged their supporters to use gun violence against opponents in order to gain political advantage, the party thugs appropriated the *gunman discourse* as a means of expressing *hegemonic masculinity* or gaining independent wealth. In this regard, both PNP and JLP politicians have to accept responsibility for setting in motion the process of 'blood for blood' and 'fire for fire', one of the most disastrous processes since slavery to have muddied the sociopolitical streams of this '*land of wood and water*' that the Tainos called Xaymaca. In the present era, the pervasive, cynical opinion is that 'there is one kind of justice in this country for the rich and another for the poor' (Jones, 1995: 34-35). Although it is still not clear what legal measures could, or should be, taken to bring the culpable party politicians to book, there is room for them to make redress in the implementation of humanitarian measures. Such initiatives will ensure that the systematic underdevelopment of the communities in question be curtailed and turned around.

Jamaican politicians of the past 40 years also stand accused by their public record of playing lackey and furthering the neo-colonial best interests of foreign political powers over the interests of their own local nation. Their passive acceptance of international loans and trade agreements with terms clearly not in the best interest of Jamaica, smacks of dereliction of duty in some cases, or bribery and corruption in others. One of the historical moments captured by the excellent 2001 video documentary *Life & Debt*, was former prime minister, the late Michael Manley, admitting for posterity that to have had to sign an IMF (International Monetary Fund) agreement, 'was one of the bitter, traumatic experiences of my public life.' Economically, that IMF agreement gave Jamaica a straw basket to carry water and the Manley administration was aware of that before signing the dotted line, but they signed on it any way for political expediency. Succeeding administrations, both PNP and JLP, have been equally visionless and weak-kneed in accepting agreements and financial plans designed to hinder Jamaica's economic options, reduce its local production and lock the island helplessly into the New World Order.

The *Life & Debt* documentary takes an unapologetic look at the New World Order from the perspective of Rastafari commentators/observers, as well as ordinary Jamaican workers, farmers, Jamaican government members and IMF/World Bank policy officials, and reveals the devastating reality of globalisation from the ground up. This gem of a film by a White American independent producer from New York, Stephanie Black, documents the ongoing paradox in paradise with a voiceover narration written by Jamaica Kincaid and adapted from her book *A Small Place*. The film's *illuminating discourse* is reinforced by an original Reggae music soundtrack with Mutabaruka (performing the title track), Peter Tosh, Bob Marley, Ziggy Marley & the Melody Makers, Luciano, Buju Banton, Sizzla and Anthony B among others. Tuff Gong produced and distributes the soundtrack. In the documentary, life as experienced from arrival to departure by typical tourists in Jamaica is contrasted with life as experienced by ordinary Jamaicans living day to day on the Reggae Rock. The journey takes you out to the small farmers in the Jamaican countryside, showing how the island's local production has been discouraged and stifled to further the cause of globalisation and to consolidate the North American 'free trade' area. *Life & Debt* illustrates how Jamaica's economy was deliberately targeted by foreign political/ economic forces, and the traumatic effects on the island's economy when its ability to compete competitively on the world market was eroded by IMF/ World Bank structural adjustment programmes.

The film shows how national economies, traditional societies and whole cultures can be subverted and destroyed by the stroke of a pen – literally. It highlights the agricultural sector – the banana, potato, onion and carrot industries; looks into dairy farming, meat production, poultry farming and egg production; examines the over-proliferation of American fast-food chains in Jamaica and the controversy between the local McDonald's and the US-based chain of the same name; and goes in depth into the Free Zone fiasco in which poor Jamaican workers, mostly women, were used, abused and then refused (i.e. laid off) in brand-name garment assembly sweathouses at the very aptly renamed 'Kingston Slave Zone'. The industrial and human rights of the poor, inner-city women working in the West Kingston Free Zone were prostituted by government bureaucrats who totally failed in their duty to protect the interests of the workers, not to speak of the socioeconomic interests of Jamaica.

IMF/World Bank policies are supposed to benefit the economies of Developing Countries by integrating them seamlessly into the global market. As the movie shows clearly, however, what actually happens is that poor people suffer while commercial banks in the North collect ridiculous amounts of interest. As a result, only an estimated five percent of the money that Jamaica has borrowed since 1977 has been able to stay inside the island country. Most of whatever remaining wealth is generated in the 'deal' is sucked out of the island financially in the form of so-called 'foreign debt'.

In this regard, Michael Manley's most important contribution to the world community during his first tenure as Jamaican prime minister, was his noble effort to initiate a still very necessary new international economic order based on more equitable terms of global trade. Implementing that unfinished task for the future benefit of the island's exports is the legacy of present-day Jamaican diplomats in the international arena. On the local scene, all ministerial and junior-level Jamaican politicians face the same task of protecting the human, civil and industrial rights of all of Jamaica's citizens. It is thus clear, that the country needs and deserves a new breed of politicians who are committed to providing adequate education, affordable housing and healthcare for all citizens, and most of all, politicians committed to providing economic opportunity, as in new jobs that will continue to reduce the unemployment rate in real terms.

Main Labour Force Indicators 2015–2017[166]

	Oct-15	Jan-16	Apr-16	Jul-16	Oct-16	Jan-17
BOTH SEXES						
TOTAL POPULATION	2,727,500	2,728,900	2,730,300	2,731,800	2,733,100	2,734,600
Population 14 & over	2,087,100	2,088,200	2,089,300	2,090,400	2,091,500	2,092,600
Labour Force	1,325,400	1,342,000	1,353,900	1,363,200	1,355,500	1,358,300
Employed Labour Force	1,146,800	1,163,800	1,169,000	1,187,000	1,180,800	1,185,700
Unemployed Labour Force	178,600	178,200	184,900	176,200	174,800	172,600
Outside The Labour Force	761,700	746,200	735,400	727,200	736,000	734,300
Employment Rate	86.5	86.7	86.3	87.1	87.1	87.3
Unemployment Rate	13.5	13.3	13.7	12.9	12.9	12.7
Job Seeking Rate	8.9	8.4	9.1	8.1	8.6	8.1
% Pop under 14 years	23.5	23.5	23.5	23.5	23.5	23.5
% Pop 14 years & over	76.5	76.5	76.5	76.5	76.5	76.5
% Pop 14 + Outside LF	36.5	35.7	35.2	34.8	35.2	35.1
LF as a % age of Total Pop	48.6	49.2	49.6	49.9	49.6	49.7
LF as a % age of Pop 14+	63.5	64.3	64.8	65.2	64.8	64.9
Employment:Population	54.9	55.7	56	56.8	56.5	56.7

Currently, prime Jamaican real estate and strategic utilities and businesses are being sold out to foreigners – North Americans, Europeans, Trinidadians and Chinese etc. – at an alarming rate. Thus, the country needs, and deserves, a new breed of politicians who will seek to regain local control of basic utilities, promote self-reliance, kick-start local production and stimulate manufacturing in place of the gross over-reliance on imported foreign consumption items. The country needs, and deserves, a new breed of politicians who are committed to fulfilling their responsibility for bringing greater socioeconomic equity and a more peaceful environment to ordinary Jamaican citizens in their homeland. But, most of all, Jamaica needs and deserves a new breed of leaders who are statesmen and stateswomen more than they are partisan politicians. In order to facilitate a reduction in partisan hostilities, special efforts should be made to arrive at a détente between the political parties. As many social reformers have suggested,

---

166 Source: http://statinja.gov.jm/LabourForce/NewLFS.aspx (retrieved June 01, 2017).

this movement for reconciliation could be designed along the lines of the controversial Truth and Reconciliation Commission that was set up in South Africa, supposedly to heal the wounds in the post-apartheid period of transformation. This proposal for compromise should enable whichever party forms the government to concentrate on generating positive activities in communities like Southside. Developing a focus on reform is vital in order to translate grand visions about inner-city renewal into meaningful initiatives that are designed to eliminate the chronic distrust with which many efforts that are made to realise this objective are regarded. However, one cannot relinquish the visions for creating change; as Jamaican National Hero Marcus Garvey reiterated, 'where there is no vision, the people perish'.

In anticipation of the establishment of an ideal accord for political regeneration, even among politicians who share party affiliation, it would be helpful if a systematic programme of self-help projects were to be generated from the partisan perspective as viable alternatives to crime. The *political will* to really act in the public interest will be a welcome innovation to match the indefatigable efforts that non-government and community-based organisations have been making over the years to achieve this very same objective. This challenge might seem ludicrous if one only considers the short-sightedness of political practices that have been rolled out since the realisation of political independence in 1962. However, it is a challenge which has been identified as a government responsibility since 1932 by none other than Marcus Garvey himself.

> We are having lots more of criminal actions and attacks than we have ever heard of before in the history of the country. If the Government is at fault we hope before it becomes more serious, efforts will be made to curb this new evil. We stated before that it is the duty of government and society to influence the life of the citizen for good, and we can see no reason why there should not be an organized event to prevent the development of greater criminal tendencies among the would-be criminal element than has been made up to the present time. When people by neglect are encouraged to take on to crime as a profession, the result generally becomes serious.

Garvey established Jamaica's first political party, the People's Political Party (PPP), in 1929, over a decade before the eventual formation of the JLP and the PNP. Garvey also set the standard for the role expected to be fulfilled by politicians, truly in the service of the people. Since the 1940s, Jamaica has basically been a two-party state, and third parties – from the Communist Workers Party of Jamaica (WPJ) to the National Democratic Movement (NDM) – have traditionally had relatively little impact on the way politics is conducted on the streets of Jamaica. However, after over 50 years of inactivity, the Marcus Garvey People's Political Party was revived in 2002. In its short lifespan, the renewed PPP seems to have already started making a difference in terms of helping to lower the levels of violent confrontation that usually occurs when opposing political partisans encounter each other on the campaign trail or in other circumstances. According to PPP President Ras Michael Lorne, the Garvey Party, by definition and for the sake of poor people, cannot implement its political programme using the same divisive and violent methods as is customary in Jamaican politics.

Speaking about the Coloured/Negro political (mis)leaders of his day, Garvey is quoted in the second edition of his *Philosophies and Opinions* as saying: 'The fraternity is heartless, crafty and corrupt. They exist for themselves only and give no thought to the future, or the condition of the people, except to exploit the said condition to their political benefit. The leaders of the race are visionless and selfish. They think of none but themselves.' Unfortunately, much the same could be said for far too many of the politicians Jamaica has seen since gaining its independence. We, therefore, urge the new generation of political aspirants to use Marcus Garvey as their role model and encourage them to follow the PPP's lead in their street politics by promoting community cooperation over community confrontation.

Furthermore, it must be fairly obvious that the damage that has already been done can only be superseded if those who control the state and its institutional apparatuses exert the necessary effort to throw down or take up the gauntlet, as the case might be. This view was reinforced by an editorial in the *Jamaica Observer* newspaper on Monday, January 31, 2005, which said:

> There is no simple, or single solution to the grave problem of violent crime in Jamaica. Intervention must be multi-disciplinary, involving all sectors of the society. Even as we are strengthening our policing arrangements and improving our ability to detect and catch the criminals, so too must we create an economic environment in which there is economic growth and the creation of jobs. People who have jobs and are productively engaged are less likely to be involved in crime. We have also to ensure the development of a social infrastructure and support systems that will underpin a message that this is a caring society in which there is room for hope.

Of course, the proof of that pudding is in the fundamental paradigm shift on which this ideal is predicated, which means that '[t]he minds of those who believe that they have a God-given right to rule, because they have the power of class, gender or money to support them must be transformed' (Jones, 1995: 41).

The unprecedented and historic *'One Love' Peace Truce* of 1978 began spontaneously in the inner-city communities, with a change in the *verbal discourse* and *body language* of the gunmen themselves as well as of other grassroots leaders, all interacting under the cultural consciousness and leadership of dreadlocked disciples of the *Rastafari Livity*. Ultimately, the *Peace Truce* failed because the political puppet masters, fearful of losing their community power/control to Rastafari-oriented community leaders, withheld their material and practical support from the peace initiative, virtually forcing the young gunmen to return to their old ways as pawns to political patronage, just for their economic survival.

At the end of the day, the *'Peace and Love'/'One Love'/'One Blood'* philosophy of Rastafari, which was instrumental in producing the *Peace Truce*, has to be invoked once again in order to develop the spirit of forgiveness that is a pre-requisite for spawning healing vibrations and action. It may be the only way of counteracting the 'blood for blood' and 'fire for fire' mentality. This is, admittedly, a tough pill for Jamaican high society to swallow, but the implementation of this regenerative spirit is desperately needed on political, socioeconomic, gender and sexual levels. By invoking such a sensibility and more community involvement in communal power sharing, we can metaphorically and in practice, plant the seeds of political administration and participation – with a conscience – plant the seeds in the fertile soil of people-centred community development policies. With this kind of a political policy orientation, we can be more confident that systems of social justice are more likely to flourish.

In the meantime, a 2005 global survey/Gallup poll which was commissioned by Transparency International found that corruption is on the increase in most countries and that poor people in poor nations are often the hardest hit. Overall, those surveyed rated political parties as the most corrupt institutions, along with customs departments, the police and legal/justice systems. Jamaica clearly fits this profile. The bottom line of this obvious social malaise is clear: Jamaican politicians as a group definitely do have a crucially important and pivotal role to play in initiating a reduction in national corruption specifically, and also in helping or hindering sociopolitical change generally. Only time will tell if the politicians have the *political will* to be true to their mandate and if they will fulfil their leadership role in helping to reclaim and redeem '*Jamaica land we love*'.

The Role for The Security Forces (Especially The Police)

The police, as a group, are next in line to the politicians in the crucial importance of their institutional role in helping or hindering social change. In their role as 'peace officers', members of Jamaica's 8,500-strong police force are supposed to proactively protect and serve the ordinary citizen, including inner-city residents. More often than not, however, in their role as 'Law Enforcement Officers', the police tend to act proactively with maximum physical prejudice in executing the hegemonic policies of the politrickal and ruling-class puppet masters…even when no just cause exists for their extreme methods.

The long-standing propensity of ordinary police officers to routinely use unnecessary violence on ordinary (read, 'Black') Jamaicans was proved once and for all, to all doubters of police brutality, years ago when Brazilian soccer star Pelé made his first appearance in 1971 at the National Stadium in Jamaica. When the visiting Brazilian team eventually scored a goal against Chelsea FC near the end, some of the team members of the Jamaica National Juvenile football squad, who were sitting in a VIP section on the cycle track, raced onto the field in celebration. They were chased off the pitch by a number of Harmon Barracks (riot) policemen who started indiscriminately beating one of the unfortunate young team members with batons, beating him to the ground and continuing the beating even after he was down and helpless. All this, in front of a stadium full of over 30,000 people, with TV cameras, dignitaries and visiting celebrities looking on. The beating did not stop until Pelé himself ran over and physically put his own body between the policemen and the young football player/fan. Of course, there was a near riot in the stadium that night, as a torrent and a virtual thunderstorm of bottles and objects hailed out of the bleachers and rained down on the police and security personnel ringing the cycle track. Suffice it to say that a lot more people got beaten by the police outside the stadium that night.

As can be easily imagined, this propensity of policemen to beat and terrorise ordinary citizens is even greater on the dark and narrow streets away from dignitaries, foreigners and the gaze of TV cameras and thousands of people. That same police propensity to extreme violence against inner-city residents must be changed first if there is to be any prospect of a general ceasefire and peace between the police and the garrison communities.

There can be no dispute, therefore, that the security forces are sometimes major contributors to the prevailing discourse of extreme urban violence. Whether legally or illegally, and with monotonous regularity, some Jamaican police and some of the 3,500 JDF soldiers repeatedly contribute to the tragic toll of blood, bullets and dead bodies that plague Kingston. In view of this, the suggestions and recommendations made here for the police and soldiers, take on added importance, precisely because of the direct involvement of the security forces (police and soldiers) in the phallic (gun) fire for (gun) fire confrontations and the bloody displays of violent masculinity backed up with guns and armoured vehicles.

As can probably be appreciated by those familiar with the recent day-to-day runnings in Kingston, it has been an ongoing challenge for us to keep the figures for the number of murders up to date. Whatever year-to-date figures we have put down over the course of completing this work have been seriously outdated within a week because of the ridiculous rate at which people are being killed of late. We can, however, speak conclusively about the year 2004. After chalking up some 975 murders in 2003, Jamaica experienced a deadly 2004 with a record body count of 1,471 persons murdered. Many of the murders were gang-related and took place in the St. Andrew south and St. Catherine north police divisions where troubled communities such as Olympic Gardens and the especially volatile Spanish Town are located.

2005 started off with more than 175 persons murdered in the first 46 days of the year. That number, 175, also included the 30 people killed over the Bob Marley birthday weekend in early February, despite pleas for a cessation of violence in honour of the beloved Reggae maestro's 60th Earthday celebration on February 6, 2005. Four months later, in crime statistics made available for June 27, 2005, the Constabulary Communication Network (CCN) reported that 32 people were murdered in Jamaica the previous week, bringing the total for the month to 115. At that time, with another six months to go in the year, the total number of murders for 2005 stood at an alarming 845. By July 17, 2005, the latest murder total stood at 926, compared to 741 for the corresponding period in 2004. It seemed almost certain even from then therefore, that the total number of murders for 2005 would eclipse the record 1,471 figure for 2004. And indeed, with the final murder tally for 2005 standing at an unprecedented 1,669 persons, Jamaica earned the dubious distinction of being one of the top three murder capitals in the world. Clearly, with a reported 50 percent increase in gang and drug-related murders in 2005 over 2004, the problem of extreme violence is still growing.[167]

The Jamaica Constabulary Force said the country had at least 1,192 slayings in 2015, a roughly 20 percent increase from the previous year. There were 1,005 killings in 2014, the lowest annual total since 2003 in this country that has long struggled with violent crime.[168]

---

167   It is relevant to note that at time of re-vision of this edition of the book, the 2007 official murder statistics, just released, puts the murder figure for 2007 at 1574.

168   http://www.jamaicaobserver.com/news/Jamaica-homicides-jump-20-per-cent--highest-level-in-5-years_48331; see p. 9

In the meantime, it is typical that in situations such as exist in Southside, the security forces and the gangsters alike 'often become part of the problem, adding to the sum total of violence' (Prothrow-Stith and Weissman, 1991: 76). Historically, in Jamaica, hostilities have always characterised the relations between the police and grassroots people; communication has been particularly problematic between the police and inner-city residents in general and between the former and the urban gangsters in particular.

However, there have also been heroic attempts to develop a system of community policing and soldiering, an initiative which needs to be encouraged as a vital trust building mechanism in the process of social change. Admittedly, it is a very tall order to erase the bitterness that inner-city residents feel towards the security forces. This sentiment results from harsh experiences which have produced the perception that this executive arm of the state treats the poor differently from the rich, thereby mitigating the possibilities for the realisation of social justice at the subaltern level. This street wisdom persists because typically,

> [t]he police are inextricably involved in the violence that bedevils poor communities. Many people blame the police for instigating violence and for failing to curtail violence in their communities. They think that if the police really cared they would restore order and end the mayhem on city streets... They interpret the search-on-sight policies of many urban police forces as proof that the police despise and assail Black manhood.

> (Prothrow-Stith and Weissman, 1991: 194-95)

The criminalisation of the gangsters, who are constructed as the enemies of the state, has legitimised the use of extreme state violence, by the security forces, against the gunmen in particular and inner-city residents in general. Exacerbating this sad state of affairs, from the beginning of the 1990s to the present, drug-related turfism has introduced an added element of viciousness among the gangsters, which has compounded the crisis for the residents in these urban enclaves. The security forces have responded with predictable aggressiveness, a state strategy that is also an expression of the project of hegemonic masculinity. This compounds the dilemma of social exclusion experienced by citizens in this sector of the society. The ongoing war in Southside as well as in other inner-city communities has therefore created a complex culture of fear, particularly in these neighbourhoods, but also in the wider society as well.

If we were to get into the figures for police shootings of citizens, that would be as frightening as the general murder statistics are. In fact, Amnesty International has reported that Jamaica currently has the highest police homicide rate per capita in the world. So another real community fear is the fear of the police. Another frightening development is the fact that well-to-do citizens no longer have any confidence in the constabulary. Thus, upper-class residents in the suburbs no longer call or depend on the police for their residential security concerns and needs. When faced with crime or criminals at their residencies, they call fast-response private security firms instead of calling the police, whom they fear may cause more problems than they solve.

However, the police do have a crucial role to play in righting the wrongs that have been perpetrated in the name of the law. At present, Amnesty International is hounding the Jamaican police force because of its reputation of being a virtual, or indeed a real, killing machine. Whatever the case, this dangerous image still militates against the valiant efforts that the Jamaica Tourist Board makes to sell the 'island paradise' of Jamaica as a key holiday destination for foreign visitors. In order to make their contribution to removing the nagging trouble that spoils the inner-city areas of this tropical island paradise, the government security forces have to develop more respectful relations with the citizens they claim to represent in the society the particularly in the urban grassroots. The official security forces also need to exercise more discretion, for example, in incidents involving the simple use or possession of ganja (marijuana), for example, even in advance of the proposed and hotly debated decriminalisation of the wisdom weed. That, alone, would go a long way to begin the healing process between the public and the police.

In an article entitled 'How Crime Creates Poverty' published in the *Sunday Gleaner* on December 1, 2002, journalist Ian Boyne made a number of astute and insightful observations concerning the security forces. He wrote:

> The fact is that we do have a problem with handling power in this society... When a police officer – who out of his uniform is seen as a nobody who has no money to "flash it" – has the power, you had better know your place. And there seems to be a particular psychopathology of the Jamaican soldier. Arrogance, aloofness and bloated self-importance seem integral to the personality type. Throwing him out in these inner-city communities can create problems...

> This long-held perception of the army as a group of disciplined, self-controlled individuals wears thin sometimes when these men interface with inner-city communities, and the fight against crime will be seriously compromised if their behaviour confirms the human rights activists' suspicion that their presence would bring more harm than good. But there are some realities that we must face. The decent, law-abiding people in the inner-cities are already under oppression from the criminals and terrorists. People talk a lot about how poverty creates crime, but very few focus on the equal fact that crime creates poverty. It's a vicious circle. People who raise howls about the presence of the military in certain communities speak as though the innocent people in these communities are living with complete freedom of movement and association, which will be disturbed by the presence of the military or by curfews. The constitutional rights of many poor, innocent inner-city people are violated every day without the alarms we hear about the proposed military presence...

> Bright, creative youth from the inner-city who could advance themselves economically and professionally are held back because they live in certain communities and employers are afraid that if they are employed and there is a dispute, their criminal friends could snuff out their lives...Crime perpetuates the poverty and hopelessness. If we could find a way to rid these areas of the violence and savagery associated with them, over time people might not be so afraid to employ people from these communities. It is not every single inner-city area where people find it hard to get uptown jobs. There are some poor areas where people can still get jobs outside

simply because the names of those communities are not constantly on radio and television as being a part of gang and political warfare. If the police and the military can succeed in restoring calm and peace to some of these communities, the poor there will benefit. If they are left under the control of the criminals and the terrorists who operate their drug bases from there, there will be no hope for the decent, law-abiding poor.

If we can just control some of these idiots in the police and military who are mesmerised by power, and discipline them when they fall out of line, the proposed police/military action on a sustained basis can be a major help to the inner-city communities, once that is coupled with economic and social renewal...

Let the congregation say, 'Amen' to that. Jamaica needs much more than just new police flying squads like the now defunct Echo Squad, and more than special operations like Operation Kingfish and the distasteful Shiprider operation that gave US and British naval vessels legal jurisdiction in territorial waters. What should be more than obvious by now is the need for new thinking, new policy measures, new tactics and strategies, new methods of training and field deployment, and new blood. And, because the politicisation of the police force is a major problem, what Jamaica needs most of all is a police force which is free of political interference and political manipulation by the incumbent party and its partisan ministers. The island also deserves a police force and army that is free of the rampant corruption involving bribery, extortion, drug dealing and smuggling, stolen motor vehicles and the like that now abounds.

Some prominent businessmen have already called for the establishment of a new multidisciplinary force that is relevant to the current and future needs of Jamaica. Bank of Nova Scotia (BNS) managing director, William 'Bill' Clarke, made such a call while also demanding the abolition of the 134-year-old Jamaica Constabulary Force (JCF) and the Jamaica Defence Force (JDF). He suggested that this new force should be accountable to Parliament without ministerial jurisdiction, and that a council of persons should be appointed to protect citizens' rights and civil liberties. Mr. Clarke was speaking at a police awards banquet at the Jamaica Pegasus Hotel in New Kingston and was reported in the press as also saying that the current crime wave is 'a very real internal threat' that could cause Jamaica to descend into 'chaos and mayhem'.

Other prominent people have called for the introduction of American law enforcement to Jamaica to beef up the muscle of local security officials. Given the prior ganja-eradication efforts by visiting US Drug Enforcement Agency personnel and associated US police-related agencies, that particular call is still controversial and unpopular in grassroots and rural marijuana-growing communities. Thus, the idea of importing American police remains open for public debate. Be that as it may, at the time of writing, Jamaica's fight against crime and violence had just received a traditional kind of boost as of March 1, 2005, when senior British police officers started arriving in the island to officially join the ranks of the JCF. According to Jamaica's National Security Minister, Dr. Peter Phillips, under a new security assistance agreement between London and Kingston, British police are expected to help flush out the criminal dons by providing Jamaica with technical expertise in the areas of investigative techniques and case preparation.

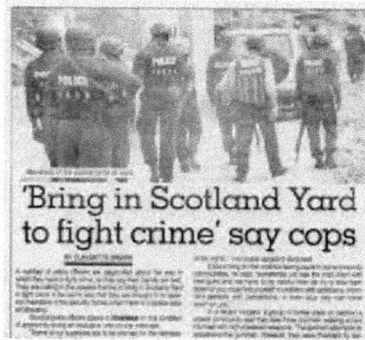

Figure 11.1 Newspaper reports say Jamaican police welcome help from England's Scotland Yard.

The British have also, reportedly, committed to giving support to the establishment of a Professional Standards Branch and to the implementation of anti-corruption policies and strategies within the Constabulary. They are also expected to post Scotland Yard specialists in Jamaica on rotating assignments and provide specialised training for selected senior members of the JCF's officer corps. Jamaica has long received substantial assistance from the British Government in the area of law enforcement, including involvement in a programme that places Jamaican police at airports in England to help identify and arrest drug traffickers from Jamaica. These days, British cops are more interested in gathering intelligence on the origins and activities of the *Yardie* crime gangs plaguing England, in their native habitat – Kingston.

Jamaica Hotel and Tourist Association President Godfrey Dyer, whose organisation has been one of the leading voices calling for overseas assistance for the JCF, described the introduction of British law enforcement personnel as a positive step in the right direction. However, the most important thing to remember about this introduction of 'colonial cops' is something that local human rights watchdog Jamaicans For Justice emphasised: namely, that this desperate measure is only a short to medium-term solution at best.

In the meantime, one of the long-term messages that need to be emphasised in the new age of policing is that the days of the legendary Jamaican 'super-cops' are over. In their days, 'super-cops' like Joe Williams and Keith 'Trinity' Gardiner, and to a lesser extent Renato Adams more recently, were/are the extreme macho models of the kind of super-aggressive, ballistically loaded, no-nonsense type of law enforcement personnel that were seen as necessary to keep poor, Black, inner-city people in line. Thus these 'super-cops' became heroes to other policemen and role models and examples for what younger upcoming officers wanted to become. Wrong! That macho image and identity is now very much passé. Such dominant and uniformed masculinities, 'super-cops' with badges and guns and an unspoken licence to kill, became the worst nightmare of not only the criminals and gunmen, but of the average inner-city resident as well. In the ghettos of Kingston there are endless anecdotes and stories based on fact, but sometimes bordering on fable, about the extensive number of mass and individual arrests, or unreported and uncompensated beatings, or raids on dancehalls, or alleged lethal shootings perpetuated by lawmen like these. Thus fear of and violence by name-brand policemen has often been the order of the day in the streets for the young and the old, the employed and the unemployed, and for men and for women.

Even other policemen with less power and prestige were afraid of the physical harm that could be inflicted on their bodies by those in the 'super-cop' bracket, especially Inspector/Superintendent Joe Williams back in his day. So along with all the other necessary administrative changes, new police recruits must be taught from training school that the old 'super-cop' image and its corresponding violence-prone 'bad-boy police' identity, is gone for good. This change in the mindset of the average policeman, would by itself be a huge accomplishment if it can be implemented. The unanswered question is, does the present police high command have the desire, the motivation, or the *political will* to begin the required changes? Only time will tell.

In the meantime, not all of the changes that need to be made in the Constabulary are new. Some are in fact old measures that were discarded along the way and just need to be reinstituted. For instance, it has been proven that 'familiarity breeds contempt' on both sides of the fence. Thus when policemen (and soldiers too) reside in the same areas that they are scheduled to patrol in, their lives are not only endangered when they are off duty, but they are often treated with contempt by the area gangsters even when they are armed and in uniform. On the other hand, community rivalries and 'blood for blood' vendettas are sometimes settled while innocent citizens are treated with contempt, unnecessarily roughed up or even arrested by policemen in uniform with chips on their shoulders or grudges to settle with people from their own or neighbouring areas. The solution to the problem of familiarity is to systematically station officers of all ranks in areas far removed from their places of residence and to give them tours of duty in areas where there is less chance of any pre-existing personal bad blood between them as policemen and citizens.

Taking such well-defined steps on this sociopolitical recovery track will, hopefully, replace the ass of the legal system with an owl of wisdom. Of course, instituting such changes will undoubtedly be a painful process for many. Change will inevitably entail replacing officers who are too entrenched in old mindsets with the new blood of officers who are more sensitive to preserving human dignity in the line of duty. Officers who accept the fact that preserving the human rights and dignity of civilians is the best practice and role for them as heavily armed and uniformed 'peace officers' occupying the powerful space between government (i.e. the politicians) and the people.

Those in authority must realise that, *no pain, no gain*, and must be clear that this kind of revamping strategy is necessary if the security forces are to legitimately claim that the institution they represent constitutes a humane constabulary system. And those in authority in both the JCF and the JDF must summon the necessary *political will* to make the difficult changes that are necessary. But, most important, members of the JCF and the JDF should be trained and equipped to truly start protecting and serving local communities – urban and rural. Only then will they be deserving of respect both at home and abroad.

The Role for the Tourism Sector

The government, police and the Tourist Board make every effort and spare no available security resources to ensure that the average tourist visiting Jamaica is safer than the average Jamaican. As a result, crime in the heavily patrolled resort areas is very low and vacationers seldom see the dangerous under belly of Jamaican street life. Although much of the promotional focus is on Americans and their 'Yankee Dollars', Europe is still a major source of visitors to Jamaica and the Jamaica Tourist Board has run television ads in key markets like England, Germany and Italy for years. As a result, European visitors to Jamaica increased by 22 percent in 2003 despite the initial downturn in travel and tourism following the 9-11 (September 11, 2001) attack on the World Trade Center in New York. Thus, surprisingly, 2004 still proved to be a bumper year for tourism in Jamaica, in spite of the Bush administration's ongoing so-called global war on terror.

According to the Caribbean Tourism Organisation (CTO), the island's 2004 tourist arrivals increased by some 4.8 percent, with a total of 1,326,918 foreign stopover arrivals, an increase of more than 60,000 bodies. Visitors from the US were listed as 996,131; some 241,925 came from Europe; and another 105,623 people came from Canada. With some 17 commercial airlines flying into Jamaica, both the CTO and Ministry of Industry and Tourism were, reportedly, expecting a similar performance in 2005, with an 8.0 percent anticipated increase in airline arrivals bringing some 1.5 million visitors to the island.

As we saw at the start of Chapter 3, Jamaica has long been popular as a sex tourism destination to those in the know. These days, Jamaica earns the bulk of its foreign exchange profits from the tourism industry. This begs the question of whether there is a *de facto* complicity between national growth policies and the sex trade, which is part and parcel of the tourism sector of the economic development apparatus. It is common knowledge that rent-a-dreads and girls are readily available in north coast resorts particularly in Negril, enabling even the female tourist to live out the fantasy of the ultimate consumption strategy while on vacation – that temporary respite from reality. In a warped reversal of the colonial norm, the local gigolos or prostitutes masquerade as temporary lovers, the ultimate hegemonic charade. The cultural assumptions resulting from this dynamic are as crude as they are predictable; because of the easy availability of sex trade protagonists, there is a popular perception propagated by popular tourism discourse, that Black bodies – male and female – are available to tourists for casual sexual encounters. This is just another reflection of the retention of race-determined social perceptions and relations in the corridors of discursive power. The class stratification inherent to the Jamaican society also permeates the sex-tourism sector making it extremely difficult to unravel the complex mysteries that agents of change would have to solve in order to realise some alternative to the poverty that feeds the needs of those embedded in this archetype of the Jamaican sexual politics that we have explored.

Unmistakably, the political interests that are vested in tourism result in the value-loaded differentiation of the urban version of prostitution from the accepted sex-work syndrome that is inherent to the tourism sector. This hypocrisy perpetuates the interlocking of racism, sexism and classism in a matrix of power that is the bane of Jamaica's development potential. Naturally, any serious suggestion for ameliorating the poverty and violence desiccating the urban landscape has to take into consideration the larger political context in which this problematic is located. It is time that policy-makers come to realise the insidious impact that marketing Jamaica as a sex tourism destination has on the already fragmented identity landscape of the majority of the island's population. It is also time for them to compensate the disenfranchised masses for the island's self-inflicted national self-abnegation, if even just for economic expediency, by consciously and actively contributing to the creation of a system of social justice.

One tangible means of so doing is by pumping some of the earnings from the sex trade (tourism) sector into the creation of development options for the industry's *workers*. Policies of protectionism could go a long way towards preventing these workers from being super-exploited at the hands of visiting guests, and could instead expose the workers to opportunities for personal development. Given that the fragile tourism trade is vulnerable to social image disruptions caused by the scourge of violence stalking the urban ghettoes, the powers-that-be are also obliged to contribute to efforts being made to tackle the problem of urban degradation and its attendant contradictory gender relations. Advocates and agents of change should also lobby for resources earned from tourism to be invested in devising mechanisms to satisfy the *needs and wants* that propel objects of domination (i.e. the workers) into pathways of social dysfunction. This is a huge challenge considering the high proportion of revenue that currently goes from the income earning industries like tourism towards servicing the perennial national debt.

A major source of contention with ordinary Jamaicans is the discriminatory treatment they receive at north coast hotels and resorts. Local residents, especially the more dark-skinned ones, are all too often rebuked for their presence or denied service if they try to check in, use the restaurant or go to the beach in tourist zones. However, despite the prevailing crime and violence, the assertion that Jamaicans are a warm and friendly people is no mere tourist propaganda gimmick. It is true. Therefore the Jamaica Tourist Board really needs to recruit the general population into the never-ending effort to make Jamaica more attractive, more memorable and more hospitable to vacationers. The JTB can do that by providing residents with access to some of the benefits generated by the industry, a move which could conceivably help make Jamaican streets safer for locals and tourists alike, even in Kingston and Spanish Town.

This would be one of the most far-reaching changes that could be introduced in the Jamaican Tourism arena, along with a kind of decentralisation process away from the almost exclusive focus on the all-inclusive style resort and all-inclusive style of vacation marketing. Cultural community activists have for decades advocated integrating the tourist industry into local communities by promoting 'cultural tourism', a Jamaican brand of eco-tourism. In such a scenario, vacationers would no longer be isolated primarily in the exclusive so-called 'all-inclusive' resorts, where they are served the same type of meals that they could get in New York, Miami, or Los Angeles. And vacationers would not be limited to going to the same few official craft markets and seeing the island's routine famous beauty spots.

Rather, 'cultural tourism' involves encouraging a significant percentage of vacationers to stay in private homes with ordinary families/residents, where they can experience the thrill of a traditional Jamaican breakfast, lunch or dinner, prepared the hometown way and interact with the real people. In homes where they can get abundant access to jelly coconuts, sugarcane, mangoes, watermelon and a range of other fresh fruit galore. Qualified, certified and approved homeowners working in the cultural tourism programme would be paid a standardised fee to cover food, the rental of their rooms, transportation expenses, time and miscellaneous costs, depending on circumstances. The host families would be responsible for taking their visiting guests around to the Blue Mountain Peak, the beaches, markets, historical sites, theatrical productions, art shows, jazz concerts, Reggae shows, or where ever they desire or agree to go. At the least it would be an economical net increase in room capacity, and would give the island the ability to simultaneously accommodate more foreign bodies seeking sun while circulating more foreign exchange.

Weekly or monthly island-wide talent shows featuring community performers could be organised in a number of local squares and community centres that should be designed and equipped for the performing arts. There is already a tradition of street dances in Jamaica, and that concept could be broadened into an ongoing and diverse series of events in multiple locations that also cater to vacationers. This would be one practical way of spreading around an increase in the trickle-down economic benefits of tourism to the average Jamaican, and would start to give ordinary citizens an investment – a vested interest – in the industry. Ordinary residents are likely to be a lot less tolerant of unnecessary crime and unwanted threats against foreigners and non-Jamaican vacationers if they stand to directly earn some much-needed income by the presence of visitors. Friendships would be built, encouraging the return of happy visitors and a continued long-term recirculation and infusion of foreign currency and goods (gifts) into the Jamaican economy at nearer to subsistence levels of the society.

Such inclusive policies will be necessary if Jamaica is to achieve a really sustainable tourism product. The way that the local tourism product has been structured up to now, is really unsustainable in the long term, not only socially or economically, but environmentally as well. Channels have been blasted in the sea to allow sightseeing, glass-bottom boating, jet-skiing, waterskiing and parasailing, which are all popular activities with tourists. But the ecologically damaging development of such tourist infrastructure on Jamaica's north coast has destroyed much of the natural beauty there, including coral reefs, wetlands, waterfalls, neighbouring forest cover as well as the great abundance of tropical fish, animals and birds that used to live there.

This dire situation makes it all the more imperative that the Ministry of Tourism's proposed Master Plan for Sustainable Tourism Development embark on a different path using a different model in its future plans, especially for western and southern Jamaica. Remember, visitors come to Jamaica for the fish and the fauna and the famed natural beauty of the island, as well as for the hospitality of the people; so the true sustainability of both elements is very important. Thus environmentally speaking, there is a great need to ensure the preservation of as much of the south coast's biodiversity and natural habitats as possible.

A safe, interactive, sustainable environment like this, with visitors having full access to the people, the music, the food, the sea, the marijuana, the mountains, the coffee, the culture...would transform *'Jamaica land we love'* into a true tourist paradise. These are only some of the alternative ideas floating in the ether, but the main point is, a fresh approach to the island's sexual economics and a fresh approach to the local vacation business is definitely necessary. Again, the million-dollar question is whether the executives in the tourist industry have the vision and the *political will* to overcome the inertia and resistance to change that is coming from those benefiting most from the status quo as it is now.

The Role for The Community
(Especially The Entertainers)

Jamaicans, and not only those who reside in the inner-city communities, have become virtual 'prisoners in paradise' due to rampant home invasions by gangsters and the prevalence of break-ins by thieves. Thus Jamaican houses in both urban and rural areas are encaged by wrought iron – iron grills over their carports and iron burglar bars over all their doors and windows. As the violence and siege-like conditions increase, stores and businesses, especially those in downtown communities, have cut the working day short, shutting shop, closing down operations and starting to leave the area from as early as four p.m., leaving commercial districts like ghost towns by five p.m. This is bad for both business and recreational pleasure.

Under these dire circumstances, the paramount role for the community to play at home and on the streets today is in creating positive and non-violent role models for inner-city teenagers and even for younger boys and girls to emulate. Next, residents of each area have to reduce if not entirely eliminate, the vicious cycle of 'blood for blood' and 'fire for fire' retaliations. Residents have to work really hard to increase the peace on the streets by trying to restore the lost sense of community that once used to exist. That sense of communal living and sharing which was conveyed in old Reggae songs by lyrics talking about cooking cornmeal porridge (for a host of hungry mouths in a tenement yard), about eating ital stew together, and about playing cricket and football as brothers. That kind of kindred community brotherhood/sisterhood is all but totally gone. Nowadays, far too many community residents are their own and their neighbours' worst enemies, and their gun-talk and vitriolic verbal dialogue, divisive body language and partisan political tribalism prove that without a doubt.

Therefore, community leaders as well as singers and DJs, have to begin the process by trying to reduce the high level of verbal, physical and political interpersonal aggression, which is increasingly characteristic of urban youngsters today. And area dons have to find smarter ways of helping their community and have to move away from the rampant and wildly indiscriminate extortion that is increasingly inflicted on helpless neighbourhood businesses, bus drivers, taxi operators, contractors, informal commercial traders (aka higglers), medical professionals and even musicians and singers. Although extortion is a billion-dollar, almost government-sanctioned racket in today's Jamaica, it is still very counterproductive and short-sighted. Ultimately, as businesses close and professionals move out, the extortionists deprive their very own residential area of easy community access to a wide variety of necessary products and essential services. This fact is increasingly bad for business and pleasure also.

To paraphrase a popular saying, you can take the body of a person out of the ghetto, but it is much harder to take the ghetto mentality out of the mind of that same person. So whether it is the inner-city ghettoes that are being renovated and upgraded, or whether people are relocated to better residential areas with more facilities, the critical ingredient for sustained community improvement is the raising of individual consciousness and the emancipation of the consciousness from the typically conflicted ghetto mindset. Given the adverse international conditions and the seeming lack of *political will* on the part of local civil administrators, it will of course be a very tall order to try and change the mass mentality of inner-city communities in any meaningful way, especially without resources, but try we must. Right now, Jamaica has no other choice.

City planners should also recognise that they have little choice but to start establishing a network of urban agricultural enterprises with designated growing zones. This is very necessary for a number of reasons. Most obviously, urban agricultural production will help to alleviate food shortages and to bring down unemployment rates. In the long run, urban growing zones could prove to be an integral part of plans for achieving sustainable inner cities in the future. Far too many poor people, even those with land in the rural communities, are not planting food to feed their hunger, but are begging, stealing or doing nothing instead. Community leaders need to encourage people in their areas to do real work, starting with feeding themselves where possible.

Currently, an unproductive freeness mentality abounds in the inner city as it does in much of Jamaica. Thus people expect to get well paid for little or no work. The bling-bling mentality (i.e. the flaunting of gaudy extravagant jewellery) is very prevalent too, along with the consumerist mindset in which wanton greed abounds and petty thievery is not a problem. Or people with nine-to-five employment, not only waste time on the job, but pilfer and steal from their own work place, unconsciously hastening the day when, after losing money, their employer will be forced to close the business and lay off them and their co-workers as a matter of course. This kind of petty thievery has now turned into an endemic epidemic in Jamaica. Also pandemic among today's youth is a coarse vulgarity, a non-traditional lack of good manners and a crass commercialism. All of these backward, outdated and counter-productive attitudes and patterns of behaviour are bad for business and bad for the service industry and have to be changed.

Figure 11.2: Tony Young, former station manager of Roots 96.1 FM, the community radio station where I broadcast material from this project.

Most crucially, inner-city communities have to get away from the music and media-driven hype and over-glorification of the so-called 'ghetto', 'ghetto living' and 'gangster lifestyles'. Incessant 'big-ups' from Dancehall entertainers and misguided media personnel have desensitised both individuals and the society at large to the really horrific conditions that poor people live in. The bad condition is why so many people living there are trying to move out of the ghetto – except those that love the war. The incessant gun-talk and 'big-ups' have also desensitised everyone to the fatal futility of the gangster lifestyle and to the long list of ghetto-famous gun hawks who have lived and died by the gun. Therefore, such 'big-ups' of negative environments, negative lifestyles and negative products (firearms) only foster the false belief that social inequality and dysfunctionality of such magnitude below the poverty line is normal or acceptable.

According to Elaine Wint-Leslie, veteran journalist and chair of the women's arm of an organisation called the One Love Healers, 'We don't have the Jamaica we want, but perhaps the Jamaica we deserve.' The One Love Healers was formed in 2004 by American author Robert Roskind and his wife Julia, who solicited a mix of socially conscious personalities including Abijah, Luciano, Ernie Smith, Cherry Natural, I'ngel Chanta, Mackie Conscious and Swade, to help in the group's aim to restore healing to Jamaica. The organisation designated Bob Marley's 60th birthday anniversary, February 6, 2005, as a Violence Free Day and joined with the government to put on a concert on that day. The One Love Healers have hosted over 30 of their special concert events all throughout Jamaica, from inner-city schools to schools in rural areas.

Likewise, we urge radio and television personalities to use their media profile to promote a more enlightened national verbal and musical discourse. And entertainers have to once again become the conscience of the community and lead the way to a more productive way of thinking and behaving. They have to stop feeding their egos by seeking the 'ray ray' of crowds of people. The new generation of performers like Luciano the Messenjah, Mikey General, Morgan Heritage, Bushman, Jah Cure, I-Wayne, Chuck Fender, Richie Spice, Junior Kelly and Turbulence, among others, must be praised for their conscious discourse, and their careers must be used as examples of what is expected of Reggae/Dancehall singers and DJs in the future. Music still has the uncanny ability to soothe savage hearts and presently there seems to be a glimmer of light in the dark tunnel of crime and violence, with the positive public response to the *lyrical discourse* of the newest young artists. For instance, I-Wayne's popular 2004/2005 hit tune, 'Living In Love', speaks directly to many of the points that are being made in this chapter.

Living In Love (excerpts)

I love to see my people living in love
I hate to see them fighting and swimming in blood...

Politicians ah talk
Certain things them nah mention
Sey ah drugs and gun
The people tax money spend pon
Come with plastic smiles
And dem wicked intention
Inna yuh hand
Ah whey dem put dem evil invention
Turn gun modeller
Seeking attention...

By most accounts, the island's problem with crime and violence, already aggravated by the popular badness/Shotter mentality, has been made worse by the constant stream of deportees who have been sent back to Jamaica in the past few years, mainly from the US, followed by England and Canada. Although not all deportees are criminals, some of them have lived most of their lives abroad and have no family or friends in Jamaica, and being utterly rootless in an alien environment, even they may be naturally inclined to indulge in extreme and lawless behaviour. The number of returning deportees for 2003 was approximately 2,700, and many of these individuals were in fact old-time inner-city *Posse* and *Yardie* political gang members, or have 'graduated' in the field of crime in the country that is a virtual crime incorporated university – America. These hundreds of returning 'professional thugs' have only hastened the dubious process of Americanisation and foreign-style criminalisation that has been taking place below the poverty line in Jamaica.

The problem of chronic crack use took hold on predominantly Black inner-city communities in US cities in the 1980s. By the 1990s, crack cocaine had also become a major problem in the predominantly Black inner-city communities of Kingston. Over the past 15 to 20 years, the scourge of crack-cocaine along with even more high powered firearms have been slowly added to the equation of dire poverty, not only in inner-city areas of Kingston, but all throughout Jamaica. The process has been hastened however, thanks to the international transshipment of cocaine and guns through Jamaica to North and South America; thanks to the enforced return to the island of coke-head and/or crack-dealing *yardie* and posse deportees from England, Canada and the US; and thanks to the cocaine using and cocaine dealing 'tourists' who frequent the island all too regularly.

All in all, therefore, the public in inner-city areas of Kingston has internalised all of the dysfunctional, violent and illusionary 'gangster' lifestyles that they see in the North American programming that floods their big and small screens. In Jamaica, people brainwashed into the crass consumerism and commercialism of America are said to have 'foreign minds'. There are literally hundreds of thousands, if not a million-plus native bodies, walking around Jamaica with such a foreign mindset crippling their brains. Thus, Jamaicans on the whole, and poor Jamaicans in particular, love, adore and copy anything coming from 'foreign' (i.e. from abroad): the newest name-brand shoes, jeans, shirts, caps, cars, clothes, hairstyles, jewellery, guns, tattoos, body piercings, you name it. Even new and taboo 'downlow' homosexual 'preferences' too. If it's known and done in 'foreign', they have got it and are doing it in JA too.

The biggest counterbalance to the cultural imperialism of the North American mass media could prove to be Reggae/Dancehall music. It all depends on the entertainers themselves, whether they really want to be musicians or badmen/gunmen. It is well known that infant children are able to learn the lyrics of popular songs with heavy airplay very quickly and word-for-word. Thus the tremendous power and importance of the *lyrical discourse* of popular music can easily be seen. And people are also watching the entertainer's actions, their body language, as well as listening to their words, so both have to match. Therefore, entertainers, the singers and especially the Dancehall DJs, have a huge and far-reaching responsibility and role to play in either promoting 'Love & Unity' or in pushing 'War & Crime'. The entertainers need to promote the desired 'Oneness' in their studio recordings, live on stage, and in real life off-stage in the communities where they live. Anything and everything else is hypocrisy on their part.

The young politrickally or criminally inclined shotters of today should remember, or learn about, the fate of Jamaica's two most feared, powerful, larger-than-life and pre-eminent name-brand political gunmen. Claudie Massop of the JLP and George 'Feathermop' Spence of the PNP, both rose to the top of their trade and in effect commanded the street armies of gunmen loyal to each respective party. Both were ghetto role models in their day and both met similar fates, seemingly at the hands of their own. Massop, the Tivoli Gardens don, standing on Spanish Town Road with his arms raised above his head, was shot 54 times and killed 'legally' by policemen allegedly linked to the JLP. No one was charged for the killing of the JLP don and there were no reprisal shootings. The flamboyant Spence, known as 'Feathermop' because of his healthy crown of dreadlocks, was in a bar in a PNP area on Laws Street in downtown Kingston, when an 'unknown' gunman walked in and shot him three times. Once in the head, once in the chest and once in the stomach. The gunman then calmly walked out into obscurity. No one was held or charged in the killing of the PNP don and there were no reprisal shootings. The word on the streets was that both top-ranking political gunmen had become too powerful for their own good, so their own parties eliminated them. Even the politically protected 'Jim Brown' supposedly ended up burnt to death, mysteriously, in a GP prison cell. Evidently there is a literal dead end waiting for ghetto gunmen at the top of the partisan political totem pole.

As we have noted throughout, another part of the community problem is the fact that many former 'political' gunmen have become 'criminal' gunmen. Thus, at one time in the recent past, the talk of the town in Jamaica and the local media was the alleged relationship between the JLP's Olivia 'Babsy' Grange and the One Order Gang of Spanish Town. At the time, the One Order Gang was terrorizing businesses in Spanish Town and the wider St. Catherine area, forcing market people, shop owners, bus operators and others to pay 'protection money' to the gang. The leader of this gang of extortionists was high on the police's most-wanted list and when he was murdered, while driving a car of another gang member, a mini political scandal ensued. It seems that all the car papers showed Babsy Grange as the co-owner of the vehicle and there was a great public outcry denouncing her involvement with the gang. For her part, Ms. Grange was adamant that she was just a guarantor to the loan, as she was only doing a favour for one of her constituency members. Similar examples can be cited for other political leaders from both the PNP and the JLP.

Because of the politrickal *'garrisonisation'* of Kingston throughout the 1970s, 1980s and 1990s, and because of Jamaica's proximity to the USA, there are guns a plenty in inner-city communities. Judging from the facts of inner-city street life, the illegal guns in the community will not be turned in easily or any time soon under the present circumstances. Fortunately, not all of the gunmen (i.e. men possessing guns) are criminals, thieves or political partisans. Some men use their guns mainly as the only way to protect their community turf from physical assault and invasion by outside forces, whether law enforcement or opposing political goons or gangs. In a probable worst-case scenario in which guns are not totally eliminated from the streets, the best that can probably be hoped for is that the young men with guns use Dennis 'Copper' Barth – Jamaica's own 'Robin Hood' – as their role model as a last resort, instead of patterning criminal dons like Lester Lloyd 'Jim Brown' Coke and Joel Andem,[169] or the original political dons like Massop and Feathermop.

Copper was Jamaica's most-wanted man at one time during the late 1970s, widely accused of robbing banks and other business establishments in Kingston. Copper succeeded in eluding capture by the police for years because of the strong support he received from ghetto communities all over Kingston. This was because the heavily armed Copper played the role of a Robin Hood, literally robbing the rich and giving to the poor. Common criminal gunmen rob rich and poor alike, and political gunmen frequently injure or kill poor innocent bystanders in the crossfire of their indiscriminate shooting. In contrast, Copper saw himself as an armed revolutionary, and after targeting mainly the rich and well-to-do, he shared his illegally gotten wealth with a large number of people in poor inner-city communities. While taking a lot of care not to unnecessarily terrorise poor communities, the colourful Copper put food on the tables of many fatherless homes and financed the schooling of a legion of children.

Of course, Copper's maverick example was something the government, both political parties and the security forces feared and could not let continue indefinitely. His example was dangerous to their designs. Eventually, Copper was killed in a shootout at Caymanas Park race track after being betrayed and setup by the covert behind-the-scenes political manipulation of other loyal partisan gunmen. So even the immensely popular revolutionary gunman, ended up on the list of deceased dons. The fatal moral of such sad stories should be more than clear at this stage of the book.

Thus, inasmuch as those men who have survived as the protagonists of political and gang violence, can be considered victims of an unjust class system, they also have to take responsibility for their brutal actions. At the same time, it is also important to develop mechanisms for addressing the psychosocial rehabilitation of those who have experienced the trauma of losing loved ones in the ongoing versions of the war. Healing is also vital for those who are too duped by paltry gains from patronage politics to recognise the folly of their actions or to see how they solidify the entrenched power structures in the society through their violent and/or criminal acts.

Such curative processes will enhance the possibilities for social transformation, but are also dependent on a constant exposure and highlighting of the political and pragmatic dimensions of the constitution of urban poverty and violence. As Manuel Castells argues,

> [i]f urban problems are indeed the result of the development of contradictions structurally rooted in the economic and political interests of capital (and thus of the bourgeoisie), they do not rest on a direct contradiction between the bourgeoisie and those of the working class, but between the interests of the bourgeoisie and those of the popular classes, who both submit to

---

169   Gang leader Joel Andem was freed of a murder charge (one of twenty-six other charges) in the Home Circuit Court after the prosecution's only witness firmly told the court that he would not testify for fear of his life. Police say that Andem's gang, known as the Gideon Warriors, was involved in more than 22 murders, kidnapping, extortion, robbery, gun-running and contract killings.

the mode of organisation of daily life imposed by the logic of capital. It is precisely this multi-class character of urban contradictions which makes them strategically fundamental for a transformation of social relations, for they objectively generalise the sources of opposition to the dominant class for the great mass of the people.

(Castells, 1978: 37)

A contingent consideration is the rampant gender inequalities compounding the structural power arrangements in which the grassroots communities, particularly in the urban areas, are so deeply embedded and on which prevailing political arrangements are predicated. Thus, it is also important that these proposals for social change incorporate an awareness of the gendered dimensions of the community problem.

A Gender-Sensitive Approach to Development

Although the gender-power regime of hegemonic masculinity in Southside presupposes a converse relationship with subordinate femininity, it is also clear from the discussions in which we have engaged, that this does not represent gender power in its entirety. While some women (and men) defer to the hegemonic deployment of masculinity, particularly in its violent interpretation, the compliance is often more strategic than real. That said, the women and men who have internalised and acted out the discourse of violence need to come to consciousness about more effective ways of exercising agency, thereby making their own contribution to creating an alternative ethos of social relations.

On the other hand, one cannot ignore the structural factors that create the conditions for the intense and often violent competition for scarce resources in the urban enclaves of Kingston. These conditions limit the opportunities available to the disadvantaged and dispossessed subjects in these areas, thereby encouraging them to seek material and symbolic recourse in survival strategies such as participating in patronage politics and exchanging sex for materiality.

As my interview with Alicia Taylor showed, there was a moment of development epiphany in Southside in the 1970s, when the then ruling party of the PNP experimented with implementing innovative strategies of community renewal.

Although reflecting elements of political expediency, this initiative was able to facilitate significant improvement in the quality of life at the ground level by concentrating on securing the well-being of women and children. The implementation of this strategic partiality proved to be effective as a method of improving the quality of life for families as a whole. The current practices of institutions like the Parents of Inner City Kids (PICK), which grew out of this process, remains a beacon of hope, which shows that bolstering the mechanisms of family support is crucial to adopting an integrated approach to poverty and violence reduction in Jamaica's inner-city communities.

One also has to validate the myriad ways in which subordinated subjects have *come to voice* (Collins, 1990) by using their embodied discourses of power to disrupt

306

bourgeois notions about embodied aesthetics (Cooper, 1993; Meeks, 1996). The highly colourful self-consciousness of the Dancehall Queens is a classical case in point. These women's embodied performances illustrate the creative potential of those who are objects of domination to develop embodied media of discursive self-expression. Their self-representations have effectively defied prevailing discourses of domination, which constitute them as *other*. And, while they contradictorily reproduce sexist norms through their embodied performances, the Dancehall Queens also present an unequivocal challenge to the dynamics of social stratification and the prevailing political economy of embodiment that undergirds it (Meeks, 1996: 133).

This imaginative/creative capacity has tremendous value in the context of stimulating pressure from *below* to encourage the political changes above, that are necessary in order for the overall status of socially excluded personae in Jamaica's *civil* society to change to active participation. The women's movement has a poignant role to play in this process of community change.

The Role for The Women's Movement

The essential presence of women in social and governmental roles of influence and authority is a developmental need which is still being overlooked and disregarded in many countries around the globe. Hence, a clear and acknowledged role for the women's movement in the sociopolitical scheme of things is often downplayed or just plain ignored by those planning and implementing policy. Equally trivialised despite lip service to the contrary, is the question of the fundamental Human Rights of women. According to a recent United Nations report, many women around the world are worse off today than they were 10 years ago. The report was compiled by the Women's Environment and Development Organization, and represents the work of women's rights activists in 150 countries. The report's message was clear: 'The women of the world don't need any more words from their governments – they want action, they want resources and they want governments to protect and advance women's Human Rights.'

The fact of the matter is that while the trafficking of women and children into bonded labour, forced marriage, forced prostitution, and domestic servitude has become a lucrative global phenomenon, national governments are not making any significant efforts to combat these crimes. According to June Zeitlin, the executive director of Women's Environment and Development, 'Governments need to respond very strongly to counterbalance these trends and push the Beijing platform to further women's rights.'

The UN report documents powerful socioeconomic trends like growing poverty, inequality, growing militarisation and fundamentalist opposition to women's rights, trends which are harming millions of women worldwide. It stated, 'Across all regions, women are often still considered unequal to men – in the workplace, at home, in government – and assigned roles accordingly.' The report also said that violence against women remains an 'acute problem' which affects some two-thirds of women in relationships worldwide. For example, in Kazakhstan, over 60 percent of women have suffered from physical or sexual violence at least once in their lifetime. In the United States, 31 percent of women report being sexually abused by a husband or boyfriend. And, in 2000, 44 percent of married women in Colombia suffered from violence inflicted by a male partner.

Thus, in view of the overriding insensitive international climate towards women's affairs, the women's movement in Jamaica has little option other than to continue and increase its ongoing self-sponsored community based social improvement work, while still seeking and encouraging governmental and non-governmental assistance where available and appropriate. An estimated 70 percent of Jamaican university students are female, so the women's movement – women – are very important and may yet prove to be the hidden master key that will unlock crucial communal doors leading to an end to Jamaica's urban war; or at least to a significant reduction in inner-city violence, as well as in domestic violence and child abuse. But the first thing the women of the women's movement should do is to help themselves and their sisters reprogramme their minds and re-inscribe their bodies into a more positive identity and image than they currently have of themselves.

This is why we have highlighted notable womanists of our soil like Nanny of the Maroons, Una Marson and Amy Jacques Garvey, who did much to minister to their people and their gender. Nanny played a pivotal role as military strategist and community shepherdess in elaborating feminist traditions carved out under the arduous yoke of slavery and inlaying the foundations of women's activism as a tool of liberation. Similarly, accomplished writers like Una Marson and Amy Jacques translated everyday forms of womanism and political activism under colonialism into more sophisticated letters and discourses.

Over the years since then, the Black woman in the inner-city areas of Kingston has been consistently bombarded and belittled by lethal and suggestive media-propelled images of idealised blonde hair, blue eyes, silicone breasts, flat butts and white skin. While enduring this mass media driven assault on her identity and beauty, this very same Black woman has been carrying her community on her head, her race on her back and unborn generations in her belly, just like she has always done anywhere she resides in the Pan-African Diaspora.

Grassroots women in Jamaica have been persistent in their struggles to undermine if not completely erase, *discourses of domination* which have shaped their embodied and social identities. While there have been moments when their knowledge production devices have resulted in open confrontation with those who control the structures of power, in many other instances, their resistance has taken the form of acts of dissimulation and have therefore been nuanced into the processes of everyday life. However, a paradigm shift in defining resistance (Scott, 1985: 27) is mandatory; this insight opens a window onto the richness of the various methods that have been employed at the subaltern level to redefine women's subjectivity and their methods of exercising independent agency.

Sistren Theatre Collective's epic method of organising for change in the 1970s and 1980s was effective because the media of popular culture, particularly drama, were utilised to generate interest in gender inequalities. Despite tremendous challenges, the ultimate of which was the razing of their home-office by fire in 2004, they have valiantly continued to facilitate community development through creative popular theatrical and educational methods. In the past, this collective effectively combined grassroots and upper-class women to organise to analyse the ways in which women suffer and to organise for change. This effort speaks to the need for alliances among women across barriers of race/colour, class or local community. Such collaboration is necessary in order to effectively politicise the issues related to women's oppression and exploitation in ways that challenge the structural differences that are socially inscribed on women's bodies.

Undoubtedly, the differences among the women in the collective demonstrated that although they formed a vibrant group, they were not homogeneous. Perhaps the internal differences in the collective also contributed to the diminishing of the political energy of the group. In respect of the need for coalition building, individual Rastafari sistren who have been playing vital roles within the *Livity*, and in the non-governmental organisation community as well as in mainstream organisations, should also consider playing a more active role in the Association of Women's Organisations in Jamaica (AWOJA). Their embodiment of the guerrilla queen prototype should enable them to make a valuable contribution in more general forms of organising and in developing strategies for the emancipation of grassroots women.

Thus, there is clearly room for baton carriers and torchbearers to revive the glowing embers of the oppositional discourses. These counter-discourses of power have long been burning at both macro- and micro-levels. PICK in Southside is a demonstration that sisters who are 'doing it for themselves,' as the popular song advocates, are shouldering this challenge. Such organised grassroots feminist action should be a catalyst for more fire to blaze[170] against not only structures of power but also against the gender inequalities which crisscross frontiers of race/colour and class to mark the bodies of disadvantaged women as a much contested identity region. As the primordial healing trope, this fire should also go a long way towards generating the sexual healing that is also such an urgent requirement in the social spaces of the inner-city communities.

Another good example of what needs to be done in the here and now, is the annual 'Women In Reggae' presentation, a combination discourse of song and speech. Spearheaded by Sandra Alcott of the Jamaica Association of Female Artistes (JAFA) and Carolyn Cooper of the Reggae Studies Unit of the UWI, the event is designed to foster an atmosphere of peace, especially in inner-city communities. The programme features females centre stage before the bright lights, backstage behind the lights and everywhere else in between. So there are women on the podium, women playing the instruments, women singing and deejaying, and women speaking from firsthand experience about bringing about peace in the community. It's like the Fab-5 band predicted in one of their songs: 'Woman gonna run this country in the 21st century'. Despite the fact that, as anticipated, popular PNP politician Portia Simpson-Miller, a woman who defied her humble class background to ascend to the country's highest

---

170 *More fire*, as I explained elsewhere, is a popular phrase used by Dancehall artists to denounce taboo practices. Here I use it with deliberate irony to reinforce the refusal by women to succumb to the application of any form of hegemony.

office of Prime Minister, this development did not rock the boat of dire disadvantage for people of African descent in general and women in particular. Neither the now retired veteran politician nor her inner circle possessed the consciousness or will to drive the proverbial stake into the heart of capital and patriarchy, the combination of which subvert the inalienable rights of the majority class.

Finally on this topic, we must recall the valiant and heroic women of South Africa and use them as role models, and their experiences during the dark days of apartheid as examples for the Jamaican women's movement. The South African women of the liberation movements, characterised by Nana Winnie Mandela, were the ones who continued the community resistance and the anti-apartheid struggle in the streets while their fathers, uncles, brothers, husbands, sons, cousins and nephews were being imprisoned or killed. The women of the liberation movements found a way to support their families and keep them together in the absence of most of their menfolk and in the face of vicious and cruel state security repression. They proved that an enormous wellspring of community strength and endurance rests with the females of the African species.

There was a profound saying that was made famous during the infamous 'Pass Law Demonstrations' by African women in South Africa in the 1950s. It is a truism about the innate power of Black women that speaks for itself.

Now you have struck the women
You have struck a rock.
You have dislodged a boulder
You will be crushed!

In many significant instances and in various ways, men commit violence either to satisfy the perceived needs and wants of women, or extend the war (violence) to impress women and to receive their adoration and enjoy their charms. However, if women were to diplomatically use their influence and 'feminine charms' on their own men in the cause of peace and a ceasefire, the results could be truly surprising and amazing, not to speak of being enjoyable too. This would only require that the women from opposing sides first find common ground and mutually agree to change the nature and direction of their *feminine discourse* in favour of peaceful and non-violent methods of communal conflict resolution. Then it is just a question of domestic '*pussy politics*' and of imposing '*pussy power*' over the phallic power of the penis/gun on both sides of the fence. Does that sound too simple to ever be true or possible? Once again, fact – the truth of the matter – may prove to be much stranger than fiction, but only if inner-city women can muster the necessary *political will*.

Validating Children's Voices

A growing number of unfortunate Jamaican children are having their young voices silenced. These unfortunate pre-teens are having their innocence and childhood silently stolen away from them as they are prematurely forced to assume the varied roles and responsibilities of adults. Too many of them are orphans and have serious issues with abandonment and trust. Too many of them engage in gun-talk because they have been victims of 'blood for blood' and 'fire for fire' reprisals. Too many of them have become emotionally callous and cold-hearted because of all the killing and suffering (blood and bodies) their tender eyes have seen, and because of all the M-16 and AK-47 gunshots (bullets) they have heard. As a result, a significant number of young boys have become hardened young gunmen (Shotters) themselves, from as early an age as 10 and 11 years old. Seemingly heartless and intellectually unreachable, such teen gunmen are ready and willing to 'tu'n yuh inna duppie' (i.e. turn you into a ghost), as in kill you, in the blink of an eye.

Meanwhile, an increasingly alarming number of other pre-teen children have been forced to become sellers on the urban streets in Jamaica to help make ends meet at home. Three out of four of them don't know who their father is. Many of them wipe windshields at traffic lights and wash cars and still others beg. Some of the children are given various items to sell, but others are known to sell sex, sometimes of their own volition and sometimes on the instructions of their parents or guardians. And some are already hooked on crack cocaine. This is the vicious social cycle that needs to be broken by our ongoing validation of our children and their voices. It should be obvious from the copious evidence I have presented throughout the book that children do, indeed, learn what they live. In other words, children are socialised by what they see and hear, and they learn and adopt the ways of their environment at home, at school and in all social settings. It should be equally obvious that thereafter, children also live what they have learnt. That is, children will eventually mirror and act out all that they have seen and heard and all that they have been taught by word and deed (body language).

As an estimated 75 percent of Jamaica's population is under the age of 25, the phenomenon of 'children having children' only compounds a vast problem, as a majority of such teenage or young adult parents are still emotionally and intellectually children themselves, and are unfit and ill-prepared to raise children of their own. Thus, if we are to break the vicious cycle of social schizophrenia plaguing the inner-city on a long term basis, one of the best places to start is with the youth and the children. Children need to get love and respect from adults first, in order for them to then be able to know and appreciate love and respect themselves; before those same children can finally give love and respect back to the world. Teenage children also need to be taught not to assume adult responsibilities like having infant children of their own before they have a stable family situation and the financial ability to raise them properly.

The following recommendations and suggestions are therefore as much for the youngsters as for their caregivers, be they parents, babysitters, teachers, healthcare providers, whomever. In view of the well-known African proverb that says 'it takes a village to raise a child', these suggestions are also very much for the politicians, the security forces, the media, the Rastafari, as well as for the entire community at large. With the advent of the Industrial Revolution in the 1800s, child-rearing started becoming what it is today: arguably the hardest and most time-consuming job in the world. In essence, the job is to maximise the potential of the country's most precious resource: its children. Skilled people are the basic raw material of the present post-industrial economy. The World Bank estimates that almost 60 percent of all wealth in developed countries is created by what economists call 'human capital', in other words, by people.

It is a well-substantiated fact that the earliest years of children's lives are the most important in terms of developing their human capabilities. By this token, mothers (fathers) and other early childhood teachers are the most important wealth producers in the society. But it is only when women have reproductive freedom to have just the number of children they want to have and can adequately care for, that they can produce the kind of children who can be equipped to succeed in the modern world. In today's complex world, therefore, parents cannot just have babies; they have to raise children too. All this means a much bigger job for parents.

Parents have to remember that having children is not a joke and their first responsibility is to make time for their little ones; time to touch them, time to talk to them and time to teach them. Children need guidance in general and nurturing in particular, while big people need to accept that children are not little adults. Therefore parents and adults should not project their adult attitudes and fears onto children. Children learn and discover things by playing and so need adequate time of their own to play, and they should be exposed to as many different experiences and environments as possible: the bus, the beach, the market, the library etc. In other words, caregivers have to provide a stimulating environment, constant/consistent care, proper nutrition and responsible supervision. Children also deserve praise when they do well and deserve to work in smaller rather than bigger groups in classroom-type situations.

Positive, regular and adequate mental stimulation from early infancy is essential to the proper development of any youth. Current brain research data indicates that stimulating experiences or the lack of such experiences between birth and three years old, establish the quality and quantity of the neural pathways developed in young brains, pathways that influence and shape their intellect and behaviour for the rest of their lives.

'Recalling that, in the Universal Declaration of Human Rights, the United nations has proclaimed that childhood is entitled to special care and assistance,' I am sure that even a cursory examination of the Convention on the Rights of the Child (Resolution 44/2), which was adopted and ratified by the UN General Assembly on November 20 1989, will be an eye-opening and highly instructive experience for most people. The Assembly was '[c]onvinced that the family, as the fundamental group of society and the natural environment for the growth and well-being of all its members and particularly children, should be afforded the necessary protection and assistance so that it can fully assume its responsibilities within the community.' The Rights of the Child Convention should actually be compulsory reading for all parents and childcare providers as well as for government policy-makers. It is a lengthy document, but following are a few particularly pertinent excerpts which speak for themselves and sum up much that we have been discussing in this strange story regarding children and family.

PART I

Article 2

1. States Parties shall respect and ensure the rights set forth in the present Convention to each child within their jurisdiction without discrimination of any kind, irrespective of the child's or his or her parent's or legal guardian's race, colour, sex, language, religion, political or other opinion, national, ethnic or social origin, property, disability, birth or other status.

Article 3

1. In all actions concerning children, whether undertaken by public or private social welfare institutions, courts of law, administrative authorities or legislative bodies, the best interests of the child shall be a primary consideration.

Article 5

States Parties shall respect the responsibilities, rights and duties of parents or, where applicable, the members of the extended family or community as provided for by local custom, legal guardians or other persons legally responsible for the child, to provide, in a manner consistent with the evolving capacities of the child, appropriate direction and guidance in the exercise by the child of the rights recognized in the present Convention.

Article 13

1. The child shall have the right to freedom of expression; this right shall include freedom to seek, receive and impart information and ideas of all kinds, regardless of frontiers, either orally, in writing or in print, in the form of art, or through any other media of the child's choice.

Article 14

1. States Parties shall respect the right of the child to freedom of thought, conscience and religion.

Article 17

States Parties recognize the important function performed by the mass media and shall ensure that the child has access to information and material from a diversity of national and international sources, especially those aimed at the promotion of his or her social, spiritual and moral well-being and physical and mental health. To this end, States Parties shall:

(a) Encourage the mass media to disseminate information and material of social and cultural benefit to the child and in accordance with the spirit of article 29;

(c) Encourage the production and dissemination of children's books;

(e) Encourage the development of appropriate guidelines for the protection of the child from information and material injurious to his or her well-being, bearing in mind the provisions of articles 13 and 18.

Article 18

1. States Parties shall use their best efforts to ensure recognition of the principle that both parents have common responsibilities for the upbringing and development of the child. Parents or, as the case may be, legal guardians, have the primary responsibility for the upbringing and development of the child. The best interests of the child will be their basic concern.

Article 19

1. States Parties shall take all appropriate legislative, administrative, social and educational measures to protect the child from all forms of physical or mental violence, injury or abuse, neglect or negligent treatment, maltreatment or exploitation, including sexual abuse, while in the care of parent(s), legal guardian(s) or any other person who has the care of the child.

Article 24

1. States Parties recognize the right of the child to the enjoyment of the highest attainable standard of health and to facilities for the treatment of illness and rehabilitation of health. States Parties shall strive to ensure that no child is deprived of his or her right of access to such health care services.

2. States Parties shall pursue full implementation of this right and, in particular, shall take appropriate measures:

(a) To diminish infant and child mortality;

(b) To ensure the provision of necessary medical assistance and health care to all children with emphasis on the development of primary health care;

(c) To combat disease and malnutrition, including within the framework of primary health care, through, inter alia, the application of readily available technology and through the provision of adequate nutritious foods and clean drinking-water, taking into consideration the dangers and risks of environmental pollution;

(e) To ensure that all segments of society, in particular parents and children, are informed, have access to education and are supported in the use of basic knowledge of child health and nutrition, the advantages of breastfeeding, hygiene and environmental sanitation and the prevention of accidents;

Article 27

1. States Parties recognize the right of every child to a standard of living adequate for the child's physical, mental, spiritual, moral and social development.

Article 28

1. States Parties recognize the right of the child to education, and with a view to achieving this right progressively and on the basis of equal opportunity, they shall, in particular:

(a) Make primary education compulsory and available free to all;

(c) Make higher education accessible to all on the basis of capacity by every appropriate means;

(d) Make educational and vocational information and guidance available and accessible to all children;

(e) Take measures to encourage regular attendance at schools and the reduction of drop-out rates.

Article 31

1. States Parties recognize the right of the child to rest and leisure, to engage in play and recreational activities appropriate to the age of the child and to participate freely in cultural life and the arts.

2. States Parties shall respect and promote the right of the child to participate fully in cultural and artistic life and shall encourage the provision of appropriate and equal opportunities for cultural, artistic, recreational and leisure activity.

Article 32

1. States Parties recognize the right of the child to be protected from economic exploitation and from performing any work that is likely to be hazardous or to interfere with the child's education, or to be harmful to the child's health or physical, mental, spiritual, moral or social development.

Article 34

States Parties undertake to protect the child from all forms of sexual exploitation and sexual abuse. For these purposes, States Parties shall in particular take all appropriate national, bilateral and multilateral measures to prevent:

(a) The inducement or coercion of a child to engage in any unlawful sexual activity;

(b) The exploitative use of children in prostitution or other unlawful sexual practices;

(c) The exploitative use of children in pornographic performances and materials.

Article 35

States Parties shall take all appropriate national, bilateral and multilateral measures to prevent the abduction of, the sale of or traffic in children for any purpose or in any form.

Article 38

1. States Parties undertake to respect and to ensure respect for rules of international humanitarian law applicable to them in armed conflicts which are relevant to the child.

2. States Parties shall take all feasible measures to ensure that persons who have not attained the age of fifteen years do not take a direct part in hostilities.

4. In accordance with their obligations under international humanitarian

law to protect the civilian population in armed conflicts, States Parties shall take all feasible measures to ensure protection and care of children who are affected by an armed conflict.

PART II

Article 42

States Parties undertake to make the principles and provisions of the Convention widely known, by appropriate and active means, to adults and children alike.

Once again, I have to emphasise the critical importance of early childhood – infant, kindergarten and primary – education and the need for the government to allocate the necessary human, financial and material resources into this particular area of its education budget. Also necessary are more community institutions like the old-time Boys' Town which provided sporting and other opportunities for poor ghetto youths. Today's new Boys' and Girls' Towns should provide educational, trade training and musical instruction along with the expected athletic and sporting opportunities. And both the government/police and the dons and gunmen in various local communities really do share a collective responsibility to provide and ensure proper security at all schools and other youth training facilities, so that classes are not disrupted and so that staff and students are not raped, robbed or otherwise terrorised.

In the meantime, the public relations chairperson for the School Governance and Human Rights advocate, former talk show host and political aspirant Betty-Ann Blaine once observed that Jamaica's young people – especially those at the bottom of the income ladder – are having too much sex. According to Ms. Blaine, sex and poor family planning are contributing factors to the criminal activities that are gripping Jamaica today. In a report published in the *Jamaica Observer* newspaper on September 6, 2004, Blaine is quoted as saying that: 'There is so much sex – it is unbelievable. The birth rate in the poor communities is phenomenal, and most of the births taking place today are births to teenagers who live in the poorest communities.' Speaking at the 2004 Sandals Special Achievers' Core Scholarship presentation ceremony at the Sandals Montego Bay Hotel, she pointed out that 'Crime does not fall from the sky...If we don't intervene in their (the children's) lives they are going to become criminals.' Ms. Blaine recommended that collective effort and sacrifices from all sectors of the Jamaican society should be made in order to tackle the problem.

Even though Blaine's remarks were made over a decade ago, they are even more relevant today because in a study I spearheaded for the Ministry of Justice in 2011 entitled 'Gender, Barriers to Justice', research participants from Granville, Tower Hill, May Pen and Spanish collectively concluded that threats of sexual violence were more commonplace than threats on their lives. This calls into question the budget allocations for crimes like murder and shooting, considered harder crimes than those deemed of a 'sexual' nature.

Therefore, much more support needs to be put behind a number of vital endeavours – programmes like the Citizens' Security and Justice programme (CSJP) and the Inner City Housing Project (ICHP), both of which I have personal knowledge of, which used an empowerment approach to leverage the sustainable development potential of at-risk communities. However, rather than merely deploying resources to practitioners at the ground level, governance practitioners should acknowledge the historical roots of present day threats to citizen security and apply affirmative action (such as the ICHP did) in order to ensure that the most underserved communities enjoy basic need facilities.

There needs to be more support for the Child Care and Protection Act for children who are at risk. Children's advocacy groups say the act lacks the requisite teeth and backing to effectively do what it was designed to do: protect Jamaica's children from abuse and neglect.

It is now taken for granted in development circles that inasmuch as children are passive recipients of policies, programmes, institutional and social authority measures, they are also active agents in the enactment of their own lives. Children are obviously influenced by the cultural norms and taboos and the *daily discourses* into which they are socialised from birth, but they are also critical thinkers about many taken-for-granted rules and regulations. The development of their critical consciousness should be encouraged because of their unique role as bearers of the contradictory cultural elements crisscrossing the various spaces that come under consideration when we seek to define inner-city communities. Children are most strongly impacted by the perennial violence we have analysed and have to exercise superhuman effort to countervail the hypnotic pull of the rewards of engagement in the social dysfunctionality that characterises the s/heroics of rude boys and rude girls. Therefore, the introduction of violent foreign video games like *Grand Theft Auto* to Jamaican children only adds deadly fuel to the fire.

Many of the actors being programmed in this script have conceded to the inevitability of a *state of mind* that correlates with the desolateness of the environment. Children growing up in the shadow of death in *garrison communities* like Southside are intimately acquainted with the vicious necessity of survival despite chronic material and psychosocial lack. Some of them have come to know that they constitute the most critical constituency to participate in the process of social change. During a segment of the research process, in a summer workshop, groups of boys and girls produced the following poems, which reflected their feelings, experiences and visions of a reformed society. These discourses show that for these architects of the future, life does not consist of unmitigated disadvantage, but is coloured by rich visions that transcend the psychosocial trauma that is associated with their everyday realities. They show that there may yet be hope for what many older people consider to be a modern generation of vipers whose teeth have been set on edge by the social sins of their fathers and mothers.

A World Without Sadness

In the morning, my world brings happiness to one and all
as early as the alarm sounds[171]
you can hear the cocks crowing
the dogs barking
the trees rustling
and the beautiful birds humming
to an endless tune
that brightens up the morning
the market people getting ready
to go to market with all their baskets
it is a wonderful sight to see
in the morning you can also see people
of all sizes, shapes and colours
big, small, fat, tiny, Black, White or Brown
rushing to go to work
but after all that rushing
the place is quiet
as if it was a world without people

The whimsical tone of this collective treatise to peace is not without its edge of cynicism; it is widely known that the monotonous regularity of the passage of the spectre of death in the squalid streets of the inner city makes it prohibitive for all except the foolhardy or the Shotter to venture out after acknowledged boundaries of safety have been sealed off for the day.

The next pièce de resistance, another collective effort, again promises cleansing and renewal after the passing of the current siege of crisis.

As I Rise

As I rise in the morning
and I look outside
I see the sun coming out
like a ball of fire
ready to explode
the breeze joined with the sun
to create a cool feeling
on my skin
I smell the new day coming
I taste the dew drops on the leaves
the sun goes down and
the night draws near
and the stars appear in the sky

---

171 It is remarkable that the gong which sounds at seven o'clock every morning at the General Penitentiary prison which is located in the community, is the institutionalised reference to time to which people in Southside awaken every morning. It is an ominous reminder of the historical experiences of violence, which have been projected onto the contemporary social landscape.

Given the agency that children demonstrated during my research encounters, it is vital that the tremendous knowledges of youth be validated by those who dominate the academic space as well as by the policy-makers who are responsible for developing strategies for social change. This inclusive approach is necessary if the idealised notion of social justice is to be realised. This, along with the successful implementation of all the social strategies outlined in this chapter, is essential in as much as the long-term solution to the prevailing crime and violence is dependent on stable, productive and sustainable family life for inner-city and all children.

Remember, an estimated 75 percent of Jamaica's present population is said to be 25 years old and younger. Seventy-five percent! Obviously, we fail to validate these young voices – most of the nation – at our own peril. Thus, critics of angry and violent young people should remember that the youth of today cannot be blamed for the pre-existing conditions of their own socialisation. It is fitting therefore to leave the final words of this segment with Wailer Peter Tosh, who was an ardent and articulate advocate and validator of youth in particular and of Black people in general.

You Can't Blame The Youth

You teach the youth about Christopher Columbus
And you said he was a very great man
You teach the youth about Marco Polo
And you said he was a very great man
You teach the youth about the pirate Hawkins
And you said he was a very great man
You teach the youth about the pirate Morgan
And you said he was a very great man...

All these great men were doing
Robbing, raping, kidnapping and killing
So-called great men were doing
Robbing, raping, kidnapping...

When every Christmas come
You buy the youth a pretty toy gun
When every Christmas come
You buy the youth a fancy toy gun

So You can't blame the youth
You can't fool the youth
You can't blame the youth
You can't fool the youth
So you can't blame the youth
You can't fool the youth
You can't blame the youth
(Save the children)
You can't fool the youth
Don't blame them
Not their fault!

Peter Tosh (You Can't Blame The Youth)

The Role for the Media

Freedom of speech and of the press is supposedly still alive and well in Jamaica, which is served by a number of television and radio stations plus a variety of print publications. However, in this digital information age, characterised by instant messaging and soundbite-short attention spans, the island's mass media by necessity have a very crucial role to play in the national process of deconstructing inherent binary oppositions and reversing the social marginalisation of those victimised by virtue of their race, class, gender or age. What I, as one person, have been able to do, both within academia and also out on the streets, gives a good indication of what should be possible and even probable, if adequate media resources and sufficient man/woman power is injected into the inner-city equation.

In that same vein of multimedia *cultural communications*, a number of my own self-produced video documentaries including Is *Poverty a Crime?*, *Living, Loving and Losing in Southside*, *Rastafari Youth and the Nguzo Saba*, and the 1990 production *Gender Relations in Rastafari*, have been screened in community gatherings, on cable television stations in Jamaica and on national television in Antigua and Barbuda. Along very similar lines,

In its present form, **Blood, Bullets and Bodies** the book, is a prototype of the consciousness-raising literary form of *cultural communications*. Indeed, my overt role as a multimedia practitioner specialising in *cultural journalism*, has been very critical to every phase of this entire process.

Firstly, my multimedia experience was essential to the project in view of the research techniques that I used to gather and document the information, namely, by *cultural communications* and verbal discourses in the form of intimate (recorded or videotaped) interviews, poetry, theatre, dancing, local art (i.e. public graffiti) etc.

Secondly, my multimedia perspective also accounts for the unique kind of format chosen to present the initial written thesis version of this project, a book format which included academically unusual elements like poems and pictures. I used this formula to enhance the presentation by making it speak to the traditional communication objectives of being educational, informative and entertaining. Those communication objectives have been distilled and enhanced even further in this rewritten/re-edited General Reader version of **Blood, Bullets and Bodies**. Once again therefore, this preferred book presentation format has allowed me to communicate more effectively with you the reader in the best technological and cultural vernacular suited for corresponding effectively in today's increasingly visual world.

Finally, the multidimensional usefulness of multimedia technology as a teaching tool, makes it an indispensable component in the implementation of any culturally based or culturally sensitive strategy to positively change and improve conditions in the inner-city environment. As should be very clear by now, cultural expressions such as music, poetry, theatre, dance, fashion, art etc., greatly enhance the effectiveness of the multimedia approach to community development and collective empowerment. This is what makes bi-directional multimedia technology and *cultural communications* techniques, two areas that have become virtually inseparable from and indispensable to each other.

During class lectures at the University of the West Indies, I have consistently used multimedia products like my *African Spirituality* documentary and the Mama Cash film, *Who is She* which featured me in an episode. I have found that such multiply reflexive tools are particularly powerful in demonstrating to graduate students the real value of audiovisual documentation as a technique of reinforcing reflexive critical consciousness in both researcher and subjects of study. Ideally, the tool should help the community participants to reflect critically on their lives and in the process, allow them to experience a sense of empowerment. This is the kind of self-confidence that is required to galvanise communities into action to improve their own situation.

That explains why ethically, intellectually and professionally, I had and have no other real option besides immersing my own self, bodily, into the research environment and data, as well as into the strategies being proposed to improve the social situation in the inner city. The fact that I have been able – in the only way I know how – to compile and reproduce easily understood knowledge in forms/formats that potentially have a practical and beneficial usefulness to a wide ranging audience in general and to a specific audience in particular, is all the justification/validation I think I need for my decision to use multimedia technology and *cultural communications* techniques as a part of this project.

Admittedly, this is a very unusual and unique approach, but it allows for the exciting and original presentation of research data in a way which has its own internal logic and consistency, from start to finish. Further, it makes it possible to tell an exciting, tragic and strange story like **Blood, Bullets and Bodies** as graphically and artistically as I have. For me, this project has always been much more than just a mere academic exercise. Therefore, inserting myself into the equation as a researcher/catalyst, has enabled me, not only to make this story real, but also to, as they say on the streets, '*keep it real*' by proposing practical remedies to the social ill. This is the best validation of my novel multimedia approach – its practical utility and ultimately, its ability to motivate readers to actual action.

Thus, there is obviously an immensely important role to be played by the mass media in general and by individual and independent media practitioners in particular, in facilitating the emergence of the voices of those who are chronically disenfranchised by the various *discourses of domination* which are at large in the Jamaican society. My own personal experience and the living data included in this explosive story, prove that the full potential of mutable media methodology – i.e. the combining of multimedia technology and cultural communications techniques – needs to be properly recognised by media practitioners and correctly utilised as the invaluable resource that it truly is.

The Role For Rastafari

As we have become more familiar with the various characters involved in this dangerous drama that I have entitled **Blood, Bullets and Bodies**, Rastafari has emerged as one of the surprise and unforeseen heroes/heroines of this strange story. We have clearly seen throughout this book, that Rastafari has fulfilled the role of an essential catalyst and *voice of resistance* in the ongoing struggle by Black people in Jamaica – and indeed worldwide – to obtain their full human and civil rights; to obtain social and economic justice; and for the reclamation of their fractured African Identity and the redemption of their exploited African Bodies. Rastafari is consistently and correctly identified by sociologists and researchers from abroad as an important source of cultural identification for the island's Black majority and as a stabilising force for those straddling or below the poverty line in the violence prone Jamaican social environment.

In Chapter 1, we documented the fact that Rastafari members and Rastafari consciousness were key elements in reducing the level of inner-city fire fights and blood-letting by their brokering of the historic Peace Treaty of 1978. Chapter 4 chronicled the role of Rastafari as the primary Jamaican successors of Marcus Garvey and his philosophy and mission of African (Black) redemption. And Chapter 5 provided copious evidence that Rastafari messages and entertainers have also been the mainstay of the old school cultural Reggae music. Yet it is to the continuing amazement and dismay of many in supposedly polite Jamaican society, that Rastafari in all its myriad manifestations, has attracted so much interest from White historians and anthropologists, as well as from marijuana lovers, Whites seeking Reggae music, or foreign tourists seeking sex from the island's infamous rent-a-dreads.

However, in its present state in the early twenty-first century, the Rastafari Movement is, itself, seemingly fraught with serious contradictions as it faces many complex philosophical, political and economic challenges with very far-reaching and long-term implications. Dr. (Ras) Ikael Tafari detailed many of these issues in his book *Rastafari In Transition*. Practised as a *Way of Life* by its founders, Rastafari has been turned into a virtual religion, and an overly dogmatic one at that, by many of its present-day adherents. And, once almost exclusively the domain of Jamaica's poorer, Black working classes (with a sprinkling of well known Indian and Chinese members too), Rastafari is propagated internationally these days, not only in the Caribbean (where the racial demographics of the Movement are roughly the same as in Jamaica), but all over the globe by disciples of every body type (i.e. ethnicity and nationality) you can think of. However, it is increasingly evident that locks (the hairstyle) in all forms, including dreadlocks, are not an automatic representation of Rastafari and African spirituality as it once used to be.

Many foreigners, in particular, are also just finding out that not all Reggae music is Rasta music, as in being conscious, *old school, message music*. Many such people are also surprised to find out that not everybody in Jamaica wears dreadlocks, and even if someone does, that it does not necessarily mean that they are real Rastafarians. And of course, ganja/marijuana is used in myriad ways for a variety of purposes by a host of people (internationally) other than Rastas, and always has been. So when watching

DVDs with news footage of Jamaican criminal activity, if you see old footage of most-wanted criminal Joel Andem and his warrior gang of killers smoking ganja in a chalice and supposedly praising Jah Rastafari, do not be confused or misled. Many millions of people all over the world say 'Jesus Christ!' inappropriately every day, and most of them doing that are not true Christian disciples of the Hebrew Nazarite Messiah either.

Although just shy of 90 years old and still relatively young as a 'religious' movement, Rastafari has already begun the inevitable evolution in thinking that comes with the passage of time, an evolution that has already started shifting the Rasta paradigm and mindset. In its early incarnation, the Rastafari Livity called for total separation from the Babylon system, but these days, relatively very few Rasses are living exclusively in the hills anymore. Over time, it almost seems that integrating/investing into the Babylon system has come to be an objective by default. In addition, most people including Rastafari, cannot totally separate themselves from new technological innovations.

Yet, for every Rastafari employed in a mainstream job or idolised as a Reggae singer, there are far too many more who are marginalised and/or excluded. But do Rastafari want to be involved in civil society? Or do they still want to create a separate or even parallel social existence like the Black Muslims/Nation of Islam once did? Although there have been numerous calls for the establishment of schools, hospitals, churches, farms and other organisations/businesses exclusively for Rastafari, these initiatives have never been seriously pursued (apart from the exceptional and unusual case of the farms, supermarkets, trucks and boats once run by the Zion Coptic Church[172] during the 1970s). In other words, the Rastas have never collectively clarified who precisely should take responsibility for initiating the delinking from the mainstream system and how it should be done. Rastafarians need to revisit this issue and decide what direction the movement really wants to take and/or what options they have.

Initially regarded as a localised Black Nationalist Movement peculiar to Jamaica, the Movement has successfully spread throughout the English, French, Spanish and Dutch Caribbean at a grassroots level. It even has a small number of indigenous disciples in Castro's communist Cuba. However, although Rastafari is now undoubtedly a Pan-Caribbean Movement, it appears to have stalled in its transition into becoming a truly Pan-African force with any political and economic leverage. Traditionally, Jamaica's Rastafari Movement has been apolitical in terms of the island's local partisan politics, although both the PNP and the JLP have co-opted Rastafari/Reggae slogans, slangs and songs for their own partisan purposes. Individual Rastafarian Brethren starting with Ras Sam Brown in the early 1960s, Ras Steve McDonald in the 1980s and more recently, Ras Astor Black does not enjoy either popular or Rastafari support and neither does the Stephen Golding-led Universal Negro Improvement Association (UNIA) or the Michael Lorne-convened Peoples' Progressive Party (PPP), the latter both reincarnations of Marcus Garvey's political activism. Progressives who do not support the PNP and JLP are therefore wandering in a virtual no-[erson's-land as far as finding solace for developing a politics of transformation is concerned.

---

172 The organisation more properly known as the Ethiopian Zion Coptic Church, was started in Jamaica but made national news in the U.S. when Thomas 'Brother Louv' Reilly and other White American members of the so-called 'Ganja Church', resident at the Church's U.S. 'embassy' at 43 Star Island in Miami, Florida, were convicted of 'dope' smuggling in 1981. (See 'Louv Story' in Miami Herald newspaper, August 2, 1981)

In the meantime, failing to have impacted conventional politics in an overt and practical way like the Rastafari Movement did in Grenada during the historic 1979 bloodless revolution there, Jamaican Rastas are in jeopardy of remaining politically irrelevant and powerless *en bloc* to influence the future of their own community, much less the future of Jamaica or even Africa. And the notion or practical utility of Repatriation and the struggle for Reparations have been sidestepped by many so-called 'Rastas', who perceive this struggle to be beyond the boundaries of their immediate personal survival needs and wants. Thus in many ways, the Rastafari Movements in the Eastern Caribbean islands are much more politically advanced and economically organised in their local environments compared to Rastas in Jamaica.

Clearly, then, the agenda of the Rasta/African survival struggle needs to be properly thought through and strategised by this new generation of Jamaican Rastafari Elders. Everyone has a mouth and wants a soapbox to use it, but often times it looks like hands and hearts are lacking when there is real work to be done. Thus, many Rasta groundations and conferences turn out to be just mere talk shops. However, for the Rastafari *voice of resistance* to have any real meaning and purpose, the Rastafari will have to successfully translate their words (principles and philosophies) into deeds, because words without works is dead. And cliché though it is, it is also a truism that no one is free until all are free. This makes the Nana Rita Marley spearheaded 'Africa Unite' concert and conference series, which began in Ethiopia to mark Bob Marley's 60th birthday anniversary in February 2005, and continued in Ghana during February 2006, all the more timely and highly significant – symbolically and socially.

Addressing the relevance of Africans in the Diaspora making the meta-physical return to the Continent, Sister Imakhus of One Africa,[173] located between the Christiansborg and Elmina Enslavement Castles on the Ghana Coast, was vehement in her demand that this benchmark of transitional justice should be recognised as an inalienable human right.

> We are not talking about dual citizenship; there has to be acknowledgement that you or I or any one of us that was taken away has the right to return to the land of our Ancestors. That is our inalienable right. So for years we fought for that. They gave us the Joseph Project, they gave us PANAFEST they gave us Emancipation Day Celebrations, everything except the right of return but on the Twenty-eighth of December, [2016], John Dramani Mahama [former President, ousted in the December 7, General Elections] said a few times that we Africans who were taken away as a result of the enslavement trade and I do say Arab and European slave trade, that we are Africa's children and we have the right to return. In doing that, he has granted us the right to return.[174]

As we have explained, education has long been recognised as the key route for upward social mobility. Hence, Rastafari also need to emphasise education's utility as a tool for creating the critical consciousness which is vital for the kind of struggle

---

173 One Africa Guest House and Health Resort, http://www.oneafricaghana.com/, retrieved March 17, 2017.
174 Interview conducted January, 2017.

in which they are engaged. And, like it or not, critical consciousness is something that the Rastafari community has often been sadly lacking in recent times. I have worked with experiential education programmes, and I know that it is by how we skilfully combine academic issues with social responsibility and participation, that we facilitate students/citizens in becoming agents of social change. Because progressive social change is the real issue here, and because revolution is just another radical word for cyclic change, we also have to propose implementing practical mechanisms for achieving this objective. Although Jamaican society has made undoubted gains in terms of dreadlocked Rastafari youths gaining admission into the school system as a legal issue, it is much harder to tackle the prevailing psychosocial attitudes that keep the old-time prejudice intact. In 1990, I was involved in a campaign in Antigua and Barbuda to enable Rasta youths to enter the school system there. At that time, Rastafari had to design empowerment workshops to help enable the youth who had been denied education, new opportunities and abilities for them to go to school with more confidence.

It is very important, therefore, for Rasta Elders to help facilitate the schooling of their youth, because as Marcus Garvey emphasised, 'Education is the medium by which a people are prepared for the creation of their own particular civilisation and the advancement and glory of their own race.' Accordingly, Rastas have to develop their own schools urgently, because they cannot seriously expect what they see as Babylonian-oriented schools in Jamaica, or the Caribbean, or the Americas, or Europe, or Africa or anywhere else, to teach Rastafarian children to think independently, to live Afrocentric lives, or to be real Rastafarian revolutionaries. Nor can Babylonian schools be expected to nurture a love of Africa, nor a love of the Black self, nor a spirit of Pan-African resistance and activism in dreadlocked youngsters. Only Rastafari Elders can do that for Rasta youths. Only Rastafari Elders can encourage Rastafarian youth to take up subjects like mathematics, engineering, chemistry, physics, biology, architecture and the like, because as Marcus Garvey himself encouraged: 'In your homes and everywhere possible you must teach the higher development of science to your children: and be sure to develop a race of scientists par excellence, for in science and (culture) lies our only hope to withstand the evil designs of modern materialism.'

Thus, the education of Rastas as adults and the education of their children, especially, should be actively grounded in the social, economic and scientific concerns that affect them as individuals and as members of specific communities within the wider society. One specific proposal related to this issue, therefore, would be for Rastafarians to actively participate in the existing education system as a first means of empowering themselves to acquire the additional skills necessary for nation building. The onus is on Rastafari to develop new systems of collaboration that will allow them to combine academic and experiential expertise in order to enable them to tackle the structures of power from a position of more strength than they can currently muster. Thus, the bu'n fire crew (i.e. fundamentalist Rastas) need to think clearly and sensibly before they blaze up and verbally *fire bu'n* those of their brethren and sistren who attend schools, colleges and universities, or those who seek higher academic qualifications.

To the Rastas, ganja is not a drug, and so the still unchanged legal restrictions on the cultivation and use of the *International Herb* otherwise known as ganja, marijuana or cannabis, continues to expose the Rastafari community in Jamaica and most parts of the Caribbean (and in Africa too) to the injustice of excessive, unnecessary, embarrassing and sometimes fatal harassment from the security forces. Although the Ombudsman has recommended decriminalising small amounts of the Herb in Jamaica for personal and/or sacramental use, economic and political threats, coming mainly from the US Government, have brought parliamentary movement on this issue to a virtual standstill. A positive ruling on the decriminalisation of marijuana for personal use could also help to enhance the social security and quality of life for Rastas in particular, and for Jamaicans in general, by alleviating and minimising instances of unnecessary police harassment and civilian incarceration.

Serious and coordinated pressure needs to be brought to bear on respective Caribbean and African governments to change the unjust policies which make the anti-ganja laws into tools of neo-colonial repression and downpression – laws which deliberately turn otherwise law-abiding Rastafari brethren and sistren into so-called 'criminals' and give them the media profile of *posse* members. Given increasing public acceptance of medical marijuana propositions in the USA and new decriminalisation legislation overseas in places like England, Canada and Spain, we have to question why Caribbean society and laws are being held to a different standard than is now fashionable in an increasing number of *developed* nations. While living and studying in the Netherlands for some time, it was interesting for me to note that the Dutch integrate the decriminalised use of marijuana into their tourism product. In other words, the government allows coffee shops, a euphemism for bars where the herb is marketed. We could therefore use the example of the Netherlands as a successful case in point when we suggest a more Rastafari-friendly/tourist-friendly policy to the use of cannabis *sativa/ganja* as either a spiritual or recreational sacrament.

Finally, I need to re-emphasise the critically important but potentially explosive topic of gender relations and gender injustice in Rastafari. This is the main instance in which the injustice we are discussing is self-inflicted, which makes this problem all the more insidious and all the more difficult to cope with. Certain things have to and are already changing in the relationship between the Rasta man and the Rasta woman, but glaring contradictions remain. This has nothing to do with man-bashing or a White Western version of women's liberation. It has to do rather, with an embracing of *womanism*, i.e. gender consciousness, from the perspective of a woman of colour with critical and empathetic political standpoints.

Traditionally, most sisters have come into the knowledge of Rastafari through a relationship with a Rasta man. This is a primary reason why a number of sisters desert the *Rastafari Way of Life* after breaking up with their man. However, regardless of domestic disputes, females need to remain committed to the *Rastafari trod* because this *Way of Life* is about more than just having a relationship with a Kingman. For the woman as for the man, Rastafari is about having an African Identity; it is about seeing the Almighty in oneself and experiencing a fusion with that One; it is about sharing a cosmic consciousness, exploring spirituality and finding holistic self-realisation.

Gender relations in the wider social contexts in which Rastafari operate, have exhibited changes over the past 30 years or so. More and more women are becoming economically independent as the dictates of capital shift the demand and supply dynamics in the labour market. This dovetails into social-relation dynamics that have seen the splintering of a number of nuclear and extended family units. The Rastafari community has not been immune to these changes as demonstrated by the growing trend of single-parent households headed principally by sistren, or by brethren who are raising children on their own. These factors have power implications and therefore affect how sistren and brethren relate to each other as they move on with their lives and attempt to establish new unions or deal with the challenges of being single parents.

Domestic relations are of course critically important to the power relations that exist between brethren and sistren in Rastafari and without doubt, a divide exists between the ideal of brethren performing the role of breadwinner/head of the household, and the reality that in a lot of modern-day cases, this obligation has become a female responsibility. Just like for the wider society, the man's role as head of household in Rastafari is usually described in economic terms, with absolutely no value being ascribed to the many other domestic contributions that the man may make in terms of looking after the children, cooking for the family etc. Thus, without a consistent or sizeable income flow, the Rasta man may be perceived as incompetent or as being less of a man. Obviously such economic issues tend to pit the genders against each other more often than not.

At the same time, physical, emotional and psychological abuse by men against women is still endemic to Jamaican society. Everyone who has been socialised to accept domestic violence as the norm since their childhood will perpetuate such abuse despite religious or philosophical persuasions. This applies to adult Rastafarians – male and female – who are all acting out roles taught and learned from childhood. Remember, values imprinted in someone's conscious and unconscious mind from early in their development, remain with them for life. We cannot blame the victims. However, it is obvious that unless and until sistren themselves are prepared to begin to break the cycle of internalised downpression and domestic violence, patriarchal practices will continue to influence social and power relations within the Rastafari family and community.

It is clear therefore that the contradictions of race, class and gender distinctions all operate as insidiously within the Rastafari culture as they do in the wider society. Emancipation from this kind of 'mental slavery' is vital to the true liberation of the Rasta woman and Black woman and to maintaining their integrity and ability to contribute to the Rasta family and community. A lot of work remains to be done in this regard. Rastafari needs to develop discussion spaces where they can collectively consider the ramifications of these developing permutations of social interactions or lack thereof. However, to give the Rasta man his due in this context, he was the first race-conscious Black man in the twentieth century to fully re-elevate the ideal (of a) Black/African woman to her traditional status as Queen, Empress and *Goddess*. This kind of Rasta woman can fill any role from Midwife to Matriarch or from Wife to Warrior, and are Queens who can participate in fulfilling partnerships in all their social relations.

Rastafari will have to rationalise how they need to shift their rhetoric – their words – to reflect their reality and they will have to let that reality be didactic of a paradigm shift whose time is long overdue. Fundamental to this mental realignment is a recognition and endorsement of woman-power – the sacred *feminine*[175] – as being central to the evolution of the Livity as a viable socioeconomic and political institution. There is no question that these material dimensions have to keep pace with the spiritual, in order for balance to be realised. Meanwhile, the Willie Lynch syndrome, which works insidiously to ensure that Africans/Black people do not trust each other enough to work effectively together to achieve our goals, is yet another vicious cycle that has to be broken. And the Rastas are the ones who have to break down this syndrome, because it only benefits the slave system when Rastafari brethren and sistren cannot get along with each other. Thus, as a well established and vibrant community, Jamaica's Rastafari need to develop a collective approach to resolving conflicts by ensuring that they adopt viable measures of personal and community healing and by working together.

In addition, the Rastafari vision of *African Redemption* and *Black Liberation* needs to be clearly articulated and practically implemented. The Rastas need to be clear about what exactly they want to achieve in order to be able to systematically pool their human and material resources towards realising their stated aims. In addition, just like other races, nations and societies do, Rastafarians definitely have to encourage their children to take up the batons that the Elders have to pass on, in order to ensure continuity. In the long run, it is only by remaining true to and by actually achieving its wider Pan-African objectives, that Rastafari can maintain the non-partisan credibility and local neutrality, necessary for retaining their unique role as sociopolitical peace makers in Jamaica and Africa. However, once again we are still left with more questions than answers. Another of the still unanswered questions is whether Rastafari brethren and sistren really do have the inner will in addition to the *political will*, to rouse themselves to the level of cohesive collective action that is so urgently required by the deteriorating sociopolitical conditions in Jamaica and in Africa.

---

175 See The da Vinci Code

Ethical Consideration

> The minority cannot permit itself the luxury of tolerating the unification of the people, which would undoubtedly signify a serious threat to their own hegemony. Accordingly, the oppressors halt by any method (including violence) any action which in even incipient fashion could awaken the oppressed to the need for unity.
>
> (Freire, 1970: 137)

It is a given truism that all real social change first begins with a change in the attitude and mindset of individuals, which then leads to a change in the language and bodily actions of those same individuals. That is spontaneous social activism. Social activism is necessary in order to address outstanding community problems in a proactive rather than a reactive manner. For my own part, I am committed to participating in the struggle for the sociopolitical emancipation that I suggest is crucial for the research subjects and indeed, for any community facing similar conditions of social disadvantage and exclusion. I have consistently affirmed the usefulness of immersing myself in the process as being congruent with my ability to exercise critical consciousness in consideration of the issues being addressed. I also encouraged a similarly reflexive gaze in participants with whom I interacted, as a method of building the fragile self-esteem of some participants as far as the validation of their knowledges/power was concerned.

This commitment to consciousness-raising and critical thinking allowed me to participate in the research process with the subjective advantage of epistemic privilege, yet from an insider/outsider perspective (Lal, in Wolf (ed.), 1996: 193). To occupy this location of 'hybrid identities' (ibid.: 199), between empathetic commitment and critical consciousness, is therefore one of the major challenges of a project of this nature, but is also one of its strengths. While I recognise the importance of institutionalising the kinds of structural changes that I outlined above, the issue of ethical balance (conscientisation) in self-esteem building is basically an issue of praxis.

One of the drawbacks to self-sustained change, however, is that because of the complexity of the problems they experience, the poor are so preoccupied with the daily demands of hand-to-mouth survival, that it is difficult for them to focus on much else. In other words, their 'state of alienation hinders the emergence of consciousness and critical intervention in a total reality. And without this critical intervention, it is always difficult to achieve the unity of the oppressed as a class' (Freire, 1970: 139). Nevertheless, the encouragement of this consciousness-raising improves the ethical dimensions of ethnographic engagements, which would otherwise border on exploitation. And because such ethical consciousness and conscientisation is congruent with bell hooks' advocacy of cultural criticism, it is worthwhile quoting her at length, to reiterate the value of the political partiality that comes from this standpoint.

> Merging critical thinking in everyday life with knowledge learned in books and through study has been the union of theory and practice that has informed my intellectual cultural work. Passionately concerned with education for critical consciousness, I continually search for ways to think,

teach, and write that excite and liberate the mind, that passion to live and act in a way that challenges systems of dominant racism, sexism, class elitism...Not only did I find in cultural studies a site where I could freely transgress boundaries, it was a location that enabled students to enter passionately a pedagogical process firmly rooted in education for critical consciousness, a place where they feel recognised and included, where they could unite knowledge learned in classrooms with life outside.

(hooks, 1994: 2-3)

hooks is, by her own admission, tremendously influenced by Paulo Freire, to whom I am also indebted for his legacy of critical consciousness through reflexivity and the politicisation of the research/education processes. Freire warns however, that engaging in the conscientisation process is not without its dangers and almost superhuman challenges. Furthermore, the difficulties are intensified because Freire puts the onus of liberation on the oppressed. And so he should, for no matter how concerned the sociopolitical activist is to facilitate the ideal of social transformation, it cannot happen without those who have experienced disadvantage making the effort to break the vicious cycles of power and control, which keep them from experiencing emancipation in all its meanings. Therefore, as Freire suggests with conviction,

the great humanistic and historical task of the oppressed [is] to liberate themselves and their oppressors as well. The oppressors who oppress, exploit, and rape by virtue of their power, cannot find in this power the strength to liberate either the oppressed or themselves. Only power that springs from the weakness of the oppressed will be sufficiently strong to free both...In order to have continued opportunity to express their 'generosity', the oppressors must perpetuate injustice as well. *An unjust social order is the permanent fount of this 'generosity', which is nourished by death, despair and poverty. That is why the dispensers become desperate at the slightest threat to the source of that false generosity.*

(Freire, 1972:21, emphasis added)

Ideally, therefore, the subjects of Southside should come to the self-consciousness that it takes to challenge the syndrome of 'false generosity' as Freire names it. This is a process that can only be facilitated and not imposed; the onus is on those who experience subordination to make their own efforts to shake off the timeworn shackles of domination. Unfortunately, the daily survival routine of the poor pre-disposes them to marking time below the poverty line by default. As Bob Marley sings in *Redemption Song*, 'emancipate yourselves from mental slavery, none but ourselves can free our minds,' a view resoundingly echoed in Lucien Jones' *Options for Renewal*.

The minds of those who are lacking in self-worth and self-esteem as a result of the historical process, their status in the society and the dehumanising conditions in which they live must be transformed. Until this happens, they will be captives of doubt, and hopelessness, unable to fulfil their true potential and unleash their creative energies for the benefit of themselves and their country.

(Jones, 1995: 40)

Current governmental thrusts to realise the ideal of urban renewal provide beacons of hope that finally, sustainable development for inner-city residents is being pursued via a comprehensive inner-city housing project, even if it is only to foster commercial development in the downtown Kingston business district. I was the social development manager of this project when it started, and although it continued for a decade, it did so without the fundamental change to the scripts of racialisation, sexism, classism and their intersectionalities addressed in this project. This unprecedented attempt to combine technical and social development into a model of sustainability has not been repeated and strikes the naysayers as according to many benefits to the under-served citizens who are not seen as deserving of these basic necessities. This mindset is what desperately needs to be adjusted – in leaders and the general populace alike. Paradoxically however, the greatest challenge to the success of this project are the psychosocial obstacles that have long prevented the urban poor in Jamaica from developing the political consciousness to act as a class, and within gender categories, to struggle for the realisation of their sociopolitical freedom.

In the final analysis, therefore, sustainable social change below Jamaica's poverty line requires a triple-barrelled approach. Firstly, ideological hegemonies, like the prevailing *discourse of violence*, which undermine the emancipation potential of the disadvantaged, need to be eradicated. And since bodies and minds have been the terrain for the application of hegemonic power mechanisms, these power-drenched territories need to be reclaimed and nurtured in the sexual and social healing processes that I recommend. Secondly, social transformation can be realised by combining multimedia *cultural communications* techniques, which promote collective consciousness and community action, along with the redistribution of power – economic and otherwise – by people who are in administrative control of the state and its apparatuses. The urgent need for a shift in gender power dynamics also requires rigorous critical reflections on the popular cultural discourses like Reggae/Dancehall music, which shape the body politic. Thirdly, I encourage the flourishing of the *creation principle*, as an alternative perspective to the prevailing *discourse of violence* in the inner city. My symbolic and practical suggestions for *Peace and Love* politics advocates the use of strategic essentialism to show that lessons for cessation of strife in Southside – world peace even – can be learnt from the embodied *discourses of resistance* that I examined.

To elaborate further, under the prevailing circumstances, the need for liberation in all forms becomes quite acute and the imperative for education that is designed to reverse the systematic process of mental slavery that has been the bane of the existence of the African majority, becomes even more urgent. This is the point where *cultural communications* disseminated by multimedia methods could prove very effective as a means of empowering inner-city citizens, by educating and equipping them with the critical knowledge necessary for them to cease marking time below the poverty line; and by empowering them to regain the *political will* they need to unify and mobilise themselves economically and otherwise. It started happening once before, spontaneously, in Kingston during the Peace Truce in 1978, and it could happen again now, but only if the right social circumstances can be cultivated.

If this crisis in the psychosocial constitution of the subjects under consideration is not tackled, then we will continue to pose the futile and rhetorical question of whether the desired nihilistic end (emancipation) justifies the means (violence). If violence is the means by which the oppressed seek to assert their power, does the ethical question become subverted to the overarching necessity to escape, by whatever means necessary from the combined yoke of the 'death, despair and poverty', which resounds in the citation from Freire above? Such questions could provide the entry point for a self-conscious praxis, but only when the oppressed themselves analyse the political interests that are served by this method of expressing gender power and partisan political ambition.

Accordingly, until these individual voices unite into a collective chorus of *Redemption Songs*, the orchestra of domination will continue to play the downpressive tunes of their everyday identity and survival dances. Ultimately, both micro- and macro-level changes are urgently required, virtually simultaneously, to undermine the prevailing prejudices that perpetuate the ongoing marginalised positioning of people based on their embodied identities. The fact that these balkanising classifications of personhood are part and parcel of the discourse of bourgeois democracy makes the prospect of resolving the prevailing power paradoxes a thorny thicket in which the poor are firmly embedded.

In the meantime, further efforts to improve the ethical consciousness and conscientisation of the community have to be encouraged in order to strengthen the subordinated subjects themselves to work towards achieving this goal. This project and book, **Blood, Bullets and Bodies**, is therefore a practical contribution to the cacophony of dissent which challenges entrenched structures and discourses of power. As a unique literary project, **Blood, Bullets and Bodies** clearly serves as a major indictment of old-guard Jamaican politicians and social elitists. It also serves as a direct indictment of the imperialist/neo-colonialist minded boardroom policy-makers in the political and financial capital cities of North America and Europe.

Undoubtedly, the ideas and concepts presented in this book may be hard pills to swallow, but swallow and digest we must. The data presented supports my view that sustainable social change below the poverty line in Jamaica is only attainable by utilising *multimedia cultural communications* techniques to promote collective community action, combined with the restitution and redistribution of power – economic and otherwise – by people who are in administrative control of the state and its apparatuses. Until that happens and we stop marking time below the poverty line by not taking appropriate action, the present political economy of violence, power, gender and sexual embodiment within Jamaica's inner city, will remain rigidly in place, no doubt leading to even more blood, bullets and bodies for those unfortunately trapped by circumstances in the urban wilderness.

Further Research

Blood, Bullets and Bodies has highlighted the fact that Jamaica has become the Caribbean's major transshipment locale in the middle of a new criminal triangular trade involving the movement of drugs, guns, money and illegal migrants between South America (Colombia, Brazil and Guyana), North America (the US and Canada), and Europe (England) in particular. The book has documented in detail how the increasing intercontinental transshipment of poverty-inducing products like guns and drugs through Jamaica, has only increased the matrix of violence which is currently exploding on the inner-city streets of Kingston. As a result, gun violence is now virtually out of the control of the Jamaican security forces, who are themselves responsible for the highest police homicide rate per capita in the world.

Nevertheless, as comprehensive as this project has been, there are numerous areas that I could not possibly have addressed even if the space and time had allowed. This begs the question of whether further research needs to be done in order to produce more insights into what is certainly the most pressing development problem in Jamaica today. Clearly, the answer is a big, resounding, 'Yes!'

The relationship that exists between poverty and crime in Jamaica's inner city has been established (Moser and Holland, 1996; Levy, 1996), but other nuances of this relationship need to be explored. For example, a detailed analysis of the impact of poverty and violence on children, and on their capacity to maximise their academic and social potential under such conditions, needs to be tackled as an urgent development issue.

Secondly, although I made an attempt to address the psychosocial dimensions of the trauma of living with the combined factors of social exclusion, poverty, violence and emotional loss, my exploration was tailored to the limitations of the thesis behind my account of this strange story. A more comprehensive study should address the intellectual/emotional impact on the individual of these combined distressing factors, as well as strive to suggest mechanisms for institutionalising the rehabilitative mechanisms, which, in my view, are also crucial components of the strategies of community rehabilitation that I cited above.

The increasing incidence of hard drug trading, and the abuse of crack cocaine in poor communities in particular, act as additional intervening variables which compound the already complex situation that I have studied. Further research needs to be done on the extent to which inner-city youth are using this avenue as a means of making money as well as of escaping from the harsh realities of everyday life. In this situation of double jeopardy, it is also important to research the possibilities for developing treatment facilities, which address the causal factors that propel unemployed youth into drug trading, use and abuse, as well as the mechanisms by which the demand factors can be reduced. In 1993, I participated in an island-wide study of this problem, which was initiated by the National Council on Drug Abuse, but which was prematurely aborted due to lack of funds. A revival of this initiative is obviously long overdue, and is urgently needed in the entire circuit of the inner city.

Finally, in the interest of promoting the well-being of residents in communities like Southside, a number of studies have been done (see Stanigar, 1996; and Chen-Young, unpublished), which identify the need for a housing policy that encourages the residents to own the spaces where they live. This proposal has been advanced in order to develop a systematic approach to improving the deplorable physical conditions under which people have been living. To date, however, the powers-that-be in government and private sector circles, have prevaricated instead of adopting this blueprint as a development priority.

Despite the urgent need for rehabilitation projects like the ICHP, business leaders – with the exception of pioneers like Dr. Henley Morgan who boldly relocated to Trench Town in particular – have not responded positively to repeated efforts of successive governments to persuade them to provide sustainable investment for the waterfront capital. Corporate giant Digicel broke the spell of minimal construction activity by building its headquarters on the Kingston waterfront, but too many abandoned buildings still yawn in frustration at the palpable fear to put down new buildings with the real threat that immediate or even medium-term returns may be slow materialise.. As a result, the waterfront capital, which boasts one of the best natural harbours in the world becomes a virtual ghost town by night and is haunted during the day by the constantly lurking shadows of fearsome illicit activities. This threat is a legitimate one but grounded in the constant factor of unassuaged needs and wants.

In the final analysis, it is clear that any hope of success in solving the triple problems of poverty, crime/drugs and violence on the island and of bringing peace to *Jamaica land we love*, depends on enlightened leadership; enlightened leadership with a practical and well thought out plan (i.e. *options for development*); enlightened leadership with the long term commitment, the budget, the infrastructure and the popular community support to implement that plan. The usual political 'lip service' will not do. The dire situation demands that we all work to ensure that words promising that 'better must come' are transformed into practical deeds that meet the most urgent needs of the society.

Without a doubt therefore, the ultimate research project that is mandatory at this time in this tragic scenario, is an even more critical examination of and multimedia exposé about the factors that are subverting the *political will* of Jamaica's political and community leaders from acting in the best interest of the poor, even when explicit just cause exists for such altruistic action to take place urgently. Such an exposé is the only way to end the ongoing partisan patronage and sexual intrigue that permeate the politics of the poor and to kick-start desperately needed improvement programmes. Until that happens, the hard facts of this strange story will continue in play and the flood of blood, bullets and bodies that is overwhelming the streets of Jamaica's inner cities, will no doubt continue to rise rampantly on both sides of the poverty line.

EPILOGUE

As a practising politician, my initial reaction to *Blood, Bullets and Bodies* is as a painful critique, in fact an indictment, of our contemporary politics. We have at best failed to effectively address, and perhaps are even responsible for, the degeneration of our community life and gender relations.

But on further reflection, perhaps Imani's book may signal an inflection point in the course of our development. A great achievement for a society can be its recognition of its own dysfunction, if it also signals the beginning of the healing and the recovery from that sickness.

It is my sincere hope that *Blood, Bullets And Bodies* is a step towards that recovery.

Peter Bunting
Financial Expert, Member of Parliament &
Former General Secretary, People's National Party,
Jamaica, August 2008

BIBLIOGRAPHY

Aalten, A. (1997), 'Performing the Body, Creating Culture' in K. Davis (ed.), *Embodied Practices: Feminist Perspectives on the Body*, Sage Publications Ltd., London, California and New Delhi, pp. 41-58.

Agnew, V. (1996), *Resisting Discrimination: Women from Asia, Africa and The Caribbean and The Women's Movement in Canada*, University of Toronto Press, Toronto, Buffalo and London.

Ahmed, S. (2000), *Strange Encounters: Embodied Others in Post-Coloniality*, Routledge, London and New York.

Alcock, P. (1997), *Understanding Poverty (Second Edition)*, Campling (ed.), Macmillan, London and Companies and representatives throughout the world.

Alcoff, L. (1997), 'Cultural Feminism versus Post-Structuralism: The Identity Crisis in Feminist Theory,' in L. Nicholson (ed.), *The Second Wave: A Reader in Feminist Theory*, Routledge, London and New York, pp. 330-355.

Alcoff, L. and Potter E. (1993) *Feminist Epistemologies*, Routledge, New York and London.

Alessandrini, A.C. (1999), 'Introduction: Fanon Studies, Cultural Studies, Cultural Politics', in A.C. Alessandrini (ed.), *Frantz Fanon: Critical Perspectives*, Routledge, London and New York, pp. 1-17.

Allen, C.F. (1998), 'Caribbean Bodies: Representation and Practice,' in C. Barrow, (ed.), *Caribbean Portraits: Essays on Gender Ideologies and Identities*, Ian Randle Publishers, Kingston, in association with the Centre for Gender and Development Studies, University of the West Indies, Mona, pp. 276-293.

Alleyne, M. (1988), *Roots of Jamaican Culture*, Pluto Press, London.

Alonso, A. M. (1992), 'Gender, Power, and Historical Memory: Discourses of Serrano Resistance,' in J. Butler and J.W. Scott (eds.), *Feminists Theorise the Political*, Routledge, New York and London, pp. 404-425.

Anderson, P. and Witter, M. (1994), 'Crisis, Adjustment and Social Change: A Case Study of Jamaica,' in E. LeFranc (ed.), *Consequences of Structural Adjustment: A Review of the Jamaican Experience*, Consortium Graduate School of the Social Sciences, Kingston, pp. 1-55.

Anthias, F. and Yuval-Davis, N. (1992), *Racialised Boundaries: Race, Nation, Gender, Colour and Class in the Anti-Racist Struggle*, Routledge, London and New York.

Asante, M.K. (1988), *Afrocentricity*, Africa World Press, Inc., Trenton.

Barrow, C. (1996) *Family in the Caribbean: Themes and Perspectives*, Ian Randle Publishers, Kingston and James Currey, Publishers, Oxford.

Barrett, M. (1990), 'Feminism's Turn to Culture' in *Woman: A Cultural Review*, pp. 22-24.

Barrett, M. (1991), *The Politics of Truth: From Marx to Foucault*, Stanford University Press, Stanford.

_____ (1999), *Imagination in Theory: Essays on Writing and Culture*, Polity Press, Cambridge and Oxford.

Bartkowski, F. (1988), 'Epistemic Drift in Foucault,' in I. Drummond and L. Quinby (eds.), *Feminism and Foucault: Reflections on Resistance*, Northeastern University Press, Boston, pp. 43-60.

Bartky, S.L. (1988), 'Foucault, Femininity and the Modernisation of Patriarchal Power,' in I. Drummond and L. Quinby (eds.), *Feminism and Foucault: Reflections on Resistance*, Northeastern University Press, Boston, pp. 61-86.

Beauregard, R.A. (1995), 'If Only the City Could Speak: The Politics of Representation,' in H. Liggett and D.C. Perry (eds.), *Spatial Practices*, Sage Publications, Thousand Oaks, London and New Delhi, pp. 59-80.

Beckford, G. and Girvan, N. (1989), *Development in Suspense: Selected Papers and Proceedings of The First Conference of Caribbean Economists*, Friedrich Ebert Stiftung (FES) in collaboration with the Association of Caribbean Economists (ACE), Jamaica.

Beckford, G.L. (1972), *Persistent Poverty: Underdevelopment in Plantation Economies of the Third World*, Oxford University Press, New York, London, Toronto.

Beckford, G. & Witter M. (1991), *Small Garden...Bitter Weed: Struggle and Change in Jamaica*, Institute of Social and Economic Research, Kingston.

Beckles, H.McD. (1998), 'Historicising Slavery in West Indian Feminisms,' in P. Mohammed (ed.), *Rethinking Caribbean Difference: Feminist Review*, Number 59, Summer, pp. 34-56.

_____ (1998), 'Centring Woman: The Political Economy of Gender in West African and Caribbean Slavery,' in *Caribbean Portraits: Essays on Gender Ideologies and Identities*, Ian Randle Publishers, Kingston, in association with The Centre for Gender and Development Studies, University of the West Indies, Mona, pp. 93-114.

Benhabib, S. (1995), 'Subjectivity, Historiography and Politics: Reflections on the Feminism/ Postmodernism Exchange', in *Feminist Contentions: A Philosophical Exchange*, Routledge, London and New York, pp. 107-126.

Bennett, L. (1966), *Jamaica Labrish*, Sangster's Book Stores, Jamaica.

Berezin, M. (1994), 'Fissured Terrain: Methodological Approaches and Research Styles in Culture and Politics,' in D. Crane (ed.), *The Sociology of Culture: Emerging Theoretical Perspectives*, Blackwell Publishers, Massachusetts and Oxford (U.K.), pp. 91-116.

Birke, L. (1986), *Women, Feminism and Biology: The Feminist Challenge*, Wheatsheaf Books Ltd., Brighton.

Black, M. (1996), *Children First: The Story of UNICEF, Past and Present*, Oxford University Press, New York.

Blackwood. E., and Wieringa, S. (1999), 'Sapphic Shadows: Challenging the Silence in the Study of Sexuality', in *Female Desires: Same Sex Relations and Transgender Practices Across Cultures*, Columbia University Press, New York, Chichester, West Sussex, 9, pp. 39-66.

Blanc, C.S. (1994), 'Introduction,' in C.S. Blanc et al, *Urban Children in Distress: Global Predicaments and Innovative Strategies*, United Nations Children's Fund, Yverdon, Victoria, Paris, Berlin, Reading, Tokyo, Amsterdam, Pennsylvania, pp. 1-53.

Blok, A. (2000), 'The Enigma of Senseless Violence,' in G. Ajimer and J. Abink (eds.), *Meanings of Violence: A Cross-Cultural Perspective*, Berg, Oxford and New York, pp. 23-38.

Bordo, S. (1999), *The Male Body: A New Look at Men in Public and Private*, Farrar, Straus and Giroux, New York.

_____ (1993), 'Feminism, Foucault and the politics of the body,' in C. Ramazanoglu ed.) *Up Against Foucault: Explorations of some tensions between Foucault and Feminism*, Routledge, London and New York, pp. 179-202.

Bourdieu, P. (1989), 'Social Space and Symbolic Power,' *Sociological Theory*, Vol. 7, pp.14-25.

Boyden, J. (1994), 'Children's Experience of Conflict Related Emergencies: Some Implications for Relief Policy and Practice', *Disasters: The Journal of Disaster Studies and Management*, Vol.18, No. 3, September, pp. 254-267.

Boyne, R. (1990), *Foucault and Derrida: The Other Side of Reason*, Unwin Hyman Ltd., London, Boston, Sydney, Wellington.

Bradley, H. (1996), *Fractured Identities: Changing Patterns of Inequality*, Polity Press, Cambridge (U.K.), Cambridge, (USA), Oxford.

Braidotti, R. (1994), *Nomadic Subjects: Embodiment and Sexual Difference in Contemporary Feminist Theory*, Columbia University Press, New York.

_____ (1991), *Patterns of Dissonance: A Study of Women in Contemporary Philosophy*, Polity Press, in association with Basil Blackwell, Cambridge and Oxford.

_____ (1994) 'Toward a New Nomadism: Feminist Deleuzian Tracks; or, Metaphysics and Metabolism,' in C.V. Boundas and D. P. Olkowski (eds.), *Gilles Deleuze and the Theatre of Philosophy*, Routledge, New York and London, pp. 157-186.

Brathwaite, E. (1974), *Contradictory Omens: Cultural Diversity and Integration in the Caribbean*, Savacou Publications, Mona.

Brodber, E. (1989), Socio-Cultural Change in Jamaica,' in R. Nettleford (ed.), *Jamaica in Independence: Essays on the Early Years*, Heinemann Caribbean, Kingston and James Currey, London, pp.55-74.

Brooks, A. (1997), *Postfeminisms: Feminism, Cultural Theory and Cultural Forms*, Routledge, London and New York.

Brown, G.A. (1989), *Patterns of Development and Attendant Choices and Consequences for Jamaica and the Caribbean*, Grace Kennedy Foundation Lecture, Grace Kennedy Foundation, Kingston.

Brownmiller, S. (1976), *Against Our Will: Men, Women and Rape*, Penguin Books.

Bulbeck, C. (1988), *One World Women's Movement*, Pluto Press, London.

Burton, R.D.E. (1997), *Afro-Creole: Power, Opposition and Play in the Caribbean*, Cornell University Press, Ithaca and London.

Bush, B. (1990), *Slave Women in Caribbean Society 1650-1838*, Heinemann Publishers (Caribbean), Kingston; Indiana University Press, Bloomington and Indianapolis; James Curry, London.

Butler, J. (1990), *Gender Trouble: Feminism and the Subversion of Identity*, Routledge, New York and London.

Butler, J. (1995), 'Contingent Foundations,' in *Feminist Contentions: A Philosophical Exchange*, Routledge, New York and London, pp. 35-58.

_____ (1997), 'Performative Acts and Gender Constitution: An Essay in Phenomenology and Feminist Theory,' in K. Conboy et al (eds.), *Writing on the Body: Female Embodiment and Feminist Theory*, Colombia University Press, New York, pp. 401-419.

Calderone, M.S. (1984), 'Above and Beyond Politics: The Sexual Socialisation of Children,' in C. Vance (ed.), *Pleasure and Danger: Exploring Female Sexuality*, Routledge and Kegan Paul, Boston, London, Melbourne and Henley, pp.131-137.

Campbell, H. (1985), *Rasta and Resistance: From Marcus Garvey to Walter Rodney*, Hansib Publication Limited, London.

Caplan, P. (1987), 'Introduction,' in P. Caplan (ed.), *The Cultural Construction of Sexuality*, Tavistock Publications, London and New York, pp.1-30.

Carmichael, S. and Thelwell, E.M., (2005), *Ready for Revolution: The Life and Struggles of Stokely Carmichael (Kwame Ture)*, Scribner Books, New York, London, Toronto, Sydney, Singapore.

Cassell, P. (ed.), (1993), *The Giddens Reader*, Macmillan, Hampshire and London.

Castells, M. (1977), *The Urban Question: A Marxist Approach*, Edward Arnold, London.

_____ (1978), *City, Class and Power*, The Macmillan Press Ltd., London and Basingstoke, Delhi, Dublin, Hong Kong, Johannesburg, Lagos, Melbourne, New York, Singapore and Tokyo.

_____ (1983), *The City and the Grassroots: A Cross-Cultural Theory of Urban Social Movements*, Edward Arnold, London and Australia.

_____ (1997), *The Power of Identity*, Blackwell Publishers, Massachusetts and Oxford.

Caverno, A. (1992), 'Equality and Sexual Difference: Amnesia in Political Thought,' in G. Bock and S. James (eds.), *Beyond Equality and Difference: Citizenship, Feminist Politics and Female Subjectivity*, Routledge, London and New York, pp. 32-47.

Chamberlain, M. (1995), 'Gender and Memory: Oral History and Women's History,' in V. Shepherd et al, (eds.), *Engendering History: Caribbean Women in Historical Perspective*, Ian Randle Publishers, Kingston; James Currey, London, pp. 94-110.

Chambers, I. (1996), 'Signs of Silence, Signs of Listening,' in I. Chambers and L. Curti (eds.), *The Post-Colonial Question: Common Skies, Divided Horizons*, London and New York, 116, pp. 47-64.

Chambers, R. (1998), 'Foreword,' in J. Holland and J. Blackburn (eds.), *Whose Voice: Participatory Research and Policy Change*, Intermediate Technology Publications, London.

Chant, S. (1997), 'Single-parent Families: Choice or Constraint? The Formation of Female-headed Households in Mexican Shanty Towns,' in L. Duggan, L. Nisonoff and N. Wiegersma (eds.), *The Women, Gender and Development Reader*, Zed Books, (London and New Jersey), University Press Ltd. (Dhaka), White Lotus Co. Ltd. (Bangkok), Fernwood Publishing Ltd. (Halifax, Nova Scotia), and David Philip (Cape Town), pp. 155-161.

Charles, N. (1996), 'Feminist Practices: Identity, Difference, Power,' in N. Charles and F. Hughes-Freeland, *Practising Feminism: Identity, Difference, Power*, Routledge, London and New York, pp. 1-37.

Chen-Young, P. and Associates (1996), *KRC Strategic Community Development Programme, Final Document*, July, unpublished.

Chevannes, B. (1998), 'Rastafari and the Exorcism of the Ideology of Racism and Classism in Jamaica,' in N.S. Murrell et al (eds.), *Chanting Down Babylon*, Temple University Press, Philadelphia, pp. 55-71.

_____ (1999), *What we Sow and What we Reap: Problems in the Cultivation of Male Identity in Jamaica*, The Grace Kennedy Foundation, Kingston.

_____ (1990), 'Rastafari and the Exorcism of the Ideology of Racism and Classism in Jamaica,' *Caribbean Quarterly*, University of the West Indies, Kingston, pp. 59-82.

Chow, E.N. (1996), 'Introduction: Transforming Knowledge Race, Class and Gender,' in E. Ngan-Ling Chow et al (eds.), *Race, Class and Gender: Common Bonds, Different Voices*, Sage Publications, London and New Delhi, pp. xiv-xxvi.

Chow, R. (1992), 'Postmodern Automatons,' in J. Butler and J.W. Scott (eds.), *Feminists Theorise the Political*, Routledge, New York and London, pp. 101-117.

_____ (1999), 'The Politics of Admittance: Female Sexual Agency, Miscegenation, and the Formation of Community in Frantz Fanon,' in A.C. Alessandrini (ed.), *Frantz Fanon: Critical Perspectives*, Routledge, London and New York, pp. 34-56.

Christian, B. (1985), *Black Feminist Criticism: Perspectives on Black Women Writers*, Pergamon Press, New York, Oxford, Toronto, Sydney, Paris and Frankfurt.

Clarke, C.J. (1975), *Kingston, Jamaica: Urban Development and Social Change, 1692-1962*, University of California Press, Berkeley, Los Angeles and London.

Collins, P.H. (1990), *Black Feminist Thought: Knowledge, Consciousness and the Politics of Empowerment, Perspectives on Gender, Volume 2*, Harper-Collins Academic, London.

Collins, P.H. (1993), 'The Sexual Politics of Black Womanhood' in P.B. Bart and E.G. Moran (eds.), *Violence Against Women: The Bloody Footprints*, Sage Publications, Newbury Park, London, New Delhi, pp. 85-104.

_____ (1994), 'Shifting the Centre: Race, Class and Feminist Theorising about Motherhood,' in E.N. Glenn et al (eds.), *Mothering: Ideology, Experience and Agency*, Routledge, New York, London, pp. 45-66.

_____ (1997), 'Defining Black Feminist Thought,' in L. Nicholson, (ed.) *The Second Wave: A Reader in Feminist Theory*, Routledge, New York and London, pp. 241-259.

_____ (1998), 'The Social Construction of Black Feminist Thought,' in K.A. Myers et al (eds.), *Feminist Foundations: Towards Transforming Sociology*, Sage Publications, Thousand Oaks, London, New Delhi, pp. 371-396.

Connell, R.W. (1987), *Gender and Power*, Polity Press, Cambridge and Oxford.

_____ (1994), 'Gender Regimes and the Gender Order,' in *The Polity Reader in Gender Studies*, Polity Press, Cambridge and Oxford, pp. 29-40.

_____ (1995), *Masculinities*, Polity Press, Cambridge and Oxford.

Connolly, W.F. (1984), 'The Politics of Discourse' in M. Shapiro (ed.), *Language and Politics*, Basil Blackwell, pp. 139-167.

Conway, J.K. (1987), 'Politics, Pedagogy, and Gender,' in J.K. Conway et al (eds.), *Learning About Women: Gender, Politics and Power*, The University of Michigan Press, Ann Arbor, pp. 137-152.

Conway, J.K., S.C. Bourque and J.W. Scott, (1987), 'Introduction,' in J.K. Conway et al (eds.), *Learning About Women: Gender, Politics and Power*, The University of Michigan Press, Ann Arbor, pp. XXI-XXIX.

Cooper, C. (1993), *Noises in the Blood: Orality, Gender and the 'Vulgar' Body of Jamaican Popular Culture*, Macmillan Education Ltd, London and Basingstoke.

Cornell, D. L. (1992), 'Gender, Sex and Equivalent Rights,' in J. Butler and J.W. Scott (eds.), *Feminists Theorise the Political*, Routledge, New York and London, pp. 280-296.

Coward, R. (1983), *Patriarchal Precedents: Sexuality and Social Relations*, Routledge and Kegan Paul, London, Boston, Melbourne and Henley.

Cox, A., Furlong, P. and Page, E. (1985), *Power in Capitalist Societies: Theory, Explanations and Cases*, St. Martin's Press, New York.

Cox, R.W. (1993), 'Gramsci, Hegemony and International Relations: An Essay in Method,' in S. Gill, (ed.), *Gramsci, Historical Materialism and International Relations*, Cambridge University Press, pp. 49-66.

Crane, D. (1994), 'Introduction: The Challenge of the Sociology of Culture to Sociology as a Discipline,' in D. Crane (ed.), *The Sociology of Culture: Emerging Theoretical Perspectives*, Blackwell Publishers, Massachusetts and Oxford (U.K.), pp. 1-20.

Crompton, R. (1998), *Class and Stratification: An Introduction to Current Debates*, Polity Press, Cambridge, Oxford and Malden.

Davies, C.B. (1994), *Black Women, Writing and Identity: Migrations of the Subject*, Routledge, London and New York.

Davies, M.L. (1990), *Childhood Sexual Abuse and the Construction of Identity: Healing Sylvia*, Taylor and Francis, London and Bristol.

Davis, A. (1982), *Women, Race and Class*, The Women's Press, London.

Davis, K. (1991), 'Critical Sociology and Gender Relations' in Davis, K. et al (eds.), *The Gender of Power*, Sage Publications Ltd., London, California and New Delhi, pp.65-86.

_____ (1997), 'My Body is My Art: Cosmetic Surgery as Feminist Utopia?' *The European Journal of Women's Studies*, Vol. 4, No. 1, pp. 23-38.

_____ (1997), 'Embodying Theory: Beyond Modernist and Postmodernist Readings of the Body,' in K. Davis (ed.), *Embodied Practices: Feminist Perspectives on the Body,* Sage Publications Ltd. London, California and New Delhi, pp. 1-26.

Davis, K. and Fisher, S. (1993), 'Power and the Female Subject,' in S. Fisher and K. Davis (eds.), *Negotiating at the Margins: The Gendered Discourses of Power and Resistance*, Rutgers University Press, New Brunswick, New Jersey, pp. 3-22.

Davis, S. and Simon, P. (1992), *Reggae Bloodlines: In Search of the Music and Culture of Jamaica*, Da Capo Press, New York.

De Haan, A. (1998), 'Poverty and Social Exclusion in North and South,' *IDS Bulletin*, Vol. 29, No. 1, pp. 1-9.

_____ (1998), 'Social Exclusion': An Alternative Concept for the Study of Deprivation?' *IDS Bulletin*, Vol. 29, No. 1, pp. 10-19.

Dean, J. (1996), *Solidarity of Strangers: Feminism after Identity Politics*, University of California Press, Berkley, Los Angeles, London.

Deere, C.D., Safa, H. and Antrobus, P. (1997), 'Impact of the Economic Crisis on Poor Women and their Households,' in, L. Duggan, L. Nisonoff and N. Wiegersma (eds.), *The Women, Gender and Development Reader* Zed Books, (London and New Jersey), University Press Ltd. (Dhaka), White Lotus Co. Ltd. (Bangkok), Fernwood Publishing Ltd. (Halifax, Nova Scotia), and David Philip (Cape Town), pp. 267-276.

Delaney, J., Lupton, M.J., and Toth, E. (1988), *The Curse: A Cultural History of Menstruation*, University of Illinois Press, Urbana and Chicago.

Delsing, R. (1991), 'Sovereign and Disciplinary Power: a Foucauldian Analysis of the Chilean Women's Movement' in K. Davis et al (eds.), *The Gender of Power*, Sage Publications, London, Newbury Park, New Delhi, pp. 129-153.

Diamond, I. and Quinby, L. (1988), 'American Feminism and the Language of Control,' in I. Diamond and L. Quinby (eds.), *Feminism and Foucault: Reflections on Resistance*, Northern University Press, Boston, pp. 193-206.

Dietz, M.G. (1987), 'Context is All: Feminism and Theories of Citizenship,' in J.K. Conway et al (eds.), *Learning About Women: Gender, Politics and Power*, The University of Michigan Press, Ann Arbor, pp. 1-24.

Dogan, M. and Pahre, R. (1990), *Creative Marginality: Innovation at the Intersections of Social Sciences*, Westview Press, Boulder, San Francisco and Oxford.

Dogopol, U. (1998), 'Rape as a War Crime: Mythology and History,' in I.L. Sajor (ed.), *Violence Against Women in War and Armed Conflict Situations*, Asian Centre for Women's Human Rights (ASCENT), Quezon City, pp. 122-147.

Eade, D. (1997), *Capacity Building: An Approach to People Centred Development*, Oxfam, U.K. and Ireland.

Edie, C.J. (1991), *Democracy by Default: Dependency and Clientilism in Jamaica*, Lynne Rienner Publishers, Boulder and London, Ian Randle Publishers, Kingston.

Elgersman. M. G. (1999), *Unyielding Spirits: Black Women and Slavery in Early Canada and Jamaica*, Garland Publishing Inc., New York and London.

Ennew, J. (1994), 'Defining the Girl Child: Sexuality, Control and Development,' *Vena Journal*, Vol. 6, No. 2, pp. 51-56.

Estes, C.P. (1992), *Women Who Run with the Wolves: Contacting the Power of the Wild Woman*, Rider, London, Sydney, Auckland, Johannesburg.

Evans, D.T. (1993), *Sexual Citizenship: The Material Construction of Sexualities*, Routledge, London and New York.

Evans, M. (1997), *Introducing Contemporary Feminist Thought*, Polity Press, Cambridge, Oxford and Malden.

Fanon, F. (1963), *The Wretched of the Earth*, Grove Press Inc., New York.

_____ (1967), *Black Skins White Masks*, Grove Press Inc., New York.

_____ (1992), 'The Fact of Blackness' in Donald and A. Rattansi (eds.), *Race, Culture and Difference*, Sage Publications in association with the Open University, pp.220-242.

Finzi, S. V. (1992), 'Female Identity Between Sexuality and Maternity,' in G. Bock and S. James (eds.), *Beyond Equality and Difference: Citizenship, Feminist Politics and Female Subjectivity*, Routledge, London and New York, pp. 126-145.

Fisher, S. and Davis, K. (1993), 'Power and the Female Subject,' in Fisher, S. and Davis, R. (eds.), *Negotiating at the Margins: The Gendered Discourses of Power and Resistance*, Rutgers University Press, New Brunswick, New Jersey, pp.3-20.

Fiske, J. (1993), *Power Plays Power Works*, Verso, London and New York.

Fonseka, L. and Malhotra, D.D. (1994) 'India: Urban Poverty, Children and Participation,' in C.S. Blanc et al, *Urban Children in Distress: Global Predicaments and Innovative Strategies*, United Nations Children's Fund, Yverdon, Victoria, Paris, Berlin, Reading, Tokyo, Amsterdam, Pennsylvania, pp. 161-216.

Ford-Smith, H. (1986), in *The Potential of the Arts in Caribbean Education: Alternatives in Education IV, Final Report; Workshop on Cultural Relevance in Curriculum Development*, Kingston, Jamaica, 19-23 May, Cultural Training Centre, pp. 120-123.

Ford-Smith, H. (1986), (ed), *Lionheart Gal: Life Stories of Jamaican Women*, Sistren with Ford-Smith, The Women's Press Ltd., London.

_____ (1995), 'An Experiment in Popular Theatre,' in in Zed Books, *Subversive Women: Historical Experiences of Gender and Resistance*, London and New Jersey, pp. 147-164.

Foucault, M. (1980), *The History of Sexuality: Volume 1: An Introduction*, Vintage Books, New York.

_____ (1980), C. Gordon (ed.), *Power/Knowledge: Selected Interviews and Other Writings, 1972-977*, Pantheon Books, New York.

_____ (1984), 'The Order of Discourse,' in M. Shapiro (ed.), *Language and Politics*, Basil Blackwell, pp. 108-138.

_____ (1986), 'Disciplinary Power and Subjection' in S. LU.K.es (ed.), Power, Basil Blackwell Ltd. Oxford, pp. 229-242.

_____ (1986), 'Disciplinary Power and Subjection,' in S. Lukes, (ed.), *Power*, pp. 229-242, Basil Blackwell Ltd., Oxford.

Fraser, E. and Cameron, D. (1989), 'Knowing What to Say: The Construction of Gender in Linguistic Practice' in R. Grillo (ed.), *Social Anthropology and the Politics of Language*, Routledge, London and New York, pp.25-40.

Fraser, N. (1995), 'Politics, Culture and the Social Sphere,' in L. Nicholson and S. Siedman (eds.), *Social Post-modernism: Beyond Identity Politics*, Cambridge University Press, Cambridge, pp. 287-312.

Freire, P. (1970), *Cultural Action for Freedom*, Harvard Educational Review and Centre for the Study of Development and Social Change, Massachusetts.

_____ (1972), *Pedagogy of the Oppressed*, Penguin, London.

_____ (1985), *The Politics of Education: Culture, Power, and Liberation*, Macmillan Houndmills, Basingstoke, Hampshire and London.

French, J. et al, *No! to Sexual Violence*, Sistren Theatre Collective and Friends of Sistren (undated pamphlet).

French, J. (1995), 'Women and Colonial Policy in Jamaica after the 1938 Uprising,' in S. Wieringa (ed.), *Subversive Women: Historical Experiences of Gender and Resistance*, in Zed Books, London and New Jersey, pp.121-146.

French, J. and Ford-Smith, H. (1983-1985), *Women, Work and Organisations in Jamaica, 1900-1944, Research Project, Women and Development*, Institute of Social Studies, The Hague.

French, M. (1994), 'Power/Sex,' in H. L. Radtke and H. J. Stam (eds.), *Power/Gender: Social Relations in Theory and Practice*, Sage Publications, London, Thousand Oaks and New Delhi, pp. 15-35.

Friedman, J. (1994), *Cultural Identity and Global Process*, Sage Publications Ltd., London, California and New Delhi.

Frith, S. (1996), 'Music and Identity,' in S. Hall and P. duGay (eds.), *Questions of Cultural Identity*, Sage Publications, London, California and New Delhi, pp. 108-127.

Fuller, N. (January 2001), 'The Social Constitution of Gender: Identity Among Peruvian Men,' in, M.C. Gutmann (Guest Editor), *Special Issue: Men and Masculinities in Latin America*, Sage Publications Inc. Volume 3, Issue 3, pp. 316-331.

Fuss, D. (1989), *Essentially Speaking: Feminism, Nature and Difference*, Routledge, New York and London.

Gabriel, J. et. Al (1988), 'Empowerment Matters: Understanding Power,' in J. Gabriel et al (eds.), *Women and Power: Fighting Patriarchies and Poverty*, Zed Books, London and New York, pp. 19-45.

Galbraith, J.K. (1983), *The Anatomy of Power*, Houghton Mifflin Company, Boston.

Garvey, M. (1995), 'The Future as I See It,' in L. Hord (Mzee Lasana Okpara) and J.S. Lee (eds.), *I Am Because We Are: Readings in Black Philosophy*, University of Massachusetts Press, Amherst.

Garvey, M. (1973), 'The Race Question in Jamaica (1916)' in D. Lowenthal and L. Comitas (eds.), *Consequences of Class and Colour: West Indian Perspectives*, Anchor Books, New York, pp. 4-12.

Gearing, J. (1995), 'Fear and Loving in the West Indies: Research from the heart (as well as the head),' in D. Kulick and M. Willson, (eds.), *Taboo: Sex: Identity and Erotic Subjectivity in Fieldwork*, Routledge, London and New York, pp. 186-218.

Gibbs, S. (1994), 'Post-War Social Reconstruction in Mozambique: Reframing Children's Experience of Trauma and Healing,' *Disasters: The Journal of Disaster Studies and Management*, Vol.18, No. 3, September, pp. 268-276.

Giddings, P. (1984), *When and Where I Enter: The Impact of Black Women on Race and Sex in America*, William Morrow, New York.

Gill, S. (1993), 'Epistemology, Ontology, and the 'Italian School',' in S. Gill, (ed.), *Gramsci, Historical Materialism and International Relations*, Cambridge University Press, pp. 21-48.

Giroux, H. (1992), *Border Crossings: Cultural Workers and the Politics of Education*, Routledge, New York and London.

Girvan, N., R. Bernal and N. Hughes, (1980), 'The IMF and the Third World: The Case of Jamaica, 1974-80,' *Development Dialogue No. 2*.

Girvan, N. and Jefferson, O. (1968), 'Corporate vs. Caribbean Integration,' in N. Girvan and O. Jefferson (eds.), *Readings in the Political Economy of the Caribbean*, (from *New World Quarterly*, Vol. 4, No. 2, a Collection of Reprints of Articles on Caribbean Political Economy with Suggested Further Readings, pp. 87-108.

Girvan, N. et al, (1968), 'Unemployment in Jamaica,' in N. Girvan and O. Jefferson (eds.), *Readings in the Political Economy of the Caribbean*, from New World Group, Jamaica, Pamphlet No. 3, September, in *New World Quarterly*, Vol. 4, No. 2, pp. 267-272.

Glaser, B.G. and Strauss, A.L. (1967), *The Discovery of Grounded Theory: Strategies for Qualitative Research*, Aldine Publishing Company, New York.

The Gleaner (1999), 'Government and Politics,' (September 30).

_____ (2000), 'Colombians taking over the Drug Trade,' January 23, pp. 1 and 3A.

Gledhill, J. (1994), *Power and its Disguises: Anthropological Perspectives on Politics*, Pluto Press, London and Boulder, Colorado.

Gordon, D. (1987), *Class, Status and Social Mobility in Jamaica, Institute of Social and Economic Studies*, University of the West Indies, Mona.

_____ (1989), 'Women, Work and Social Mobility in Jamaica,' in K. Hart (ed.), *Women and the Sexual Division of Labour in the Caribbean*, Consortium Graduate School of the Social Sciences, Mona, pp. 67-80.

Graham, S. (1986), in *The Potential of the Arts in Caribbean Education: Alternatives in Education IV, Final Report; Workshop on Cultural Relevance in Curriculum Development*, Kingston, Jamaica, Cultural Training Centre, 19-23 May.

Gramsci, A. (1957), *The Modern Prince and Other Writings*, International Publishers, New York.

Gray, O. (1994), 'Discovering the Social Power of the Poor,' *Social and Economic Studies*, Volume 43, No. 3, pp. 169-189.

Green, C. (1995), 'Gender, Race and Class in the Social Economy of the English-speaking Caribbean,' *Social and Economic Studies*, Vol. 44:2&3, pp. 65-102.

Gregg, N. (1993), 'Trying to Put First Things First: Negotiating Subjectivities in a Workplace Organising Campaign' in S. Fisher and K. Davis (eds.), *Negotiating at the Margins: The Gendered Discourses of Power and Resistance*, Rutgers University Press, New Brunswick, New Jersey, pp. 172-204.

Griffith, M. (1995), *Feminisms and the Self: The Web of Identity*, Routledge, London and New York.

Griffiths, V. (1990), 'Using drama to get at gender' in L. Stanley (ed.), *Feminist Praxis: Research, Theory and Epistemology in Feminist Sociology*, Routledge, London and New York, , pp. 221-235.

Grillo. R. (1989), 'Anthropology, Language and Politics,' in R. Grillo (ed.), *Social Anthropology and the Politics of Language*, Routledge, London and New York, pp. 1-24.

Grimshaw, J. (1993), 'Practices of Freedom,' in, C. Ramazanoglu (ed.), *Up Against Foucault: Explorations of some tensions between Foucault and Feminism* Routledge, London and New York, pp. 51-72.

Grosberg, L. (1996), 'Identity and Cultural Studies: Is that all There Is?' in S. Hall and P. duGay (eds.), *Questions of Cultural Identity*, Sage Publications, London, California and New Delhi, pp. 87-107.

Grosberg, L., (1996), 'The Space of Culture, the Power of Space,' in I. Chambers and L. Curti (eds.), *The Post-Colonial Question: Common Skies, Divided Horizons*, London and New York, 116, pp. 169-188.

Gross, E. (1990), 'Contemporary Theories of Power and Subjectivity' in S. Gunew (ed.), *Feminist Knowledge: Critique and Construct*, Routledge, London and New York, pp.59-120.

_____ (1990), 'Conclusion: A Note on Essentialism and Difference,' in S. Gunew (ed.), *Feminist Knowledge: Critique and Construct*, Routledge, London and New York, pp.332-344.

_____ (1995), 'What is Feminist Theory?' in H. Crowley and S. Himmelweit (eds.), *Knowing Women: Feminism and Knowledge*, Polity Press, in association with Blackwell Publishers and the Open University, Cambridge and Oxford, pp. 355-369.

Grosz, E. (1994), 'Sexual Difference and the Problem of Essentialism' in N. Schor and E. Weed, (eds.), *The Essential Difference*, Brown University, pp.82-98.

Guillaumin, C. (1995), *Racism, Sexism, Power and Ideology*, Routledge, London and New York.

Gunst, L. (1995), *Born Fi' Dead: Journey Through the Jamaican Posse Underworld*, Henry Holt and Company, New York.

Guzzini, S. (1998), *Realism in International Relations and International Political Economy: The Continuing Story of a Death Foretold*, Routledge, London and New York.

Haden, P. et al, (1971), 'A Historical and Critical Essay for Black Women,' in Collected by Edith Hoshino Altbach, *From Feminism to Liberation*, Schenkman Publishing Co., Inc., Cambridge, Massachusetts and London, pp. 125-141.

Hall, J.R. (1999), *Cultures of Inquiry*, Cambridge University Press, Cambridge and Melbourne.

Hall, L, (1994), 'Deconstructing the Monolithic Phallus,' in *The Polity Reader in Gender Studies*, Polity Press, Cambridge and Oxford, pp. 249-254.

Hall, S. (1992), 'New Ethnicities,' in J. Donald and A. Rattansi, (eds.), *'Race', Culture and Difference*, Sage Publications in association with the Open University, pp. 252-259.

_____ (1996), 'Introduction: Who Needs 'Identity?' in S. Hall and P. duGay (eds.), *Questions of Cultural Identity*, Sage Publications, London, California and New Delhi, pp. 1-17.

Hallmark. S. (1971), 'Subcultures as a Focus of Analysis,' in A.A. Said (ed.), *Protagonists of Change: Subcultures in Development and Revolution*, Prentice-Hall, Inc., Englewood Cliffs, N.J., pp. 10-22.

Hammonds, E.M. (1997), 'When the Margin is the Centre: African American Feminism(s) and Difference,' in J.W. Scott et al (eds.), *Transitions, Environments, Translations: Feminisms in International Politics*, Routledge, New York and London, pp.295-309.

Hanif, N.Z. (1995), 'Male Violence Against Women and Men in the Caribbean: The Case of Jamaica,' *Wand Occasional Paper*, CARICOM and the International Planned Parenthood Federation.

Harding, S. (1991), *Whose Science? Whose Knowledge? Thinking from Women's Lives*, Open University Press, Milton Keynes, Buckingham.

Harker, R. et al, (eds.), (1990), *An Introduction to the Work of Pierre Bourdieu: The Practice of Theory*, Macmillan, Hampshire and London.

Harré, R. and Gillett, G. (1994), *The Discursive Mind*, Sage Publications, Inc., Thousand Oaks, London and New Delhi.

Harrigan, J. (1975), 'Political Economy and the Management of Urban Development in Brazil,' in W.A. Cornelius and Felicity M. Trueblood, (eds.), *Urbanisation and Inequality: The Political Economy of Urban and Rural Development in Latin America*, Sage Publications, California and London.

Harriott, A. (2000), *Police and Crime Control in Jamaica: Problems of Reforming Ex-Colonial Constabularies*, The University of the West Indies Press, Barbados, Jamaica, Trinidad and Tobago.

Harris, I.A. (1995), *Messages Men Hear: Constructing Masculinities*, Taylor and Francis, Bristol.

Hartsock, N. (1981), 'Fundamental Feminism: Process and Perspective,' in *Building Feminist Theory: Essays from Quest*, A Feminist Quarterly, Longman Inc., New York, pp. 32-44.

_____ (1981), 'Staying Alive,' in *Building Feminist Theory: Essays from Quest*, A Feminist Quarterly, Longman Inc., New York, pp. 111-122.

_____ (1996), 'Community/Sexuality/Gender: Rethinking Power,' in N.J. Hirschmann and C. Di Stefano (eds.), *Revisioning The Political: Feminist Reconstructions of Traditional Concepts in Western Political Theory*, Westview Press, A Division of HarperCollins Publishers, Colorado and Oxford, pp. 27-50.

_____ (1997), 'The Feminist Standpoint: Developing the Ground for a Specifically Feminist Historical Materialism,' in L. Nicholson (ed.), *The Second Wave: A Reader in Feminist Theory*, Routledge, London and New York, , pp. 216-240.

Hart, K. (1987), 'Commoditisation and the Standard of Living', in A. Sen et al, G. Hawthorn (ed.), *The Standard of Living: The Tanner Lecture Series, Clare Hall, Cambridge, 1985*, Cambridge University Press, 103-112.

Hart, R. (1997), *Children's Participation: The Theory and Practice of Involving Young Citizens in Community Development and Environmental Care*, Earthscan Publications Limited, New York.

Hearn, J. (1987), *The Gender of Oppression: Men, Masculinity, and the Critique of Marxism*, Wheatsheaf Books, Brighton.

Hebidge, D. (1987), *Cut 'N' Mix: Culture, Identity and Caribbean Music*, Methuen and Co., in association with Methuen Inc., New York.

Heckman, S.J. (1995), *Moral Voices, Moral Selves: Carol Gilligan and Feminist Moral Theory*, Polity Press, Cambridge and Oxford.

Henderson, M. G. (1992), 'Speaking in Tongues: Dialogics, Dialectics and the Black Woman Writer's Literary Tradition,' in J. Butler and J.W. Scott (eds.), *Feminists Theorise the Political*, Routledge, New York and London, pp. 144-166.

Hennessy, R. (1993), *Materialist Feminism and the Politics of Discourse*, Routledge, New York and London.

Henriques, F. (1953), *Family and Colour in Jamaica*, Eyre and Spottiswoode, London.

Hewitt, R. (1989), 'Creole in the Classroom: Political Grammars and Educational Vocabularies,' in R. Grillo (ed.), *Social Anthropology and the Politics of Language*, Routledge, London and New York, pp.126-144.

Himmelweit, S. (1987), 'Abortion: Individual Choice and Social Control' in *Sexuality: A Reader*, Feminist Review (ed.), Virago, pp. 98-104.

Hindess, B. (1996), *Discourses of Power: From Hobbes to Foucault*, Blackwell Publishers, Oxford and Cambridge, Massachusetts.

Holton, RJ. (1992), *Economy and Society*, Routledge, London and New York.

Honig, B. (1992), 'Toward an Agnostic Feminism: Hannah Arendt and the Politics of Identity,' in J. Butler and J.W. Scott, (eds), *Feminists Theorise the Political*, Routledge, New York and London, pp.215-238.

hooks, b. (1981), *Aint I a Woman: black women and feminism*, Pluto Press, London.

hooks, b. (1984), *Feminist Theory: From Margin to Center*, South End Press, England.

hooks, b, (1989), *Talking Back: Thinking Feminist, Thinking Black*, Sheba Feminist Publishers, Boston and London.

hooks, b. (1990), *Yearning: race, gender, and cultural politics*, South End Press, Boston.

hooks, b. (1994), *Teaching to Transgress: Education as the Practice of Freedom*, Routledge, New York and London.

hooks, b. (1994), *Outlaw Culture: Resisting Representations*, Routledge, New York, London. hooks,

b. (2000), *Feminism is for Everybody: Passionate Politics*, Pluto Press, London.

James, S.M. (1993), 'Mothering: A Possible Black Feminist Link to Social Transformation?' in S.M. James and A.P.A. Busia (eds.), *Theorizing Black Feminisms: The Visionary Pragmatism of Black Women*, Routledge, London and New York, pp.44-54.

Jamaica Survey of Living Conditions 1997 (1998), A Joint Publication of the Statistical Institute of Jamaica and The Planning Institute of Jamaica, Kingston, October.

Jefferson, O. (1968), 'Jamaica's Post-War Economic Development,' in N. Girvan and O. Jefferson (eds.), *Readings in the Political Economy of the Caribbean*, (from New World Group, Jamaica, Pamphlet No. 3, September, 1967) in New World Quarterly, Vol. 4, No. 2, pp.109-120.

Jones, K.B. (1988), 'On Authority or Why Women Are Not Entitled to Speak,' in I. Drummond and L. Quinby (eds.), *Feminism and Foucault: Reflections on Resistance*, Northeastern University Press, Boston, pp.119-134.

Jones, L. (1995), *The Jamaican Society: Options for Renewal*, Grace Kennedy Foundation, Kingston.

Kandiyoti, D. (1991), 'Bargaining with Patriarchy,' in J. Lorber and S. Farrell (eds.), *The Social Construction of Gender*, Sage Publications, Newbury Park, London, New Delhi, pp. 104-118.

Kandiyoti, D. (1998), 'Gender, Power and Contestation: Rethinking Bargaining with Patriarchy' in C. Jackson and R. Pearson (eds.), *Feminist Visions of Development: Gender, Analysis and Policy*, Routledge, London, pp.135-152.

Katzin, M.F. (1959), 'The Jamaican Country Higgler,' *Social and Economic Studies*, Volume 8, Number 4, December, pp. 421-435.

Kelly, L. Burton, S. and Regan, L. (1996), 'Beyond Victim or Survivor: Sexual Violence, Identity and Feminist Theory and Practice,' in *Sexualising the Social: Power and the Organisation of Sexuality*, British Sociological Association, pp. 77-101.

Kirton, C. (1992), *Jamaica: Debt and Poverty*, Oxfam.

Komter, A. (1991), 'Gender, Power and Feminist Theory,' in K. Davis et al (eds.), *The Gender of Power*, Sage Publications Ltd. , London, California and New Delhi, pp. 42-64.

Kozol, J. (1996), *Amazing Grace: The Lives of Children and the Conscience of a Nation*, Harper Perennial, A Division of HarperCollins Publishers, New York.

Kulick, D. (1995), 'The Sexual Life of Anthropologists: Erotic Subjectivity and Ethnographic Work' in D. Kulick and M. Willson, (eds.), *Taboo: Sex: Identity and Erotic Subjectivity in Fieldwork*, Routledge, London and New York, pp. 1-28.

Lacey, T. (1977), *Violence and Politics in Jamaica, 1960-70: Internal Security in a Developing Country*, Manchester University Press, Oxford.

LaForest, M.H. (1996), 'Black Cultures in Difference,' in I. Chambers and L. Curti (eds.), *The Post-Colonial Question: Common Skies, Divided Horizons*, London and New York, 116, pp.115-122.

Lal, J. (1996), 'Situating Locations: The Politics of Self, Identity and "Other" in Living and Writing the Text', in D.L. Wolf (ed.), *Feminist Dilemmas in Fieldwork*, Westview Press Inc., Boulder and Oxford, pp. 185-214.

Landy, R.J. (1995), 'The Dramatic World View: Reflections on the Roles Taken and played by Young Children' in S. Jennings (ed.), *Dramatherapy with Children and Adolescents*, Routledge, London and New York, pp. 7-27.

Lang, Beryl (1997), 'Metaphysical Racism (Or: Biological Warfare by Other Means' in N. Zack (ed.), *Race/Sex: Their Sameness, Differences and Interplay*, Routledge, New York and London, pp. 17-28.

Lawler, S. (2000), *Mothering the Self: Mothers, Daughters, Subjects*, Routledge, London and New York.

Laws, S. (1985), 'Male Power and Menstrual Etiquette,' in H. Homans (ed.), *The Sexual Politics of Reproduction*, Gower Publishing Company Limited, Aldershot and Vermont, pp. 13-29.

Layder, D. (1994), *Understanding Social Theory*, Sage Publications Ltd., London, California and New Delhi.

Leo-Rhynie, E. (1993), *The Jamaican Family: Continuity and Change*, Grace Kennedy Foundation and Institute of Jamaica Publications Limited, Kingston.

Leo-Rhynie, E. (1998), 'Socialisation and the Development of Gender Identity: Theoretical Formulations and Caribbean Research,' in C. Barrow, (ed.), *Caribbean Portraits: Essays on Gender Ideologies and Identities*, Ian Randle Publishers in association with the Centre for Gender and Development Studies, University of the West Indies, Kingston, pp. 234-254.

Leo-Rhynie, E. B. Bailey and C. Barrow (eds.), (1997), *Gender: A Caribbean Multi-Disciplinary Perspective*, Ian Randle Publishers in association with the Centre for Gender and Development Studies, University of the West Indies and The Commonwealth of Learning, Kingston and Oxford.

Lewis, O. (1967), *La Vida: A Puerto Rican Family in the Culture of Poverty – San Juan and New York*, London, Secker and Warburg.

Levy, H. (1996), *They Cry 'Respect': Urban Violence and Poverty in Jamaica*, Centre for Population, Community and Social Change, University of the West Indies, Mona, Kingston.

Lipton, M. (1976), *Why Poor People Stay Poor: A Study of Urban Bias in World Development*, Temple Smith, London.

LU.K.es, S. (1986), 'Introduction,' in S. Lukes, (ed.), *Power*, pp. 1-18, Basil Blackwell Ltd., Oxford, pp. 1-18. Lushena Books (1999), The Willie Lynch Letter and the Making of a Slave, Lynch Lushena Books, Chicago.

MacCannell, D. and MacCannel, J.F. (1993), 'Violence, Power and Pleasure: a Revisionist Reading of Foucault from the Victim Perspective,' in C. Ramazanoglu (ed.) *Up Against Foucault: Explorations of some tensions between Foucault and Feminism*, Routledge, London and New York, pp. 203-238.

MacKinnon, C. (1997), 'Sexuality,' in *The Second Wave: A Reader in Feminist Theory*, Routledge New York and London, pp. 158-180.

Maharaj, N. (1995), 'Pathology and Power: The Failure of Democracy in the Caribbean,' in J. Hipler (ed.) *The Democratisation of Disempowerment: The Problem of Democracy in the Third World*, Pluto Press with Transnational Institute, London and Amsterdam.

Mann, K. and Rosneil, S. (1999), 'Poor Choices: Gender, Agency and the Underclass Debate,' in G. Jagger and C. Wright (eds.), *Changing Family*, Routledge, London and New York, pp. 98-118.

Marcus, S. (1992), 'Fighting Bodies, Fighting Words: A Theory and Politics of Rape Prevention,' in J. Butler and J.W. Scott (eds.), *Feminists Theorise the Political*, Routledge, New York and London, pp. 385-403.

Marre, J. and Charlton, H. (1985), *Beats of the Heart: Popular Music of the World*, Pluto Press, in association with Channel Four Television Company Limited, London and New South Wales.

Martin, B. (1988), 'Feminism, Criticism and Foucault,' in I. Drummond and L. Quinby (eds.), *Feminism and Foucault: Reflections on Resistance*, Northeastern University Press, Boston, pp. 3-20.

Martin, G. (2000), 'The Tradition of Violence' in Colombia: Material and Symbolic Aspects, in G. Ajimer and J. Abink (eds.), *Meanings of Violence: A Cross-Cultural Perspective*, Berg, Oxford and New York, pp. 161-182.

Martin-Jones, M. (1989), 'Language, Power and Linguistic Minorities: The Need for an Alternative Approach to Bilingualism, Language Maintenance and Shift,' in R. Grillo (ed.), *Social Anthropology and the Politics of Language*, Routledge, London and New York, pp. 106-125

Marx, K. (1976), *Capital, Vol. 1*, trans. Ben Fowkes, Penguin, Harmondsworth.

Massiah, J. (1989), 'Women's Lives and Livelihoods: A View from the Commonwealth Caribbean,' *World Development*, Vol.17, No. 7, pp. 965-977.

Matsumoto, V. (1996), 'Reflections on Oral History: Research in a Japanese American Community' in D.L. Wolf (ed.), *Feminist Dilemmas in Fieldwork*, Westview Press Inc., Boulder and Oxford, pp. 160-169.

May, Las, (1996), 'Map of Kingston,' *The Gleaner*, (September 25).

McClintock, A. (1995), *Imperial Leather: Race, Gender and Sexuality in the Colonial Contest*, Routledge, New York and London.

McCord, J. (1997), 'Placing American Urban Violence in Context,' in J. McCord (ed.), *Violence and Childhood in the Innercity*, Cambridge University Press, Cambridge U.K., New York and Melbourne, pp. 78-115.

McGregor, S. (1981), *The Politics of Poverty*, Longman, London and New York.

McNay, L. (1992), *Foucault and Feminism: Power, Gender and the Self*, Polity Press, Cambridge.

_____ (2000), *Gender and Agency: Reconfiguring the Subject in Feminist and Social Theory*, Polity Press, Cambridge, Oxford and Malden.

McRobbie, A. (1996), 'Different, Youthful Subjectivities' in I. Chambers and L. Curti (eds.), *The Post-Colonial Question: Common Skies, Divided Horizons*, London and New York, 116, pp. 30-46.

Meeks, B. (1996), *Radical Caribbean: From Black Power to Abu Bakr*, The Press, University of the West Indies, Barbados, Jamaica, Trinidad and Tobago.

Melkonian, M. (1996), *Marxism: A Post-Cold War Primer*, Westview Press, Boulder and Oxford.

Meyers, D.T. (1994), *Subjection and Subjectivity: Psychoanalytic Feminism and Moral Philosophy*, Routledge, New York and London.

Mies, M. (1986), *Patriarchy and Accumulation on a World Scale; Women in the International Division of Labour*, Zed Books, London.

Miller, E. (1991), *Men at Risk*, Jamaica Publishing House Ltd., Kingston.

Miller, E. (1990), *Marginalisation of the Black Male: Insights from the Development of the Teaching Profession*, Canoe Press, Barbados, Jamaica and Trinidad and Tobago.

Millet, K. (1984), 'Beyond Politics? Children and Sexuality' in C. Vance (ed.), *Pleasure and Danger: Exploring Female Sexuality*, Routledge and Kegan Paul, Boston, London, Melbourne and Henley, pp. 217-231.

Milner, A. (1999), *Class*, Sage Publications, London, Thousand Oaks and New Delhi.

Mills, C.W. (1991), 'Marxism and Caribbean Development: A Contribution to Re-thinking,' in J. Wedderburn (ed.), *Rethinking Development*, Consortium Graduate School of the Social Sciences, University of the West Indies, pp. 14-53.

Mills, G.E. (1997), *Westminster Style Democracy: The Jamaican Experience*, Grace Kennedy Foundation Lecture, Kingston.

Milward, B. (2000), *Marxian Political Economy: Theory, History and Contemporary Relevance*, MacMillan Press Ltd. and St. Martins Press, Inc., Houndmills, Basingstoke, Hampshire, London and New York.

Mohammed, P. (1988), 'The Caribbean Family Revisited,' in P. Mohammed and C. Shepherd, (eds.), *Gender in Caribbean Development*, The University of The West Indies Women and Development Studies Project, Mona, Jamaica; St. Augustine, Trinidad and Tobago; Cave Hill, Barbados, pp. 170-182.

_____ (1998), 'Towards Indigenous Feminist Theorising in the Caribbean,' in P. Mohammed (ed.), *Rethinking Caribbean Difference: Feminist Review*, Number 59, Summer, pp. 6-33.

Mohanty, C.T. (1997), 'Under Western Eyes: Feminist Scholarship and Colonial Discourses,' in L. Duggan, L. Nisonoff and N. Wiegersma (eds.), *The Women, Gender and Development Reader*, Zed Books, (London and New Jersey), University Press Ltd. (Dhaka), White Lotus Co. Ltd. (Bangkok), Fernwood Publishing Ltd. (Halifax, Nova Scotia), and David Philip (Cape Town), pp. 79-85.

_____ (1995), 'Feminist Encounters: Locating the Politics of Experience,' in L. Nicholson and S. Siedman (eds.), *Social Postmodernism: Beyond Identity Politics*, Cambridge University Press, Cambridge, pp. 68-86.

Moors, A. (1991), 'Gender, Property and Power: Mahr and Marriage in a Palestinian Village, in K. Davis et al (eds.), *The Gender of Power*, Sage Publications, London, Newbury Park, New Delhi, pp. 111-128.

Morris-Brown, V. (1993), *The Jamaica Handbook of Proverbs*, Island Heart Publishers, Mandeville.

Morrissey, M. (1989), *Slave Women in the New World: Gender Stratification in the Caribbean*, University Press of Kansas, Lawrence.

_____ (1998), 'Explaining the Caribbean Family: Gender Ideologies and Gender Relations, 'in C. Barrow, (ed.), *Caribbean Portraits: Essays on Gender Ideologies and Identities*, Ian Randle Publishers Kingston in association with The Centre for Gender and Development Studies, University of the West Indies, pp. 78-90.

Morawska, E. and Spohn, W. (1994), 'Cultural Pluralism' in Historical Sociology,' in D. Crane (ed.), *The Sociology of Culture: Emerging Theoretical Perspectives*, Blackwell Publishers, Massachusetts and Oxford (U.K.), pp. 45-90.

Moser, C. and Holland, J. (1996), *Research Report on Urban Poverty and Violence in Jamaica*, World Bank.

Mouffe, C. (1992), 'Feminism, Citizenship and Radical Democratic Politics,' in J. Butler and J.W. Scott (eds.), *Feminists Theorise the Political*, Routledge, New York and London, pp. 369-384.

Muellbauer, J. (1987), 'Professor Sen on the Standard of Living,' in A. Sen et al, G. Hawthorn (ed.), *The Standard of Living: The Tanner Lecture Series, Clare Hall, Cambridge, 1985*, Cambridge University Press, pp. 39-58.

MU.K.erji, C. (1994), 'Towards a Sociology of Material Culture: Science Studies, Cultural Studies and the Meaning of Things,' in D. Crane (ed.), *The Sociology of Culture: Emerging Theoretical Perspectives*, Blackwell Publishers, Massachusetts and Oxford (U.K.), p. 143.

Munroe, T. (1983), *The Politics of Constitutional Decolonisation: Jamaica, 1944-62*, Institute of Social and Economic Research, University of the West Indies.

Mutiku, M. and Mutiso, R. (1994), 'Kenya: The Urban Threat for Women and Children,' in C.S. Blanc et al, *Urban Children in Distress: Global Predicaments and Innovative Strategies*, United Nations Children's Fund, Yverdon, Victoria, Paris, Berlin, Reading, Tokyo, Amsterdam, Pennsylvania, pp. 217-258.

Naples, N.A. (1996), 'Activist Mothering: Cross-Cultural Continuity in the Community Work of Women from Low-Income Urban Neighbourhoods,' in E. Ngan-Ling Chow et al (eds.), *Race, Class and Gender: Common Bonds, Different Voices*, Sage Publications, London and New Delhi, pp.223-245

Nash, K. (1994), 'The Feminist Production of Knowledge: Is Deconstruction a Practice for Women?' *Feminist Review*, No. 47, London, pp. 65-75.

Nettleford, R., (1973), 'National Identity and Attitudes to Race in Jamaica,' in D. Lowenthal and L. Comitas (eds.), *Consequences of Class and Colour: West Indian Perspectives*, Anchor Books, New York, pp. 35-56

_____ (1978), *Caribbean Cultural Identity: The Case of Jamaica, Centre for Afro-American Studies and UCLA Latin American Centre Publications*, University of California, Los Angeles.

Newman-Williams, M. and Sabatini, F. (1997), 'Child centred development and Social progress in the Caribbean,' in N. Girvan (ed.), *Poverty, Empowerment and Social Development in the Caribbean*, Canoe Press, University of the West Indies, Barbados, Jamaica and Trinidad and Tobago, pp. 50-78

Newton, J. (1990), 'Historicisms in New and Old: Charles Dickens meets Marxism, Feminism and West Coast Foucault', *Feminist Studies*, pp. 449-470, Vol. 16, No. 3.

Nicholson, L. (1995) 'Interpreting Gender,' in L. Nicholson and S. Siedman (eds.), *Social Postmodernism: Beyond Identity Politics*, Cambridge University Press, Cambridge, pp.39-67.

_____ (1997), 'Feminism and Marx: Integrating Kinship with the Economic,' in L. Nicholson, (ed.), *The Second Wave: A Reader in Feminist Theory*, Routledge, New York and London, pp. 131-145.

Nkululeko, D. (1987), 'The Right to Self-Determination in C. Qunta (ed.), *Research: Azanian Women,' in Women in Southern Africa*, Allison and Busby Ltd., London and New York, in association with Skotaville Publishers, Johannesburg, pp. 88-106.

Oakley, A. (1993), 'Becoming a Mother,' in S. Jackson et al (eds.), *Women's Studies: A Reader*, Harvester Wheatsheaf, New York, London, Toronto, Sydney, Tokyo, Singapore, pp. 198-201.

_____ (2000), *Experiments in Knowing: Gender and Method in the Social Sciences*, Polity Press, Cambridge and Oxford.

Oldersma, J. and Davis, K. (1991), 'Introduction,' in K. Davis et al (eds.), *The Gender of Power*, Sage Publications Ltd., London, California and New Delhi, pp. 1-18.

Olsen, M.E. and Martin N. Marger (eds.), (1993), *Power in Modern Societies*, Westview Press, Boulder, San Francisco and Oxford.

Panton, K. (1994), *Leadership and Citizenship in Post-independence Jamaica: Wither the Partnership?*, Grace Kennedy Foundation Lecture.

Parker, I. (1992), *Discourse Dynamics: Critical Analysis for Social and Individual Psychology*, Routledge, London and New York.

Parker, R.G. and John H. Gagnon (eds.) (1995), *Conceiving Sexuality: Approaches to Sex Research in a Postmodern World*, Routledge, New York and London.

Pateman, C. (1992), 'Equality, Difference, Subordination: the Politics of Motherhood and Women's Citizenship,' in *Beyond Equality and Difference: Citizenship, Feminist Politics and Female Subjectivity*, G. Bock and S. James (eds.), Routledge, London and New York, pp. 17-31.

Pathak, Z. (1992), 'A Pedagogy for Postcolonial Feminists,' in J. Butler and J.W. Scott (eds.), *Feminists Theorise the Political*, Routledge, New York and London, pp. 426-441.

Patton, C. (1995), 'Refiguring Social Space,' in L. Nicholson and S. Siedman (eds.), *Social Postmodernism: Beyond Identity Politics*, Cambridge University Press, Cambridge, pp.216-249.

Payne, A.J. (1994), *Politics in Jamaica*, Ian Randle Publishers, Kingston, Jamaica.

Payne, G.K.(1977), *Urban Housing in the Third World*, Leonard Hill, London and Routledge and Kegan Paul, Boston.

Poland, F. (1990), 'The history of a 'failed' research topic: the case of childminders,' in *Feminist Praxis: Research, Theory and Epistemology in Feminist Sociology*, Routledge, London and New York, pp. 80-90.

Pollard, V. (1985), 'Dread Talk – The Speech of the Rastafarian in Jamaica,' in *Caribbean Quarterly Monograph: Rastafari*, University of the West Indies, Kingston, pp. 32-41.

Poovey, M. (1992), 'The Abortion Question and the Death of Man,' in J. Butler and J.W. Scott, (eds.), *Feminists Theorise the Political*, Routledge, New York and London, pp.239-256.

Porio, E. et al (1994), 'Philippines: Urban Communities and their Fight for Survival, in C.S. Blanc et al, *Urban Children in Distress: Global Predicaments and Innovative Strategies*, United Nations Children's Fund, Yverdon, Victoria, Paris, Berlin, Reading, Tokyo, Amsterdam, Pennsylvania, pp. 101-159.

Post, K. (1978), *Arise Ye Starvelings: The Jamaican Labour Rebellion of 1938 and its Aftermath*, Martinus/Nijhoff, The Hague, Boston, London.

_____ (1981), *Strike the Iron: A Colony at War: Jamaica 1939-1945, Volume I and Volume II*, Humanities Press, New Jersey, in association with The Institute of Social Studies, The Hague.

_____ (1996), *Regaining Marxism*, MacMillan Press Ltd and St. Martin's Press, Inc., Houndsmills, Basingstoke, Hampshire and London; and New York.

Poster, M. (1984), *Foucault, Marxism and History: Mode of Production versus Mode of Information*, Polity Press, Cambridge, Oxford and New York.

Poulantzas, N. (1986), 'Class Power,' in S. Lukes (ed.), *Power*, Basil Blackwell, Oxford, pp. 144-155).

Probyn, E. (1993), 'Choosing Choice: Images of Sexuality and "Choiceoisie" in Popular Culture', in S. Fisher and K. Davis (eds.), *Negotiating at the Margins: The Gendered Discourses of Power and Resistance*, Rutgers University Press, New Brunswick, New Jersey, pp. 278-294.

Prothrow-Stith, D. & Weissman, M. (1991), *Deadly Consequences: How Violence Problem*, Harper Collins Publishers, New York.

Qunta, C. N. (1987), 'Preface' in C. Qunta (ed.), *Women in Southern Africa*, Allison and Busby Ltd. London and New York, in association with Skotaville Publishers, Johannesburg, pp. 11-19.

Radtke, H.L. and Stam, H.J. (1994), 'Introduction' in H. L. Radtke and H. J. Stam (eds.), *Power/Gender: Social Relations in Theory and Practice*, pp.1-14, Sage Publications, London, Thousand Oaks and New Delhi.

Ramazamoglu, C. (1990), *Feminism and the Contradictions of Oppression*, Routledge, London and New York.

_____ (1993), 'Introduction,' in C Ramazanoglu (ed.), *Up Against Foucault: Explorations of some tensions between Foucault and Feminism*, Routledge, London and New York, pp. 1-28.

Ramazanoglu, C. and Holland, J. (1993), 'Women's Sexuality and Men's Appropriation of Desire,' in C. Ramazanoglu (ed.), *Up Against Foucault: Explorations of some tensions between Foucault and Feminism*, Routledge, London and New York, pp. 239-264.

Reddock, R. (1986), 'Some Factors Affecting Women in the Caribbean Past and Present,' in P. Ellis (ed.), *Women of the Caribbean*, Zed Books Ltd. London and New Jersey, pp.28-31.

Reid, T.L. (1997), *KU.K.umaka: The African-Jamaican Most Ancient Connection: Language, Historical and Other Perspectives*, Reid, Spanish Town.

Reinharz, S. (1992), *Feminist Methods in Social Research*, Oxford University Press, New York, Oxford.

Risseeuw, C. (1991), 'Bourdieu, Power and Resistance: Gender Transformation in Sri Lanka' in K. Davis et al (eds.), *The Gender of Power*, Sage Publications, London, Newbury Park, New Delhi, pp. 154-179.

Rizzini et al (1994), 'Brazil: A New Concept of Childhood,' in C.S. Blanc et al, *Urban Children in Distress: Global Predicaments and Innovative Strategies*, United Nations Children's Fund, Yverdon, Victoria, Paris, Berlin, Reading, Tokyo, Amsterdam, Pennsylvania, pp. 55-99.

Rodney, W. (1969), *Groundings With My Brothers*, Bogle-L'Ouverture Publications, London.

_____ (1973), *How Europe Underdeveloped Africa*, Bogle-L'Ouverture Publications, London, Dar-es-Salaam.

Rose, N. (1996), 'Identity, Genealogy, History,' in S. Hall and P. duGay (eds.), *Questions of Cultural Identity*, Sage Publications, London, California and New Delhi, pp. 128-150.

Rosenthal, R. (1993), 'Skidding/Coping/Escaping: Constraint, Agency and Gender in the Lives of Homeless Skidders' in Fisher, S. and Davis, R. (eds.), *Negotiating at the Margins: The Gendered Discourses of Power and Resistance*, Rutgers University Press, New Brunswick, New Jersey, pp. 205-234.

Ross, L.J. (1993), 'African-American Women and Abortion: 1800-1970,' in S.M. James and A.P.A. Busia (eds.), *Theorising Black Feminisms: The Visionary Pragmatism of Black Women*, Routledge, London and New York, pp. 141-159.

Rothfield, P. (1990), 'Feminism, Subjectivity and Sexual Difference,' in S. Gunew (ed.), *Feminist Knowledge: Critique and Construct*, pp.121-146, Routledge, London and New York.

Rothman, B.K. (1994), 'Beyond Mothers: Ideology in a Patriarchal Society,' in E.N. Glenn et al (eds.), *Mothering: Ideology, Experience and Agency*, Routledge, New York, London, pp. 139-160.

Rowe, M. (1998), 'Gender and Family Relations in Rastafari: A Personal Perspective,' in N.S. Murrell, W.D. Spencer and A. A. McFarlane (eds.), *Chanting Down Babylon: The Rastafari Reader*, Temple University Press, Philadelphia, pp. 72-88.

Rowley, H. and Grosz, E. (1990), 'Psychoanalysis and Feminism,' in S. Gunew (ed.), *Feminist Knowledge: Critique and Construct*, pp.175-204, Routledge, London and New York.

Rubin, G. (1984), 'Thinking Sex: Notes for a Radical Theory of the Politics of Sexuality,' in C. Vance (ed.), *Pleasure and Danger: Exploring Female Sexuality*, pp. 267-285, Routledge and Kegan Paul, Boston, London, Melbourne and Henley.

Rushing, A. B. (1993), 'Surviving Rape: A Morning/Mourning Ritual,' in S. M. James and A.P.A. Busia (eds.), *Theorising Black Feminisms: The Visionary Pragmatism of Black Women*, Routledge, London and New York, pp. 127-140.

Ruth, S. (1989), 'A Feminist World View,' in R.D. Klein and D. L. Steinberg, *Radical Voices: A Decade of Feminist Resistance from Women's Studies International Forum*, Pergamon Press, Oxford, New York, Beijing and Frankfurt, pp. 171-181.

Said, E. (1991), *Disciplining Foucault: Feminism, Power and the Body*, Routledge, New York and London.

Sawicki, J. (1988), 'Identity, Politics and Sexual Freedom: Foucault and Feminism,' in I. Drummond and L. Quinby (eds.), *Feminism and Foucault: Reflections on Resistance*, Northeastern University Press, Boston, pp. 177-192.

Scheper-Hughes, N. (1992), *Death Without Weeping: The Violence of Everyday Life in Brazil*, University of California Press, Los Angeles and Oxford (U.K.).

Schudson, M. (1994), 'Culture and the Integration of National Societies,' in D. Crane (ed.), *The Sociology of Culture: Emerging Theoretical Perspectives*, Blackwell Publishers, Massachusetts and Oxford (U.K.), pp. 21-44.

Scott, J.C. (1985), *Weapons of the Weak: Everyday Forms of Peasant Resistance*, Yale University Press, New Haven and London.

_____ (1990), *Domination and the Arts of Resistance*, Yale University Press, New Haven and London.

Scott, J. W. (1992), 'Experience,' in J. Butler and J.W. Scott (eds.), *Feminists Theorise the Political*, Routledge, New York and London, pp. 22-40.

Scott, J. W. Scott, (1996), 'Introduction.' In J. W. Scott, (ed.), *Feminism and History*, Oxford University Press, New York.

_____ (1987), 'History and Difference,' in J.K. Conway et al (eds.), *Learning About Women: Gender, Politics and Power*, The University of Michigan Press, Ann Arbor, pp. 93-118.

Segal, L. (1997), 'Sexualities' in *Identity and Difference*, Sage Publications, London, Thousand Oaks and New Delhi, in association with The Open University, Milton Keynes, pp. 183-238.

Senior, O. (1991), *Working Miracles: Women's Lives in the English-speaking Caribbean*, Institute of Social and Economic Research, University of the West Indies, Cave Hill, Barbados, in association with James Currey, London and Indiana University Press, Bloomington and Indianapolis.

Sewell, T. (1990), *Garvey's Children: The Legacy of Marcus Garvey*, The Macmillan Press Ltd., London and Basingstoke.

Shapiro, M. J. (1984), 'Literary Production as a Politicising Practice,' in M. Shapiro (ed.), *Language and Politics*, Basil Blackwell, Oxford.

Sheehan, M. (1996), *The Balance of Power: History and Theory*, Routledge, London and New York.

Sheridan, A. (1980), *Michel Foucault: The Will to Truth*, Tavistock Publications, London and New York.

Shilling, C. (1997), 'The Body and Difference,' in *Identity and Difference*, Sage Publications, London, Thousand Oaks and New Delhi, in association with The Open University, Milton Keynes, pp. 63-120.

Shorey-Bryan, N. (1986), 'The Making of Male-Female Relationships in the Caribbean,' in P. Ellis (ed.), *Women of the Caribbean*, Zed Books Ltd., London and New Jersey, pp. 69-73,

Silvera, M. (1992), 'Man Royals and Sodomites: Some Thoughts on The Invisibility of Afro-Caribbean Lesbians,' *Feminist Studies*, Vol. 18, No. 3, Fall, pp. 521-532.

Skeggs, B. (1994), 'Refusing to be Civilised: Race, Sexuality and Power,' in H. Afshar and M. Maynard (eds.) *The Dynamics of 'Race' and Gender: Some Feminist Interventions*, Taylor and Francis, London, pp. 171-181.

Sobers, Y.M. (1997), *Wholeness for our Children*, Bernard van Leer Foundation, Kingston, January 30.

Stanigar, P. (1993), *The Southside Empowerment Project*, Kingston.

Sobo, E.J. (1993), *One Blood: The Jamaican Body*, State University of New York Press, Albany.

Social and Economic Studies, Volume 8, Number 4, (1961), 'Partners: An Informal Savings Institution in Jamaica,' pp. 436-440.

Solow, R.M. (1995), 'Mass Unemployment as a Social Problem,' in K. Sen, K. Basu et al (eds.), *Choice, Welfare and Development: A Festchrift in Honour of Amartya*, Clarendon Press, Oxford, pp. 313-322.

Spivak, G. (1993), 'The Question of Cultural Studies,' in S. During (ed.), *The Cultural Studies Reader*, Routledge, London and New York, pp. 169-188.

Smith, M.G. (1989), *Poverty in Jamaica, Institute of Social and Economic Research*, University of the West Indies, Mona.

_____ (1996), *The Southside Lot Development Project*, Kingston.

Stanley, L. and Wise S. (1990), 'Method, methodology and Epistemology in Feminist research processes' in *Feminist Praxis: Research, Theory and Epistemology in Feminist Sociology*, Routledge, London and New York, pp. 20-62.

Stephens, E.H. and Stephens, J.D. (1986), *Democratic Socialism in Jamaica: The Political Movement and Social Transformation in Dependent Capitalism*, Macmillan Education Ltd., Basingstoke and London.

Stone, C. (1973), *Class, Race and Political Behaviour in Urban Jamaica, Institute of Social and Economic Research*, University of the West Indies, Mona.

_____ (1983), 'Decolonisation and the Caribbean State System: The Case of Jamaica,' in P. Henry and C. Stone (eds.), *The Newer Caribbean: Decolonisation, Democracy and Development*, Institute for the Study of Human Issues, Philadelphia, Pennsylvania, pp. 37-61.

_____ (1986), *Class, State and Democracy in Jamaica*, Praeger, New York, Connecticut and London.

_____ (1987), 'Crime and Violence: Sociopolitical Implications' in P. Phillips and J. Wedderburn (eds.), *Crime and Violence: Causes and Solutions*, Department of Government, University of the West Indies, Mona.

_____ (1989), 'Power, Policy and Politics in Independent Jamaica,' in R. Nettleford (ed.), *Jamaica in Independence: Essays on the Early Years*, Heinemann Caribbean, Kingston and James Currey, London, pp.19-54.

_____ (1989), *On Jamaican Politics, Economics & Society: Columns from the Gleaner, 1987-88*, The Gleaner Company Ltd. Kingston.

Storey, J. (1993), *An Introductory Guide to Cultural Theory and Popular Culture*, Harvester Wheatsheaf, New York, London, Toronto, Sydney, Tokyo, Singapore.

Storrocks, R. (1997), *An Introduction to the Study of Sexuality*, St. Martins Press Inc., New York.

Strinati, D. (1995), *An Introduction to Theories of Popular Culture*, Routledge, London and New York.

Suttles, G.D. (1972), *The Social Construction of Communities*, The University of Chicago and London.

Tafari, I. (2001), *Rastafari In Transition; The Politics of Cultural Confrontation in Africa and the Caribbean (1966-1988)*, Research Associates School Times Publications/Frontline Distribution Int'l Inc and Miguel Lorne Publishers, Chicago, Jamaica, London, Trinidad & Tobago

Tafari, I. J. (1996), *A Rastafari View of Marcus Mosiah Garvey: Patriarch, Prophet, Philosopher*, Greatcompany Inc., Fort Lauderdale, Chicago.

_____ (2002), 'Life and Debt,' *Rootz Reggae & Kulcha Magazine*, Volume 5 #1, Fort Lauderdale, Florida, pp. 32-33

Tafari-Ama, I. (1988), 'Shadow of Death: Growing up in a Jamaican Garrison Community,' in V. Johnson et al (eds.), *Stepping Forward: Children and Young People's Participation in the Development Process*, Intermediate Technology Publications, pp. 263-266.

_____ (1988-89), *An historical analysis of grassroots resistance in Jamaica: A case study of Participatory Research on Gender Relations in Rastafari*, MDS, ISS, The Hague.

_____ (1998), 'Rastawoman as Rebel: Case Studies in Jamaica,' in N.S. Murrell, W.D. Spencer and A.A. Mc-Farlane (eds.), *Chanting Down Babylon: The Rastafari Reader*, Temple University Press, Philadelphia, pp. 89-106.

Taylor, B. (1992), *Free For All? – A Question of Morality and Community*, Grace Kennedy Foundation Lecture, Kingston.

Thiongo, N. wa, (1993), *Moving the Centre: The Struggle for Cultural Freedoms*, James Currey, London; EAEP, Nairobi; Heinemann, Portsmouth.

Thomas, C.Y. (1988), *The Poor and the Powerless: Economic Policy and Change in the Caribbean*, Latin America Bureau (Research and Action) Limited, London.

Thomas, M. and Boot, A. (1982), *Jah Revenge: Babylon Revisited*, Eel Pie Publishing Limited, London.

Tong, R.P. (1998), *Feminist Thought: A More Comprehensive Introduction*, Westview Press, A Division of HarperCollins Publishers Inc. Boulder, Colorado and Cumnor Hill, Oxford.

Torfing, J. (1999), *New Theories of Discourse: Laclau, Mouffe and Zizek*, Blackwell Publishers, Oxford and Massachusetts.

Tornquist, O. (1999), *Politics and Development: A Critical Introduction*, Sage Publications, London, Thousand Oaks, New Delhi.

Turshen, M. (1998), 'Women's War Stories,' in M. Turshen and C. Twagiramariya (eds.), *What Women Do in Wartime: Gender and Conflict in Africa*, Zed Books Ltd., London and New York, pp. 1-26.

Twagiramariya, C. and Turshen, M. (1998), 'Favours to Give and 'Consenting' Victims' in M. Turshen and C. Twagiramariya (eds.), *What Women Do in Wartime: Gender and Conflict in Africa*, Zed Books Ltd., London and New York, pp. 101-118.

Tornquist, O. (1999), *Politics and Development: A Critical Introduction*, Sage Publications, London, Thousand Oaks, New Delhi.

UNICEF, (1990), *Children and Development in the 1990s: A UNICEF Sourcebook, on the occasion of the World Summit for Children*, United Nations, New York, (29-30 September).

Van Dijk, T. A. (1998), *Ideology: A Multidisciplinary Approach*, Sage Publications, London, Thousand Oaks, New Delhi.

Van Dijk, (1997), *Discourse as Social Interaction: Discourse Studies: A Multidisciplinary Introduction, Volume 2*, Sage Publications, London, Thousand Oaks, New Delhi.

Vance, C.S (1984), 'Pleasure and Danger: Toward a Politics of Sexuality' in C. Vance (ed.), *Pleasure and Danger: Exploring Female Sexuality*, Routledge and Kegan Paul, Boston, London, Melbourne and Henley, pp.1-28.

Vansina, J. (1985), *Oral Tradition as History*, Heinemann Kenya, Nairobi: Kenya, Uganda and Tanzania and James Currey Ltd., London.

Vansina, J. (1995), 'Social Construction Theory: Problems in the History of Sexuality,' in H. Crowley and S. Himmelweit (eds.), *Knowing Women: Feminism and Knowledge*, pp. 132-145, Polity Press, in association with Blackwell Publishers and the Open University, Cambridge and Oxford.

Vickers, J. (1994), 'Notes toward a Political Theory of Sex and Power,' in H. L. Radtke and H. J. Stam (eds.), *Power/Gender: Social Relations in Theory and Practice*, Sage Publications, London, Thousand Oaks and New Delhi, pp. 174-193.

Violi, P. (1992), 'Gender, Subjectivity and Language,' in G. Bock and S. James (eds.), *Beyond Equality and Difference: Citizenship, Feminist Politics and Female Subjectivity*, Routledge, London and New York, pp. 164-176.

Wacquant, L.J.D. (1992), 'Toward a Social Praxeology: The Structure and Logic of Bourdieu's Sociology,' in Bourdieu, P. and Wacquant, L.J.D. *An Invitation to Reflexive Sociology*, Polity Press, pp.1-6.

_____ (1992), 'Epistemic Reflexivity,' in P. Bourdieu, and L.J.D. Wacquant, *An Invitation to Reflexive Sociology*, Polity Press, pp. 36-46.

_____ (1994), 'The New Urban Colour Line: The State and Fate of the Ghetto in Post Fordist America,' in C. Calhoun (ed.), *Social Theory and the Politics of Identity*, Blackwell Publishers, Massachusetts and Oxford, pp. 231-275.

Walby, S. (1990), *Theorising Patriarchy*, Blackwell, Oxford U.K. and Cambridge USA.

Weedon, C. (1999), *Feminism, Theory and the Politics of Difference*, Blackwell Publishers, Oxford and Massachusetts.

Weeks, J. (1994), 'The Body and Sexuality,' in *The Polity Reader in Gender Studies*, Polity Press, pp. 235-239.

Weeks, J. (1985), *Sexuality and its Discontents: Meanings, Myths & Modern Sexualities*, Routledge and Kegan Paul, London, Melbourne and Henley.

Wekker, G. (1992), *I Am Gold Money: The Construction of Selves, Gender and Sexualities in a Female, Working Class, Afro-Surinamese Setting*, Ph.D. Dissertation, University of California, Los Angeles.

Wieringa, S. (1991-1992), 'Methods and Power: Epistemological and Methodological Aspects of a Feminist Research Project,' *Women and Development Programme*, Reading Session B, Course MWC103 (Research Methodology).

Williams, B. (1987), 'The Standard of Living: Interests and Capabilities' in A. Sen et al, G. Hawthorn (ed.), *The Standard of Living: The Tanner Lecture Series, Clare Hall, Cambridge, 1985*, Cambridge University Press, pp. 94-102.

Wilson, M. (1989), 'The Status of the Jamaican Woman, 1962 to the Present,' in R. Nettleford (ed.), *Jamaica in Independence: Essays on the Early Years*, Heinemann Caribbean, Kingston and James Currey, London, pp.229-256.

Wiltshire-Brodber, R. (1988), 'Gender, Race and Class in the Caribbean,' in P. Mohammed and C. Shepherd, (eds.), *Gender in Caribbean Development*, The University of The West Indies Women and Development Studies Project, Mona, Jamaica; St. Augustine, Trinidad and Tobago; Cave Hill, Barbados, pp. 142-155.

Witter, M. and C. Kirton, (1990), *The Informal Economy in Jamaica*, Institute of Social and Economic Research, University of the West Indies, Mona.

Witter, M. (1991), 'Some Reflections on the Economic Development of Jamaica,' in J. Wedderburn (ed.), *Rethinking Development*, Consortium Graduate School of the Social Sciences, University of the West Indies, pp. 101-119

Wolf, D.L. (1996), *Feminist Dilemmas in Fieldwork*, Westview Press, Boulder and Oxford.

Wolfensperger, J. (1991), 'Engendered Structure: Giddens and the Conceptualisation of Gender,' in K. Davis et al (eds.), *The Gender of Power*, Sage Publications, London, Newbury Park, New Delhi, pp. 87-110.

Wood, L. A. and Kroger, R.O. (2000), *Doing Discourse Analysis: Methods for Studying Action in Talk and Text*, Sage Publications Inc. Thousand Oaks, London and New Delhi.

Woodhull, W. (1988) 'Sexuality, Power, and the Question of Rape,' in I. Drummond and L. Quinby (eds.), *Feminism and Foucault: Reflections on Resistance*, Northeastern University Press, Boston, pp.167-176.

Woodward, K. (1997), 'Motherhood: Identities, Meanings and Myths,' in *Identity and Difference*, Sage Publications, London, Thousand Oaks and New Delhi, in association with The Open University, Milton Keynes, pp. 239-298.

Woollett, A. and Marshall, H. (1997), 'Reading the Body: Young Women's Accounts of their Bodies in Relation to Autonomy and Independence,' in K. Davis (ed.), *Embodied Practices: Feminist Perspectives on the Body*, Sage Publications Ltd., London, California and New Delhi, pp. 27-40.

Wright, R. (1995), *Native Son*, Picador (an imprint of Macmillan General Books).

Young, K. (1997), 'Gender and Development,' in L. Duggan, L. Nisonoff and N. Wiegersma (eds.), *The Women, Gender and Development Reader*, Zed Books, (London and New Jersey), University Press Ltd. (Dhaka), White Lotus Co. Ltd. (Bangkok), Fernwood Publishing Ltd. (Halifax, Nova Scotia), and David Philip (Cape Town), pp. 51-53.

Yeatman, A. (1993), 'Voice and Representation in the Politics of Difference,' in S. Gunew and A. Yeatman (eds.), *Feminism and the Politics of Difference*, Allen and Unwin, New South Wales.

Yuval-Davis, N. (1997), *Gender and Nation*, Sage Publications Ltd., London, California, New Delhi.

Newspapers

Abeng, (1969), Volume 1, No. 5, March 1.

The Gleaner, several editions

Records

Banton B. (1998), 'Destiny,' on *Reggae Gold*, VP Records Inc., Catalogue No. 0 54645-1529-2-1.

Capleton, (1999), 'Things are Happening,' on *Reggae Hits '99*: Various Artists, Jamdown Records, Catalogue No. 6 5685-40017-2 6.

Eccles, C. (1996), 'Rod of Correction,' on *Joshua's Rod of Correction*, Intermusic S.A., Catalogue No. 8 712177024117.

_____ (1996), 'Power for the People (Version 2),' on *Joshua's Rod of Correction*, Intermusic S.A., Catalogue No. 8 712177 024117.

Elephant Man, Log On Holt, J. (1997), 'She Want It,' on *In the Midnight Hour*, Catalogue No. FMCG, 5 031 773 004624

Kelly, A. et al (2001), 'Chi Chi Man,' Produced by Tony C.D. Kelly, Catalogue No. LOVPD1002-3, Platinum Records, Kingston.

Marley, B. 'Small Axe,' on *It's Alright*, Mega Sound, Catalogue No. 5 028421 501222.

Shaggy, (1997), 'John Doe,' on *Midnite Lover*, Virgin Records Ltd., Catalogue No. 7 24384 45222 3.

Spragga Benz, (1998), 'She Nuh Ready Yet,' on *Reggae Gold*, VP Records Inc., Catalogue No. 0 54645-1529-2-1.

Vegas, (1998), 'Heads High,' on *Reggae Gold*, VP Records Inc., 0 54645-1529-2-1.

INDEX

www.ingramcontent.com/pod-product-compliance
Lightning Source LLC
Chambersburg PA
CBHW050330270326
41926CB00016B/3393